THE

ORIGIN AND HISTORY

OF THE

FIRST OR GRENADIER GUARDS.

FROM DOCUMENTS IN THE STATE PAPER OFFICE,
WAR OFFICE, HORSE GUARDS, CONTEMPORARY
HISTORY, REGIMENTAL RECORDS, Etc.

BY

LIEUT.-GEN. SIR F. W. HAMILTON, K.C.B.,

LATE GRENADIER GUARDS.

IN THREE VOLUMES.

VOL. II.

WITH ILLUSTRATIONS.

LONDON:
JOHN MURRAY, ALBEMARLE STREET.
1874.

LONDON :
BRADBURY, AGNEW, & CO., PRINTERS, WHITEFRIARS.

JOHN, DUKE OF MARLBOROUGH, K.G.

Commander in Chief of Her Majestys Forces.
7th Colonel of the First Regiment of Foot Guards.
1704 - 1712.   1714 - 1722.

CONTENTS.

CHAPTER XII.

CHAPTER XIII.

CHAPTER XIV.

CHAPTER XV.

CHAPTER XVI.

CHAPTER XVII.

CHAPTER XVIII.

CHAPTER XIX.

CHAPTER XX.

CHAPTER XXI.

CHAPTER XXII.

CHAPTER XXIII.

CHAPTER XXIV.

ORIGIN AND SERVICES

OF THE

GRENADIER GUARDS.

CHAPTER XII.

WHILE one battalion of the First Regiment of Guards was reaping much honour and glory under Marlborough in Germany in the year 1704, the services of a portion of the home battalions, both of the First and Coldstream regiments, were called for during the summer of the same year in Portugal, where the campaign had not hitherto been successful for the British arms. Mainhardt, Duke of Schomberg, brother to the former colonel of the First Guards, had been during the previous year, and still was, at the commencement of the year 1704, in command of the British contingent in that country, and as the war was increasing in importance the government had sent out early this year some reinforcements drawn from the regiments of the line in Flanders. To these was added a detachment of 150 men of the First Guards, under Captain Peachy, drawn from the home battalions of the regiment, which sailed in the month of January. Schomberg, however, had been unable to gain

1704.
Spain.

any advantage over the Duke of Berwick, to whom he was opposed, and having quarrelled with the Portuguese he at length resigned his command. The queen appointed as his successor the brave and gallant Rouvigny, a French refugee, who, without desiring the honour, promptly obeyed the royal command, but at the same time requested an increase of forces from England, a demand which was readily complied with, and, in

July, 4000 troops were ordered to hold themselves in immediate readiness for foreign service; amongst these was a combined battalion of 600 men, formed from the several home companies of the First and Coldstream Guards, the command of which was given to Colonel Richard Russell of the First Guards, now a brigadier, and next in seniority to Colonels John Seymour and Gilbert Primrose, who accompanied the battalion to Cadiz and Vigo in 1702.

The senior officers of the First Guards were now employed as follows :—

Major-Gen. Henry Withers, the Lieut.-Colonel, commanding a Brigade in Flanders.

   ,,   ,,   Shrimpton, 1st Major, commanding a Brigade in Portugal and subsequently at Gibraltar.

John Bristow, 2nd Major, commanding the Home battalions in London.

John Seymour.

Gilbert Primrose had been commanding the Flanders battalion, but having been wounded at Schellenberg was now at home.

Richard Russell, commanding combined battalion of Guards in Portugal.

Charles Gorsuch, commanding Flanders battalion, *vice* Primrose, wounded.

To facilitate the recruiting of the several companies, upon the above draft being made from the home battalions, the Lord Mayor of London was requested to allow the officers of the Foot Guards to enlist into the regiment such insolvent debtors as would be willing to serve in it.

The combined battalion, under Colonel Russell, received directions to march from London so as to reach Portsmouth on the 26th of July, and upon joining the remainder of the reinforcements, the expedition immediately set sail, arriving at Lisbon on the 4th of August, shortly after which the whole army was reviewed by Rouvigny, now created Earl of Galway, and on the 28th of August it moved in a north-easterly direction to the frontiers of Portugal. On proceeding to Almeida, above 200 miles from Lisbon, Lord Galway found the Duke of Berwick with a large force advantageously posted on the river Agueda, and after holding a council of war, in which it was considered advisable not to risk a battle, he returned with his forces to Portugal, and the combined battalion of Guards with several of the English regiments remained quartered in Lisbon until called upon in the month of December, under the following circumstances, to form part of the garrison of Gibraltar.

In the summer of 1704, Admiral Sir George Rooke, who was cruising in the Mediterranean in search of the French fleet, had captured that important fortress in a most gallant manner, whereupon the Spaniards collected an army under Villadarias to attempt its recovery, and the French, sent a fleet to their assistance, but were unable during the winter to prevent the arrival of reinforcements, either from England or from Portugal.

With the view to strengthening its garrison, the British Government towards the end of the year directed the combined battalion of Guards, then at Lisbon, together with Barymore's and Donegal's regiments, the 13th and 35th of the line, under the brigade command of Major-General Shrimpton, first major First Guards, together with one Dutch and one Portuguese regiment, to proceed there; they embarked accordingly at Lisbon on the 12th of December, and landed on the rock on the 19th of the same month.

No sooner had they arrived than the Guards were engaged, on the 22nd, in a successful sortie against the enemy's works, which were too extensive for the number of troops that Villadarias had at his command, and the French court, impatient at the slow progress of the siege, superseded the Spaniard by the French Marshal Tessó, who had an additional force of men placed under his orders.

705.
.7.
Tessé, during the month of January, 1705, was less successful even than the Spaniard, and the attempt made on the Round Tower on the 2nd of February failed, but it was followed a few days later, on the 7th, by a more determined assault, when six hundred Frenchmen, under Lieutenant-Colonel de Thong, ascending an unprotected part of the rock during the night, lay concealed till dawn, and upon the withdrawal of the British night guard made a rush at the works. The defenders, under Colonel Borr, were at first overwhelmed, and the enemy pushed on till they met a company of the Queen's Marines, under Captain Fischer, who with Lieutenant-Colonel Rivett of the Coldstreams and twenty grenadiers of the Guards and Barymore's battalion, having all clambered up the rock, held the enemy in check till the remainder of the battalions of Guards and Marines came to their assistance, when the French were driven back with considerable loss. After this unsuccessful attack no further attempt on the rock was made by the enemy, and the British admiral having cleared the sea from all obstacles to the entrance of supplies, the French and Spaniards, after having in vain fired 8000 shells and 70,000 cannon shot into the fortress, raised the siege and withdrew their troops into the interior.

The services on this occasion of Brigadier-General Shrimpton of the First Guards were recognized by the queen in the following year, by the grant of the sum of 500*l.* as a mark of her majesty's royal favour.

Before reverting to the campaign in Flanders of 1705, and the movements of the first battalion First Guards in that country, we will continue the record of events that occurred that year in Spain, in which the combined battalion of the First and Coldstream Guards continued to take a part.

The queen and British government having resolved upon more energetic action in the Peninsula in the interests of Charles of Austria, appointed the gallant Earl of Peterborough, in April, 1705, to the command of another expedition, consisting of six regiments of the line, with Major-General

EAST COAST
OF
SPAIN
to illustrate Campaigns
of
1705, 1706, 1707.

SKETCH OF
BATTLE OF ALMANZA
April 25th 1707.

Cunningham second in command, and to which Colonels Thomas Brudenell and James Stanhope, the future peer, were appointed brigadiers. The combined battalion of Guards under Colonel Richard Russell, now at Gibraltar, ultimately joined these forces and was attached to the brigade of the above Brigadier-General Stanhope. The expedition with the six regiments of the line sailed from Portsmouth early in June, touching at Lisbon on the 30th, where it took on board King Charles of Spain, his suite, and two dismounted regiments of dragoons. On his arrival at Gibraltar, Peterborough landed some of his young soldiers, and embarked in their place three regiments of the line, as well as the combined battalion of Guards under Colonel Richard Russell, which, as Cox relates, had recently been distinguishing itself in the defence of that fortress.

The Prince of Hesse Darmstadt, who had assisted in the capture of Gibraltar, and had lately been Viceroy of Catalonia, also joined the expedition, and by his advice the fleet, on leaving Gibraltar, continued its course to Barcelona, the capital of that province, where the friends of the Austrian cause were said to be very numerous. On the voyage, the fleet was joined by a Dutch contingent, increasing the strength of the expedition to 6000 men.

Barcelona was at this time strongly fortified, and occupied by a Spanish garrison more numerous than the invaders, commanded by two determined men, Don Francisco de Velasco and the Duke de Popoli. Above the town rose the fortress of Montjuick, which nature, assisted by art, had rendered almost unapproachable. The British fleet arrived off the coast of Catalonia on the 16th of August, and in anticipation of the Catalans joining in large numbers, the army was landed at Mataro, about twenty-five miles to the north-east, and marched to the Llobregat river, within five miles of the town, where an entrenched camp was formed. General Stanhope's brigade, including the Guards, as well as the rest of the troops, were now for three weeks daily employed in the trenches, but owing to the nature of the

Aug. 16.

soil little progress was made for some time, and the Catalans showed but few signs of sympathy. Lord Peterborough, however, who detected that the garrison of Montjuick, relying on the strength of the works, had become careless, secretly formed his own plans, which he communicated to no one. He ordered the artillery and stores to be embarked, to the great indignation and despair of King Charles, the Prince of Hesse, and their officers, but to the infinite joy of the garrison of Barcelona, who immediately organized public rejoicings at these prospects of

Sept. 13. a speedy release, when suddenly, on the night of the 13th of September, Peterborough called the Prince of Hesse from his tent and showed him his army turned out, ready to march to the assault of the outworks of Montjuick. At dawn of day this was successfully accomplished, though with the loss of the Prince of Hesse himself, who was killed by the side of Peterborough. A panic however seized the men who had so gallantly taken possession of the works, but the reserve under Stanhope, including the combined battalion of Guards, coming up at this critical moment, order was soon restored, the works maintained, batteries

Sept. 15. erected against the keep, and on the 15th of September, an explosion occurring in the magazine, which killed the officer commanding, and made a serious breach in the walls, Fort Montjuick fell into the hands of the British. The siege of the town then progressed with rapidity, and Velasco the governor, touched by a chivalrous act of Lord Peterborough's in rescuing the Duchess of Popoli from insult, surrendered

Oct. 9. on the 9th of October.

Catalonia now declared for Charles, who was proclaimed king, and numbers came forward offering him their services. He was making himself universally popular, but being unwilling to submit to the fiery counsels of the active-minded Peterborough, he detached him on a separate expedition to Valencia, while the battalion of Guards, now reduced by the casualties of war to little more than 300 men, remained during the winter of 1705-6 in Barcelona as a body-guard to the Spanish king, enjoying the festivities of the Spanish court, where we will leave them and revert to the progress of events in Flanders.

CAMPAIGN IN FLANDERS.

The enthusiasm in England consequent upon the victory of Blenheim had much facilitated the progress of recruiting, which was all the more urgently needed, that, in addition to the filling up the vacancies caused by the many casualties in the last year's campaign, the establishment of companies abroad was augmented, that of the First Guards being raised by an order of the 17th of March by ten men per company. With the view to increasing to that extent the establishment of the service companies of the Guards in Flanders, the men of the two companies commanded by Colonel Highmes and Colonel Ferrers were drafted into the remaining eleven, while those officers were sent home to raise two new companies; the strength of the first battalion at the opening of the campaign of 1705 was 32 officers besides the staff, and 858 non-commissioned officers and men.* Colonel Charles Gorsuch continued in command of the service companies now divided into two battalions, and Colonel Primrose of the home battalions, and the latter officer was, on the 24th of March, appointed second major of the regiment.

At the end of April, Marlborough arrived at Maestricht, where the army was by that time assembled. The French still occupied Flanders and the greater part of Brabant, and he thought that by a rapid march into the Duchy of Luxembourg, he would be enabled to co-operate with the Margrave of Baden on the Moselle, take Saar Louis, invade France from that side, and thus force the French to abandon their conquests in Brabant. He therefore left Overkirk with a portion of the Dutch troops at Petersburg, near Maestricht, and marched with about 40,000 men, including the First Guards, towards Luxembourg, with the intention, of awaiting

---

* In detail—9 Captains (the Col.'s and Lieut.-Col.'s cos. were both present, and had no other Captain), 13 Lieutenants, 9 Ensigns, 1 Adjutant, 33 Sergeants, 33 Corporals, 22 Drummers, 770 Privates; being 70 to each of the 11 companies, besides the usual staff of officers and non-commissioned officers.

1705.

June.

the arrival of the Margrave beyond Consaarbruck, but the
Margrave did not make his appearance, and as Marlborough
was too weak alone to attack Villeroy, who had 55,000 troops
under him, he determined to retrace his steps into Brabant,
more especially as the French, taking advantage of his
absence, had seized upon Huy and Liege.   At midnight
accordingly, on the 17th of June, the troops commenced their
march northwards, having lost three weeks waiting in vain
for the Margrave.   At ten the next morning they reached
Consaarbruck, the First Guards marching in the second
column, commanded by General Churchill, but they had not
gone far when, in consequence of demonstrations on the
part of the enemy, the Guards, and part of Churchill's
brigade, were ordered to halt and form up to the rear.   The
French who had stolen out of their lines, checked by this
sudden menace to attack them, hurried back to their camp
and gave Marlborcugh the advantage of two days' start.

There was indeed no time to be lost, for the French were
threatening Maestricht, and Overkirk possessed far too few
troops to offer any effectual resistance ; Marlborough
therefore pressed forward both cavalry and infantry, and
appeared on the Meuse before the French expected him.
Villeroy thereupon withdrew his troops behind the lines
which for three years he had been constructing for the
defence of those parts of Flanders and Brabant, so unjustly
appropriated before the war commenced, and which extended
from Marché aux Dames on the Meuse along the two
Gheet rivers and the Demer as far as Antwerp.   They
were now manned by 70,000 Frenchmen, and Villeroy
transferred his head-quarters to Mierdorp, on his right, a
short distance within those lines, near the Mehaigne.
Marlborough was not long in deciding upon his plan of
operations to force them.   The Guards had crossed the

July 2

Meuse at Viset on the 2nd of July, and on the 3rd all
the divisions of the army joined Overkirk at Haneffe, north
of Huy, only fifteen miles from the French head-quarters at
Mierdorp ; these still felt themselves secure behind their
formidable works, though the fortress of Huy in front of

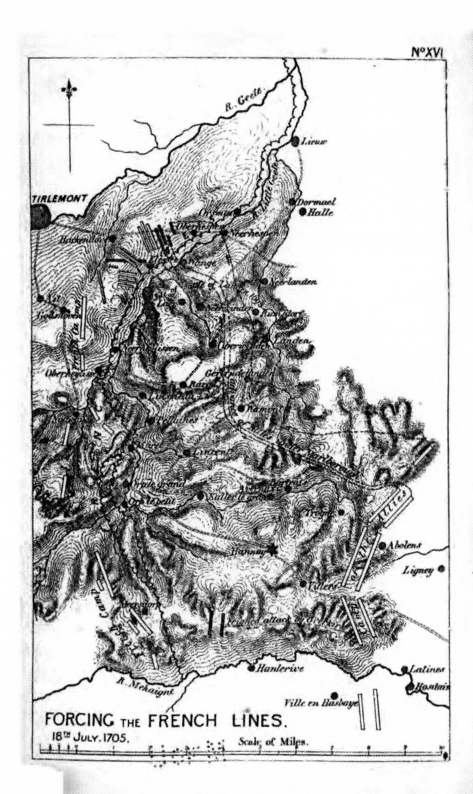

FORCING the FRENCH LINES.
18TH JULY. 1705.   Scale of Miles.

their right was soon recaptured by the Dutch, and wherever
the allied troops approached the enemy, they heard the jeer-
ing notes of the air, " Malbrook s'en va t'en guerre," repeated
by the bands and voices of the French regiments.

Acting on information he had received, Marlborough at
length determined to force the French lines between Lieuwe
and Heylissem. Overkirk, who alone was entrusted with
the secret, was detached on the 16th of July with the left
wing of the allied army towards Mierdorp, as if to turn the
French right, whereupon Villeroy quickly assembled all his
forces on the 17th at the menaced spot. No sooner did
Marlborough see that he had deceived the enemy, than
while recalling Overkirk from opposite the French right, he
moved off silently and rapidly in the foggy morning of the
18th of July towards his own right flank, and passing over
the site of the battle of Landen, crossed the little Gheet
unperceived, and was in possession of the enemy's advanced
posts before the stratagem was discovered. The allies
seized the barriers, levelled the obstacles, and enabled the
duke to ride in at the head of his light horse without
difficulty; the infantry followed and maintained itself
within the lines, notwithstanding the subsequent strenuous
efforts of the French to retrieve the fortunes of the day. The
struggle was desperate, but the French after ten hours'
fighting were forced to retire and take up another defensive
position behind the Dyle, when Marlborough urged instant
pursuit, but the Dutch pleaded exhaustion, and the army
bivouacked that night near Tirlemont. On the following
day the allies marched to the Dyle, and finding the enemy
posted on the opposite side, Marlborough encamped his
army near Louvain. The two battalions of the First Guards
took their share in the glories of the day in forcing these
famous lines, now lost to the French for ever, and on the
troops encamping near Louvain, they took up a position in
line with the rest of the army, round Parke Abbey, in the
village of Vlierback, two miles to the north-east of the town,
where Marlborough fixed his head-quarters.

As the enemy remained for some time on the further

banks of the Dyle, Marlborough formed a project to cross that river and force his way to Brussels. At tattoo, on the 7th of August, the Guards, with the rest of the British infantry, having received sudden orders to march, proceeded to the banks of the Dyle, above Heverle, a few miles south of Louvain, when bridges were laid, and fifteen battalions, including the Guards, crossed unopposed, but the Dutch generals refusing to traverse the intervening swampy ground, the duke at dawn was compelled to withdraw those that had already crossed. Thereupon the army marched to Meldert, on the road to Tirlemont, and remained there till the 14th of August. At this camp the whole army was formed in two lines, the infantry in the centre, the cavalry on the flanks; the Guards here were not placed in line with the rest of the army, but were encamped at the duke's head-quarters at the Château de Meldert, in rear of the right wing. A subsequent attempt of Marlborough to turn the French right at Overysche, near Waterloo, by moving round the sources of the Dyle, failed in consequence of the inexcusable conduct of General Slangenberg, who blocked up the road with his artillery; the allies, consequently, returned to their former quarters, and Marlborough ordered the demolition of the famous lines that he had forced.

October.   As the season was advancing, the camp was ordered to be broken up, and the Guards, marching by Herenthals to Breda, went into winter quarters in that latter town at the end of October.

The glorious success in breaking the enemy's lines, though unrecorded as a brilliant victory, was productive of great results, and when the news was taken to England by Colonel Durel* of the First Guards, adjutant-general of the army, it was received with delight, and a *Te Deum* was sung at St. Paul's, where the queen went in state, between two lines of troops composed principally of the battalions of the household brigade.

* He had exchanged into the First Guards in January, 1703.

Many of the officers of the First Guards, while their 1705.
battalions were in winter quarters, received leave to return
to England. Amongst them were,—

Major-Gen., Henry Withers.	Capt. Alexander Deane.
Lieut.-Col. Selwyn.	„ Thomas Brown.
Capt. Edward Colston.	Ensigns, Nicholas Guibert.
„ Francis Howard.	„ John Deane.
„ George Ivey.	„ — Rengall.
„ Richard Seymour.	„ Henry Skelton.
„ — Hall.	„ John Cholmley.

These officers all received orders to rejoin their battalions 1706.
in Flanders, previous to the opening of the ensuing campaign, and Captain Thomas Brown, on coming out at the
end of March, brought with him a draft of 120 men from
the home companies, and twenty additional recruits followed
ten days later.

The ensuing campaign of 1706 was one of the most successful in its results that Marlborough ever conducted, as
the French were thereby forced from almost every stronghold in Brabant and Flanders, and it was the good fortune
of the First Guards, under Colonel Gorsuch, who were that
year brigaded with the Royals, 8th, 23rd, 28th, and Dalrymple's regiments, all under Brigadier Webb, to continue
to share in the triumphs of their colonel. At the end of
April Marlborough drew his troops out of winter quarters,
and the garrisons of Breda and of the neighbouring places
were directed to move in a south-easterly direction, towards
Tongres and Maestricht, where, by the middle of May, all
his forces, amounting to about 60,000 men, were collected.
Marlborough's first object was to endeavour to take Namur
by surprise; and on the 22nd of May he advanced with
his whole army towards the little Gheet river, halting for
the night with his right at Borchloen, and his left at Cos-
waren, not far from the spot where he broke through the
French lines in the previous year; but the French were on the
alert, and Villeroy, now also 60,000 strong, marching south
from Judoigne and Mont St. André, was first to arrive in
the field, on an elevated plateau, above the sources of the

May 22.

May 23.
Battle of
Ramillies.

little Gheet, where he took up a position, intending to await the advance of the allies. The French line was formed in a curve, with its left resting on the marshy ground near Anderkirk,* the low hill of Foulz in its front, on the allies' side of the stream; the village of Ramillies in front of his centre was converted into a strong post, while his right extended near to the Mehaigne river, resting on the high ground above the village of Tavières.

Marlborough determined at once to attack, and on Whit Sunday, the 23rd of May, he advanced in ten columns against the enemy, with his cavalry on the two flanks. The infantry, on reaching the plateau, was formed in two lines, the right of which consisted of Meredith's and Lord North and Grey's brigades, in first line, supported in second line by Webb's, with the First Guards, and by Macarthy's brigades. This wing advanced over the hill of Foulz, against the left of the enemy's position at Anderkirk, carrying pontoons with the view to crossing the stream; but when the first line had advanced half way down the exterior slope it was halted, and retired again to the summit, while the second line, its movements being concealed from the enemy by the hill, wheeled to its left, and joined the remaining troops in the great attack against the centre of the French position at Ramillies. Villeroy, upon first observing the false attack on the left of his position at Anderkirk, had, with the view to strengthening that flank, considerably weakened the centre of his line at Offuz, but soon perceived that the real attack was on his right and centre, where a hard struggle was going on. Marlborough had massed on his left the greater part of the Dutch and Danish cavalry, besides some infantry under Overkirk. This cavalry repeatedly charged the household cavalry of France, and eventually forced it to retreat. In the meantime the first attack against the centre of the position at Ramillies, by twenty battalions under General Schultz, had failed in driving the enemy from that post, but being sub-

* French "Autreglise."

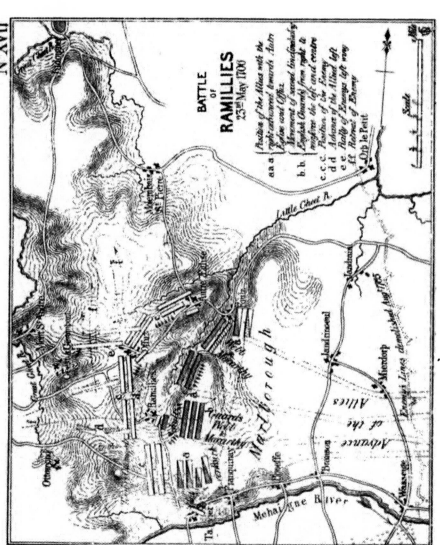

BATTLE
OF
RAMILLIES
23rd May 1706

Plate XVII bis

PLAN
OF
CAMPAIGN IN FLANDERS
1706

Scale of English Miles

Bruges
Ghent
BRUSSELS
Louvain
Tirlemont
Namur
Ypres
Lille
Tournay
Mons
Ath
Oudenarde

A   First encampment of the Allies at Borchlen.   May 21
B   Battle of Ramillies, remains of French Army retire to
      Dendermonde, thence to Tournay, Menin and Ypres behind
      the lines constructed in 1606
C.D.E.F. Successive positions taken up by the Allies at Wherle, Alost
      Gavre near Ghent, Deynse and Arsel, between 27th May and 5th June

sequently joined by Webb's and Macarthy's brigades,
withdrawn by the duke from the right, the attack was
renewed, and as the First Guards and the rest of Webb's
brigade advanced, the French began to give way. The brigade
then forming line, charged the retreating foe, who was at
the same time met by the victorious cavalry of the left wing,
whereupon all chances of the enemy retrieving the day were
lost, as he could not reform. The English cavalry on the
right had succeeded at last in crossing the little Gheet, and
after the infantry had driven the left of the French from their
position above the village of Anderkirk, they continued the
pursuit of the foe for five leagues, to Judoigne, on the road
to Louvain. The right wing of the enemy, taking a westerly
direction, retired towards Nivelles, but baggage waggons
encumbered the roads, and 6000 men, besides 600 officers,
were taken prisoners ; 8000 of the enemy were killed in the
field, and their total losses, with wounded and deserters,
amounted to not less than 20,000 men ; 50 guns, 120 colours
and standards, and several pairs of kettle drums were
the trophies of this victory. The losses of the allies were
comparatively small ; officers killed, 60 : wounded, 232 ;
men, killed, 1070 : wounded, 2467. The casualties in each
corps are not known, so that no approximate return of the
losses of the First Regiment of Guards can be given.

That night the army bivouacked at Bavechem, and on the
following day crossed the Dyle, and encamped at Bethlem,
near Louvain, whence the road was open to the capital,
and the whole country lay at the feet of the Duke of
Marlborough.

The allies advanced, on the 27th, across the Senne River,
encamping to the west of Vilvorde, near Brussels ; and on
the 28th of May Marlborough entered that town in triumph ;
when the three estates acknowledged Charles as their king.
Antwerp soon after fell without a blow, and the army continued its advance, clearing the country of the enemy. It
crossed the Dender on the 30th of May, encamping that
night to the west of Alost. The next day it reached the
Scheldt, and in the first week of June entered the country

1706.

June 28.

Aug. 25.

beyond the river Lys.   Many towns now fell in succession before the allied arms.   Cadogan took Ghent, Bruges, and Arsele; Overkirk took Ostend, and the Prince of Holstein Beck captured Courtrai.   On the 19th of June the allied army was encamped to the north-west of Rousselaer, towards Hoglede, with the battalion of Guards on duty at the duke's head quarters, on the extreme left of the line, to the east of Rousselaer, on the road to Rimbeck.   On the 28th of June the army moved to Meldert, not far from Tirlemont; shortly afterwards a corps, including a battalion of the First Guards, was detached to the west, and from the 1st to the 11th of July was quartered near Harlebec, the Guards being in the town; thence they proceeded to Helchin, on the Scheldt, south-east of Courtrai, to act as a covering force, while General Salisch invested Menin. While here they effectually prevented the French, under Vendome, who had now succeeded Villeroy, from succouring the town, which was stormed and taken on the 25th of August; whereupon the French fell back behind the Lys. General Churchill took Dendermonde, lying east of Ghent, on the 3rd of September; and on the 16th the British, under Marlborough, moved to Grametz, while Overkirk attacked and took Ath.   On the 13th of October the allies moved to the camp of Cambron, lying not far from Soignies, between Mons and Ath, when the First Guards, with North's and Lalo's, the 10th and 21st, regiments, were quartered near the abbey of Cambron.   Here Marlborough remained till the 26th of October, in hopes of drawing out Vendôme to a general action, but failing in that he proceeded to Gieslingen, behind Ath; and on the 31st of October the troops went into winter quarters, the First Guards proceeding to Ghent, where, after six months' hard campaigning, they were glad of the repose that there awaited them.   The victory of Ramillies, thus successfully followed up, had enabled Marlborough to clear almost the whole of Spanish Flanders of the enemy, and to recover many of the places that Louis XIV. had unjustly seized before the war begun.

CAMPAIGN IN SPAIN.

The combined battalion of First and Coldstream Guards reduced to about half their original strength, were left at Barcelona, in the winter of 1705-6, doing duty at the court of the Spanish King Charles of Austria, and as it was not to be expected that the French would leave Charles in un-disturbed possession of this fortress, steps were taken to reinforce the garrison. Amongst other troops ordered out from England, was a draft of 310 men from the Guards, being ten men from each of the seventeen and fourteen home companies of the First and Coldstream Guards respec-tively; they were placed under the command of Colonel Bisset, of the Coldstreams, and embarked at Gravesend the 3rd of March, on board Sir John Leake's fleet, which March. 3. shortly sailed to the coast of Catalonia. Sir Charles O'Hara, now lieutenant-general, was sent out about the same time, to act as second in command under Lord Peter-borough, and to join King Charles in Catalonia, or where-ever he might be found, according to advices he should receive on his way out. Long before they arrived however, the Spaniards and French, trusting that the capture of Charles would put an end to the war, had laid siege to Barcelona both by sea and land, determined to retake it. The garrison was still very weak, for the British Guards were not yet reinforced, and the newly raised regiment of Spanish Guards, which did duty at the royal palace on alternate days with the British Guards, was not yet suffi-ciently organised for active service. The greatest enthu-siasm, however, prevailed; the priests urged all who were able, to bear arms, and the women formed themselves into companies for working and watching. The French blockading squadron consisted of thirty ships, under the Count de Toulouse, and Philip's besieging army, commanded by Mar-shal Tessé, was 20,000 strong. The besiegers broke ground on the 8th of April, and directed their batteries against April 8. Montjuick, but the firm resistance made by the British and Dutch retarded the progress of the siege, and it was not till Lord Donegal and most of his men were killed that the fort fell. This occurred on the 25th of April, and on the same day an attack was made by the French on the western outworks of the town, where they overthrew the Spanish Guards, but on reaching the post of the English Guards they were first checked, and then driven back to their trenches.

Lord Peterborough, who, on hearing of the siege of Barcelona, had hurried back from Valencia, had been unable to throw his division into the town, but he remained in rear of the besieging force, daily harassing and annoying the French camp as much as possible, till at last the British fleet, with reinforcements from England, made its appearance on the coast. Peterborough immediately communicated with the admiral, and having made all necessary arrangements embarked his own force on board the fleet, which made sail direct for the bay of Barcelona, entering it without opposition; for, on its arrival, the Count de Toulouse, with his French squadron, at once withdrew, and Tessé, without loss of time, raised the siege, retiring into the interior. The First and Coldstream Guards, now increased to their original strength, had thus not only formed part of the besieging force which had taken Barcelona, but, while much reduced in numbers, had materially contributed to resisting, with success, the combined French and Spanish attempts to regain it.

Peterborough now renewed his proposal for an immediate advance on Madrid, but many days were spent in deliberations before the proposal was agreed to, and it was then decided that Charles, with his Spaniards, should proceed in the direction of the capital, by the circuitous route of Saragossa; while Peterborough, taking with him the chief part of the English and Dutch infantry, including the combined battalion of Guards, now raised to 600 men, should sail for Valencia, and advance on the capital from that quarter. On his arrival there he left the Guards and some other troops, under Brigadier Richard Russell, of the First Guards, to follow according to circumstances, and advanced

with the remainder through the provinces of Valencia and
New Castile towards Madrid. Lord Galway, who had now
recovered from the severe wound received at the siege of
Badajos in October, 1705, and the Portuguese General das
Minas had joined in this combined movement from Portugal,
and reached Madrid; but finding themselves unsupported by
the inhabitants were compelled to leave it, and march to
Guadalaxara, about thirty miles north-east of the capital,
where, on the 5th of August, they fell in, both with the Aug. 5.
troops under Charles that had marched by Saragossa, and
with those under Peterborough from Valencia.

The Guards remained for a time at Valencia, and it was
not till July that, together with 2400 other troops, principally
British, they left that town for the general rendezvous at
Guadalaxara, under the command of Lieutenant-General
Edmund Windham, who had served most of his early years
in the First Regiment of Guards. Lord Peterborough
having given Windham discretionary powers as to the route
he should take to join the main body of the army, this
officer left Valencia on the 28th of July, his men in high July 28.
spirits, and wearing boughs in their caps as the distinguishing badge of the English forces. He halted at St. Jago,
sixteen miles from Valencia, where he was delayed by the
explosion of his magazines, but collecting what powder he
could in the village, he pushed on to Requena, a town lying
amongst the hills separating Valencia from New Castile,
where he was received by a warm fire from the walls of the
place; but while deliberating on his plans, the town capitulated, and the combined battalion of Guards was ordered to
take possession of the gates. Leaving some companies of
friendly Spaniards to take charge of Requena, Windham
then marched with the Guards and the rest of the troops to
Cuença, which town, after a few shots were fired, also surrendered. In the meantime Lord Peterborough finding his
counsels disregarded, and being superseded in his command
by Lord Galway, resolved to quit the army in Spain, and
proceed to Italy. He arrived at Huette, with an escort of
300 dragoons, but lost his baggage on the road, owing to his

convoy being surprised by some Spaniards; his anger was, however, diverted from that personal loss by hearing of a horrible outrage perpetrated near Campelo on a detachment of Guards, under an officer of the Coldstreams, who had all lately left hospital, and were on the march to join their battalion; the men were suddenly seized, many of them slain, and the survivors thrown down a well. Peterborough having discovered the leader of the band engaged in these atrocities, and having ordered him to be hung to the knocker of his own door, proceeded on his road to Valencia, and sailed for Genoa. Windham continued his march with the Guards and the rest of his detachment, and joined the army at Chinchon, a town twenty six miles south-south-east of

Aug. 11. Madrid, on the 11th of August, having been a fortnight on the road, but so much time had now been lost, that an advance upon Madrid was out of the question, and as the Duke of Berwick barred the road to Portugal, it was resolved, after many councils of war, and much unnecessary delay, that the army should return to the coast of Valencia. The troops left Chinchon on the 9th of September, crossed the Tagus at Fuente Duena, and continued their march over the mountains to Valencia, where the Guards and rest of the army took up their winter quarters.

1707.

Spain. A council of war assembled at Valencia in the beginning of February in the following year, 1707, at which Lord Rivers, who had landed some reinforcements at Alicant on the 28th of the previous January, was present, and a proposal of General Stanhope's to march upon Madrid was generally approved and decided upon; but though every effort should have been made to secure the success of such an expedition, it was no sooner settled, than Lord Rivers left for England, Charles left for Catalonia, taking with him 600 Dutch troops, and the governor at Barcelona refused to allow the three English regiments remaining in that garrison to proceed to Valencia; these however were only the natural

forerunners of the subsequent disaster of Almanza.
Amongst the officers of the First Guards that took part in
this year's campaign in Spain, were the following, viz.:—

The senior regimental Major, Major-Gen. Shrimpton, commanding
        a Division.
Lieut.-Col. Richard Russell, as Brigadier-General.
  ,,   Edward Austin.   Captain Henry Pulteney.
  ,,   Philip Talbot.   ,,   ,,   Fogg.
Captain William Peachey.

    The road towards Madrid was now no longer open to the
British troops as it had been in the previous campaign, for
the Spaniards under Berwick advancing through Castile had
crossed the frontiers into Valencia. Previous to Lord Galway moving from the coast he directed Lieutenant-General
Erle, who was commanding at Alicant, to advance with the
troops under his command, and their two corps effected a
junction on the 31st of March near Caudete, about sixteen March 31.
miles south-east of Almanza, when Lord Galway found
himself at the head of 15,500 men, amongst whom were
the combined battalion of British Guards and 4500 cavalry.
The Duke of Berwick, who had been watching the movements of the allies, finding himself not strong enough to
encounter them, retreated further into the interior, abandoning stores of provisions at Yula, which were most
welcome to the allied army; for two days every one was
allowed to help himself, and the remainder were destroyed.
On the 18th of April, Lord Galway laid siege to the castle
of Villena, but receiving information that the French,
strengthened by the arrival of detachments, meditated an
attack upon him, he determined to be beforehand with
them, abandoned the siege, and on the 24th of April April 24.
marched his army in three columns to the Torre de Bour-
garres, where information was received that the Dukes of
Orleans and Berwick were encamped at Almanza; the
Duke of Orleans, however, had left the camp, not expecting
an attack.

    At three in the morning of the 25th of April, Lord Gal- April 25.
way moved his army in four columns over a difficult and

1707.

Battle of
Almanza.
April 25.

hilly country, and on arriving in the plains beyond, in sight of the enemy, he formed his troops in line of battle.

The British infantry with the combined battalion of Guards formed the centre, under the command of Lieutenant-General Erle and Major-General Shrimpton, both under the supreme command of the impetuous Das Minas. The wings consisted of cavalry and infantry intermixed; the left wing was composed of English and Dutch under Sir Charles O'Hara, now Lord Tyrawley; the right, of Portuguese under the Conde de Atalaya. The French and Spaniards were somewhat similarly disposed. The Count d'Avarez commanded the cavalry on the right, the Duke di Popoli the Spanish Horse Guards on the left, while Berwick principally superintended the movements of the infantry in the centre.

Galway, perceiving that the superior force of the enemy's cavalry on their right enabled them to threaten the British left under Tyrawley, moved against that wing, and a furious encounter ensued, in which he himself was badly wounded by a sabre cut over the eye, and notwithstanding the efforts of Lord Tyrawley and his subordinates, the British and Dutch squadrons were forced to retire. The Anglo-Dutch infantry, however, in the centre, amongst which were the British Guards, advancing steadily against the enemy, drove all before it, and penetrated their first line, forcing it back on its supports; and the Guards and Portmore's battalion, which were leading, advanced close up to the walls of Almanza. Here the struggle was most obstinate, and the victory still doubtful, notwithstanding the defeat of the left wing of the allies, when the right wing, composed of Portuguese under Atalaya, fled almost at the first fire of the enemy, without even returning it, and both their cavalry and infantry left the field. The body of English and Dutch infantry that had hitherto not only gallantly resisted, but driven back the troops opposed to them, were now charged on both flanks by the enemy's horse under D'Avarez and Popoli. Das Minas, commanding the allied centre, though himself severely wounded, was everywhere urging on and supporting his men, who, upon the repeated charges of the enemy's cavalry, formed squares, and in that formation gradually withdrew in perfect order from the field of battle. Thirteen battalions, including the Guards, reached the wood of Caudete, but the men had no more ammunition left, and all were without food; they had been marching and fighting all day, and could offer no further resistance, whereupon a council of war was held attended by Major-General Shrimpton, Colonel Bretton, Colonel Hill, Brigadier Macartney, and the Dutch brigadiers. These officers saw that there were no means of procuring food; they were isolated from the cavalry which had ridden off the field, and they knew not which way to go. The men, disheartened, were open to an attack from the combined forces of the enemy, and the council decided that there was nothing left for them but to surrender. At dawn the next morning they sent to the Duke of Berwick desiring honourable terms, who granted the same that were allowed to the French battalions at Blenheim, viz., that the men should be prisoners of war till exchanged; that the officers should retain their swords; and that they should get all their baggage before they marched further. Other battalions had surrendered on the field, making twenty-three in all. The loss of the allies was very great, for including the killed, wounded, and prisoners, no less than 10,000 men were missing out of the 16,000 who marched to the attack. Amongst the casualties in the First Guards, were Lieutenant-Colonel Austin and Captain W. Peachey, killed; Major-General Shrimpton, Lieutenant-Colonel Philip Talbot, and Captains Henry Pulteney and Fogg, of the First Guards, besides five officers of the Coldstreams, surrendered as prisoners. As soon as the baggage arrived they were marched to France, many of the English remaining in the vicinity of Paris till the end of the war. The small remains of the army that escaped made their way to Alcira, and there embarked for Barcelona. After this disaster the province of Valencia declared for Philip, and the crown of Spain was lost to Charles. The conduct of Lord Galway

1707.

April 25.

Almanza.

1707.   and the other generals was much censured in England, and
their excuses of want of provisions were thought insufficient
to justify such a capitulation.   In considering the failure
at the battle of Almanza, it does not appear to be at all
attributable to any shortcomings on the part of the British
infantry, which, posted in the centre, successfully carried
out the duties imposed upon it, gallantly breaking through
the enemy's line and advancing up to the walls of the town,
when if the wings had been equally successful the overthrow
of the enemy would have been certain.   The complete
defeat of these wings, however, caused the British infantry,
including the Guards, to be surrounded on three sides, a
position from which they gallantly extricated themselves by
forming squares to repel the repeated charges of the enemy's
cavalry, and having reached a place of safety, they might
have continued to defend themselves with success, if their
commanders had taken the necessary precautions to ensure
a due supply of provisions, failing which, a capitulation
was a necessary consequence.   The conduct of all ranks in
the Guards left nothing to be desired, and that of Colonel
Richard Russell the 2nd major of the First Regiment, under
whose command the combined battalion of Guards had left
England in July, 1704, appears to have met with so much
approbation from the authorities, that in a subsequent
warrant granting him a certain sum of money, it is stated
to be in consideration of his exemplary services and conduct,
and the losses he sustained in the queen's service in Spain.
It is a curious fact that in this action the British troops
were commanded by a Frenchman, Rouvigny, Lord Galway,
and the French, by an Englishman, the Duke of Berwick.

This severe misfortune in the Spanish Peninsula was not
Flanders. redeemed by any brilliant operations in Flanders, where
scarcely a shot was fired, or any great advantage gained on
either side, but the very fact of not being beaten by
Marlborough was considered by the French as a favourable
circumstance, for it enabled them to reorganise their army
after its defeat the previous year at Ramillies, and gave
spirit to the soldiers.   Louis XIV. had given to Vendôme

the command of his armies, 80,000 strong, which were distri- 1707.
buted in a new series of lines of a formidable character
thrown up along the French frontier.

Marlborough, who in the early part of the year had been
much occupied with negotiations, had, by a well-timed visit
to Charles XII. of Sweden, won over that sovereign to the
side of the allies, and about the middle of May he had May 15.
75,000 troops assembled at Anderlecht, near Brussels.
The Duke led this army, on the 27th, towards Nivelles,
where a small corps of French would have been surrounded, but that the field deputies insisted on discussing
the plan of attack, thereby allowing the enemy to escape,
and nothing more was effected during the summer months.
On the 11th of August the Guards marched to Florival, August.
and after three days joined the rest of the army at Jemappes,
whence it proceeded to Soignies, but very heavy rains prevented the continuance of operations, and Vendôme retired behind his lines. Marlborough, unable to take his
enemy at a disadvantage, retired in October, and placed his October.
troops in the same winter quarters as those occupied by
them the preceding year, the First Guards proceeding to
Ghent.

Captain William Barrell, who had been adjutant of the
First Guards battalion at Blenheim, was promoted this
summer to a company, and was succeeded in his office by
Captain William Blakeney from the 18th Royal Irish,
who subsequently rose to be Governor of Gibraltar.
Barrell was rough in manner, but an excellent soldier, and
devised a system of exercising the men by the sound of the
bugle and the waving of colours. Colonel Gorsuch submitted this new exercise to Major-General Withers, the
lieutenant-colonel of the regiment, who with its colonel,
the Duke of Marlborough, witnessed the evolutions while
quartered at the camp of Meldert, and both expressed their
entire approval.

A warrant was issued in England, in October, 1707, to
make good the losses sustained by the Guards at Almanza;
it stated that as the 600 men that had been detached from

1707.

the several companies at home of the First and Coldstream
Guards had been entirely reduced by that battle, and other
accidents, the several companies should be forthwith recruited again, viz., 310 men to the seventeen home companies
of the First Guards, and 290 to the fourteen companies of
the Coldstreams. After this the First Guards sent no more
reinforcements to Spain during the remainder of the war,
and the establishment of the home companies remained at
fifty privates each, while that of the service companies continued at seventy.

1708.

A change occurred in the following year (1708) among
some of the senior officers of the First Guards. Major-
General Shrimpton, first major of the regiment since 1696,
who, though released after having been taken prisoner at
Almanza, was incapacitated for the time from serving,
retired from the corps on the 9th of March, and William
Tatton, a brigadier-general in the army since the 1st of
January, 1707, was brought in as first major in his place.
Brigadier Gilbert Primrose retired from the regiment at
the same time, and was succeeded as 2nd major by Colonel
Richard Russell, who became a brigadier-general in 1710.

The following officers were in the regiment on the 9th
of March, 1708, after the above changes took place :—

OFFICERS OF HER MAJESTY'S FIRST REGIMENT OF GUARDS,
9TH OF MARCH, 1708.

John Duke of Marlborough, Colonel.
Major-Gen. Henry Withers, Lieut.-Colonel.

CAPTAINS AND LIEUT.-COLONELS.

Brigadier W. Tatton, 1st Major.	Thomas Ferrers.
Lieut.-Col. Thos. King.	Henry Durel.
Richd. Russell, 2nd Major.	James Dormer.
Charles Gorsuch, Col. pr. Brevet.	John Pococke
Andrew Wheeler.	Sir John Mathews.
John Maurice, Col. pr. Brevet.	John Guise.
Francis Sydney.	William Lloyd.
George Etheredge.	William Barrell.
Andrew Windsor.	Thos. Harrison.

CAPTAINS AND LIEUT.-COLONELS—*continued.* 1708.

Thomas Sidney.
    Egerton.
Mich. Richards.
Phil. Talbot.
John Selwyn.

A. Oughton.
Sir Robert Rich, Bart.
Lt.-Col. Edw. Stanhope, Capt.-Lt.
    24 Aug., 1707.

LIEUTENANTS AND CAPTAINS.

Charles Lewis.
Anthony Hastings.
Richd. Berkely.
Wm. Bodenham.
Henry Browne.
Gilbert Nicholetts.
George Reede.
Thos. Brerewood.
George Docwra.
Den. Pujolas.
George Smith.

Edwd. Colston.
Richd. Seaman.
Thos. Wade.
George Wilmon.
Henry Andrews.
Henry Wingfield.
Harvey Wolstenholme
James Gould.
David Eyton.
Jeffrey de Culant.

John Southby.
Willm. Alehorn.
Archd. Primrose.
Robt. Townsend.
Nich. Herne.
    Armstrong.
Henry Pulteney.
James Phil. Moreau.
James Pettit.
    Saubergue.

ENSIGNS.

Edwd. Leighton.
George Chudleigh.
Thos. Woodcock.
Thos. Poultney.
Char. Sibourg.
John Deane.
John Cholmeley.
Henry Skelton.

George Brett.
Richd. Pearson.
Phill. Shrimpton.
George Oglethorpe.
Rowland Reynolds.
Nich. Guibert.
Francis Rodd.
Wm. Oakely.

Fra. Cleaver.
Charles Wightwicke.
Robt. Shapleigh.
Henry Murcott.
Willm. Lancaster.
Daniel Tanner.
George Wallis.
    Fogg.

STAFF OFFICERS.

Capt. Charles Lewis,
  ,, Wm. Oakley, 24th March 170⅞, ⎱ Adjutants.
  ,, Richd. Berkely,   ⎰
  ,, Gilbt. Nicholetts,
  ,, Willm. Bodenham,   ⎱ Quartermasters.
Ensign David Eyton,   ⎰
  Mr. Benjamin Sweet .   .   . Solicitor.
  Doct. James Smallwood .   . Chaplain.
  Mr. Archd. Harris   .   . Chirurgeon.
  Mr. Charles Harris .   .   . Chirurgeon's Mate.
  Mr. Roger Burroughs, .   . Drum Major.
  Mr. Thos. Morphey .   .   Deputy Marshal.

Among the above captains of companies are two whose names came prominently forward towards the end of the present reign, for, as strong supporters of the Hanoverian succession, they were threatened with the loss of their commissions, viz., Lieutenant-Colonel Egerton, brother to the Earl of Bridgewater; and Lieutenant-Colonel Sidney, brother to the Earl of Leicester, and nephew to Henry Sidney, Earl of Romney, late Colonel of the regiment.

Political intrigues had for some time been effecting modifications among the counsellors of the queen, and the influence of the Tories had increased, while the Duke of Marlborough had proportionately sunk in the queen's favour. This change of opinions at court filling the Jacobites with false hopes, a plot was concocted in Paris early in 1708 for the invasion of Scotland. A fleet under
the Chevalier de Forbin, bearing an army commanded by General de Gacé, was assembled at Dunkirk awaiting Prince James, who at this critical moment was attacked by the measles, and the delay caused thereby enabled the governor of Ostend to be made aware of the plan, which he immediately communicated to the government in England, and to Marlborough. The greatest consternation prevailed in London; drafts about to start for Spain were counter-manded, troops were directed to march to Edinburgh, and a combined battalion of Guards, 450 strong, composed of five of the home companies of the First Regiment and four
of the Coldstreams, was despatched on the 15th of March from London to the north, with two troops of Life Guards, and the Duke of Northumberland's regiment of horse (the Blues). These companies marched through Northampton, Leicester, Nottingham, and Doncaster, and reached York, after fifteen days' march, at the beginning of April.

Upon the news of the intended invasion reaching Marlborough, he directed General Lumley, who was in command of the troops at Ghent, on the 8th of March, to take the whole of his garrison, including the eleven companies of the First Guards, together with the British regiments at Bruges, by canal boats to Ostend. Accord-ingly, the First Guards, under Colonel Gorsuch, the first battalion of Orkney's, Argyll's, Webb's, North and Grey's, Howe's, Godfrey's, Ingoldsby's, Lalo's, and Primrose's *

* 1st, 3rd, 8th, 10th, 15th, 16th, 18th, 21st, and 24th Regiments of the line.

regiments, all under Lieutenant-General Withers, embarked
on board the fleet commanded by Admiral Baker, and sailing northwards, anchored on the 21st at Tynemouth; here
they remained weather-bound, suffering much from the want
of provisions and covering, till the 30th of March; at
which time the combined battalion of Guards from London
was arriving at York. On the 2nd of April, after a fair
passage, the fleet entered the Leith roads, having missed the
French ships which had been dispersed by a storm, and
were making the best of their way back to Dunkirk after
the loss of some of their transports, especially of the
" Salisbury," on board of which were many distinguished
Jacobites, a French general officer, and 450 troops,
besides a crew of 200 men. The First Guards had suffered
much from the discomfort of the passage to Scotland,
owing to the crowded state of the transports, and on the
6th of April, Colonel Gorsuch succeeded in getting his
battalion transferred from the wretched old ship " Bonaven-
ture " to the line-of-battle ship " Dreadnought," carrying
the flag of Admiral Baker. The danger over, the fleet
sailed southwards on the 21st of April, and on its arrival
at Ostend, General Withers' force disembarked to the great
joy both of officers and men. In the language of an officer
of the First Guards, by name Deane, who kept a journal of
this campaign preserved to the present day, "continued
destruction was in the foretop, the plague between decks,
hell in the forecastle, and the Devil at the helm. The
allowance was short, the purser was blessed with soldiers'
prayers, who rejoiced when they knew they were about to
leave the wooden world, and find themselves once more on
terra-firma." There is no doubt that many of the transports
were ill-fitted for carrying troops, and that in the hurry of
the hour they were badly victualled, and Parliament, admit-
ting the excuse of the emergency, voted a sum of money to
make good the losses experienced by men and officers in
the course of the voyage. On the 22nd of April the troops
re-entered their former quarters at Bruges and Ghent, the
Guards proceeding to the latter town, having been absent

1708.   only five weeks on this expedition. The following were the
captains of companies of the First Guards' battalion at the
commencement of the ensuing campaign :—

Lieut-Col. Ch. Gorsuch, Comg.	Lieut.-Col. Thomas Harrison.
„ Francis Sydney.	„ Michael Richards.
„ George Etheridge.	„ John Selwyn.
„ James Dormer.	„ Adolphus Oughton,
„ John Pococke.	and the Colonel's company, of
„ John Guise.	which Lieut.-Col. E. Stanhope
	was Captain and Lieutenant.

April 29.   As from the complete failure of the invasion there was
but little probability of such an attempt being repeated, the
troops had all been recalled to their former stations, and
it was resolved to detach one more battalion of Guards from
England to join the First Guards battalion in Flanders.
The combined battalion of First and Coldstream Guards,
which, as long as danger threatened, had remained at York,
received orders accordingly on arriving at Northampton to
march to Colchester, for further proceeding to the Continent, being at the same time augmented by 136 men, so
as to consist of the same numbers as the First Guards
battalion already abroad.   Brigadier Braddock of the Coldstreams was under orders to accompany this battalion, but
as he was senior to Colonel Gorsuch, who had commanded
the first battalion of the First Guards on service for four
years, the Duke of Marlborough desired that neither
Braddock nor any officer senior to Gorsuch should be sent
out.   The combined battalion was accordingly put under
the command of Lieutenant-Colonel Andrew Wheeler of
the First Guards, who stood next junior to Colonel Gorsuch,
and marching to Harwich in the middle of May, this bat-
May 20.   talion embarked on the 20th for the Continent; landed
at Ostend on the 22nd of May, and joined the service
battalion at Terbank.

Before the opening of the campaign of 1708, which commenced shortly after the return of the Guards and other
troops from the expedition to Scotland, the allies held Ath
and Oudenarde with their most advanced troops, while
Bruges, Ghent, Brussels, and Louvain formed a second line

1708.

in support. The French were massing their troops between
Mons and Tournay, as though to threaten Brussels, and on May 11.
the 11th of May the garrison of Ghent with the battalion of
First Guards received orders to take the field. Marching
through Bellinghem, ten miles south of Ghent, where the
Duke of Marlborough joined them, they arrived on the 18th
at St. Renelle, in front of Hal, thus effectually stopping any
further advance of the French in that quarter, who had by
that time reached Soignies.* The French now made a movement to the right, as if with the view of turning the left of
Marlborough's position, and gaining the road to Louvain,
upon which, while Marlborough sent a detachment of
cavalry to secure the pass leading direct to that town, he
directed the Guards and the rest of the infantry to march
to Anderlecht near Brussels, and the Guards had no sooner
arrived there than they were ordered to proceed without loss
of time to Louvain.• They accordingly made a forced march
during that day and the following night, and on the 23rd
reached Louvain, where the duke fixed his head-quarters at
Closter Terbank, the First Guards being all quartered at
that place.   While here, the Elector of Hanover, the future
king of England, arrived, and was received with great consideration by the duke. The combined battalion of the First June.
and Coldstream Guards from England also joined the First
Guards battalion in this camp of Louvain on the 15th of
June, their arrival being much welcomed by their comrades.   This, however, was not the first time that a detachment of Coldstreams had been sent over to join in the
campaigns under Marlborough, for in the spring of the
previous year, when a draft of fifty-one men, three men per
company, was sent out from the seventeen home companies
of the First Guards, there was added a draft of three
drummers and twenty-eight men, or two from each of the
Coldstream companies, to make up the required strength.
There were now of the First Guards, sixteen companies in
Flanders, and twelve at home; of the Coldstream, four in

---

* While in this camp of St. Renelle, Captain John Cholmeley was promoted
to be captain and lieut.-colonel of a company, *vice* James Dormer.

1708.

Flanders, and ten at home. The several battalions of Guards were now formed into a brigade, and placed under the command of Colonel Charles Gorsuch.

The French, under Vendôme and the Duke of Burgundy, finding all attempts against the left of the British line of no avail, suddenly changed their tactics, and endeavoured to take advantage of the comparatively more defenceless state in which Marlborough had left the right of his position, to threaten that point, notwithstanding the risk of advancing so far into Flanders; Marlborough on hearing of this movement ordered the British troops at Louvain early on

June 24.

the 24th of June to march suddenly through Brussels to Anderlecht, their left wing resting on Hal; but the enemy had already reached Alost, Ordeghem, and Dendermonde, thus cutting off the duke from Ghent and Bruges, and two days later he had the mortification to hear that those two towns had fallen into the enemy's hands.

Before turning his thoughts to recovering these places, Marlborough determined to meet Vendôme in the field. He laid his plans with Prince Eugene, who met him at Asche, a few miles in advance of Anderlecht, and feeling certain he had caught the enemy in a trap, from which he could not extricate himself without hazarding an action, he determined, after crossing the Dender higher up, to advance on the Scheldt, and place himself between the French and their frontier. Upon the troops being accordingly ordered to move towards Ath, the brigade of Guards moved at six in the morning of the 28th of June, O. S. (8th of July, N. S.), to Herselingen, whence, after waiting some hours for the main body, they continued their march and bivouacked for the night.

July 9.

The next day, while the main body with the Guards advanced in four columns, and crossed the Dender at Lessines and Ath, where they halted for the night, General Cadogan was sent forward, through Lessines, about five leagues further, with a strong force of cavalry, infantry, and artillery, to secure the passage of the Scheldt at Oude-narde. Cadogan successfully accomplished this task, and

having left four battalions to watch the bridges, took up
a position the same evening on the western side of the
Scheldt, between the villages of Heyne and Bevern.

At break of day on the morning of the 10th of July, the
main body followed Cadogan ; the Guards and the rest of the
infantry reaching Oudenarde, a distance of fifteen English
miles, about 2 p.m., and, after waiting for some cavalry,
crossed the Scheldt by the bridges he had constructed below
the town, and as each brigade came up, it formed in line of
battle, extending the line that had been taken up the night
before between Heyne and Bevern.   The brigade of Guards
was ordered to occupy this latter village, in performing
which task, these battalions with two other brigades found it
necessary to dislodge the advanced guard of the enemy,
whom they found in possession.   The allies were now in
position, with 80,000 men in line, intercepting the communications of the French army, to secure which object
still more effectually, Marlborough directed most of his
cavalry to advance on the left, and check any movement of
the French to retire by their right flank.

When Vendôme, with his army of 86,000 men, in
position between Ghent and Dendermonde, became aware
of Marlborough's plan to cut him off, he hastened across
the Scheldt at Gavre, to anticipate if possible the allies
in crossing it, and to maintain his own communications ;
but he was too late for the first, and was forced to fight
to attempt to secure the second.   He accordingly drew up
his army in a strong position facing the allies, between
Asper and Wareghem, and had he remained stationary, the
allies would not—tired as the troops were with a long
march—have molested him that day ; such, however, was
not Vendôme's intention ; it was near five o'clock before the
attack commenced, when he threatened Marlborough's left,
with the view to cutting off his communication with Oudenarde, and the severest part of the fighting was in that
wing, where Marlborough, anxious for its safety, placed
himself, while he entrusted his right to Prince Eugene,
who, leaving his own army at Maestricht, had come to

offer his assistance, and share in the glories of his comrade in arms.

The Duke of Argyll commanded the centre, composed principally of British infantry with the Guards. As the evening drew on, the contest here also became very severe, and the infantry after a hard struggle drove the enemy from hedge to hedge. After a time, the brigade of Guards and two other brigades, in advancing upon the French, received their fire without its doing much damage, upon which the Guards returned a murderous volley into the enemy's ranks, causing them to turn and retreat from the field. Vendôme and the Duke of Burgundy, it is said, had been at cross purposes the whole day, to which their defeat may be partly attributable ; but the French officers themselves were ready to allow that Marlborough had forced victory to his side by the able disposition he had made of his forces, and by bringing fresh bodies of troops to every part of the field as they were required. The French were now beaten and in full retreat, for though Vendôme attempted to retrieve the day by leading on his men on foot, all his efforts were useless ; he posted some regiments to arrest the pursuit, and then remounting, rode off to Ghent.

The allied army lay that night on the wet ground, and on the following day the two battalions of Guards were ordered to take up their quarters in Oudenarde.

The loss of the French in this action was 6000 killed and wounded and 9000 prisoners, that of the allies about 5000 killed and wounded. In the First Regiment of Guards, Lieutenant-colonel Sir John Mathew and Ensign John Deane were killed : and the loss of men, though not recorded, is stated to have been severe. Ten pieces of cannon, fifty-six pairs of colours, fifty-two standards, and eight pairs of kettle-drums were the trophies of this victory. On the receipt in England of the news, a national day of thanksgiving was ordered, and, on the 19th of the following August, the queen proceeded in state to St. Paul's, on which occasion a combined battalion of 500 men from the

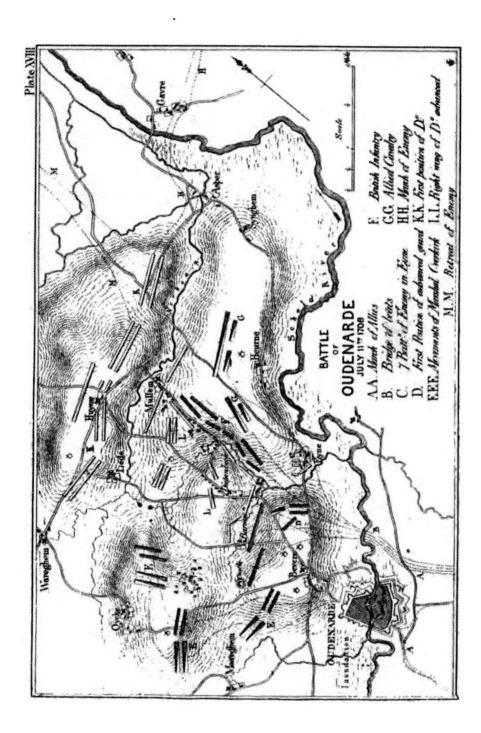

Plate XVIII

BATTLE
OF
OUDENARDE
JULY 11ᵀᴴ 1708

AA. Mead of Allies
B. Bridge of Boats
C. 7 Point of Enemy in View
D. First Position of advanced guard
EEE. Movements of Marshal Overkirk
F. British Infantry
GG. Allied Cavalry
HH. Mead of Enemy
KK. First position of Dᵗ
I.I. Right wing of Dᵗ advanced
M.M. Retreat of Enemy

Scale

U of M

First and Coldstream Regiments of Guards were in attendance on her majesty.

Marlborough now found himself between Vendôme's beaten army and France, and having 70,000 men with him in splendid condition, proposed to march with them direct upon Paris; but this bold plan was opposed even by the daring Eugene, and after a consultation with the field deputies, it was decided that Prince Eugene, whose army had now arrived at Brussels from Maestricht, should undertake the siege of the famous frontier fortress of Lille, while Marlborough covered his operations. An itinerary of the Guards, during Prince Eugene's siege of Lille, is still extant, from which it appears that the brigade was on continuous duty wherever Marlborough fixed his head-quarters. On the 14th of July the army moved July 14. up the left bank of the Scheldt, and, after a thirteen miles' march, reached Helchin, whence a detachment was sent on to the River Lys to secure Menin, and destroy the enemy's lines there, before the Duke of Berwick, who had come from Spain, could arrive to reinforce the French. The Guards then proceeded to Werwick, the duke making it his head-quarters, where they remained, till the 12th of August, when they returned to their former camp at Helchin for ten days. Part of the British troops were now detached to assist Eugene in the siege, while the remainder were on the 19th reviewed by Marlborough Aug. 19. in presence of the Elector of Hanover. On the 23rd, the Guards moved across the Scheldt, and during the next six days were encamped at Amougies, the duke fixing upon the neighbouring Château de Montpensier as his head-quarters for the time. They were returning to Helchin on the 29th, when, in consequence of the enemy appearing in force in the direction of Lille, they were countermanded, and marched the next day to Pont d'Epierres, thence on the 1st of September to Peronne, lying in the plain between Lille and Tournay, as an attack was expected, and, on the 4th, the whole army advanced across the Sept. 4. plain, but the enemy declined an engagement, and the

1708.

troops encamped, the duke fixing his head-quarters at Château Fretain, two miles from Peronne, where he remained with the Guards till the 16th, during which time, owing to their proximity, frequent small affairs took place with the enemy. On the 8th, the 15th Regiment was engaged in driving them from a post, in which they suc-

Sept. 18.

ceeded, but not without great loss; on the 18th, all the grenadiers of the army were engaged in forcing them from a position at St. Pleuss, and the Guards, who moved up in support, occupied the post after assisting in the operation. The Guards then advanced still further on the road to Lille, passing by Sanghain and Templeuve, and on the 20th were encamped at Lannoy, all places rendered memorable, eighty-seven years later, by the gallant conduct of the brigade of Guards under very adverse circumstances.

Sept. 22.

On the 22nd of September, detachments of grenadiers were made from the covering army to supply the losses incurred the day before by the besiegers, and, on their arrival, were encamped, together with Godfrey's, Primrose's, Sabine's, and Ingoldsby's regiments, within the general line of contravallation in the neighbourhood of the Abbey of Loos, three miles W.S.W. of the town. The principal attack was directed from the north against the two hornworks and the intermediate defences, all of which were surrounded by wet ditches, and from this period till the capitulation of the town on the 22nd of October these additional troops shared in all the labours of the siege. A party of five grenadiers of the First Guards particularly distinguished itself on the occasion of its being required to cut the chains of a drawbridge of one of the works. These men, amongst whom was one of the name of William Lettler, volunteered to make the attempt; and in swimming across the ditch to execute their task, under a galling fire from the ramparts, three of his comrades were killed; Lettler succeeded in the attempt, survived, and for this gallant action was promoted to an ensigncy in his own regiment; he rose in the same corps to be captain and lieutenant-colonel of a company of grenadiers, to whom he had shown such a brilliant example

of cool determination and courage, and died in the regiment **1708.**
in 1742, honoured and respected by all his brother-officers.

The duke being anxious to open a communication with
Ostend, the battalion of First Guards marched on the 23rd Sept. 23.
of September, eight miles to Roncq, near Menin, to which
village the duke was about to transfer his head-quarters,
while the combined battalion was left at Lannoy, in
attendance upon his Grace. On the 29th the duke came to Sept. 29.
Roncq, and the whole army encamped in its neighbourhood,
while the French at Tournay, taking advantage of this
movement, moved up, and cut off the communication of
the allies with Brussels; notwithstanding which, the duke
carried out his former project, and with a view to protecting
the convoy coming from Ostend, the troops continued their
march northwards on the 7th of October, encamping at
Rousselaer; on the 8th they advanced in four columns to
meet the enemy, who retired, cutting the sluices, and
inundating the country to such an extent, that Marlborough
was unable to proceed; the convoy was obliged to retire to
Ostend, and, on the 9th, the Guards and the rest of the Oct. 9.
army returned to Rousselaer, where the duke remained for
more than six weeks. While Marlborough's army was in
this camp, news arrived that the town of Lille had surrendered to Prince Eugene on the 22nd of October, and that
Boufflers had retired into the citadel with 5000 men. A
month later, information being received that the enemy
had appeared before Brussels on the 22nd of November, Nov. 22.
Marlborough ordered a rapid advance to save that town,
and the Guards, with the rest of the covering army,
were sent off in that direction. On the 25th they
marched to Harlebec, where they crossed the Lys; on the
26th and 27th Marlborough forced the passage of the
Scheldt in two places, above and below Oudenarde, at
Asper near Graves, and at Kerkhoven—he himself with
the Guards and the main body, and accompanied by Prince
Eugene, crossing at the latter place; the enemy was surprised
at both, and retired without offering any serious resistance,
and the Guards, after crossing, proceeded to the heights

1708. above Oudenarde, where Marlborough rested for the night.

Nov. 28. At break of day on the 28th, the cavalry were sent with all speed towards Brussels, while the two battalions of Guards were despatched to make a forced march of twenty miles, and seize upon the bridges over the Dender at Alost. Marlborough personally commanded the brigade of Guards on this occasion, so anxious was he for the success of the manœuvre, and it was performed with so much alacrity that the Guards occupied the town before the enemy's arrival, and effectually barred their passage by that route. The main body of the army, exhausted by previous toil, had been unable to keep up with this rapidly executed movement, and came up the following day.

The French under the Elector had attacked Brussels on the 26th of November, but were driven back by the ten regiments in garrison there; and as the Elector was not prepared to resist the attack of the allies under Marlborough, he precipitately retreated, leaving behind him both stores and cannon. Brussels being thus relieved, the brigade of **Nov. 30.** Guards, on the 30th of November, marched westward again, to Baeleghem, where Marlborough remained till the 11th of December, when, on hearing that the citadel of Lille had capitulated, he resolved, as his army was no longer required as a covering force, and as his anger at the loss of Ghent had not abated, to lay siege to that town before the close of the campaign, notwithstanding the advanced period of the season; for this purpose he advanced to Melle, within **Dec. 11.** a few miles of Ghent on the 11th, and to Harlebec, still nearer, on the 19th of December, where the Guards continued in attendance upon him, while Prince Eugene, who had arrived with part of his army from Lille, on the 18th, placed himself so as to cover the operations of the siege.

Dec. 24. On Monday night, the 24th of December, the first battalion First Guards, first battalion Orkney's, and five other regiments approached as close as they could to the glacis, and covered the working parties that first broke ground; these worked with such diligence, that by dawn a long trench sheltered the whole force. But the enemy had opened a heavy fire during the night, from which the Guards suffered some loss. The First Guards, in particular, had to lament the loss of their commanding officer and brigadier, Colonel Charles Gorsuch, who had now commanded them on service during five campaigns, ever since the battle of Blenheim, and with whose conduct Marlborough was so well satisfied, that he would not allow a senior officer to come out and supersede him. He was mortally wounded in the trenches, and died a few days afterwards ; only one private soldier of the Guards was killed, while Captain Hearne and four privates were wounded. On the following day, the 25th, the second or combined battalion Dec. 25. of Guards relieved the first in the trenches, and, on the 28th, the first battalion entered the trenches again, on which occasion it lost one serjeant, one corporal killed, and three men wounded.

The place was strong, well provisioned, and had a good citadel ; a protracted siege might, therefore, have been expected ; but the Count de la Motte, willingly listening to the suggestion of a Swiss captain that the place was untenable, capitulated on the 30th of December, and, on the 2nd of January, twenty-nine battalions and nineteen squadrons marched out with all the honours of war. By the articles of capitulation, Bruges, Plassendahl, and Lessinghem were given up, and Marlborough thus became master of the greater part of Flanders.

The two battalions of Guards marched to Alost on the 3rd of January, and thence on the following day to Jan. 3. Brussels, where they went into winter quarters. Thus ended a campaign in which Marlborough had exhibited as much skill, judgment, and perseverance as in any previous year.

CHAPTER XIII.

1709.

1709. ALTHOUGH the standing army of Great Britain had not
been in existence fifty years, many abuses which required
to be repressed had crept into the military system. The
practice of bestowing commissions upon children, instituted
with the charitable purpose of providing for the sons of
officers who had lost their lives in the service, was per-
verted into a base exercise of patronage, and henceforward
these children's commissions were to be restricted to two in
any one regiment. Another abuse that had crept in was
that of officers who had been granted brevet promotion
ceasing thereupon to perform any regimental duty, but this
evil on Marlborough's remonstrance was also amended.
The original order on the subject of the 12th of July, 1708,
applied only to certain regiments of cavalry and infantry of
the line, but by a subsequent order of the 2nd of August of
the same year, the three regiments of Foot Guards were
included with others in its operation. Colonel Shrimpton,
however, who had held the post of brigadier in Spain, had
already left the regiment in the previous month of March,
so that this order did not affect him. The practice of
enlisting debtors to screen them from their creditors,

was also shown up, and put a stop to, and a law was enacted that when an action was brought against any soldier for a debt of not less than twenty pounds, he should either be discharged and proceeded against as a civilian, or else be sent to serve abroad.

There are, perhaps, no better proofs of the continued successes of Marlborough hitherto, than the successive sites chosen by the French to construct their lines of defence, each year nearer and nearer to their own frontiers, till during the last winter, owing to the loss of Lille, they were forced to construct them on their own soil for the defence of French territory. The site now chosen, selected with the view to preventing a direct advance of the allies upon Paris from Lille, extended from Douay to Bethune, and behind these lines the French had assembled, at Pont à Vendin, an army of 112,000 men, under Villars. The allies had made equal exertions to bring a large body of men into the field, though had it not been for Marlborough's strong remonstrances, the British Government, anxious to redeem the failure of Almanza, would have detached seven battalions from the army in Flanders to Spain. A wet spring delayed the assembling of the allied army, but when united, in June, it reckoned 110,000 men. A reconnaissance June. of the French lines showed them to be too strong for an attack in front; Marlborough therefore resolved on the siege of Tournay, in which seven English battalions out of sixty to be so employed were selected to take part, and General Withers the lieutenant-colonel of the First Guards was entrusted with the command of the British troops, viz., the two battalions of Guards, Argyll's 3rd, Temple's, Evans's, and Meredith's 37th. On the 23rd of June, the Guards, who had assembled with the rest of the army near Ath, marched thence to Leuze on the road to Tournay; and Marlborough, after making a feint to advance upon the French lines, whereby Villars was induced to detach part of the Tournay garrison to strengthen the threatened point, decamped in silence on the night of the 27th from Leuze, June 27. and marched upon Tournay, which was immediately invested,

and, while Eugene covered the operations by stationing
himself at Pont à Tressin, the siege commenced. The
two battalions of Guards, encamped at Villemeau, took
their share of duty in the trenches during the whole
period of the siege, and in the attack to the south-east of
the citadel, which was carried on under the direction of
General Lottum. The town itself surrendered on the 5th
of August, when De Surville, who commanded, retired
into the citadel. The siege of this fortress was terribly
destructive, and the loss of life from the explosion of mines
and countermines enough to appal the stoutest hearts; but
the allies never slackened their exertions, and the citadel
was ultimately surrendered on the 3rd of September.
The casualties in the First Guards during this siege are
not recorded. Lieutenant-Colonel Withers is thus spoken of
in a letter of the time, published in the "Tatler": ... "the
correspondent hopes to have an opportunity of thanking
Mr. Withers for the service he has done his country. No
man deserves better of his friends than that gentleman, whose
distinguished character it is that he gives his orders with
the familiarity, and enjoys his fortune with the generosity, of
a fellow-soldier."

Marlborough's next object was the siege of Mons, and,
anticipating the fall of Tournay, he dispatched a strong
division, under Orkney and Cadogan, on the morning of the
3rd, to take St. Ghislain, lying six miles west of that town
on the Haisne, and thus secure the passage of that river, while
the Prince of Hesse Cassel, moving round Mons, succeeded in
penetrating the French lines of the Trouille at Espienne,
about six miles to the south-east of the same fortress. The
whole army followed and formed up on the heights of
Jemappes, thus interposing itself between Mons and Marshal
Villars, who, upon hearing of the advance of the Prince of
Hesse, hurried forward from the south with 95,000 men and
eighty guns, by Quievrain and Bavai, towards Mons, but was
too late to prevent the investment of that town on the side
of France, by Marlborough. Villars then drew up his army
on the heath of Malplaquet, between the woods of Lagnière

Plate XIX

BATTLE
OF
MALPLAQUET
SEP.ᵀᴴ 11ᵀᴴ 1709

A. Attack on end of Breading penetrating to 'a'   G. Gen.ˡ Withers' corps attacking
B. Attack on the other flank of angle of wood   Enemy's left
C. Attack on the redans in Enemy's centre   HHH. Enemy's infantry behind
D. Dutch troops attacking the right   their intrenchments
E.E. Allied cavalry sustaining the infantry   KK. Their cavalry
F. Cavalry in reserve.

Scale

on his right and of Tasnières on his left, and commenced
without delay to throw up a strong line of entrenchments
along his front.

The allies, 93,000 strong with 105 guns, observed the
gradual approach of the enemy, and Marlborough was
anxious to attack him before he had time to strengthen his
position, but the field deputies objected until the forces
under Cadogan, engaged at the siege of St. Ghislain, should
have come up; that fortress fell on the 10th, but in the
meanwhile the French had thrown up batteries and parapets
so judiciously that it rendered the approach to their position
what they justly termed a *trouée d'enfer*, notwithstanding
which, Marlborough and Eugene were resolved to attack the
following day, and made their dispositions accordingly.
Eugene commanded the right under Schulemberg and
Lottum, who were destined to attack the French left,
strongly entrenched in the wood of Tasnières; Marlborough
commanded the left and centre. The centre was composed
chiefly of infantry, the British troops, under Orkney, being
in first line, the two battalions of Guards on the extreme
right, and therefore in their advance much exposed to the
flank fire from the wood of Tasnières; the Dutch were in
second line in front of the wood of Ivry.

Sept. 10.

At three o'clock on the morning of the 11th September,
after divine service, the troops marched to their appointed
stations, in the midst of a dense fog; but as the sun broke
out at half-past seven, the allied artillery opened fire on the
woods of Tasnières and Sart. The attack was begun by the
two columns on the right under Schulemberg and Lottum,
while Orkney, in the centre, advanced in two lines on the left
of Lottum, detaching the three right battalions of his second
line under Argyll to the assistance of that latter officer.
The conflict in the woods became very severe, and Lottum
was unable at first to make head against the "Brigade du
Roi," which manned the entrenchments at the edge of the
wood of Tasnières, but D'Auvergne's cavalry, led by Marlborough, coming to his assistance, he eventually carried the
works, and penetrating the woods, joined Schulemberg,

Sept. 11.
Battle of
Malplaquet

when these together drove back the left wing of the French army. On the left, the Prince of Orange, who led his troops against some of the strongest of the enemy's works, was not only unable to make any impression upon them, but was himself nearly defeated, and sustained a great loss of men, when Marlborough came up from the right and restored order, forbidding any further attack till Orkney's infantry in the centre was more advanced. Marlborough at length desired Orkney to lead his troops forward; these consisted of the two battalions of Guards, the Royals, 1st Ossory's, Argyll's 3rd, Temple's, Ingoldsby's 18th, Evans's, Godfrey's 16th, Webb's 18th, Primrose's 24th, and Lalos's 21st regiments. Upon the order being given they dashed forward at the entrenchments, carrying all before them, supported by Rantzau's and Vincke's brigades in second line, while the cavalry of D'Auvergne, Wood, and Bulow were formed in rear; the British infantry and two battalions of Guards stormed the works and overpowered the Bavarians and the Cologne guards, but suffered severely in doing so. Many officers and men were killed in the attack, and Lieutenant-Colonel Rivers of the Coldstreams, commanding the second or combined battalion of Guards, who early in the day had been carried off the field in a fainting state from the effects of a wound, and returned at this period to resume his command, was shot dead. The attack on the left was renewed with varying fortune, till the enemy's cavalry was at last checked by the fire of the British infantry, who lined the ditches of the entrenchments they had just carried. A final charge of Bulow's cavalry, under Marlborough, drove the French back, and Boufflers, hearing that the left had already retired, ordered a general retreat, covered by the gardes du corps, under La Vallière, whereupon the French army retired to Bavay with a loss of fourteen thousand men.

The allies halted at Tasnières, where thanks were offered up for the victory; their losses were greater than those of the vanquished, for they had the harder task of storming the works. Nearly 18,000 were either killed, wounded, or

MAP
ILLUSTRATING
CAMPAIGNS
— IN —
1710, 1711, 1712.

Scale of English miles

H A I N A U L T

F R E N C H A M P S

C O M P S   O F   T H E   A L L I E D   A R M I E S

LILLE

Tournay

Bethune

ARRAS

Douai

Cambrai

SIONS

Binche

Maubeuge

Avesnes

Landrecies

le Cateau Cambresis

le Capelet

Valenciennes

Bouchain

Papaume

Villers Brouillian

Avesnes le Comte

Aubigny

Lens

Ath

Orchies

St Amand

Marchiennes

R. Scarpe

R. Sensee

FR. EUGENE

ORMOND

Quesnoy

R. Selle

R. Scheldt

R. Lys

R. Lyne

missing. Of the Guards, Captain James Gould of the grenadier company of the first regiment was killed; Lieutenant-Colonel Andrew Windsor and Ensign George Chudleigh, of the same regiment, were slightly wounded, the former near the eye, the latter received a contusion on the chest. After this action the enemy made no further attempt to molest the besiegers : the investment was completed on the 25th of September, and the place fell on the 26th of October, after which the army went into winter quarters, the Guards proceeding to Brussels, where they arrived at the beginning of November, and Marlborough returned to England, where, notwithstanding the successes of the late campaign, he found he was out of favour both with the court and government.

1710.

During the winter there were some attempts at negotiations for peace, but they came to nothing, and in April, 1710, the army in Flanders again took the field, when the Guards, moving out with the rest of the troops from Brussels, marched to Tournay, where Marlborough resumed the command of the forces. No great action was fought during the ensuing campaign, the attention of the allied commanders being directed to the reduction of the several frontier strongholds of Douay, Bethune, St. Venant, and Aire. General Cadogan was engaged with the British infantry in reducing the first of these fortresses; trenches were opened on the 5th of May, and on the 25th of June it surrendered. The Guards were employed in this siege, as well as in those of Bethune, St. Venant, and Aire, which fell on the 28th of August, 29th of September, and 12th of November respectively. The excessive wet had not only delayed the siege of the latter place, but greatly increased the number of sick, and the troops returned to their winter quarters at an earlier period than usual. The discontent in England at the continuance of the war was now daily increasing, and Marlborough was accused of

1711.   prolonging it for his own profit.   There had been no
brilliant victory to dazzle the eyes of the people in the
late campaign, and the increased cost of the war alarmed
the economists.   Marlborough, however, was well received
by the people, as well as by the queen, though her majesty
had shown in the early part of the year some coldness towards him in consequence of not having been enabled to
carry out her wish to give a certain regiment to her own
nominee, Marlborough having promised it to General Meredith, who was accordingly gazetted to the colonelcy of the
21st Royal Scots Fusileers. Though the queen had to give way
in this, she shortly afterwards deprived Marlborough's son-
in-law, Lord Sunderland, of the office of secretary of state,
and gave the seals of office, in June, to Lord Dartmouth,
and subsequently made other changes in the ministry,
adverse to Marlborough's friends and to the Whigs, so that
on Marlborough's return he again met with some coldness
from the new ministers.

1711.

In order to make up the numbers of companies in the
combined battalion to the same as in the First Guards

March.   battalion, it was proposed in the month of March, 1711,
that two more companies of the Coldstreams should be sent
over to Flanders.   The queen sanctioned the arrangement,
and Lieutenant-General Withers was authorised to send
them off if the London duty admitted of such a reduction.

April.   They were ordered in April to embark, but a counter-order
was subsequently received, owing to a representation of
Major-General Braddock commanding the Coldstreams, to
the effect that he had not sufficient men left to perform
the Tower duties.

Early in the year, the services of several sergeants of
experience and ability being required abroad, who were to
receive ensigns' pay and commissions of lieutenants in the
army, three sergeants of the First Guards were, on the

Jan. 17.   17th of January, selected for this purpose out of the thirty-

seven required, viz., Sergeant William Matthews, Thomas   1711.
Garland, and Alexander Cleland; but owing to a subsequent
reduction of the numbers required to thirty, the two first
only received commissions. Six weeks later the name of
another sergeant of the First Guards, Sergeant Cook, was
sent in, and he also received his commission as lieutenant;
but being detained in England to give evidence before the
House of Commons in an affair of Colonel Charters, it was
too late to send him out, and his commission was surrendered.

The French in Flanders had never been in a more efficient
state than in the spring of 1711, when reinforcements had
replaced their losses of the previous year's campaign, and
with the view of protecting France from invasion, they
had been employed during the winter in throwing up lines
of defence more formidable than ever, extending from
Namur to the coast. Heavy guns were mounted on
the ramparts, and Villars, with 156 battalions and 227
squadrons, amounting to 90,000 men, between Bouchain
and Arras, defied all the efforts of the allies; and the French
troops, confident in their marshal, announced to the world
that these lines were the " *ne plus ultra* " of Marlborough's
career.

The allied troops were drawn out of their winter quarters
in April, and before the end of the month the Guards
marched to the general rendezvous in front of Orchies,
between Tournay and Douay, where they were present at April 30.
a grand review that Marlborough held of his whole army,
consisting of 141 battalions and 256 squadrons amounting
to 100,000 men, preparatory to entering into this his tenth
campaign; but the news of the death of the Emperor of
Austria, received in camp the day before, rendered the May 1.
plans of the allied powers uncertain, as Charles, the titular
King of Spain, who succeeded to the Imperial throne,
might at any time recall Prince Eugene, and a portion of
the Austrian troops, by which the forces in Flanders at the
duke's disposal would be considerably reduced.

Immediately after the review Marlborough advanced his

army from Orchies, and a two days' march in a deluge of rain, which much fatigued the troops, brought them in front of Douay.   The duke established his head-quarters at Warde, his front protected by outposts reaching as far as the abbey of Visny, which was held by Lieutenant-Colonel Cholmondeley with 300 men of the First Guards. The army remained encamped here waiting the enemy for six weeks, during which this advanced post of the Guards was, on the 30th of May, attacked by a large force, but, protected by walls, the Guards gallantly repelled the assailants, compelling them to retire with considerable loss. At the beginning of June, Marlborough was occupied in reviewing the several corps of the army, commencing with

June 8. the Prussians; and on the 8th of that month he reviewed the English and Hanoverian infantry, amongst which were the two battalions of Guards.

The French feeling secure behind their lines had lately detached several squadrons and battalions from the main army towards the Rhine ; and Prince Eugene having received instructions from his court that in such an eventuality he should also march in that direction and quit the

June 14. allied army, moved off with the Imperialists on the 14th of June towards Orchies, when the Danes, Saxons, and Hessians, that had formed part of his corps, were transferred and attached to the army under Marlborough, who left his camp the same day, moving to his right, and crossed the Scarpe at Vitry, south of Douay, encamping in the plains of Lens, with his right at Lievin and his left at Hennin-Lietard; the Prince of Hesse, bringing up the rear, was posted between Arleux and Binche.   The brigade of Guards was quartered near Lens, which the duke made his head-quarters, and which gave the name to the camp. The French at the same time made a corresponding movement to their left to Mouchy Le Preux, leaving the town of Arras between the two combatants.   The allies were now in an open plain where, as the duke wrote at the time, the enemy had a fair opportunity of attacking them if they should be so inclined.

The month of June and half of July were spent in this 1711. camp, and the army began to despond through fear that the French lines were inaccessible, and though the veterans never doubted their chief's ability, they perceived that he was cast down and sullen, and thought they observed with some misgivings that he had forgotten his usual caution, and would at times speak openly before his staff, of his intention to attack the town of Arras, which soon became known throughout the army; and as spies abounded in the camp, Villars, made aware of the duke's supposed project, prepared to lay a trap for his adversary. Marlborough, on the 20th and 21st of July, moved his army still further to the west, so as to deceive Villars as to his real point of attack, and passed in front of Bethune and Lillers, leaving Aire in his rear. After ten days spent at the camp of Cote, near Lillers, Marlborough advanced, on the 1st and 2nd of August, to Dievel and Villers-Brulin, as if to attack the left of the French lines, to which flank Villars began to mass his troops. But although the spies had given all the information in their power, they had not been able to let the French marshal know that six days' bread had been furnished to the troops, and that the garrisons of Lille and Tournay, on the 4th of August, were Aug. 4. marching to the east; nor did they perceive that on the afternoon of that day Cadogan had secretly left the camp to join the twenty-three battalions and seventeen squadrons from the above garrisons, and push on swiftly with them. Marlborough, having sent a body of horse forward on his right to alarm the extreme left of the French, suddenly retraced his steps eastward, and followed Cadogan with the main body. At five in the morning of the 5th of August, after a night's march, and completing thirty-six miles in sixteen hours, Cadogan crossed the Sauzet unopposed, and by ten o'clock the whole army, which had made a similar forced march, having passed unmolested by Vitry, Aubigny, and some forts that had been dismantled two months before by the French, was in position on high ground above Bouchain, having thus without the loss of a single man entered

1711. these famous lines.   This feint of the duke's on the enemy's left, and the sudden march to force the right of his lines, may be considered as one of the best examples of strategy ever carried out in presence of so large a force of the enemy. He was much congratulated by the ministers at home, who said that, without losing a man, he had gained an advantage which would have been reckoned as cheaply bought at the expense of several thousands.

Villars was informed of Marlborough's march at eleven

Aug. 5. on the night of the 4th to the 5th of August, and galloped off at once with a hundred dragoons to Cambray, where he suddenly found himself in the midst of the allied army. Most of his escort were captured, and he himself escaped with difficulty.   The French army arrived on the evening of the 5th, but the allies were already so strongly established that Villars deemed an attack impossible.   After some manœuvring Marlborough crossed the Scheldt, and invested Bouchain, having fixed his head-quarters at Avesnes le Sec, where the Guards were quartered.   The investment was

Aug. 23. completed on the 23rd of August, when the trenches were opened, and the batteries being completed, a vigorous bombardment commenced at the end of the month.   On the 27th, the grenadiers of the army were employed in gaining possession of a small work, commanding a passage by which the garrison had been enabled to keep up a communication

Sept. 12. with their army outside.   The fire was kept up till the 12th of September, when the garrison offered to capitulate on the terms of being allowed to march out with all the honours of war; but Marlborough refused, and on the following day they surrendered as prisoners of war to the number of 8000.   Several days were spent in the neighbourhood to repair the breaches, and the camp did not break up till towards the end of October.   Rumours of a renewal of negotiations had reached the camp, and Marlborough, who had meditated the siege of Quesnoy, was so fully convinced of the truth of these reports, though he was kept in ignorance of the intentions of the British ministry, that, unwilling to shed blood unnecessarily, he abandoned his

project of prosecuting the campaign any further, and ordering   1711.
his troops into winter quarters, took leave of the army at
Tournay on the 2nd of November; and after spending a
fortnight at the Hague settling affairs with the States-
General, he returned to England, the Guards moving into
winter quarters in Brussels.

In the previous autumn her majesty had re-established
a custom which had been adopted in the reign of Charles II.,
and the following order, signed by the Secretary of State,
is the authority upon which rests the appointment of the
present Field-Officer in Brigade waiting to the Foot
Guards :—

" Whitehall, 9th August, 1711. Aug. 9.

" Gentlemen,—Her Majesty having thought fit that a
Field-Officer of the Foot Guards be always in waiting upon
her Royal Person, in like manner as she is attended by an
Officer of the Horse Guards, I am commanded to acquaint
you with her Majesty's pleasure herein, and that she
expects compliance therewith as soon as may be.

"I am, Gentlemen,

" Your most humble Servant,

" To the Officer in Chief   " (Signed) G. Granville.
with the two Regiments of Guards."

Marlborough had no sooner arrived in England than his
enemies and the Jacobite party, perceiving his popularity
on the wane, struck a blow at his power by accusing him of
peculation, and although a careful inquiry proved his innocence, his enemies, profiting by the vague charges against
him, induced the queen to dismiss the great general of her
armies, and accordingly on the 31st of December, 1711, she
signified to him, under her own hand, that she deprived
him of all his offices, including the Colonelcy of the First
Regiment of Foot Guards. There is no published correspondence in the " Marlborough Dispatches " concerning
this event; the only reference that the duke makes to it is

1711.   in a letter to Comte Hompesch of the 28th of December
(8th Jan., 1712, N.S.), in which he says,—"Vous aurez
"appris mon sort, que la reine a trouvé bon de me
"remercier de tous mes emplois. On vient de me pousser
"encore vivement, mais pourvu que cela me procure une
"retraite à la campagne, à quoi j'ai si long temps aspiré, je
"serai content de ma destinée, et en aurai l'obligation à mes
"ennemis. Là je pourrai continuer mes vœux pour le bien
"du public, et jouir en repos de la compagnie de mes amis
"qui voudront bien me l'accorder."

The policy that had induced the queen thus to deprive
herself of the services of her most able subject and lieutenant, who had raised England to such a pitch of military
glory, was not dictated by any personal dislike, but by a
wish, shared in by many of her present ministers and subjects, that England should withdraw from the grand alliance.
Secret measures were being taken to make a separate treaty
with France, unknown to Prince Eugene and the Imperialists.
and it was well known that Marlborough would not lend
himself to such an act of deception towards his faithful
comrade in arms, and the being deprived of his high offices
at such a juncture of affairs may be looked upon as the
highest compliment that could be paid to his character;
though the ostensible reason given by the queen in thus
treating him was that his conduct might be inquired into
with more impartiality, an information having been laid
against him before the House of Commons by the commissioners of public accounts.

Prince Eugene came over to England in the winter with
the view to urging the British ministers to maintain the
alliance, and though he was received with every mark of
distinction by the nobility, he was coldly received by the
ministers and the queen. The ministers even hinted to
him that it would be well that he did not see much of the
Duke of Marlborough, a suggestion that he indignantly repelled; and to a remark addressed to the Prince by Lord
Oxford, who was entertaining him, that he was proud of
receiving the greatest captain of the age in his house, the

JAMES, 2ᴰ DUKE ᴏғ ORMOND, K.G.

Commander in Chief of Her Majesty's Forces.
8ᵗʰ Colonel of the First Regiment of Foot Guards.
1712 – 1714.

Prince pointedly replied, that if it was so, he owed it to Lord Oxford himself; alluding to his having been one of those who had induced the queen to deprive the Duke of Marlborough of his appointments.

1712.

James Butler, second Duke of Ormond, lord-lieutenant of Ireland, now in his 50th year, was, on the 1st of January, 1712, appointed in Marlborough's place, captain-general of the British armies, both at home and abroad, as well as colonel of the First Regiment of Foot Guards; other honours were heaped upon him, both by the queen and the universities; he became lord warden of the Cinque Ports, constable of Dover Castle, lord-lieutenant of Somersetshire and of Norfolk, and chancellor of the universities of Oxford and Dublin. He had received his education under Colonel O'Hara, now Lord Tyrawley, and succeeded his grandfather in the dukedom in 1688, when he was only twenty-six years of age. He learnt the rudiments of war in France, and was subsequently colonel of horse in the English army, he had served at Sedgmoor, and sided with the Prince of Orange at the time of the Revolution; was colonel of the second troop of Horse Guards from 1689, a lord of the bedchamber, and a knight of the garter; attended William III. at the battle of the Boyne, entertaining him sumptuously at his castle of Kilkenny; was wounded and made prisoner at the battle of Landen, and in 1702 commanded the Vigo expedition. Gallant, bold, generous, devoted to pleasure, fond of admiration and eager for action, Ormond, at the same time, detested business, and avoided it as much as possible. In appearance he was short, but well made and handsome. He soon had an opportunity of seeing the service battalions of his new regiment, which, with the companies of the Coldstream Guards, had been quartered during the winter of 1711-12 at Brussels. Here Lieutenant-General Withers came from Ghent, on the 14th of April, to inspect them previous to the opening of the campaign, after they had received a draft of

200 men from the home battalions, ordered out in the middle of March; and thus completed to their full establishment, and having received their new clothing, and being in every way fit to enter on another campaign, they quitted Brussels with other regiments of the garrison on the April 14. 14th of April, marching to the general rendezvous of the whole army, at Bassieux, near Tournay, where a camp was being formed. With some misgivings as to the deceitful part he was called upon to perform, Ormond came out in April, and having, according to his avowed instructions, given the States-General at the Hague the assurance that the war would be carried on with vigour, he assumed, in May, the command of a splendid army of 120,000 confederates, all in the highest spirits, to lead which against an enemy dejected and miserable, he could not but feel, was to ensure success, yet his secret instructions compelled him to remain inactive, and even to dissimulate while negotiations were still being secretly carried on. His splendid hospitality and the magnificence of his camp equipage contrasted with the homely style of the Duke of Marlborough; but although some were dazzled by the display, and although the " Duke of Ormond's march " was now played by the bands in camp in place of the recently popular " Malbrook," the troops did not forget their former chief, and looked with distrust on one who had come out " not to fight," or rather not to " act offensively."

May 13.   The First Guards were for the first time reviewed by the Duke of Ormond as their colonel, on the 13th of May, at the camp of Bassieux. The inspection took place in presence of Prince Eugene, the Earl of Albemarle, and the other general officers, who all expressed themselves extremely well satisfied with their appearance, and, in the evening, Lieutenant-General Withers, the lieutenant-colonel of the regiment, entertained at dinner their new colonel, the Duke of Ormond, who was accompanied by Prince Eugene and many others. Subsequently Ormond reviewed the right wing of the first line, consisting of all the British troops, and sixteen squadrons of auxiliaries.

The preliminaries of the treaty of peace were so un-
favourably received in England, that the ministers deemed
it prudent still to preserve secrecy with respect to the negotiations at Utrecht, where, as Louis had raised his demands,
the discussions were prolonged. No hint of these proceedings was communicated to the allies in the field, and when
Prince Eugene asked Ormond whether he might rely on his
support, the duke evaded a direct reply, but gave the prince
to understand that the armies would stand by each other.

In the subsequent campaign the lieutenant-colonel of the
First Guards, Henry Withers, and Lord North and Grey were
the two lieutenant-generals of infantry; Gilbert Primrose,
who had commanded a battalion of First Guards in the
earlier campaigns of Marlborough, Sabine, Evans, and the
Earl of Orrery, were the major-generals.

On the 26th of May the two armies advanced into the May 26.
enemy's country, the Duke of Ormond crossing the Scheldt
with his troops at Souche, between Bouchain and Denain;
while Prince Eugene crossed it at Neuville, when they took
up a position parallel to the river Selle running in their
rear. Ormond formed the right wing of the allies, and fixed
his head-quarters at Hapre, a small village south of Denain,
in rear of the right of his troops, with the Guards in his
immediate neighbourhood, Eugene extending the line to the
southward and fixing his head-quarters in rear of the centre
of his army, at Solesmes, and while here forty or fifty men
from every battalion of both armies were daily employed in
strengthening the lines between Denain and Marchiennes.

For some time Eugene had felt doubts as to Ormond's
intention to afford the necessary assistance in attacking
the enemy should an opportunity offer, and to ascertain
what he might expect under such circumstances, he proposed an immediate attack as the enemy was weakly posted;
Ormond was at length obliged to confess that he had the
queen's instructions to hazard neither battle nor siege. It
is asserted by Ormond's friends that he had received these
instructions only two days before. At all events, such a
declaration put an end to any further active operations

1712. on the part of the British, and the whole army having moved back across the Selle, put that river between them and the French.

June. Prince Eugene had already undertaken the siege of Quesnoy, when Ormond, on the 25th of June, signified to him that he had received orders to publish a cessation of arms for three months, and proposed to Prince Eugene to join in it, but so far from agreeing to such a proposition, Eugene redoubled his attacks upon Quesnoy, when Ormond declared that if he continued, he should withdraw the British forces from the neighbourhood. Eugene was not to be diverted from his purpose by such a threat, and continued. All friendly intercourse now ceased between the allied com-

July 3. manders; Quesnoy surrendered to Eugene on the 3rd of July, and on the 15th the Prince having signified to Ormond his intention of advancing the following day, Ormond replied that as he had not been consulted upon any future plan, he could not accompany him. Accordingly, on the

July 16. 16th of July, the two armies separated, and Ormond directed all British regiments and others in British pay to march to the rear. But the Danes, Prussians, Saxons, and Hanoverians, though subsidized by England, remained under Eugene, while Ormond, with five regiments of horse, five of dragoons, and twenty-four battalions of infantry, amongst which were the two battalions of Guards, making altogether 18,000 men, and eighty-six guns, proceeded to Avesnes le Sec. On the 17th Ormond published a cessation of arms, and notified that England had made a separate truce with France. When the men became aware that they had thus abandoned their allies, with whom they had fought and conquered in nine campaigns, they broke out into angry shouts and cries, and well might Marlborough rejoice that his sovereign had not called upon him to participate in such an action. As the troops marched towards the coast, they were insulted by their former allies; the gates of Denain were closed against them, they were denied admittance into Douay; and at Oudenarde, the scene of two former triumphs, they were refused a passage through the town. Ormond, finding that he would be soon excluded from every place in Flanders, took possession, on the 29th of July, with the Guards and the rest of the British and some other troops of the towns of Bruges and Ghent; the British Guards taking up their old quarters at Ghent, where they remained several weeks, while six battalions of the line were sent on to take over Dunkirk from the French, according to agreement; but the French demurred, in consequence of the German troops remaining with Prince Eugene's army, contrary to stipulation. It is impossible to defend the conduct of the British government in thus treacherously abandoning their allies while in the field before the enemy, thereby losing many of the advantages that might have been gained in a treaty of peace had the allies remained staunch to each other to the end, and the country must ever regret that most of the advantages acquired by the genius of a Marlborough should have been thus basely thrown away by the enforced treachery of an Ormond. Such a proceeding and such an inglorious termination to a series of glorious campaigns sullied for years the honour of the British name throughout Europe.

Ormond again reviewed the two battalions of Guards at Ghent on the 15th of September, and left next day for England, leaving General Lumley in command of the British troops, including the Guards, which remained in Flanders till the following spring.

Though we do not propose to follow the fortunes of the Imperialists after the British troops left the army, a reference must be made to the movements of the French and of Prince Eugene during the remainder of this campaign, for under very different auspices they were re-enacted on the same ground as a peace-manœuvre above one hundred years later by the Duke of Wellington and the allies, during the period of the army of occupation at Cambray, when the Duke of Wellington, with the British troops, enacted the part of Marshal Villars with the French army in driving a portion of the Imperialists from before Denain.

Eugene had undertaken the siege of Landrecies, and had a

force at Denain to maintain the communication between that town and Marchiennes. Villars, making a feint to relieve Landrecies, pushed his main body secretly towards Denain across the Scheldt, attacked the Dutch general who was in command of the camp there, and completely defeated him with great loss, before Prince Eugene could bring the main body to his assistance, and this misfortune was followed by the loss of all the posts on the Scheldt, as well as of Marchiennes. These losses changed the aspect of affairs in England, and showed still more clearly the consequences of withdrawing the British forces from the army, and depriving Marlborough of the command of the confederates, for Prince Eugene, unable by himself to cope with the French, was compelled to retreat, and, after lengthy negotiations, peace was eventually signed between France and Austria in 1714 ; but the British nation must ever regret that the government of the country should have recommended the sovereign to allow her prejudices for a party to influence her to such an extent as to outweigh her anxiety for the glory, character, and position of Great Britain among nations.

1713.

When the Duc d'Aumont arrived in London from Paris in January, 1713, for the purpose of settling some of the contested points in the treaty, the populace evinced their dislike of the affair, by insulting his carriage in the streets, and on the 26th of that month his house was burnt down, the whole garrison of London turning out under the Duke of Ormond, to protect his property. Some accused the Whigs of having set the place on fire, in consequence of their dislike to the peace, and their desire to annoy the Duke of Powys, the landlord ; but the story told in France was, that D'Aumont had done it himself to conceal his vast contraband dealings, and with the expectation of being amply repaid for his losses. The Foot Guards were employed in removing his property, and when he was subsequently, by the queen's desire, lodged in Somerset House, the Guards mounted guard over him, and posted sentries not only 1713. round his apartments, but even on the roof.

Orders were issued at home, on the 31st of January, 1713, Jan. 31. for the service battalion of the First Guards, 600 strong, to march to Ostend, and embark there for England, landing at Deptford, if wind would permit. Its departure was, however, delayed, and it did not reach the Thames in the transport "John and Sarah" till near the end of March, and only a small force was left in Flanders till all matters connected with trade should be settled. The two battalions of Guards, on landing in England, rejoined their respective regiments in London, and, on the 26th of March, the late March 26. service companies of the First Guards were reviewed by the Duke of Ormond on the parade in St. James's Park.

Peace was proclaimed on the 5th of May, 1713, the May 5. treaties between the different powers having been signed at Utrecht on the 31st of March, according to the provisions of which the Spanish throne, the main object of the war, was secured to the Bourbons. England gained Gibraltar and Minorca, two places actually in her possession, and the claims of the Stuart family were disavowed by Louis, while France recovered almost all her lost ground, obtaining great advantages in the commercial treaty with Great Britain. Thus, after all the toils and triumphs of British armies, the miserable conduct of a party faction forced Great Britain to accept these disadvantageous terms, and to abandon its allies to their fate.

Shortly after the withdrawal of the British troops from the alliance in the previous year, a very considerable reduction in the British army was resolved upon, and on the 17th of October, 1712, the companies of all three regiments of Guards had been reduced to sixty men. On the 16th of May, 1713, after the proclamation of peace, they were still further reduced to forty men each, but there was no reduction in the number of companies of the First Guards. The Third Regiment of Guards had taken no share in the campaigns in Flanders, nor had they till lately been quartered in the metropolis. Of the two battalions of that

1713.   regiment, at the beginning of 1713, one was quartered in the
Tower Hamlets, the other, which had just returned from
Spain, was at Dartford and Woolwich.   On the 3rd of
September, 1713, the first battalion of the Third Regiment was
sent to Windsor, while five companies of the second battalion
proceeded to Portsmouth, and three to Plymouth, where they
remained for a whole year.   The third regiment of Guards
in future performed the same duties about the sovereign as
the other two regiments, and it is noticeable that whereas
previous to this period the orders specified that the duties
should be performed proportionately (to their number of
companies), by the first and second regiments of Foot
Guards, it was for the future specified in general terms
that they should be performed by the *Foot Guards.*

In consequence of the inconvenience thus early found to
exist in the custom of *billetting* the Guards in London, by
which they were scattered all over the town, a strong memorial was presented this year to the Lords of the Treasury,
to sanction the rebuilding of the Savoy as a barrack, and
for the construction of another at the King's Mews,
Charing Cross, the Duke of Ormond having previously
given instructions to Major-General Tatton to inquire into
the subject.   The barracks at the mews were eventually
rebuilt, but no steps were taken towards rebuilding the
Savoy.

July 1.   After the peace, the Duc d'Aumont returned to England,
and made his public entry into London on the 1st of July,
1713, and on the 4th had an audience of the queen at St.
James's Palace.   The Foot Guards on duty were drawn up
in the court-yard, the officers saluting the ambassador
with pike and colour, and afterwards with their hats as he
passed, the drums beating a march.

July 31.   On the 31st of July the seven battalions of Foot Guards,
together with the Horse and Life Guards, and the Royal
Regiment of Horse, commanded by Lord Peterborough, were
reviewed in Hyde Park by the Duke of Ormond.

Towards the end of the year detachments of Foot and
Horse Guards were called out in consequence of a mutinous

spirit appearing in a disbanded corps at Canterbury. It appears that some hundreds of disbanded marines of General Wills' regiment near that town and Rochester refused to deliver up their arms, and this being exaggerated into a report of an insurrection, General Withers was desired to send a force to suppress it. Major-General Tatton, major of the First Guards, was despatched towards Canterbury with 120 of the Life Guards, 80 horse grenadiers, and 600 Foot Guards, but on reaching Woolwich he was informed that the mutineers were on their way to Greenwich, there peaceably to surrender their arms to the governor of the hospital, and the troops subsequently returned to London.

The dismissal of Marlborough, the conclusion of an ignominious peace, and the evident desire of the ministry to favour Jacobite officers, among whom the Duke of Ormond himself was not the least, were the causes of many changes amongst the officers of the Guards, who spoke their minds freely in favour of the Hanoverian succession, and drew comparisons between their present commander-in-chief and their late colonel, to whom they were devoted, and who, to escape further persecution, had been obliged to go abroad, on which occasion he took with him as his aide-de-camp Ensign Eaton of the First Guards. These expressions of opinion were disapproved by the ministry, and several officers received hints that it would be as well for them to retire. Lieutenant-Colonel Coote, who had publicly drunk the health of the Elector of Hanover, and had been very active in some rejoicings at the Three Tons Tavern on the anniversary of William III.'s birthday, was called upon to sell his company, which he did to William Blakeney, the adjutant, for the sum of 1200*l*. Captains Hawksworth, Smith, and Allison were summarily dismissed from the regiment for too great 'freedom of speech; it was deemed necessary to supplant every officer whose public devotion to the Hanoverian succession might interfere with the projects of the supporters of the Stuarts, and amongst the senior officers of the army, the Duke of

Argyll, the Earl of Stair, and General Davenport were ordered to resign their commissions about the same time.

A list of officers who were known to be well affected to the House of Hanover was made out, and in the First Guards alone there were seventeen whose dismissal on that account was to be effected if they did not retire of their own accord, and give way to men selected by Ormond. But as a wholesale dismissal of officers could not be carried out without the queen's permission, and as it would probably raise an outcry if carried into execution all at the same time, it was deemed advisable to eject the officers by degrees, and, by making the service disagreeable to them, provoke them to sell out. In 1714. April, 1714, Lieutenant-Colonel Egerton, brother to the Earl of Bridgewater, and Lieutenant-Colonel Sidney, brother to the Earl of Leicester, were desired to sell their companies in the First Guards for 1000*l.*, and were replaced by two well-known Roman Catholic Jacobites, Lieutenant-Colonels Markham and Owen. Shortly afterwards Lieutenant-Colonel Paget of the First Guards, and some officers of the Coldstream, receiving orders to sell out, remonstrated. During the delay thus occasioned the news spread that the queen was dying, and though not unexpected, the close of her life had arrived before the preparations for supporting a Stuart had been completed. As serious conflicts, however, were expected in London, the Duke of Ormond, anxious at any rate to preserve the peace, doubled all the guards, and sent a reinforcement of the Foot Guards to increase the garrison of the Tower. The queen died on the 1st of August, and, in accordance with the Act of Succession, George, Elector of Hanover, was proclaimed King of Great Britain and Ireland. The queen's funeral took place on the 24th of August, on which occasion the Foot Guards furnished the necessary duties connected with the ceremony, the details of which are recorded in MSS. Harleian, Brit. Mus. 6815.

CHAPTER XIV.

UPON the death of the late queen, preparations were at 1714.
once made to receive the new sovereign of the kingdom,
and the Lords Justices, who were named to carry on the
government of the country till his arrival, issued the following order on the subject on the 3rd of September, directed
to the colonels of the three regiments of Foot Guards :—

By the Lords Justices, Harcourt, C., W. Ebor, Shrewsbury,
Buckingham, P., Carlisle, Argyle, Abingdon, Scarborough, Townsend,
Halifax.

We do hereby direct that you cause the several companies of
grenadiers belonging to his Majesty's 1st, 2nd, and 3rd Regiments of
Foot Guards to march to Greenwich and to encamp in the Park there,
in order to mount the King's guard upon his arrival at Greenwich,
and to do duty on his Royal Person during his Majesty's continuance
in that place, and you are also to cause the remainder of the said
three regiments which shall not be upon duty on that day (to
which end the detachment now at the Tower will be relieved the
day before by a detachment of Lieut.-Gen. Webb's regt.) to line the
streets from the place where the Militia ends to the palace at St.
James's. And the officers, &c. Given at St. James's, 3rd Sept. 1714.

By order,   F. GWYNN.

1714.   To the Colonels of the three regiments of Foot Guards, and to the
officers in chief with the several companies of Grenadiers herein
above mentioned.*

Accordingly, the grenadier companies of the three regiments marched on the 16th of September to Greenwich, where, on the 18th, they received the king, and mounted guard over him while he lodged there, the bands playing by order only the English march and Scotch reveille. On Sept. 20. the 20th of September, on the occasion of the king's entry, the Tower detachment having, according to the above order, been relieved by a party of General Webb's regiment, joined the head-quarters at the West-end, and the three regiments of Foot Guards lined the streets from Temple Bar to St. James's Palace.

Amongst the first acts of George I., on attaining the crown of Great Britain, was that of restoring the Duke of Sept. 14. Marlborough to all his offices. On the 14th of September, even before his arrival in the country, the duke was, by writ of privy seal, appointed Captain-General of all the Forces, and the letters-patent of Queen Anne of the 1st of March, 1712, appointing the Duke of Ormond to that office, were at the same time revoked.

The new sovereign also immediately restored the Duke of Marlborough to the colonelcy of the First Guards, and the Sept. 26. commission to that effect, under date the 26th of September, declares that George I., reposing especial trust and confidence in his loyalty, courage, and conduct, did appoint him to be colonel of his Majesty's First Regiment of Foot Guards, whereof James Duke of Ormond was late colonel, likewise to be captain in the same, and about the same time the Duke of Argyll was appointed general of all the troops in Scotland. It will be interesting to peruse the following extracts from a memorial, drawn up immediately after the accession of the new sovereign by Lord Stair, to the Duke of Marlborough, relative to the part he was expected to take in promoting the interests of those officers

* W. O. Military Order Book.

of the Foot Guards who had suffered for their adherence to 1714.
the Hanoverian succession :—

"MEMORIAL OF LORD STAIR TO THE DUKE OF MARLBOROUGH,
CAPTAIN-GENERAL OF THE ARMY.*

" It will be expected from your Grace that you represent
to his Majesty the hardships that a very great number of
the best officers of the army, that have served with the
most distinction, be under, from their firm adherence to
the Protestant succession, and to the interests of their
country."

Several facts showing the manner in which the army had
been lately treated were mentioned in the memorial, but
those relating more particularly to the Guards will alone be
mentioned here.

"Lieutenant-Colonel Coote had his company of the Guards
taken from him for no other reason that appeared, but his
being present at the burning of the Pretender, and drinking
his present Majesty's health. Those who were suspected
of Jacobitism were courted and advanced; those who were
known to be firm to the Protestant succession were neglected, vexed, and ill-used, that they might be provoked to
leave the service; and those who were brought into the
army were, for the most part, such as professed themselves
zealous supporters of the new measures. When the queen
was ill at Christmas, 1713, and it was apprehended she
might soon die, the resolution of purging the army was
openly declared. The Duke of Argyll, the Earl of Stair, and
Major-General Davenport were ordered to leave the army.
They had successors named to them, and prices appointed.
Several captains of the Foot Guards were ordered to sell,
and two gentlemen, who had been Papists till very lately,
were brought in to be captains in the Guards." The
queen's death, however, partly put a stop to these
proceedings.

* State Papers.   George I.   Vol. ii. p. 522.   Goodwood Library, fol. 1.

1714. The joy of the Hanoverian party was now great, and officers, who had been daily expecting their dismissal, exulted in their triumph. Lieutenant-Colonel Chudleigh of the First Guards, at a dinner, where many friends of the late ministry were present, expressed his delight in loud terms, and gloried in the restoration of Marlborough to the regiment. Two days later, at the first court held by the king at St. James's, Mr. Aldworth, M.P. for Windsor, when in the presence-chamber, in a loud voice denounced Colonel Chudleigh's conduct, and said it was ungentleman-like. This was resented by several, and especially by Colonel Chudleigh of the Coldstreams, a cousin of the former, and high words led to a duel in Marylebone Fields, which took place in spite of the efforts used by Colonel Bissett of the Coldstreams to prevent it, and Mr. Aldworth was killed.

1715. Colonels Sidney and Egerton, besides many others who had been dismissed, were restored in the following year to the regiment, but there were a few officers and some men, who, attached to the Stuart faction, only awaited a propitious moment to blow any spark of discontent into a flame, and the following trivial incident, by this means, assumed undue proportions, showing the talent of the Jacobite agents in working upon the minds of soldiers, April 18. who thought they were suffering under a wrong. A review was ordered to take place in Hyde Park on the 18th of April, and the new clothing of the First Guards was not delivered till the previous evening. In the hurry the officers delivered it to the men before they had examined it, and it turned out that some articles of the clothing, especially the shirts, were so coarse, that the soldiers considered they had been cheated, and some insubordination ensued. The detachment marching to the Tower carried their shirts in their hands, exhibiting them to the shopkeepers, saying, "These are Hanover shirts." General Tatton, hearing of the disturbance, ordered all the clothing to be immediately collected at Whitehall, and the Duke of Marlborough, without loss of time, ordered a board of officers to examine and report upon the whole of it. This board reported that " the soldier had been very much abused in the shirting by the undertakers." The duke ordered two shirts of good linen to be immediately supplied to each soldier, instead of one, and likwise new waistcoats, instead of those cut out of the old coats. All the old clothing, moreover, was to remain the soldier's property. On the 2nd of June the duke June 2. inspected the regiment, and made a speech, saying, that he was concerned to find the complaint of the men so just, that the fault was not his, that he had insisted on full satisfaction, and ordered a new set of clothing, such as would in every way become his Majesty's First Regiment of Foot Guards. He alluded to having served many campaigns with some, who were then listening, and concluded with a hope that he left them good subjects to the best of kings, and that everybody was entirely satisfied. The soldiers thereupon raised great shouts to express their satisfaction, and the affair terminated by their all drinking the king's health.

The Jacobites were now very busy in concerting measures for a rising, but the steps taken for its suppression by government alarmed the party, and the Duke of Ormond, so lately the colonel of the First Guards, but now one of the principal leaders of the Jacobites, as indeed he probably had been during the previous years, fled to the Continent; he was attainted, and all his honours forfeited, while others, who could not escape, were arrested on the first indication of disaffection. The household troops were called out, and, on the 23rd of July, a camp was formed in Hyde Park under Lieutenant-General Cadogan, in which most of the Foot Guards were assembled.

In September, the adherents of the Stuarts in Scotland September. broke out in open rebellion. The forces remaining in the two kingdoms scarcely amounted to 9000 men, but with these the Government, assisted by volunteers, prepared to meet the storm till an increase was effected. It was proposed to add thirteen new regiments of dragoons and eight regiments of foot, and the companies of the First

Guards and others were increased from forty to seventy men each, making an addition of 840 men to the First Regiment. The principal military man in the cabinet was Lord Stanhope, who had begun life in the First Guards, and latterly commanded the army in Spain. He now took the chief conduct of the military arrangements, and with the advice of Marlborough retained the household troops in London. The twenty-eight companies of the First Guards had, on the first threatening of a rising as above related, been called out of their billets, and encamped in Hyde Park under the command of the first major, Brigadier-General Tatton, where they remained till the 10th of December, when the season becoming severe and the danger past, the Guards returned with the rest of the troops to their quarters. During the encampment, General Tatton had received orders, in August, to hold his regiment in readiness to take the field, and to cause all officers to provide themselves with everything necessary for the purpose, in the event of their services being required in the North. Upon the breaking up of the encampment, the duke directed that, during the present emergency, fifteen and a half companies of the regiment should be quartered in Westminster, four and a-half in Kensington, Chelsea, etc., and eight in Holborn.

In the meantime, officers who were suspected of favouring the Stuart cause were narrowly watched, and Sergeant Silver of the First Guards was apprehended on the 2nd of September for enlisting men for the Pretender's service. It transpired that his real name was Sullivan, and that he induced men to join his company with the secret understanding that they were to act for the Pretender when required. He assured his recruits of the captain's support, and when this was known, Lieutenant-Colonel Paul, the captain in question, was arrested, and confined in the gatehouse, on a charge of being concerned in treasonable practices. Sullivan was tried, convicted, and executed, but the evidence not only failed to implicate the officer, but established his innocence, so that, after some months' detention, Colonel Paul was released, and before returning to his duty kissed the king's hand in token of his loyalty. On the same day that Paul was arrested, warrants were issued for apprehending six members of the House of Commons for having engaged in a design to support the invasion. Lieutenant-Colonel Huske, who had just been promoted from a lieutenantcy in the First Guards to a company in the Coldstreams, was sent with a sergeant-at-arms to arrest Sir William Wyndham, in Somersetshire. He seized all his papers, and made Wyndham a prisoner, but on his entreating permission to visit his wife, on the eve of her confinement, and giving his word to return, Huske allowed him to enter Lady Wyndham's bed-room, from whence he effected his escape, and left Huske to gallop up to London with the intelligence of his failure.

1716.

When General Charles Wills, subsequently colonel of the First Guards, and General Carpenter defeated the rebels at Preston, and captured large numbers of prisoners, the invasion of England by the Jacobites from Scotland was checked; and the noblemen and persons of rank and influence who were taken, were sent to London in charge of Brigadier Panton and 100 men of Lumley's horse. At Highgate, the prisoners were delivered over to Major-General Tatton, of the First Guards, who, with a detachment of about 300 Foot Guards escorted his charge to town, the prisoners being pinioned, and their horses led by foot soldiers. They were to be distributed in the several prisons at the Tower, Newgate, Marshalsea, and the Fleet, and each gang being placed between a party of horse grenadiers and a platoon of Foot Guards, Tatton marched them in this manner from Highgate to the several prisons, between large crowds of people, the drums beating a triumphal march.

The rebellion was now completely crushed, and the country again at peace, but for two years the First

1716. Regiment of Guards continued at its increased establishment of seventy men per company, and the Regiments of Guards were again brought together, and encamped in
June 14. Hyde Park, in the summer of 1716, from the 14th of June to the end of August, during which they furnished a detachment of 400 men to encamp at Hampton Court, to attend upon the prince during his stay there, to be relieved by similar detachments from time to time from Hyde Park. In July, the Prince of Wales, as guardian of the realm during the king's absence in Hanover, held a review of all the troops in the park, and in August his royal highness inspected the First Guards, expressing himself well pleased with their appearance. On the
Sept. 19. 19th of September a battalion of ten companies of the First Guards was detached to Rochester for a month, returning about the 20th of October, and in January, 1717, on the return of the king from Hanover, a detachment of 170 men from the three regiments, with officers, was sent to Greenwich to receive his majesty.

1717.

1717. . The eager demands for a further reduction of the army caused the companies of the Foot Guards to be reduced in the course of the year 1717, by five men each, and in November they were still further reduced to forty-nine privates each. At a royal review of the household troops held this year, both the king and the Prince of Wales were present.

The Third Regiment of Foot Guards had not hitherto been upon the same footing as the First Regiment, with reference to the supply of drum-majors' state clothing, and
Nov. 9. other items supplied from the lord-chamberlain's department, but being now brought to London, and performing the same duties, Lord Dunmore, as colonel of the Third Guards, made a representation on the subject, and the same supply was allowed as to the other two regiments.

The system of performing the duties by the three regiments proportionately was this year carried out

in an unusual manner; a detachment of sixty or seventy
men being required in November to relieve two companies
of the line at Windsor Castle, a company was formed of one
man from every company of the brigade, under a subaltern,
with a proportion of non-commissioned officers. A detachment similarly composed was sent down again to Windsor
in January, 1718.

1718.

Towards the end of the year 1718, the insulting conduct
of Spain, her interference with British trade, and her treatment of British subjects, forced the ministry to advise a
declaration of war, which caused a brigade of Guards to be
eventually again sent abroad; and though this was deferred
for a time in the hopes of a peaceful solution of the matters
in dispute, the fleets of the two nations soon encountered
each other, when Byng inflicted a defeat upon the Spaniards,
and shortly after this, on the 17th of December, war was
declared between the two countries. Previous to the
breaking out of hostilities, the Guards were now called upon
to perform other garrison duties. A detachment of ninety
men was sent in October to Sheerness, fifty to Tilbury,
thirty to Greenwich, and, on the 1st of November, a combined battalion of the brigade, consisting of 350 men, in
seven companies, under Colonel Robert Townsend, was
sent to garrison Portsmouth, in place of Sabines' and Wills'
regiments, called elsewhere.

The Stuarts, who had always found favour in Spain,
exerted themselves to widen the breach that already
existed between that country and England; the Jacobite
Duke of Ormond prepared an expedition at Cadiz for
the invasion of this country; and stores having been
collected at Vigo and Corunna, the advanced squadron
set sail for the north, but the French government having
received intelligence of these proceedings, the Duke of
Orleans, regent of France, in a loyal manner, sent a warning to George I. of Ormond's movements. The British

1718. government, being still ignorant, however, of the ultimate destination of his expedition, deemed it advisable to dispose of the king's troops principally in the north and west of England, and called over two Swiss and three Dutch battalions to assist in the defence of the country, which, on arrival from Holland, were sent to Scotland, under Major-General Keppel. While the combined battalion of seven companies of Foot Guards, under Lieutenant-Colonel Robert Townshend, remained at Portsmouth during the winter of 1718–19, an unusual detachment was made from the several battalions of Guards in London, consisting of eighty sergeants, corporals, and drummers of the brigade; these **Jan. 17.** were relieved by orders of the 17th of January, 1719, by a similar detachment, and directions were at the same time issued that they should be relieved from London by others of equal strength as often as should be required; but it does not appear whether the sergeants and others were sent down to supply the want of efficient non-commissioned officers and drummers in other regiments at Portsmouth, or to relieve periodically the non-commissioned officers of the combined battalion of Guards during its stay at Portsmouth.

1719.

1719.   Upon receipt of the intelligence of the approach of the Spanish fleet, three more battalions of Guards, one from each **Mar. 6.** regiment, were, on the 6th of March, 1719, despatched in all haste into the west. The head-quarters of the First Guards, under Brigadier-General Richard Russell, major of the regiment, was stationed at Marlborough, whence one company was detached to Swindon, four to Devizes, and one to Ramsey. The Coldstreams were sent to Chippenham, and the Third Guards to Melksham and Devizes, where, on the 18th of March, they relieved the companies of First Guards, while the combined battalion at Portsmouth was, on the 14th of the same month, ordered back **Mar. 20.** to London, where it arrived on the 20th. Besides the Foot Guards sent into the west, three troops of Life

Guards, Wade's and Pitt's horse, Kerr's, Evans's, Gore's, 1719. and Honeywood's dragoons, were quartered in the adjacent district, the fleet, under Sir John Norris, watching the Channel. The Houses of Parliament assured the king of their support, and a proclamation was issued, offering 10,000*l.* for the capture of Ormond. A storm, however, dispersed the Spanish fleet, two ships only reached Scotland, and the invaders, having landed, were, after a short fight at Glenshiel, on the 10th of June, all made prisoners. June 10. The Guards returned to London from the west, as soon as the dispersion of the fleet was known, in time to take part in more active operations; for the ministers, not satisfied with having merely successfully defeated this attempt at an invasion, organised an expedition to assemble in July, in the Isle of Wight, to retaliate upon the enemy, and though July. the actual destination of the force was kept secret, it was generally reported that the object was to effect a landing on the coast of Spain.

Amongst the troops ordered to assemble in the Isle of Wight, was a brigade of Foot Guards, consisting of one battalion from each of the three regiments; the battalion of the First Guards, of seven companies, 415 strong, was placed under the command of Lieutenant-Colonel Guise, who subsequently rose to command the regiment. It left London with all its camp equipage on the 29th, reached Havant on the 1st of August, and Portsmouth on the 3rd, Aug. 3. when it crossed over to the Isle of Wight, and a reinforcement of 100 men, with officers and non-commissioned officers in proportion, followed a few days later, according to instructions addressed to the Duke of Marlborough to complete these battalions. On arriving in the Isle of Wight, the three battalions of Guards, all under the Earl of Dunmore, were encamped with the regiments of Wills, Chudleigh, and Hinchingbrook, and a detachment of cavalry. The whole expedition was placed under Lord Cobham as captain-general, with Lords Mark Kerr, Dunmore, and Wade as his lieutenant-generals.

On the arrival of the fleet from Ireland, with the regiments of Howard, Dormer, Hawley, and Barrell, the Guards, with the other regiments, embarked at Cowes, and the fleet, with 4000 men on board, sailed from St.

Sept. 21. Helen's on the 21st of September, convoyed by Vice-Admiral Michel.   On arrival at Corunna, on the 27th, Cobham, finding the harbour too well defended, ran along the coast

Sept. 29. to Vigo, entering that port on the 29th, and, on the same evening, the general landed with the grenadiers of the army. The remainder of the force disembarked on the following day on the south side of the river, about three miles from the town, and advanced towards it unchecked by a rapid but harmless fire of small arms from some armed peasants on a distant hill, and encamped at Bocos.   Some shots were fired at the same time by the fleet into the town, whereupon the place surrendered, and the garrison under Don

Oct. 5. Gonzales de Soto withdrew into the castle.   On the 5th of October, the village of Rodondella was burnt, and, on the 6th, the governor of the castle offered to capitulate.   Lord Cobham immediately sent Colonel Ligonier, the future Lord Ligonier and colonel of the First Guards, to demand possession of the place, but as the Spaniards replied that it would be inconsistent with their honour to surrender unless a battery were raised against the walls, two 24-pounders were at once landed from the fleet, and on the following day

Oct. 7. De Soto capitulated.   A detachment from the brigade of Guards occupied the gates, and the Spaniards marched out, taking with them only their personal baggage, when Lord Cobham took the opportunity of quartering the whole of his army within the town, as the rains had rendered the

Oct. 12. camp very uncomfortable.   On the 12th of October, Major-General Wade sailed up the river with 1000 men, took possession of Pont à Vedra, and returned with some guns and other trophies of his success.   Part of the ordnance and other stores intended for Ormond's expedition was also found lying at Vigo.   The British carried on board their ships everything that was of any warlike value, and on the 24th of October, the Guards and the rest of the troops having re-embarked, the fleet sailed for England,

and on its arrival, the troops landed at Portsmouth, the   1719.
Guards returning to London, where all the twenty-eight
companies of the First Regiment were now assembled, and
quartered in the several districts of Kensington, Chelsea,
Holborn, and Westminster.

As the Spaniards were now anxious to come to terms,
peace was concluded between the two countries in the
following month of February. In the course of the year
Colonel John Pitt, of the First Guards, was appointed one Oct. 24.
of the king's aide-de-camps, but it was specially stipulated
that he should not claim the rank of colonel, as was usual
under those circumstances, nor claim thereby any precedency
either in his own regiment or in the army generally.

1720.

The purchase system had been introduced into the British   1720.
army almost at the time of its first formation, in 1660, sixty
years before, and originated in days when all places of profit
under the crown were saleable; but abuses had by degrees
crept in. William III. had endeavoured to abolish the
practice; but, failing in the attempt, he endeavoured to
legalise the custom by establishing a regular scale of prices;
the obscurity, however, of the orders, and the want of any
authority to ensure their observance, allowed them to remain
almost a dead letter. In some cases men purchased companies who had never served as subalterns; exorbitant
prices were demanded and given by those who desired position, and a general disorder prevailed. George I., with
the view to correcting these abuses, issued regulations,
on the 27th of February, 1720, which, besides ruling that Feb. 27.
officers of any rank could only purchase into the rank immediately above them, fixed the prices of all the commissions
in the army. The following scale was established for the
First Foot Guards:—

Lieut.-Col., including co.	6000*l.*	Lieutenant . . .	900*l.*
Major, including compy.	3600*l.*	Ensign . . .	450*l.*
Captain	2400*l.*	Adjutant . . .	200*l.*
Captain-Lieut. . . .	1500*l.*	Quartermaster .	150*l.*

1720.   Some considerable misunderstanding had arisen in 1717,
———   between George I. and the Prince of Wales, the causes of
April 23. which are not necessary here to detail; the consequence, however, was, that on the occasions of the king's visiting his continental dominions, the prince was not appointed regent
during his absence, and the Guards were ordered on that
occasion to do duty over "the princesses," the Prince of
Wales' daughter, and not over him; and the Guards were
ordered by the king to be withdrawn from Leicester House,
the residence of the Prince of Wales; but in April, 1720, a
reconciliation between father and son took place, and after
an interview between them, on the 23rd, the termination
of their differences was notified to the public by the
appearance of the yeomen of the Guards and the Horse
and Foot Guards in attendance upon him at his house.

During the king's absence in the summer of 1721 in
Hanover, the lords justices directed that the officers of the
Guards on duty at Kensington Palace, or elsewhere, where
the young princesses were residing, should observe all orders
they might receive from the Countess Dowager of Portland,
their governess.

The following letter is given in full as an instance of the
authority given by the king to the gentleman usher of the
Black Rod, to call upon the commanding officers of the
Guards for the assistance, whenever required, of a guard of
soldiers to assist him in the better securing of prisoners
committed to his custody by an order of the House of
Lords :—

"WHITEHALL, 25 Jan., 17⅜.*

Jan. 25.   "MY LORDS,—Sir William Sanderson, Gentleman Usher of the
Black Rod, having made application to the king for assistance of a
guard of soldiers for the better securing of the prisoners committed
to his custody by an order from the House of Lords, his Majesty
has been pleased to give directions accordingly, and to commend me
to signify to you his pleasure that you send immediately a sergeant
and six men to Sir William Sanderson for the purpose aforesaid, and
that you likewise give it out in orders, that upon any emergency he

———
* W. O. Letter Book, 151, p. 155.

may have the assistance of any of his Majesty's Foot Guards upon duty to prevent the escape of such prisoners he now has, or may have for the future.   I am, my Lords, yours, &c.,

> "GEO. TREBY.

"To the Colonels of H. M.'s three regts. of Foot Guards, or to the officers commanding in chief those regiments respectively."

On the 4th of February, 1721, in the course of a warm debate on the South Sea affair, Earl Stanhope, the principal Secretary of State, was taken ill, and died on the following day.   The king, who greatly lamented the loss of so able a minister, ordered that the Guards should attend the funeral, and the corpse accordingly was carried from Whitehall through the City on its way to Chevening, Kent, escorted by horse grenadiers and Horse Guards, the procession being led by the second battalion of the Third Foot Guards, as youngest battalion in the brigade, and closed by the first battalion of the First Foot Guards, the officers wearing mourning scarves and cypress, and hatbands, and the drums being covered with black.   At St. George's, Southwark, the Foot Guards drew up, and the coffin, passing between the lines proceeded to its destination.

The several battalions of Foot Guards were quartered as usual in the several districts of London, Westminster, and Chelsea.

1722.

It was about this time that the South Sea scheme was apparently flourishing, and crowds were rushing to the city in the vain hope of making their fortunes ; and it is curious to observe that on the occasion of 200 or 300 men of the Guards being ordered, in May, 1722, into the Tower of London, directions were given, under the authority of the king, that the Tower Guard should at any time afford "aid and assistance," whenever required, by the directors of the Bank, the *South Sea*, or the India Company.

In the summer of this year, 1722, the First Guards had

to lament the loss of their world-renowned colonel, whose
health had been long failing.   The Duke of Marlborough
had been for some time paralytic, age had weakened that
commanding intellect, and though at times for short periods
he would recover, his infirmities increased upon him, and he
died on the 16th of June, 1722.   Now that he was gone his
faults and his weaknesses were forgotten, and crowds
hurried up to London to pay a tribute of respect to his
memory, and to witness his funeral, which was carried out
on a scale of great magnificence.   The body was brought
from Windsor Park, where he died, to Marlborough House,
where it lay in state till the funeral took place on the 9th of
August, when, at an early hour in the morning, all the
troops lined the streets.   The First Regiment of Guards
was drawn up in the Park, with its right on Buckingham
House; the other regiments of the household brigade
forming upon its left.   As soon as the procession was
formed it wended its way by St. James's Park to Hyde Park
Corner, Piccadilly, St. James's Street, Pall-Mall, Charing
Cross, and King Street, to Westminster Abbey.   The following was the order of march of the troops who took part
in the ceremony :—

> Detachments of the Horse Grenadiers, Colonel Fane ;
> Detachments of the Horse Guards, Lord Newburgh ;
> Detachments of Artillery and Train, Colonel Bour-
> gard ;
> Detachment of Third Foot Guards, Earl of Dunmore ;
> Detachment of Coldstream Guards, Earl of Scar-
> borough ;

Then followed the first battalion of the First Regiment of
Foot Guards, of which his grace had been colonel ; the first
company, led by Captain Courtney ; the second by Captain
Lee and Captain Webb abreast ; Lieutenant-Colonel Reid in
the centre, and four lieutenant-colonels in rear ; the third and
fourth companies, led by two captains abreast ; the fifth by
Ensign Worley ; the sixth by Ensign Durand ; the seventh
by five ensigns ; the eighth by Ensign Hamilton ; the ninth
by a captain and ensign ; the tenth and eleventh by two

captains each. Captain Rowland Reynolds marched as adjutant, and four lieutenant-colonels closed the rear. Major-General Tatton, as major of the regiment commanding the battalion, rode alone, followed by six hautbois. Then came ten general officers riding five abreast, followed by the Earl of Cadogan, to whom the king had now given the colonelcy of the First Guards, and who, attended by his staff, rode in front of the eldest company of grenadiers of the regiment; Captain Bagnell leading, with the drums in the centre ; Captain Herbert and Lieutenant-Colonel Pitt brought up the rear.

All the officers were in deep mourning, the colours furled and wrapped in cypress, and the arms of the men and officers reversed. The men marched eight abreast, six deep. Then came the heralds, with all the paraphernalia of state, seventy-three pensioners (the duke's age), more heralds bearing the deceased's arms, followed by his grace's household. The coffin was surmounted by banners and shields, whereon were emblazoned the victories and conquests of the great duke, and a long line of mourners in carriages and on foot was followed by a detachment of horse, which closed the procession.

Thus ended the career of one of England's greatest generals, who, from the day he joined the First Guards as ensign of the king's company, on the 14th of September, 1667, to the end of his life as its colonel, had ever interested himself in the welfare of the officers and men. Throughout his campaigns he had retained the first battalion near his person, more than once showing himself to be especially solicitous for their welfare and comfort.

Old General Withers, the lieutenant-colonel of the regiment for twenty-seven years, who had served throughout the wars of William III., as well as in every campaign under Marlborough, would never leave the corps as long as his old master and colonel lived ; but on Marlborough's death he resigned his post to the first major, Major-General Tatton, and retired to his house at Greenwich, where, surrounded by literary friends and the wits of the

1722. day, he passed the remainder of his life cheerily, in company with Colonel Disney, an old comrade of the wars. General Withers appears to have been a man of some considerable fortune, and was an early friend of Pope. The poet Gay, in recording a visit paid to him at his hospitable mansion at Greenwich, in 1720, says :—

> ———" The friend of human kind,
> More visited than either park or hall.
> Withers the good, and with him ever joined
> Facetious Disney."

Oct. 12.   Major-General William Tatton's commission as lieutenant-colonel of the First Guards is dated October the 12th, 1722, and he retained that post above seven years. He had filled the post of first major ever since 1708. Brigadier-General Richard Russell and William Lloyd succeeded now respectively to the first and second regimental majorities.

Earl Cadogan.   The king selected General the Earl Cadogan, the most faithful of Marlborough's lieutenants, and who had been colonel of the Coldstreams since October, 1714, to succeed the great duke in the colonelcy of the First Guards, the Earl of Scarborough receiving that of the Coldstreams in his place. Lord Cadogan had served throughout the campaigns of William III. in Flanders, as well as in all Marlborough's wars in the Low Countries and in Germany. At the commencement of the War of the Spanish Succession he was still a colonel, but was made a brigadier-general on the 25th of August, 1704, after the battle of Blenheim. He continued to be actively employed, and in August, 1706, on the capture of Menin by the allies, was taken prisoner, and shortly afterwards exchanged for Brigadier-General Palavicini. He was at this time acting as quartermaster-general to the army, and shortly after his exchange he received the honorary appointment of Lieutenant of the Tower, vice General Churchill, and was promoted to be major-general. In the following year, 1707, he was appointed envoy to the States of Holland, retaining his military command; and in January following held a conference with

WILLIAM, 1ST EARL CADOGAN, K.T.

9th Colonel of the First Regiment of Foot Guards
1714 - 1726.

the deputies to concert measures for defeating the projects of the French. In March, 1708, he superintended the embarcation of ten battalions at Ostend, with the view to pursuing the French fleet then preparing to sail from Dunkirk with the Pretender, who was collecting eighteen battalions to effect a descent in Scotland; and in the following August, with 14,000 men, he defeated 24,000 of the enemy near Oudenbourgh, the main army under Marlborough being at Menin.

This will not be an inappropriate place to record an anecdote concerning the late and present colonel of the First Guards, showing how thoroughly Cadogan understood and appreciated his master. It is related that one day as the Duke of Marlborough was reconnoitring the ground in front of his position, accompanied by a numerous staff, he appeared accidentally to drop his glove, and requested Cadogan to dismount and pick it up, which request was immediately attended to. On his return to camp, having dismissed his suite, he turned to General Cadogan and asked him if he recollected the spot where he had made that request, as he wished to have a battery erected on the spot, but did not wish to speak openly on the subject. Cadogan replied that he had already given orders to that effect; and upon Marlborough expressing his surprise that he should have known what he required, Cadogan replied, that he knew his grace too well not to believe him to be too much of a gentleman to have asked him to dismount to pick up his glove, were there not some good hidden reason for such a request. This occurrence is perpetuated in a piece of plate, which forms a central table ornament in possession of the present Earl Cadogan.

In 1709 Cadogan was promoted to the rank of lieutenant-general, and in September was detached from the army with a corps, two hundred guns, and fifty mortars, to conduct the siege of Mons. On the occasion of opening the trenches before that town, which was effected with great loss, he was wounded, but not so seriously as to prevent his being present at the Hague, in January following, to confer with the deputies, in his capacity of envoy to the States, upon the late proposals for peace. In April, 1710, he was again in the field, and with fifteen battalions, and some cavalry, he entered the French lines with the Duke of Wurtemberg without firing a shot. General Cadogan was ever one of the Duke of Marlborough's most faithful followers, and may be compared to Lord Hill in the Peninsula with reference to the Duke of Wellington ; in 1710 and 1711 he suffered with his master in the change that was affecting public opinion in England towards the duke, and on the refusal of Mr. Richard Hill to accept the post of envoy extraordinary to the States, was supplanted in it by the Earl of Ossory, son of the Duke of Ormond, then just appointed colonel of the First Regiment of Guards. General Cadogan continued, in 1711, actively engaged in the field, and in March had 80,000 troops assembled under him near Tournay ; but he soon shared with Marlborough the displeasure of the Queen, and in January, 1712, was succeeded in the post of Lieutenant of the Tower by Lieutenant-General Hill, brother to the Lady Masham, and in the following summer in the command of the British infantry by Lieutenant-General Withers, the lieutenant-colonel of the First Guards. On the change of policy that took place in the new reign he was, on the 11th of October, 1714, appointed to the colonelcy of the Coldstream Guards, and in the same year re-chosen member for Woodstock. In 1716 General Cadogan was raised to the peerage as Baron Cadogan, and, in 1718, advanced to the dignity of earl, with remainder, failing issue, to his brother ; and now, on the death of his former master, was appointed, on the 18th of June, 1722, general commanding-in-chief, master-general of the ordnance, and colonel of the First Regiment of Foot Guards.

In this year the Jacobites again meditated an attempt at revolution. They proposed to take advantage of the king's usual absence in the summer to effect a rising throughout the country, to seize the Tower, Bank, and public buildings, and proclaim the Pretender. Government obtained intelligence of the plot, and took all necessary preventive measures to defeat it. They induced the king to postpone his journey to Hanover, and move to Kensington Palace, where he was close to a camp formed for his security in Hyde Park, in which were assembled, besides the seven battalions of Foot Guards, four troops of Horse Guards, and two troops of Grenadier Guards, all under the command of the Earl Cadogan, now colonel of the First Regiment. Other camps were formed throughout the country, at Reading, Salisbury, Durham, York, Manchester, and Hungerford, where various regiments were assembled. Notwithstanding all these preparations, the Jacobites did not at first abandon their intentions, or their hopes of future success; they strove hard to seduce the soldiers, and in one instance believed they had succeeded. A barrister named Layer drew up a carefully arranged plan for the capture of the Tower, founded on the supposition that the sergeants of the Guards there quartered, and one of the officers on duty, would support the plot, but it does not appear that the Jacobites obtained any such support. They offered Captain Erle, a lieutenant in the First Guards, a high rank in the rebel army, on condition of his joining the cause, who immediately reported the matter to the Government. Several arrests were made, the Tower garrison was reinforced, and troops were held in readiness to act; but the feelings of the bulk of the English people were so evidently opposed to the restoration of the Stuarts that it was deemed prudent by their party to abandon any further attempts for the present, and in November the camp in Hyde Park was broken up, the troops returning to their usual quarters. Of the twenty-eight companies of the First Guards, the first battalion, of ten companies, went for the first time into *barracks* in the Tower; the second battalion, nine companies, to the Savoy; the third battalion, nine companies, to Southwark.

1722.

July 22.

Nov. 23.

1723.

Though the fears of an insurrection were allayed, the establishment of the Guards was increased according to

1723.

1723.   former orders, and from the 25th of January, 1723, each
company of the First Regiment of Foot Guards was augmented to fifty-seven privates, and all duties out of town
continued to be performed by a proportionate number of
men from each regiment.

June.   The king proceeded to Hanover in the month of June,
when a camp similar to that of the last year was formed in
Hyde Park of the household troops, both cavalry and
infantry, to which were added the following regiments of
dragoons and infantry of the line:—

REGIMENTS OF DRAGOONS.

The Royal Regiment.	Colonel Kerr's.
Colonel Campbell's.	Maj.-General Evans's.
Earl of Stairs'.	Honeywood's.
Lord Carpenter's.	Lieut.-Colonel Churchill's.

INFANTRY.

Lieut.-Gen. Wills, 3rd Regt.	Harrison's,	15th Regt.
Cadogan's,	4th ,,	Groves',	19th ,,
Montague's,	11th ,,	Sabins',	23rd ,,
Clayton's,	14th ,,	M'Carter.	
Stanwen,	12th ,,		

During its existence, detachments of various strengths from
the three regiments of Guards were sent to Windsor, Hampton Court, and the Tower, the parties when relieved returning

July.   to the camp, and in the middle of July all these detachments
were called in for a few days on the occasion of a grand
review, returning to their several country quarters on the
22nd of the same month. The camp was broken up on

Sept. 30.   Saturday, the 30th of September, when the Foot Guards
returned to their usual quarters in town. The king did not
return from Hanover till the end of December, 1723.

1724.

1724.   In the summer of 1724, the camp in Hyde Park was
again formed, and the three regiments of Foot Guards were
reviewed by his majesty on the 3rd of July, after which a
detachment of the three regiments was sent to Windsor

about the 22nd of the same month, to be present on the 1724.
occasion of an installation, but nothing beyond the usual
routine and change of quarters took place during the
remainder of the year.

1725.

A slight change was made in 1725 in the arming of the 1725.
corporals of the Guards; they had hitherto carried firelocks, Jan.
like the men, they were now ordered to carry halberts, the
same as the sergeants.

The Order of the Bath having been revived this year, an
installation of knights took place on the 17th of June, when June.
detachments from the three regiments of Foot Guards were
ordered to attend at St. James's Palace, and four battalions
of the Foot Guards proceeded on the same day to Old
Palace Yard, where, during the procession, installation, and
dining of the several knights of the Bath, they were to
follow the orders of his royal highness Prince William and
the Duke of Montague, great master of the order. These
directions being addressed to Major-General Tatton, lieutenant-colonel of the First Guards, in the absence of Lord
Cadogan, he issued the necessary orders on the subject;
but the Earl of Dunmore, colonel of the Third Guards,
remonstrated against the order not having been sent first to
him. The case was brought before the Lords Justices in
the king's absence abroad, who would give no decision in
the matter, preferring that it should be submitted to the king.

The following extract from a letter from the Secretary of
State, Henry Pelham, to Lord Townshend, in attendance
upon the king, is given as referring to the question in
dispute :—

June 22. Extract of letter from H. Pelham to the Rt. Hon. Lord June 22.
Viscount Townshend with the king abroad, giving some account of the
dispute that happened between Lord Dunmore and Major-General
Tatton in relation to the command of the Foot Guards in the absence
of Lord Cadogan.*

Upon the orders that were to be sent appointing several detachments of the Foot Guards to attend the Installation of the Knights of

---

* W. O. Letter Book.

1725.   the Bath, my Lord Dunmore conceived that he being Colonel of a
regiment, and Major-General Tatton but Lieut.-Colonel, he had a
right to have those orders sent to him as the commanding officer.
Major-General Tatton, though but Lieut.-Colonel of a regiment, yet
having long had a commission as Maj.-General asserted his right of
having the command. This being brought before the Lords Justices,
they did not care to give any final determination in the matter, but
ordered that for the present the orders should go to Mr. Tatton, and
that if my Lord Dunmore should persist in his opinion that he had a
right to command, they should then both of them draw up their pre-
tensions in writing, which I was to transmit to your Lordship, in
order to have his Majesty's pleasure upon it. Nothing having been
brought to me in writing by either of them, and my own opinion, both
with regard to the nature of the thing itself, and by all orders and
precedents that I can find in the books of the office, being very clear
against my Lord Dunmore, I did not think of giving your Lordship
any trouble about it, till I was told the Duke of Newcastle referred to
a letter that I should write upon the occasion. At present, I think
the dispute is at an end, but if Lord Dunmore should renew his pre-
tensions, I shall then have the honor of transmitting them to your
Lordship . . . .

Aug. 6.   In the absence of the king, the Lords Justices directed
Sir Charles Wills and Lord Carpenter to make the
usual annual inspection of the regiments of cavalry and
infantry in different parts of England; but they did not
think it proper to nominate any officer to review the Guards,
as they had been seen by the king in the preceding year. In
August a company of sixty-four men from the three regiments, under a lieutenant and an ensign, was ordered to
Barnet to assist in capturing the deer-stealers who were
then infesting the Enfield Chase and carrying away the
deer.

1726.

1726.   The Earl of Cadogan, having held the colonelcy only four
years, died on the 17th of July, 1726, and was succeeded as
colonel of the First Guards by Lieutenant-General Sir
Charles Wills.

Sir Charles, born about the year 1670, was son of John
Wills of St. Germans, in Cornwall; he was still a subaltern in
1693, when serving in the Low Countries under William III.,
and was present both at the battle of Landen and siege of

LIEUT: GENERAL SIR CHARLES WILLS. K.B.

10th Colonel of the First Regiment of Foot Guards,
1726 - 1742.

Namur. On the 13th of October, 1705, he was appointed colonel of the 30th Regiment, and sailed with it to Spain. He acted as quartermaster general to the troops in that country, was present at Llerida, Almanza, and Saragossa, and was made prisoner at Brihuega in 1711, with the army under General Stanhope, but was released at the end of the war. He had been appointed brigadier-general in 1707, major-general on the 1st of January, 1709, and lieutenant-general 16th November, 1710. After the peace of 1715, being in command of the troops in the midland district, he marched northward to meet the rebels from Scotland, and with the assistance of General Carpenter defeated them and took a large number of prisoners at Preston. On the 5th of January, 1716, he was appointed to the colonelcy of the third regiment of the line, and now, on the death of Lord Cadogan, was transferred, on the 26th of August, 1726, to that of the First Regiment of Foot Guards. He appears to have had a property at Claxton, and was member of parliament for Totnes. He took an active interest in the affairs of the regiment during the next fifteen years, and, when he died, left his property to Field-Marshal Sir Robert Rich, Baronet, of Rosehall in Suffolk, governor of Chelsea Hospital.

1727.

The court of Spain had of late shown symptoms of great hostility to England, and now, provoked at the measures of retaliation adopted by some captains of British men-of-war, proceeded to violent acts, seizing upon an English ship in the West Indies. Philip, King of Spain, longing to repossess himself of Gibraltar, the brightest jewel in his crown, was anxiously watching for an opportunity to regain it, and being supported in his cause by Austria, had assembled about 20,000 men, at the end of the year 1726, in the southern part of Andalusia, under the transparent pretence of repairing the castle of St. Roch. He offered the command of his army to Villadarias, but the gallant old antagonist of the British refused the honour unless he were to be supported by a fleet at sea. The Count de las Torres was then named. This Spaniard felt no misgiving, and boasted that in six weeks he would drive the heretics into the sea, and plant the standard of Spain upon the summit of the rock.

The governor of the place, the old Earl of Portmore, was in England at the time, but his place was well filled by Colonel Clayton, who with four or five regiments was prepared to hold out till more assistance came from England, and which arrived in the course of the winter. On the

Government determining to send out further reinforcements, the First Regiment of Foot Guards was increased by 128 men, or four men per company, and a battalion of that regiment was ordered on the 6th of March to prepare for foreign service, to be composed of ten companies to be selected by lot, which fell upon those commanded by the following officers, the companies being completed from others to sixty privates each:—

Lieut.-Col. John Price.	Lieut.-Col. Thos. Inwood.
„ Anth. Hastings.	„ Rich. Hele Treby.
„ Rich. Pearson.	„ James Brown.
„ Wm. Meyrick.	„ Adolphus Oughton.
„ John Duncombe.	„ Williamson.

Treby was son of the late secretary for war, governor of Dartmouth, and for some reason resigned his commission at this time, being succeeded by Colonel Richard Onslow, brother to the Speaker of the House of Commons.

The battalion was placed under the command of Colonel John Guise, major of the First Guards, and it would appear that considerable activity was displayed by him under the directions of Sir Charles Wills, the colonel of the regiment, in getting it ready for foreign service, as the following extract of a letter under date the 20th of March, addressed to Sir Charles by Mr. Pelham, secretary at war, who had succeeded Treby, fully attests:—" I was glad to find by your letter that, let other people neglect this service never so much, you are resolved it should occasion no delay in the embarkation of your battalion. I must recommend it to you to continue your orders to Colonel Guise to forward the service as much as possible."

This battalion, in all 710 strong, left London on the 23rd of March, and going down the river to Gravesend, found the transports not yet ready to receive them, whereupon the Guardsmen set to work at once to fit up their own and their officers' cabins. This willingness of the Guards in preparing their own vessels for sea only showed the zeal with which they were embarking for service abroad. On the 27th they sailed in five ships for Ports- mouth, where Lord Portmore joined them with Lord Mark Kerr, while Lord Coote, a captain in the First Guards, who was not one selected to serve, obtained permission to join the service companies as a volunteer.

After being joined by some more transports, the fleet left Portsmouth, arriving at Gibraltar on the 21st of April, before the Spaniards, under Las Torres, were in a position to commence very active operations, for sickness had been very prevalent amongst them. They had opened the trenches on the 11th of February, but could do nothing till May, when large reinforcements having joined them the total effective force of the besiegers was raised to 25,000 men, with ninety-two guns and seventy-two mortars. The garrison had not escaped the prevailing sickness, for though all the women, old men and children, had been sent away, and fresh provisions were procurable from the opposite coast, there was considerable mortality, and in the course of the year the First Guards lost through disease no less than eighty men.

In May the garrison amounted to about 6000 men, while eighty guns were in position in the batteries. All the attempts of the Spaniards against the rock were effectually checked, and on the 20th of May, the king's birthday, salvoes of double shot were fired from all the batteries, which not only did considerable execution, but spread dismay amongst the enemy's artillerymen.

While these events were occurring in Spain, the Austrians, though they had in this quarrel given their moral support to the Spaniards, had at first shown no inclination to assist them in the field; but in the spring of the year a threat was made by them of attacking the Dutch frontier towns in order to divert the attention of the British Government from Gibraltar. England was, however, determined, while giving effectual support to its troops already in Spain, to thwart the intentions of the Austrians, and George I., on the 12th of May, directed twelve more regiments of infantry to prepare for service in Holland, at the same time naming a large staff of general officers to command, amongst whom were Viscount Cobham, the Earl of Stair, Earl of Deloraine, Major-General Honeywood, and five brigadiers. Two battalions of the Foot Guards were also destined to join this expedition to Holland, and the second battalion of the First Guards and a battalion of Coldstreams forming a brigade under Colonel Robinson of the First Regiment were the two battalions selected; but this army of about 10,000 men, under Lord Cobham, never sailed, for before they left England, Las Torres, who had found that the siege of Gibraltar was hopeless, as the garrison was completely supplied from the sea, proposed a suspension of arms,

June 12. which was agreed to on the 12th of June. The siege of Gibraltar having thus failed, there was no further reason on the part of the Austrians for creating a diversion of the British forces, and after much negotiation peace was restored.

The total loss of the garrison during the siege did not exceed 400 men, whether from sickness or wounds; the casualties amongst the First Guards was four men killed and nineteen wounded, irrespective of losses through sickness.

June 10. In the midst of these occurrences, George I. died on the 10th of June, 1727, and was succeeded by his son, George II., who took the earliest opportunity of reviewing the Foot Guards, recollecting probably how, during the

lifetime of his father, the late king, they had at times
been ordered to withdraw from all attendance upon him.
A week after his accession orders were issued for this
review to take place on the 22nd of June, and in order that
the brigade should appear at its full strength, detachments
from Brigadier Kirk's and Colonel Harrison's regiments,
Second and Fifteenth of the Line, being ordered to take
the duties of the Foot Guards for that day, the several
detachments of the Guards in out-stations were ordered up
for the occasion. These orders were communicated by the
secretary for war to Sir Charles Wills as colonel of the
First Guards, who was not the senior colonel by date in
the brigade. The review of the three regiments took place
accordingly on the 22nd of June, before his majesty,
eighteen companies only of the First Guards being present
under its lieutenant-colonel, General William Tatton, the
other ten being still abroad, and the king, subsequently,
on the 10th of July, reviewed the household cavalry, on
which occasion 400 of the Foot Guards kept the ground for
them. Kirk's and Harrison's regiments, which on the 22nd
of June had done duty for the Guards, were also reviewed
on Blackheath.

1728.

Gibraltar being now considered safe from any further
attempts of the enemy, all troops beyond the regular garrison were, in the spring of 1728, ordered to England, and
the squadron under Captain Stuart, conveying the First
Guards Battalion and other regiments, anchored at Spithead on the 25th of April; but no orders having been
received for the men to land, they were detained on board
the transports till the 1st of May, when, upon Colonel Guise
receiving his orders from the secretary at war, he proceeded with his battalion by route through Petersfield,
Guildford, and Kingston, and rejoined the head-quarters of
the regiment in London.

On the 10th of May these ten service companies were
passed in review by George II., in St. James's Park, as he

1728.   had not seen them the previous year, and he was pleased to address them on the occasion, expressing his approval of their conduct at Gibraltar, and complimenting Colonel Guise on the reputation he had earned in that fortress, as well amongst his superiors as amongst his subordinates, for being a true man of honour and the soldiers' friend.

The first years of George II.'s reign were those of peace. Part of the Guards continued to occupy the Tower and Savoy barracks, while the rest of the brigade were, as formerly, billetted in the various metropolitan districts, changing their quarters periodically. Besides furnishing the duties regularly at St. James's and Kensington Palaces, and the Tiltyard, and sending detachments to Windsor and Hampton Court, as required, they were often employed in the preservation of order, in guarding criminals at the assizes, in assisting the Custom-House officers in the prevention of smuggling, in checking poaching in the royal preserves, specially in Enfield Chase, and in such like duties that are now, since the introduction of a more complete system of police, undertaken more by the civil than by the military power. A guard of 100 men, with a captain and lieutenant-colonel, a lieutenant and an ensign, was always furnished to the king's theatre in the Haymarket whenever balls were given there, when, amongst other orders the sentries received, was one not to permit any persons whatsoever to enter the said theatre in habits worn by the clergy. The king, as we have seen, occasionally reviewed his Guards in Hyde Park, and during his absence the Prince of Wales would do the same.

1729.

1729.   Early in the following year, 1729, several orders were issued under the authority of a royal warrant, regulating

April 30.   the honours to be paid by the Horse and Foot Guards, and other regiments, to general officers; the clauses specially referring to the household troops, Horse and Foot Guards, were to the effect that they should be exempted from paying any honours to the generals, except when they, the Guards, shall be in line with other troops, or mixed with them in detachments, or when they should be reviewed by a general officer under the king's special orders. To these were added regulations as to how officers of the Guards shall salute the several ranks of general officers. It was also ruled that the Foot Guards should give no guard to any general officer excepting the general commanding in chief, if of the rank of a full or lieutenant-general, in which cases the guard was to consist of a lieutenant and an ensign, with fifty men, and an ensign with forty men respectively.

About the same time when Lord Leicester was constable of the Tower a question arose as to the honours to be paid to the Tower Major by the officers of the Guards, as it was held by the latter that the above new regulations had superseded those of 1728. The question continued long in abeyance; but in 1731 it was ruled that, notwithstanding those new regulations, they were not intended to apply to the Tower, and that it was the king's wish that the same honours should be paid to the present constable, the Earl of Leicester, as had always been paid to his predecessors.

The following letter on the subject is inserted, not so much for any interest being attached to the matter contained therein, as to the fact that the writer, Sir William Strickland, who, in 1730, had succeeded Henry Pelham as secretary at war, in conveying the orders of the king to the brigade of Guards, addresses himself as his predecessor had done to Sir Charles Wills, who, though youngest colonel in point of date, takes precedence of his seniors as colonel of the First Regiment of Foot Guards, by virtue of the royal warrant to that effect issued by Charles II., in 1684, and that warrant, with other documents, under date 1737, were brought forward as precedents, ninety-six years later, in favour of the Duke of Wellington.

WHITEHALL, 19 *Aug.* 1731.

SIR,—I have represented to the King the disputes that have happened in the Tower between the Major of that garrison and the officers of the Foot Guards doing duty there with respect to the right of command, and have received his Majesty's command to acquaint you

1729.   it is his express will and pleasure, that the regulation which he was
pleased to make on the 26th of June, 1728, shall stand good and be in
force, notwithstanding the regulations which were made and signed
by him on the 30th of April, 1729, in regard the latter were never
intended to take away those that were made for the Tower of London,
but only for the duties of other garrisons.

His Majesty's further will and pleasure is, that the same honours
in every respect shall be paid from time to time in the Tower of
London to the Earl of Leicester, the present Constable of the Tower,
as have been always paid to his predecessors.

I am,

The Rt. Hon. Sir Chas. Wills.   WM. STRICKLAND.

Nov. 24.   William Tatton, who had been promoted to the rank of
lieutenant-general on the previous 1st of March, resigned
his post of lieutenant-colonel of the regiment on the 24th of
November, and Richard Russell, the first major, a brigadier
during the last years of Marlborough's campaigns, and
major-general since 1727, was promoted to the lieutenant-
colonelcy in his place. At the same time Colonel John
Guise became first, and George Read second regimental
major.

It had been customary at all times for the king's
company of the First Guards to fly the royal standard,
which was carried by that company on all state occasions,
and following former precedents such a royal standard was
supplied to the First Guards at the end of 1729. It was
of crimson silk throughout, with the king's cypher and
crown in the middle, and the arms of the three kingdoms
quartered at the four corners. The staff of this standard
was also more ornamented than that of the other twenty-
seven company colours, each of which, to the 24th, bore as
formerly, in the centre, the royal badge of former English
sovereigns. The lieutenant-colonel's colour was also of
crimson silk throughout, the remaining twenty-six colours
were the union. The issue of these twenty-eight colours
from the office of the master of the great wardrobe, forming
part of the lord chamberlain's department, was now made
every seventh year, or thereabouts; they had been issued
in February, 1728, and were again issued in December,

1736; January, 1743; May, 1751; January, 1758, and so on, at a charge of 282*l.*, or 10*l.* each. The charge of the eighteen colours to each of the Coldstream and third regiments was 162*l.*, or 9*l.* each.

1730.

At the beginning of June, 1730, the king reviewed the 1730. three regiments of Foot Guards in Hyde Park, after which each regiment sent a detachment of 100 men to Windsor June 2. and its neighbourhood to attend on his majesty during his residence at the castle. The First Guards' detachment moved there on the 10th of June, and returned on the 13th of October, having been relieved in the meantime by other detachments of similar strength.

The First Guards, under Colonel Richard Russell, again 1731. took part in a grand review of the whole brigade in Hyde Park, early in June, 1731, at which the king and queen, June 9. the Prince of Wales, Prince William, the future Duke of Cumberland, and the royal princesses were present, and previous to which detachments of General Wade's regiment of horse at Beaconsfield were ordered up on the 1st of June to Windsor and Hampton Court to relieve the Foot Guards at those stations. On the 9th of June the household cavalry was reviewed, the Foot Guards finding 400 men, with officers, to keep the ground. On the 21st of Oct. 21. October the twenty-eight companies of the First Guards were all in London as usual; sixteen companies being in Westminster.

1732.

The only duty this year that the Guards were called 1732. upon to perform beyond the usual London duty, was to send four battalions, on the 30th of June, to Old Palace June 30. Yard, to take part in the ceremony and procession connected with the installation of knights of the Bath, after which the king proceeded to Hanover, and remained there till the end of September.

1732.   The sentries placed at the doors of the offices of the Board of Trade, of the Treasury, and of the Paymaster-General, appear to have been first placed there by several orders issued in the first months of this year, for the purpose of preventing for the future the frequent riotous disturbances that happened in the streets.

1733.

1733.   In consequence of the great extent to which smuggling was carried on even in the city of London, to the prejudice of fair trade and the revenue, the secretary at war, Strick-

April 4. land, addressed a letter on the 4th of April, 1733, in the form of a warrant, to the governor of the Tower, and to the officer in command of the Foot Guards in that garrison, authorising them to furnish detachments of the Guards, upon requisitions from the commissioners of customs, to assist them in securing all contraband goods, but not to repel force by force, unless authorised by a civil magistrate accompanying the troops.

June 22. The annual review of the Foot Guards, by the king, took place this year, 1733, on Saturday, the 22nd of June, when the outlying detachments were brought up to London. The household cavalry were reviewed by the king on the following Saturday, when the Foot Guards found the usual detachments to keep the ground.

Lieutenant-Colonel Francis Fuller became second regimental major on the 5th of June this year, in the place of George Read.

1734.

1734.   In consequence of the increase of duties to be performed by the several regiments of Foot Guards, their establishment was raised, in 1734, by ten men per company, and the warrant for paying Sir Charles Wills 560*l*., or 2*l*. a head for each recruit, is dated the 21st of February of the following year.

No regimental Order Books are extant in the orderly room of the Grenadier Guards of an earlier date than the year 1734. In this one, however, has been copied the order of Charles II., under date the 6th of February, 1684, in the thirty-sixth year of his reign, regulating the precedency to be given to his own Royal Regiment of Guards (now the Grenadier Guards), viz., that the colonel thereof be always reckoned and take place as the first foot colonel. Then follow a copy of orders issued by the Duke of Marlborough, while colonel of the First Guards, for regulating the duties of officers, non-commissioned officers, and soldiers, while on duty on the several guards in London, the mode of reliefs and salutes to be given by the Guards to the king and members of the royal family at reviews and all other times; then follow instructions for the officers' and non-commissioned officers' recruiting, the first paragraph of which directs that none shall be enlisted but Britons and Protestants. It was the custom of the Guards when mounting duty to have four rounds of ball cartridge in their pouches, and for the sentries to go on duty with loaded firelocks. An order of the field-officer in brigade waiting, of December 26th, directs that the men shall draw Dec. 26 their pieces upon dismounting guard, to prevent their firing them off in the streets. Colonel Folliott, of the Coldstream Guards, who at a later period became lieutenant-colonel of the First Regiment, appears to have been a strict disciplinarian, for on the 5th of February, 1735, he declares he will break any serjeant or corporal on the parade who shall bring any men for duty under their charge who are not in perfect order, with clean good linen, square toes and arms, and accoutrements, and everything else in perfectly good order.

1735.

An order of the 13th of June, 1735, directs the regiment June 13. to be out in Hyde Park on the following Thursday, to be reviewed by Lord Scarborough. Amongst the directions given as to dress is one that the men shall appear as at a review, with *Ramilyed* wigs, according to the pattern which may be seen at the Tiltyard.

A change in the command of the regiment and batta- July 5.

lions took place on the 5th of July, 1735 : Major-General
Richard Russell retired, and Colonel John Guise succeeded
to the lieutenant-colonelcy; Colonel Francis Fuller, second
major in 1733, was promoted to first major, and Colonel
Charles Frampton to second major. From the following
Oct. 23, order of the 23rd of October of this year, Colonel Guise,
on succeeding to the regiment, would appear to have
shown himself even a stricter disciplinarian than Colonel
Folliott, for, after issuing instructions as to interior economy
and drill, he adds :—" Any soldier for the future that comes
to the parade with two shirts on, brings any necks in his
pocket or pouch, or changes his linen on guard, shall receive
one hundred lashes on the next mounting day."

1736.   Another order of the 21st of January, 1736, directs all
serjeants and corporals to wear their own hair except they
are bald, and then to have wigs like hair.

Sept. 28.   At the end of September of this year fifty-two companies
of the Guards were assembled in London, when, in consequence of disturbances amongst various classes, which at
last became very serious, it was found necessary on the
28th, with the view to preserving the peace of the metropolis, to have recourse to their services ; 100 extra men
were added to the queen's guard at Kensington, with
officers and non-commissioned officers in proportion ;
the guard at Whitehall and the Tiltyard was made up
to 150 men; that at St. James's to 100 ; that at Kensington to 200 ; 60 men at Westminster Abbey; 20 at the
Rolls' Court in Chancery Lane ; 30 on guard at Somerset
House ; and out of the twelve companies at the Tower, a
picquet of 100 men was kept ready to march, and if ordered
out, another picquet of the same strength was under orders
to be ready to relieve them. The three majors of the regiments were directed to meet at Sir Charles Wills' house in
the morning, and told off to take command of the troops at
the different stations ; the officers of the Guards were directed
to assist the civil power, and repel force by force if required
by the magistrates to do so, and the men were all served
out with ball cartridge. This state of things lasted till the

1st of October, when the minds of the people becoming
appeased, all danger of further disturbances was over, and
the extra guard at Westminster was removed; but it was not
till the 5th of that month that the remainder of the detachments were relieved, and the usual change of quarters took
place on Monday, the 25th.

The visitors to the Colour Court to witness the guard
mounting at St. James's Palace, may often even now have
their curiosity excited by witnessing an individual in a red
coat and shako, with a baton, keeping order about the band.
He is one of the marshalmen. The following order of 1736
appears to be the origin of the custom :—

The Board of Green Cloth having ordered the marshalmen to attend every day upon the parade, to prevent
beggars, &c. &c., the officers of St. James's and Tiltyard
guards are to let them have a serjeant or corporal with a
file of men to assist.

Questions of precedency appear still to have arisen
amongst the officers of the household troops which caused
the following order to be issued in the course of the year
1736 :—

" Whereas disputes have arisen between officers of Horse
and Foot Guards concerning precedency and commands.

" It is his Majesty's express will and pleasure that those
officers, in their respective ranks, who have commissions
of eldest, shall at all times precede and command all other
officers of the same rank or others in his Majesty's forces."

There had now been so long a period of peace, that it
became necessary for the colonels of the three regiments of
Foot Guards to settle amongst themselves, which battalions
of the brigade were the first for foreign service in the event
of a war, as well as upon a general system of roster for
home service; the regulations for the latter were settled
and signed, in January, 1737, by the three colonels, Sir
Charles Wills, Lord Dunmore, and Lord Scarborough. In
the month of August, 1738, the same colonels drew up a
memorandum, according to which it was settled that the
First Regiment was first for foreign service, the Cold-

streams second, and the Third Regiment third. This memorandum is signed Charles Wills, Dunmore, and Scarborough, again giving precedency to Sir Charles Wills, the colonel of the First Guards, the junior as to date of appointment.

The attention of the colonels of regiments had lately been called to the existence of a club or society, called the "Friendly Society of Military Members," that had been formed for some time, and met every Tuesday and Wednesday fortnight at a certain tavern, "The Goat," in Fuller's Rents. A continuance of it was now considered contrary to the rules of discipline, and the colonels gave directions in January, 1737, that they should meet but once more to divide their box, under a severe penalty to those who infringed this order.

On the occasion of the usual annual review of the Foot Guards by the king in 1737, the following brigade order, descriptive of the uniform worn at the time, was issued :—

July 6.   "At six o'clock to-morrow morning Colonel Pulteney will exercise the seven battalions by the wave of the colours as usual when the king sees them.

"The officers to appear in their new regimental clothes, gaiters, square-toed shoes, gorgets, sashes, buff-coloured gloves, regimental laced hats, cockades, the button worn on the left side, and twisted wigs, according to the pattern. The men to appear perfectly clean and shaved, square-toed shoes, gaiters, their hats well cocked, and worn so low as to cover their foreheads, and raised behind, with their hair tucked well under and powdered, but none on their shoulders, the point of their hats pointing a little to the left, their arms perfectly clean."

The quarrel, between George II. and his son the Prince of Wales, increased during the autumn of 1737 to such an

Sept. 12.   extent, that the king was pleased by an order of the 12th of September, to desire the withdrawal of the usual guard over his royal highness at Leicester House, and to command that none of the three regiments of Foot Guards should take any notice of the Prince or Princess of Wales, 1737. or any of their family, till further orders.

A few months later the queen of George II. died, and the November. funeral ceremony, which took place in December, was attended by the several battalions of Guards, when the following orders were issued for mourning to be worn by the officers of the three regiments :—

"Every officer to have a scarlet coat, buttoned on the Nov. 26. waist with a mourning button, and faced with black cloth; no buttons on the sleeves or pockets; black cloth waistcoats and breeches; 'plain hats with crape hatbands; mourning swords and buckles. To get crape for their sashes, to be all got ready by Sunday sevennight, the fourth of December."

Another review of the three regiments of Foot Guards 1738. was held by the king on the 20th of June, 1738, and the most minute instructions were issued as to how both officers and men were to be dressed on the occasion. Amongst the many orders was one that the men be sized six deep, as they will march before the king, but to march on the ground three deep; also, that the ensigns of the field companies are to carry the colours in the field; this last order refers apparently to the old practice of each company flying its own colour, a custom that had not yet been abolished.

Francis Fuller succeeded to the lieutenant-colonelcy of Dec. 15. the regiment on the 15th of December, 1738; Charles Frampton and William Meyrick to the two majorities.

The twenty-eight companies of the First Guards were 1739. quartered in March, 1739, nineteen in Westminster and nine in Southwark. In the summer detachments were as usual sent to Windsor and Hampton Court, and in the middle of June these were relieved by detachments of the King's Own June 16. Regiment of Cavalry, to enable the whole regiment of First Guards, now under Colonel Fuller, to be present at a review of the brigade, held by the king in Hyde Park on Saturday, the 16th of June, and on the 23rd of the same month detachments of the three regiments kept the ground while the king reviewed the several troops of Horse and Horse Grenadier Guards.

While these reviews were being held, a considerable increase in the army was ordered, consequent upon the impending declaration of war against Spain, which was formally declared on the 19th of October following. Each regiment of Guards, as well as twenty-two regiments of the line, of which ten were called over from Ireland, were augmented; the First Guards by 308 men, or eleven per company, and the others in like proportion.

November. In November, serious disturbances broke out amongst the dockyard labourers at Woolwich, and those who continued to work were exposed to insult and violence from the others. The disturbances at last assumed so formidable an aspect, that the companies of the First Guards at the Tower, and the King's Regiment of Horse at Fulham, were sent at dawn of day on the 6th to take possession of the dockyard, and to hold it till order was restored. This display of military force discouraged the **Nov. 16.** rioters, and the troops were soon afterwards enabled to return to their quarters. Colonel Francis Fuller remained but a short time at the head of the regiment, and was succeeded on the 16th of November, 1739, by Charles Frampton; Colonel William Meyrick and Richard Ingoldsby succeeding to the two regimental majorities, and to the command of the second and third battalions.

1740. The king paid one of his annual visits to Hanover in **May.** the month of May, 1740, and the Lords Justices, according to the former practice, directed the affairs of the kingdom during his absence; orders were issued by them to the household troops relative to furnishing the usual guards at St. James's and other palaces during the residence there of the princesses, and they directed that the same salutes should be given to a quorum of the Lords Justices (four in number), as representing the sovereign, as were given to the king himself.

As the political horizon on the Continent in the beginning of this year was very threatening, the government, in antici-

pation of hostilities, directed in the month of February that
an expedition should be prepared, to consist of ten regiments, to be placed under the command of Lord Cathcart,
and with a view to the greater efficiency of the army if
called upon to serve abroad, the troops were ordered to
assemble in camps in various parts of England. In March
orders were issued to Sir Charles Wills and others, to direct
their officers to provide themselves with tents, and everything needful, either for an encampment, or for such other
service as the king might think fit, and, as the season advanced, the troops at home were ordered to concentrate under
the command respectively of Sir Charles Wills at Hounslow,
General Wade at Newbury, and Lieutenant - General
Honeywood at Windsor. Sir Charles superintended the
formation of the camp on Hounslow Heath, where the
whole of the Horse and Foot Guards were to assemble, for
which purpose they paraded in Hyde Park on the morning
of the 15th of June, under Sir Charles, who had a lieutenant-general and a major-general on the staff with him,
and proceeded as a division to the encampment marked
out for them, leaving in town only a sufficient number
of men for the duties of the metropolis. The twenty-
eight companies of the First Guards, under the command of Colonel Richard Ingoldsby, second major of the
regiment, remained encamped at Hounslow from the
16th of June for several months. During this encampment
some troops had, in the month of September, been put on
board the fleet, in anticipation of their services being required
abroad ; but they were again disembarked at the beginning
of the following month.

The Guards remained in camp till the middle of
October, when, by an order of the 10th, the camp was
broken up and the several companies returned on the 14th
to their respective quarters in London.

Sir Charles Wills was now filling the post of General
Commanding the King's Forces, and had been raised to the
dignity of a Knight of the Bath.

(marginal notes:) 1740. Feb. 11. May. Oct. 10.

CHAPTER XV.

1740.   ANOTHER period of warfare, in which the British Guards took a part, was now about to commence, and the following sketch of European affairs about this period will show how England, after enjoying nearly thirty years of peace, excepting the short Spanish campaign in 1727, became gradually involved in a war for the defence of the electorate of Hanover.

Charles the Sixth, Emperor of Germany, died in October, 1740, leaving an only daughter, Maria Theresa, whose succession to the throne was guaranteed by almost all the European powers, by an act commonly known as the Pragmatic Sanction, but as Prince Eugene justly remarked, 100,000 men would have guaranteed it more safely than 100,000 treaties. Maria Theresa took possession of her inheritance at once as Queen of Hungary, at the same time making her husband, the Duke of Lorraine, co-regent, in the hopes and expectation that he would be elected Emperor of Germany, but claimants immediately sprang up in every part of Europe to contest her right. Frederick, King of Prussia, offered to support her on condition only that she ceded to him the province of Silesia; she haughtily refused, and sent an army under Count Neuperg to expel the Prussians from that district, but the Austrians were defeated at the battle of Molwitz in 1741. Charles Albert, Elector of Bavaria, another candidate for the imperial crown, was supported by Louis XV., who sent a French army, under Marshal Maillebois, into Germany, threatening Hanover, whereupon George II., becoming alarmed for his electorate, prepared to take an active part in the struggle, the British parliament promptly voting a subsidy in favour of Maria Theresa, and a considerable augmentation of the army on the English establishment. Seven new regiments of the line, from the 43rd to 48th inclusive,* and four of marines, were ordered to be raised; but as the Opposition affirmed on that occasion, that an increase in the number of the men in each company without adding to the number of officers, would be a more economical mode of strengthening the army, a division took place, and the difference of opinion ran so high, that it resulted in an attempt to impeach the minister, Sir Robert Walpole.

A general election ensued at the end of 1741, when the excited state of public feeling caused much tumult at the polling booths, and especially at Covent Garden, where it was considered necessary to call for the assistance of some companies of the First and Coldstream Guards, from the Savoy and Westminster; but this being considered an infringement on the liberty of elections, the Westminster justices, who sent for the troops, incurred a severe reprimand from the House of Commons.

More camps were this year formed in the country, the principal one being at Lexden Heath, near Colchester; but Sir Charles Wills, who was becoming infirm, was no longer able to take an active part in their superintendence, and the command devolved upon Lieutenant-General Wade, with Philip Honeywood and Thomas Howard as his lieutenant and major generals.

In December of this year General Sir Charles Wills, who had held the post of colonel of the First Regiment of Foot

---

* The 49th was raised two years later.

1741. Guards for above fifteen years, breathed his last, and was succeeded early in the following month by his royal highness William Duke of Cumberland.

1742.

1742. Prince William, second son of George II., created Duke of Cumberland when only seven years old, was now in his twentieth year, a major-general in the army, and having been brought up in England, was looked upon as a true British prince. He had received a military education, assisted, while he was still a boy, by being allowed, during the hours devoted to exercise, to drill a company of young gentlemen arrayed as grenadiers. He had been appointed to the colonelcy of the Coldstream Guards, in succession to the Earl of Scarborough, on the 30th of April, 1740, and now, on the 18th of February, 1742, was transferred to that of the First Regiment of Foot Guards, when Charles Duke of Marlborough succeeded to the Coldstreams; and the Earl of Dunmore, who had been colonel of the Third Guards for nearly thirty years, continued for ten years longer at the head of that corps.

The death of an officer of the First Guards, that took place early in 1742, must here be recorded, viz., that of Lieutenant-Colonel Lettler. He was one of five private soldiers who swam to cut the drawbridge chain at the siege of Lille, three of whom were then killed. Lettler survived, and was, as before recorded,* at once promoted, for his daring act, to an ensigncy in the First Guards; he became captain-lieutenant 27th of December, 1738, and after succeeding to the command of a grenadier company in the regiment with the rank of lieutenant-colonel on the 26th of April, Feb. 13. 1740, vice Ingoldsby, died on the 13th of February, this year.

Already in 1741, a considerable force had been ordered to hold itself in readiness for foreign service, including part of the household cavalry, eight regiments of dragoons,

* *Ante*, p. 34.

FIELD-MARSHAL WILLIAM AUGUSTUS,
DUKE OF CUMBERLAND, K.G.

11th Colonel of the First Regiment of Foot Guards.
1742 – 1757.

three battalions of Foot Guards, and twelve regiments of 1742. the line; but it was not till the spring of 1742, after Sir Robert Walpole had left the ministry, which had endeavoured to maintain a peace policy, that it was finally determined to send a British army to the Continent, under the command of Field-Marshal the Earl of Stair. The three first battalions of Guards, the first battalion of First Guards, of nine companies, being under Colonel Meyrick, were ordered in May, 1742, to be in immediate readiness, and the brigade was placed under the command of Brigadier-General Frampton, the lieutenant-colonel of the First Guards. On the 17th of May, these battalions were reviewed by the king on Blackheath, and embarked on the 26th at Woolwich, whence they sailed to Ostend, and dis- May 26. embarking 2242 strong, the brigade marched to Ghent, thence to Dieghem, in the plains near Brussels, where, by the end of summer, a British force of above 16,000 men was assembled. These consisted, besides the brigade of Guards, of the following regiments of the line, viz., 3rd, 11th, 12th, 13th, 20th, 21st, 23rd, 28th, 31st, 32nd, 37th, 39th, the regiments of Life Guards and Blues, and eight regiments of dragoons. The three lieutenant-generals commanding divisions were P. Honeywood, the Earl of Dunmore, and J. Campbell. Amongst the major-generals were Howard, J. Cope, J. Ligonier, H. Hawley, and the Earl of Albemarle. The brigadier-generals were Cornwallis, the Earl of Rothes, Earl of Effingham, R. Onslow, Pulteney, Huske, H. Ponsonby, and Frampton, the latter commanding the brigade of Guards.

In the meantime, in the course of this year, the Elector of Bavaria having, in conjunction with France, taken Prague, was crowned emperor under the title of Charles VII.

The Dutch had been earnestly pressed to furnish their quota to the service, and much time was lost in negotiations with them, as they were by no means inclined to oppose themselves to the French, and their lukewarmness prevented any offensive operations being undertaken this year, even though eventually an auxiliary force of 22,000

Hanoverian and Hessian troops was to be attached to the army under Lord Stair.

Amongst the regiments forming part of this force, was a corps of Highlanders, recently raised in Scotland, and sent thence to London, where their unusual appearance caused some astonishment. Many of these men had enlisted under the impression that they were not to leave their country, so that no sooner did the rumour reach them that they were to be sent abroad, than a considerable number determined to mutiny. After a review of the regiment, it was ordered to Greenwich, when 150 of the men, taking their arms with them, marched off towards Scotland. A combined battalion of the Guards, hastily drafted from the three regiments, was ordered to watch the remaining Highlanders, while Major-General Blakeney (the future defender of Gibraltar) and a strong force pursued the fugitives, ultimately taking them prisoners in a wood in Northamptonshire, and bringing them to London, when, on arrival at Highgate, a lieutenant and fifty men of the Guards took charge, and escorted them to the Tower. Three of the ringleaders, two corporals and a private, were tried by a court-martial, of which Colonel John Folliott, of the Coldstream Guards, who became lieutenant-colonel of the First Guards in the following year, was president. The three prisoners were convicted and executed on Tower Hill, and while some of the remainder were sent to the West Indies, the greatest number were allowed to rejoin their battalion, proceeding with it under Lord Semple to Flanders, where the corps served with great distinction.

The plan of the allies in the ensuing campaign was to hasten across the Rhine to Frankfort on the Maine, and unite with the Austrians under the Prince of Lorraine, thus anticipating the French, under De Noailles, in any attempt they should make to cross that river with the view either to moving on Hanover, or to seizing the large magazines that the Austrians had established at Mittenberg on the Maine, about twenty miles above Aschaffenburg.

Maestricht was fixed upon as the first rendezvous of the

British and Dutch troops; and the brigade of Guards, still 1743. at this period under Brigadier-General Frampton, left its winter quarters at Brussels in the month of February, and marching through St. Tron on the 17th, and thence by Feb. 17. Tongres, arrived in a few days at Maestricht, where the Guards and the rest of the assembled British troops were constrained to remain for two months, owing to the delay caused by the continued unwillingness of the Dutch to take part against the French.

1743.

A very general promotion in the army took place in 1743, 1743. while the troops were waiting inactive at Maestricht, and a April. change was made thereby both in the command of the brigade of Guards and of the First Regiment, by the retirement of Brigadier-General Frampton, whereupon Charles Duke of Marlborough, who was promoted to brigadier-general in February that year, received the command of the brigade; but he did not enter upon his new duties till he joined the army in the field, in the suite of the king, in the following month of June.*

Upon Frampton's resignation he was appointed colonel of the 30th Regiment of the line, and the lieutenant-colonelcy of the First Guards was given, on the 1st of April, to Colonel John Folliott, who had served all his life in the Coldstream Guards, having entered it as an ensign and lieutenant in the year 1704,† and for the

---

* This was Charles Spencer, fifth Earl of Sunderland, who succeeded as second Duke of Marlborough in 1733, on the death of his aunt Henrietta, Duchess of Marlborough, daughter of the first duke.

† Colonel John Folliott's previous steps in the Coldstream Guards were as follows :—

Ensign and Lieutenant,	20th March, 1704.
Lieutenant and Captain,	24th June, 1706.
Adjutant,	25th March, 1710.
Captain-Lieutenant,	12th November, 1713.
Captain and Lieut.-Col.,	23rd November, 1716.
2nd Major,	8th July, 1721.
1st Major,	3rd August, 1733.
Lieut.-Colonel,	30th October, 1734.

He was appointed Lieut.-Governor of Pendennis Castle, 19th June, 1729, and Lieut.-Governor of Carlisle, 9th July, 1739.

last nine years had been its lieutenant-colonel. The reason for the promotion not going in the regiment on this occasion does not clearly appear, for both Colonel William Meyrick and Richard Ingoldsby, the majors of the First Guards, were captains of companies in 1715, before Folliott. It may be surmised, however, that it was either from the want of funds, or that Folliott, who had risen to be second major in the Coldstream in 1721, had seventeen years advantage in that respect over Meyrick; or it may have been with the view to giving the lieutenant-colonelcy of the Coldstream to the first major of that regiment, George Churchill, a relative of the first Duke of Marlborough, who had been brigadier-general since 1739, to which rank Meyrick did not attain till the year 1744.

April.   At length Lord Stair, impatient of delay, determined at the end of April to advance with the whole British army, including the brigade of Guards, but without the Dutch, and after passing through Aix-la-Chapelle, he reached the banks of the Rhine in May. Ascending its left bank, he crossed that river at Neuvied, a few miles below Coblentz, pursued his march by Ehrenbreitstein and Ems, thence up the right bank by Cassel, opposite Mayence, and turning up the course of the Maine, reached Höchst, near Frankfort, in the middle of June, where he effected a junction with the Austrians and some Hanoverians. From Höchst he proceeded through Frankfort, up the right bank of the Maine, to Hanau and Aschaffenburg, watching the French, who had arrived on the opposite bank, after crossing the Rhine at Worms and Spires. De Noailles, who commanded the French army, hearing of the Austrian magazines at Mittelberg, sent forward a detachment of cavalry, and seized upon the whole of them. This was a serious loss to the allies, for, after quitting their depôts at Hanau, they had calculated upon these for the future maintenance of the army, as it penetrated further up the country. While in this position, confronting the French,

June 19   George II., on the 19th of June, joined the army, and took the supreme command, being accompanied by Lord Car-

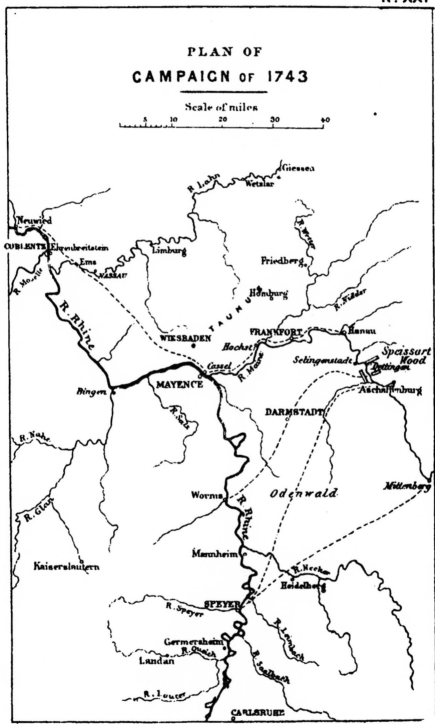

PLAN OF

CAMPAIGN OF 1743

Scale of miles

M YoU

teret, the secretary-of-state, by the young Duke of Cumberland, colonel of the First Guards, and by Charles, Duke of Marlborough, who now took over the command of the brigade of Guards from Brigadier-General Frampton.

Though Lord Stair had been unable to save the magazines at Mittelberg, he had frustrated the attempt of the French to take Aschaffenburg, where there was a bridge over the Maine, and both he and the king established their head-quarters in that town, the brigade of British as well as some Hanoverian guards being encamped in the neighbourhood. On this occasion, some jealousy was caused in consequence of the king's order that these latter should take their turn with the British Guards in doing duty at the royal quarters; and so intense was the feeling in England against the Hanoverians that, in the next session of parliament, the Lords drew up a protest referring to this circumstance as the highest dishonour to the king and the British nation, though in fact it was only following the precedent of William III. with his Dutch guards.

The hostile armies were now encamped on the two banks of the river, facing each other. The allies, 38,000 strong, were drawn up with their left at Aschaffenburg, their right extending down the river to Klein Ostheim, with the Spessart hills in their rear. The French, under De Noailles, were 58,000 strong, and extended from Stockstadt to Grostheim, with batteries erected along the river's bank, from which the allies could be taken in flank when once in motion. A retrograde movement, therefore, towards Hanau now became unavoidable, both to fall back upon the stores of provisions collected there, and to join some reinforcements of 10,000 or 12,000 Hanoverians and Hessians who had arrived in that neighbourhood; but the allied generals, recognising the danger of such a step in the presence of the French army, exposed as they would be to the flank fire of the French artillery, urged that the utmost caution should be observed. Accordingly, at a late hour in the night of the 26th of June, orders were issued to march June 26. in silence without beat of drums towards Hanau, the cavalry

1743.

June 27.

Battle of
Dettingen.

leading; and as it was the general opinion that the enemy's attack would be made on the rear of the army, from Aschaffenburg, the king ordered a considerable force, consisting of the brigade of British Guards, under the Duke of Marlborough, four battalions of Lüneburgers, and twenty-eight squadrons of Hanoverian cavalry, under Lieutenant-General Alten, together with some artillery, to remain behind in position, so as to check any attempt of the enemy to advance from that quarter, and the king, believing it would be the post of danger, remained with that body of troops. The opinion that the enemy would attack the rear of the allies was all the more confirmed by the fact that immediately upon the evacuation of Aschaffenburg by the Guards, and the withdrawal of their outposts, the French sent over five brigades to occupy it. Had the enemy carried out this idea, the whole brunt of the battle would at first have fallen upon the Guards and the rest of the rear-guard, till the main body had time to return to its support; but this was not De Noailles' plan, who was in hopes of cutting off the allies entirely from their supplies at Hanau; and no sooner was the French marshal informed, early in the morning of the 27th, that the main body of the allies was moving towards that town, than by means of two bridges, which he threw across the Maine, below Selingenstadt, he passed 20,000 men over to the other side, and drawing up his army in two lines at the village of Dettingen, near the Maine, posted himself between the allies and their base, so as to obstruct their further progress; giving at the same time strict injunctions to the commander of the troops at Dettingen not to attack till the allies were entangled in the passage of a stream with marshy banks, which ran between the hostile forces. As soon as Stair discovered that his further progress was stopped, he drew up his army in two lines, and opened fire with his artillery, whereupon the French, contrary to the strict injunctions given to them, left their cover and advanced to the attack. In the meantime, the king hearing of the action, and seeing no signs of the French advancing from

No. XXII

PLAN OF THE
BATTLE OF DETTINGEN
27th June 1743

ASCHAFFENBURG

Daum

FRENCH ARMY

Mayn Aschaff

Hochland

FRENCH

French marching to disengage the May 1854

Dettingen

Gr. Welschheim

Seeligenstadt

Scale of English miles

miles

BRITISH CAMP

Aschaffenburg, joined the troops engaged, and led them in
person against the enemy. The battle was fiercely contested, but the French were eventually completely defeated,
and driven back across the Maine, many of them, including
the French guards, attempting to save themselves by
swimming, a feat of which they did not hear the last for
many a day. No sooner had the king quitted the rear-
guard, than the Duke of Marlborough, observing all quiet
in the direction of Aschaffenburg, left the cavalry and
artillery to watch the plain, and marched the British Guards
and Lüneburgers to the extreme right flank of the allied
army, where they acted as a support to the first line, and
observing the French columns retreating in confusion to
the bridges near Selingenstadt, they joined in the general
advance. The cavalry followed the fugitives to the bank,
when Stair recalled them, for, content with his success, he
saw the danger of venturing across the river. The king
rode round the field, congratulating the officers and men
on their victory, and conferring on the spot the honour of
knight-banneret on Sir John Ligonier, who commanded
the cavalry, and who in later days was rewarded with a
peerage and the .colonelcy of the First Guards. The loss
of the allies was between 2000 and 3000 men, that of the
French between 5000 and 6000. The British Guards,
from having formed part of the rear-guard, in expectation
of an attack from Aschaffenburg, and from not arriving
in time to join in the first attack against the enemy, suffered
no loss.

The French, though still numerically much stronger than
the allies, retired to their own territory, while the latter, after
resting a few hours on the field they had so gallantly gained,
pursued their march to Hanau, where the troops were well
supplied with provisions, having been on half rations for
some days previously ; and being now strengthened by reinforcements, the whole army pursued the French across
the Rhine ; but as the Austrians, as well as the Dutch, who,
to the number of 20,000, had now joined the allies, refused
to attack the enemy, Lord Stair, after demolishing the

1743.
June 27.

Dettingen.

1743. French lines on the Quiech, near Germersheim, resigned the command of the army to Lieutenant-General Honeywood, and returned to England, for he saw that both the king and the government at home were bent on a peace policy. The Duke of Marlborough at the same time gave up the command of the brigade of Guards, when Colonel George Churchill, the lieutenant-colonel of the Coldstreams, succeeded him; but as no further operations were to be undertaken against the enemy, General Honeywood marched northwards to Mayence, with the Guards and the rest of the British and Dutch troops, when the former, embarking on Rhine boats, dropped down the river towards Holland, and Oct. 11. landing near Maestricht, about the 11th of October, proceeded to Brussels, where they took up their quarters for the winter. The first battalion First Guards was now commanded in the field by Lieutenant-Colonel Charles Russell, while Colonel R. Ingoldsby, second major of the regiment, was appointed temporarily to the command of the Guards brigade; but before the opening of the next year's campaign, this latter officer was promoted, with the rank of brigadier-general, to the permanent command of a brigade of the line, still retaining his regimental majority in the First Guards.

1744.

1744. Though France and England had not yet declared war, the battle of Dettingen sufficiently betrayed the intentions January. of Louis XV., who, at the instigation of the Jacobites, at the beginning of the following year, despatched a fleet from Brest, with the object of invading England. A British fleet was instantly sent out in search of the enemy; all the household troops were ordered to hold themselves in immediate readiness to march to the threatened point; and amongst other steps taken to secure the arsenals, the third battalion of the First Guards, of nine companies, under the command of Colonel Meyrick, the first major, Feb. 27. was sent down, on the 27th of February, to reinforce the garrisons at Chatham, Maidstone, and Sittingbourne. The

Government had recourse also to assistance from foreigners. 1744.
Three regiments of Dutch were brought over in March, and March.
200 Swiss, out of 500 of that nation residing in London,
who had offered their services in case of an invasion, were
enlisted and formed into a corps under Colonel Desjean of
the First Guards. The French fleet, finding itself unable to
cope with that of Great Britain, retired from the Channel,
and sailed back to Brest in the middle of March; and on
the 21st of that month, the third battalion First Guards, Mar. 21.
under Meyrick, was ordered back to London, and thence
to the Tower. A declaration of war on both sides soon
followed; but while the attempt of the French had thus
failed, owing to the vigilance of the British government,
the threats of an invasion had prevented England sending
the requisite reinforcements to the Continent, and the
Austrian and Dutch contingents also fell short of their
proper numbers. The service brigade of Guards, however,
still consisting of the first battalions of the three regiments
under Colonel Churchill of the Coldstreams, received considerable drafts from the home battalions in the course
of the month of May, before leaving their winter quarters
at Brussels; the drafts for the First Guards, now
under Colonel Meyrick, amounted to above 200 men,
or twelve men from each of the eighteen home companies. At the beginning of May the confederates, nearly May 3.
60,000 strong, consisting of 22,000 British troops, under
Marshal Wade, who had succeeded the Earl of Stair; of
16,000 Hanoverians, and 20,000 Dutch, were assembled at
Asche and Affligen, about six or eight miles west of Brussels,
on the road to Ghent, on which occasion the brigade of
Guards took up their position on the right of the line, near
Hekelghem, in the direction of Aalst; and here, on the 20th
of May, the brigade was reviewed by Her Imperial Highness May 20.
the Archduchess. The allied generals, however, found
themselves too weak to undertake any active operations
against the enemy, who, with 120,000 men, under Louis
XV. and Count Maurice of Saxe, had already taken the
field on the Flemish frontiers; and they spent the time

in useless discussions, while the French overran West Flanders, taking the frontier towns of Courtrai, Menin, Ypres, Fort Khock, Furnes, and Dunkirk, their light troops advancing to the neighbourhood of the allied camp, on the flank occupied by the brigade of Guards. On one occasion General Wade sent a detachment of 400 men of the Guards, under Lieutenant-Colonel Lord Robert Bertie, with a similar detachment of the line, in pursuit of these light troops, and effectually drove them off, but were prevented from carrying the pursuit any further by the appearance of a strong division of the enemy in support; whereupon the whole brigade of Guards, the Highlanders, and some Hanoverians were turned out to check any further advance of the enemy.

Fortunately for the allies, the successes of the Austrian army on the Rhine, commanded by Prince Charles of Lorraine, who crossed that river into Alsace at the head of above 70,000 men, had obliged Marshal Saxe to weaken his army in Flanders so considerably as to reduce it to 60,000 men, while the confederates were soon augmented to 90,000; but, notwithstanding this superiority, the divided counsels of the allies prevented their undertaking anything in concert, and the campaign terminated, after a succession of useless marches and countermarches, by the army retiring, on the 15th of October, across the Lys, when, after an uneventful campaign, the brigade of Guards proceeded to Ghent to take up their winter quarters.

The following are the names of the commanding officers and captains of companies of the several battalions of the First Guards as they stood in October, 1744, those of the first battalion being with their corps abroad :—*

H.R.H. the Duke of Cumberland, Colonel.
Major-Gen. Folliott, since April, 1743, Lieut.-Colonel.
Brig.-Gen. Wm. Meyrick, 1st Major.
Brig.-Gen. Richd. Ingoldsby, 2nd Major.

* The field officers' names are here given twice, viz., as field officers and captai of companies.

FIRST BATTALION (on service).

Colonel William Meyrick, Commanding.

Lt.-Col. Charles Russell.	Lt.-Col. Lord Charles Hay.
„ Henning.	„ Boscawen.
„ Sabine.	„ Earle.

SECOND BATTALION.

Lt.-Col. Lord Beauclerk.	Lt.-Col. Swann.
„ Lord Ossulton.	„ Brig.-Gen. R. Ingoldsby
„ Rambouillet.	„ Lees.
General H.R.H. Duke of Cumberland.	„ Pitt.
	„ Dury.

THIRD BATTALION.

Maj.-Gen. Folliott.	Lt.-Col. Brackley.
Lieut.-Col. Bagnell.	„ Sabine.
„ Herbert.	„ Carr.
„ Townshend.	„ Laforey.
„ James Durand.	

1745.

A detachment of 150 men, with officers from the four home battalions of Foot Guards, was sent to Windsor, on the 1st of February, 1745, as a guard for the safe custody of the French marshal, the Duke de Bellisle, and his brother, who were to be kept in honourable confinement there till further orders. These officers had been taken prisoners in the Hartz Mountains in the course of the month of January, and were sent over to England, where they arrived on the 13th of February, notwithstanding the strong protest of the French government that the capture was illegal, and contrary to the law of nations, having been effected on neutral territory. These distinguished prisoners were put under the responsible charge of Major-General Folliott, or other officer commanding the brigade. The detachment of Guards remained at Windsor till the 23rd of February, when it was relieved by five companies of Lieutenant-General Handyside's regiment, who were to receive their orders from General Folliott, or other officer of the Foot Guards who should from time to time have the custody of the marshal.

1745.
Feb. 1.

The evils of divided counsels had been so apparent in the last campaign that the allied powers concurred in the necessity of having one head, and all agreed in the selection of the Duke of Cumberland as captain-general of all the forces in Flanders.   He was young—only twenty-four—brave, energetic, and honest; and, although a strict disciplinarian, was popular both with officers and men.   Arriving at the Hague on the 17th of April, accompanied by his aide-de-camp, Lord Ancrum, of the First Guards, Lord Cathcart,

and other officers, he proceeded to Brussels on the 21st, and immediately rode out to the camp formed at Anderlecht, near the town, where the Guards and the rest of the troops were assembled, by whom he was welcomed with enthusiasm.   On the following day a review of all the troops took place, and the British in their new clothing presented a brilliant appearance.   The Dutch field contingent did not exceed 20,000 men, being far short of the promised quota ; but they had 8000 troops in Tournay, and other detachments garrisoned Oudenarde, Dendermonde, Ostend, Bruges, and Ghent.   The attention of the duke was at once turned to Tournay, which was invested, on the 26th of

April, by Louis XV., at the head of 80,000 men under Marshal Saxe, who opened trenches before it on the 30th of April.   The allied army, 60,000 strong, waiting too long before it marched to its relief, only broke up its encampment at Anderlecht on the same day, and proceeded by easy marches to Hal in two columns, thence by Soignies to Cambronne, and on the 10th of May to Brefoeuil, within fifteen miles south-west of Tournay.   Here the allies formed in two lines in order of battle, concealed by a wood from the enemy, the cavalry on the two flanks, the infantry in the centre ; the three battalions of British Guards, forming the first brigade under Churchill, were on the right of the first line, Ponsonby's and Onslow's brigades next, and further to the left were the Hanoverians, Dutch, and Austrians.   The British cavalry, under Lieutenant-Generals Sir James Campbell and Crawfurd, were drawn up on the extreme right.   The second line of British infantry was composed of three more

BATTLE
OF
FONTENOY
11th May 1745

brigades, Howard's in rear of the Guards, Bland's, and Skelton's, while Brigadier-General Ingoldsby, of the First Guards, had two regiments, viz., Durour's, of Ponsonby's brigade, and Pulteney's, of Howard's, placed under his command for a special object near the right of the line.

Marshal Saxe, aware of the approach of the confederates, left 15,000 men to guard the trenches before Tournay, and massed the remainder of his forces in position to defend the road by which the allies were advancing, his right resting on Authoin on the Scheldt, his centre thrown forward to the village of Fontenoy, while his left, covered by the wood of Barri, extended nearly to the villages of Gaurain and Ramecroix. In the midst of the French camp was a hill called Notre Dame de Justice. This position was strengthened by a line of entrenchments covered by redoubts and batteries along its whole front, and was flanked by batteries on the other side of the river. The village of Authoin was strongly entrenched and barricaded, as was also that of Fontenoy, which crossed its fire to the left at 1000 yards distant, with a redoubt near the wood of Barri, garrisoned by a battalion of the Regiment d'Eu, from which the redoubt received its name. Many of the best troops of France defended that part of the position between Fontenoy and the wood of Barri. Amongst them were the French Foot Guards and household cavalry, under the Dukes de Grammont and De Biron, supported by a second line, while more to the left of the French position beyond the line of the British attack were the Irish brigades, composed of Bulkeley's, Clare's, Dillon's, Ruth's, Berwick's, and Salby's regiments. The right of the French position was also strongly occupied, flanked by the entrenchments of Authoin and Fontenoy, and strengthened by three small redoubts between these villages.

With the exception of Königseck, the Hanoverian, who counselled a harassing warfare, the commanders of the allied troops were eager for an attack. The advanced posts of the enemy at Vezou were accordingly driven in on the evening of the 10th, and the necessary reconnaissance was completed by the Assistant Quartermaster-General Neville Tatton, when General Crawfurd suggested that the wood of Barri should at once be occupied; an advice unfortunately disregarded, and it was subsequently found full of the enemy's skirmishers.

May 11. At two in the morning of the 11th of May the several corps of the allied army were in motion to take up their **Fontenoy.** ground preparatory to a general advance on the French position. The Dutch and eight squadrons of Austrian cavalry were to assault the lines between Authoin and Fontenoy; the attack of this latter place being entrusted to a mixed corps of Dutch and Hanoverians, under Prince Waldeck, while to Brigadier-General Ingoldsby, with his two regiments, Durour's and Pulteney's, supported by some cavalry, was confided the task of capturing the Redoubt d'Eu, opposite the extreme right of the British troops. As soon as those two posts, Fontenoy and the Redoubt d'Eu, were in possession of the allies, the British infantry, under Sir John Ligonier, with some Hanoverian troops, were to advance in the interval between them and storm the French encampment. At four o'clock Sir John Ligonier commenced forming his line, a manœuvre which should have been covered by the cavalry under Sir James Campbell, but, owing to this officer having his leg shot off thus early in the day, the order was not given, and the first infantry formation was carried out under a heavy fire of artillery, which was only silenced by the duke ordering up to the front seven guns, supported by the brigade of Guards.

In the meantime the several columns advanced to the assault. The Dutch rushed without order against the lines between Authoin and Fontenoy, were received by the French infantry under the Comte de Danois, and being taken in flank and in rear by the batteries beyond the Scheldt, were put in confusion, and driven back to the nearest cover, whence they scarcely emerged during the rest of the day. Their cavalry which supported the movement also fell back in great disorder to the woods, and carried back to Hal the false report of the entire destruction of the allied army.

The centre attack on the village of Fontenoy by the
Prince of Waldeck was made in greater order, but was
equally unsuccessful, as the place, strongly barricaded, armed
with cannon, and defended by a brigade of French infantry,
defied all attempts of the Dutch.

Brigadier-General Ingoldsby had been placed on the right
of the British troops, as before explained, with Durour's
and Pulteney's regiments, to which were added the 42nd
Highlanders and Zastrow's battalion of Hanoverians; and
the first thing in the morning he received instructions from
the duke to take the Fort d'Eu, near the wood, with these
troops, supported by some cavalry. According to these orders
he commenced the advance, but had scarcely entered the
wood before his brigade was received by such a heavy musketry fire from the light troops that occupied it, that he
retreated for shelter to a hollow way in rear, sending a staff-
officer to ask for artillery; then, perceiving no cavalry near
him, he considered himself justified by his instructions in
waiting for it before he made any further advance.
Owing, however, to Sir James Campbell's wound, and to
Crawfurd and Hawley, who succeeded him, being without instructions, no cavalry was sent forward, and the
attack on the redoubt, a most vital point of the action,
was thus unfortunately delayed. The Duke of Cumberland,
in great anger at seeing that his plans were not being carried
out, rode up to Ingoldsby, gave him three guns, and desired
him again to advance; but the duke withdrew at the same
time the 42nd Highlanders, which, with the third regiment
of the line (Howard's) was sent to reinforce Waldeck in
another attempt upon Fontenoy. As Ingoldsby, however, continued inactive, Jeffery Amherst, the future Lord
Amherst, now aide-de-camp to Sir John Ligonier, gallopped
up to him from his general, who, stationary with the Guards
and other brigades under a galling fire, could not advance
till the redoubt d'Eu was taken, and asked him the cause of
the delay. He answered that he was obeying the commander-in-chief's order, and that he would advance when the
infantry of the main body pushed forward, and not till then.

The failure of the attack upon the Fort d'Eu, as well as the second one upon Fontenoy, and the loss of the Dutch against the right of the French lines, had roused the anger of the duke, who swore that he would carry the position cost what it might. He formed all the British and Hanoverian infantry into one mass, the first battalion of the First Guards, as before, under Lieutenant-Colonel Charles Russell, being on the right of the first line, which was commanded by the Earl of Albemarle; to the left of the First Guards were the 3rd Regiment and Coldstreams, under Colonels Carpenter and Needham respectively. Then came Ponsonby's and Onslow's brigades, also in first line, followed in second line by Howard's, Bland's, and Skelton's brigades, while the Hanoverians, who were on the left flank, were by the narrowness of the ground gradually crushed into a third line. Twelve guns also accompanied this column.

The French troops standing behind the ridge were unseen, and on their side could not perceive the movements of the British; but the commander, observing the guns that were being dragged up on the flanks, called the attention of the colonels to it, whereupon the officers of the French Guards exclaiming, "We must go and take those guns!" advanced with their battalions to the crest of the ridge, when the opposing lines suddenly found themselves within fifty paces of each other. Lieutenant-Colonel Lord Charles Hay, captain of the King's Company of the First Guards, stepping forward, recognised his opponents in a moment. A pause succeeded the suddenness of the meeting. Hay took out his flask and drank to them, saluting at the same time with his hat. He told them he was followed by the English Guards, adding, in a bantering tone, that he hoped they would stand till his regiment came up to them, and not swim the Scheldt as they had swum the Maine at Dettingen. Then, turning to his own company, he told them their foes were the French Guards, and that he hoped they would beat them; whereupon the soldiers gave a hearty cheer. Surprised at this strange address, the officers of the French Guards hurried

to the front, with the Duke de Biron at their head, to
return the salute of the British Guardsman, and D'Aute-
roche, captain of the grenadier company, called for a return
cheer, but it was a poor one, and given without spirit.
The French Guards then fired, when Hay was wounded in
the arm, but concealed it till later in the day. The First
Guards replied with a deadly volley, the Third Guards
took it up, and then the Coldstreams, while the First re-
loaded. Nineteen officers and a great number of men of
the French Guards fell at the first discharge, the front rank
was swept away, the second wavered, the British column
pressed forward, and the French were forced back. But the
losses on the British side were already severe. George
Churchill, commanding the brigade of Guards, had been
wounded, and the Third Guards thrown into some confusion
by the loss of many men ; when Lord Panmure, a captain
in that regiment, collecting the unbroken companies,
attached himself to the left flank of the First Foot Guards,
and the column continued its advance over the ridge, through
the French camp, towards the hill of Notre Dame de la
Justice, bearing all before it ; till at last the British
Guards stood proudly on the French position, but exposed
to the terrible reverse fire from the redoubt d'Eu, which was
still untaken ; for Ingoldsby, who had advanced at the same
time as the columns, had been wounded ; Zastrow, who
succeeded him, was not more successful in his attempt to
take it, and most of the troops engaged in that service,
finding it impracticable, pushed forward and joined the First
Guards in their advance into the French position. The
British Guards had successfully driven back into their camp
the household troops of France, when they found themselves,
with four or five other battalions, surrounded by the French
cavalry ; but a close and well-sustained fire effectually kept
off their repeated charges, and though the enemy advanced
till their horses' breasts met the British and Hanoverian
bayonets, he was eventually, by repeated volleys, driven
back, with the loss of 460 men. In the First Guards, as
well as in the other regiments, it required the utmost efforts

of the officers and men to close up the gaps in the ranks, for the columns were decimated. Lieutenant-Colonel Conway's company was nearly all destroyed, and many others suffered severely; but prominent by his exertions in the battalion, amongst all others equally brave, was Sergeant Silk, who, though shot through the hand, bound up the disabled member, and continued on duty as coolly as if he had been on parade. Had the Dutch now recommenced their attack on Authoin, or had the cavalry come up, the success of the British attack might have been maintained, and the battle have been won; but no support was at hand.

It may not be out of place here to quote two French writers, J. J. Rousseau and Marshal Saxe himself, when treating of this part of the action. Rousseau says, that in the height of that famous battle "the English, having closed the heads of their columns into one, fell furiously upon the centre of the French, where the valour of the French Guards and of the troops which supported them was forced to yield to numbers. By this movement and the suddenness of the attack the French troops gave way, and the enemy (the English) penetrated no less than 300 paces into the French camp, where they formed themselves into a kind of square battalion. The French king's household cavalry and the carabineers attacked their front, and three times were these French troops repulsed." Marshal Saxe says:—"Je ne " sais s'il y a beaucoup de nos généraux qui osassent entre- "prendre de passer une plaine avec un corps d'infanterie " devant un corps de cavallerie nombreuse, et se flatter de " pouvoir se soutenir plusieurs heures avec quinze ou vingt " bataillons au milieu d'une armée, comme ont fait les Anglais " à Fontenoy, sans qu'aucune charge de cavallerie les ait " ébranlé ou fait dégarnir de leur feu. Ce sont des choses " que nous avons tous vu, mais l'amour propre fait qu'on ne " veut point en parler, parcequ'on sait bien qu'on n'est point " en état de les imiter." *

* Published in the "Traité des Légions," fourth edition, published at the Hague, 1757, and attributed by some to General D'Heronville, a friend of Marshal Saxe, and by others to Marshal Saxe himself.

Here, then, were the British troops in possession of part
of the enemy's camp, and but little more was wanting to
secure the victory than a diversion on the part of the Dutch,
who, however, did not again come forward. Marshal Saxe,
observing the state of affairs, counselled the king to retire,
but Louis gallantly refused to move ; and, at the suggestion
of Lally and others, artillery was brought up, to fire into the
mass, on which neither the French infantry nor cavalry could
make any impression. Not satisfied with this alone, such
still appeared the indomitable bravery of the British infantry, that Marshal Saxe, reduced to his last and principal
effort to retrieve the fortunes of the day, and seeing that
the French Guards had been driven back, brought up three
fresh French regiments, as well as the Irish brigades led by
Clare and Dillon, who with a wild cheer dashed forward
against the already decimated British column of Guards and
line, who received them with a shout, and poured in so hot
a fire upon them, that in one French regiment thirty-two
officers were struck down ; but the troops on the right of
the French being no longer occupied in repelling the
assaults of the Dutch, who had long since retired from the
field, were in a position to come to the assistance of their
comrades, and to repel with overpowering forces the hitherto
successful attack of the British ; and now, unassisted, in
the middle of the plain, surrounded by cavalry and artillery,
as well as infantry, the utmost heroism was of no avail, and
the allied commanders saw with heavy hearts that further
progress was impossible, unsupported as they were by the
rest of the allied army, and they gave the order to retreat.
The French Guards, who had given way before the
first shock of the British column, now reappeared on the
field, under the command of the Comte de Chabannes, and
with fixed bayonets charged so close up to the British
infantry that the adversaries were firing at each other almost
muzzle to muzzle. The First Guards, undismayed, retired in
perfect order, keeping the enemy at bay, and made their way
to Vezout, whence they had marched in the morning. The
cavalry came up to protect the movement, and the Blues

1745.
May 11.
Fontenoy.

especially distinguished themselves on the occasion in checking all attempts at pursuit.

Throughout the day the duke had been in the hottest fire, but while his gallantry was universally applauded, his judgment was universally condemned, for the attack had been conducted under his orders in the rashest manner and in opposition to all the rules of war. The unfortunate result of the day to the allies generally, and to their cause, did not detract from the credit gained by the British army, and especially by the Guards, on the occasion; and the acknowledgment quoted above, of the superiority of the British infantry over the French troops, founded on their behaviour on this occasion, is some compensation for the unfortunate issue of the battle, which was due entirely to the want of co-operation on the part of the allies. The first battalion of the First Guards showed themselves at Fontenoy to be worthy successors of those who, under the eye of their future sovereign, stood alone against the whole French army at the battle of the Downs, in 1658, and under the eyes of a Marlborough stormed the heights of Schellenberg in 1704; and an unsuccessful attack that can extract so favourable a comparison from an enemy may surely be looked upon with almost the same regimental feeling of pride as though the attempt of the confederates generally had been crowned with success.

There were not wanting, however, some amongst the allies, who, to cover their own ignominious retreat, attempted to cast imputations upon the conduct of the British, including the Guards; but these were no sooner uttered in presence of the duke, than they were disproved, for the next morning, as the duke was witnessing the relief of the head-quarter guard, always furnished by the brigade, he observed that, contrary to his express orders, it was composed of men of all three regiments of Guards, and upon inquiry, he was informed that there were not men sufficient left in any one regiment to furnish the necessary complement. The duke, surprised, repeated the report he had heard from a Dutch officer, when the whole staff burst out into furious exclamations of anger at so unfounded a calumny, and it is not surprising to hear that his royal highness never afterwards admitted that foreign officer to his confidence.

The British casualties amounted to 4041 men ; the rest of the allies lost 3000 ; the French about 5000. The duke, in his despatch, gives full credit to the First Guards, when he states that the battalion remained the whole day without being once put into confusion, though they lost many brave officers as well as private men. Four officers, Captains Gideon Harvey, Henry Berkeley, ... Brereton, and Ensign Sir Alexander Cockburn, three serjeants, and eighty-two men were killed. Seven officers, Lieutenant-Colonel Lord Charles Hay, Captains Francis Hildesley, John Parker, Richard Pearson, and Ensigns Maurice Borland, Gustavus Nash, and Gibert Vane, nine serjeants, and one hundred and thirty-three privates were wounded. Besides these, Brigadier Ingoldsby and Lieutenant-Colonel Lord Ancram, aide-de-camp to the duke, both officers of the First Guards, were wounded. Lord Charles Hay, who was reported killed, recovered from his wounds, and was complimented on his conduct by the officers of the regiment in a letter addressed to him by the adjutant ; and also by the men of the regiment, in one addressed to him by Serjeant Owen. Captain Hildesley's conduct was also brought before the notice of the duke, who obtained for him promotion to the rank of captain-lieutenant, with the rank of lieutenant-colonel. Many of the wounded had fallen into the enemy's hands, and Ensign Borland, with 104 men of the First Guards, and more of each of the Coldstream and Third Regiments, were prisoners at Lille a few days after the battle, many of whom died of their wounds before the survivors were restored to their country.

The French showed no disposition to follow up their advantage, and on the 12th the allied army marched unmolested to Ath, arriving on the 16th at Lessines.

The news of the loss of this battle created much alarm in England, where the duke's bravery was applauded ; but the conduct of the Dutch, and Ingoldsby's failure, were severely commented on, and it being necessary to take steps, without loss of time, to repair the heavy losses sustained, various proposals were submitted to government for expediting recruiting. Three regiments, Mordaunt's, Price's, and Handyside's, were ordered to Flanders, and a draft from the brigade of Guards, consisting of three lieutenant-colonels, eight captains, eight ensigns, four surgeons, sixteen sergeants, sixteen corporals, eight drummers, and 540 privates, was ordered to prepare for immediate service—a call that was joyfully responded to by all ranks.

While the army was encamped at Lessines, inquiries took place into the alleged causes of the loss of the battle ; but these were eventually reduced, as far as the British were concerned, to the cases of Captain Watts and Brigadier Ingoldsby. The former was tried by court-martial and acquitted ; but some time elapsed before it was decided how the latter was to be dealt with, and there were rumours that the commander-in-chief did not throw any blame on the brigadier. A court-martial, or a council of war as it was then termed, was at length assembled under the presidency of Lord Dunmore, the colonel of the Third Guards, and by this tribunal Ingoldsby was found guilty of not having carried into effect the orders given to him, and was sentenced to be suspended from pay and duty during the duke's pleasure. Thereupon, the duke named three months, so as to enable him to retire ; but though the king permitted him to sell his company, he refused to allow him to dispose of the majority in the First Guards in a similar manner, and at length, on the 20th of November, Colonel John Laforey, who had been captain and lieutenant-colonel in the regiment since 1728, was appointed second major in his place.

On the 21st of May, nine days after the battle, the town of Tournay was taken by the French under Löwendahl, and

a month later the citadel capitulated. On the 4th of June the reinforcements from England, including those for the brigade of Guards, joined the army at Lessines, and were inspected by the duke, who expressed himself well satisfied with their appearance. His army, however, not being yet

strong enough to resume the offensive, he could only afford
to detach therefrom small bodies to keep his communications open, and Lord Robert Manners, with a party of the
Guards, was stationed at Scoris, to protect the convoys
from Oudenarde.

Count Löwendahl had no sooner become master of Tour-   Attack on
nay than with 15,000 men he made a dash at Ghent, where-   Ghent by
upon the Duke of Cumberland sent Lieutenant-General   French.
Moltke with 4000 men, British and Hanoverians, to intercept him. These, however, falling into an ambush, the
cavalry and Hanoverians escaped to Ghent, Brigadier Bligh,
with the British, retired to Dendermonde; and a few days   July 4.
later Löwendahl took Ghent, with the British hospitals,
stores, and 500 prisoners. Moltke himself, after having
been refused admittance to Sluys by the Dutch governor,
reached Ostend half famished, where the presence of his
cavalry was rather an inconvenience than a strength; the
officers of the garrison, however, all welcomed him as an
active general, whose counsels they hoped would influence
the wavering mind of the old worn-out lieutenant-governor,
General O'Connor. Mr. Hatton, the consul at Ostend, had
for some time been calling the attention of the authorities
at home to the defenceless state of that important town, the
principal port for communication between England and
its army in Flanders; and Lord Stair, then in England, was
so impressed with the importance of the place, and the
danger it was in, that he requested the Lords of the Regency,
in the king's absence in Hanover, to give him the command
of two battalions of Guards, and with them he undertook
to throw himself into the town, and hold Ostend against
the enemy. Rumours, however, of a Jacobite movement
at home now beginning to make themselves heard, induced
their lordships to be cautious how they reduced the garrison
of London, and they preferred waiting for the opinion of
the governor of the place, Count Chandos, who was at the
time in the Duke of Cumberland's camp. Meanwhile the
French were overrunning Flanders, and having taken
Bruges, Oudenarde, and Dendermonde, were evidently medi-

tating an attack on Ostend. The garrison consisted of the Scotch Fusiliers, under Sir A. Agnew, and Skelton's regiment, besides a Dutch, an Austrian, and a Hanoverian battalion. The commanding officer decided on immediately flooding the country round the fortress ; but scarcely had the sluice gates been open for this purpose, than they were again closed by order of the lieutenant-governor, O'Connor, in consequence of a letter he received from the Austrian minister. Chandos, the governor, under the impression that the inundation had been completed, promised to defend the town if the duke allowed one battalion from the army, and that two more were supplied from England ; and the Royal Irish being thereupon despatched from the camp, Chandos made all haste with them to reach the place before Löwendahl's army could invest it. In the meantime the English government, having sent Colonel Braddock of the Coldstream Guards to report upon the defences of Ostend, issued orders early in July for a combined battalion of Guards to be placed in immediate readiness for foreign service, when fifteen men were drafted out of each home company of the three regiments, to form a battalion about 550 strong. The commanding officers were very averse at this moment to reducing the effective strength of their regiments, as an invasion was already considered imminent, and, believing that any men would do for garrison duty, they drafted for this service their least efficient men and their oldest officers, the command of this combined battalion being given to Colonel Rowland Reynolds, of the third Guards, the junior of the three lieutenant-colonels. On the 22nd of July it was assembled on the parade at St. James's, and marched to Margate, where it embarked on the 24th, remaining some days in the offing awaiting further orders ; but as soon as the report was received in England of the Royal Irish Regiment being on the road from the camp to Ostend, the Lords Justices directed the transports carrying the Guards to sail, and the battalion was landed at

Ostend on the 18th of August.*

* The absence of this draft from London, caused some inconvenience to the

Ostend was now closely besieged, and in consequence of the neglect to inundate the country, the enemy was enabled to erect batteries on the beach towards the sea, thus preventing the British ships offering any assistance to the town. Lord.Albemarle and Brigadier Mordaunt were subsequently despatched by the duke to assist in the command of the garrison; but they were too late, and Count Chandos, seeing that his case was hopeless, surrendered on the conditions that the garrison, including the combined battalion of Guards, should be allowed to return to the army, and be conducted to Mons. On the 28th of August the garrison accordingly left Ostend, where the combined battalion of Guards under Colonel Reynolds had been stationed only ten days, and passing by Oudenarde on the 4th of September, and thence through Authoin, near the scene of the late action, reached Mons on the 11th, when the French escort, under Beaufremont, returned to its own head-quarters.

In the meantime, the allies, after the loss of Ghent, had retired to the Brussels Canal between that town and Antwerp, and the Duke of Cumberland established his head-quarters at Vilvorde, where the Brigade of Guards were encamped. While here, on the 11th of August, the troops were suddenly turned out by the sound of firing at Grimbly, whereupon the duke, taking with him the Life and Foot Guards, proceeded to the spot with Sir John Ligonier and Lord Albemarle, and found the French, under the Duc d'Aumont, already in possession of the castle, from which however they quickly retreated, upon seeing the British troops approaching in force, and the Guards eventually returned to Vilvorde, taking up their original position.

In the midst of these operations, events were occurring in Great Britain which forced the government to withdraw for a time the whole of the British contingent from the Confederate army. Positive information had been

remaining troops, who were compelled to mount duty for eight-and-forty hours consecutively, notwithstanding that the detachments from Hampton Court and Windsor were called in to head-quarters.

1745.
September.
received that the Jacobites, secretly favoured by the French, who were too glad to promote any plan that would withdraw the British troops from Flanders, were meditating an invasion of England, and Prince Charles Edward actually landed in Scotland at the end of July. The progress which he subsequently made determined the government to instruct the Duke of Cumberland to send home ten battalions with Sir John Ligonier, without loss of time, while the Dutch were called upon to fulfil their treaty engagements, by sending over 6000 men to their assistance.

Sept. 20.
The duke found himself in great difficulties in complying with these orders, for the Ostend garrison, sent off to Mons, had not yet rejoined, and he was disinclined to weaken his army to such an extent in the presence of an enterprising enemy ; but the orders were peremptory, and besides the three battalions of Foot Guards under George Churchill, seven regiments under Major-General Pulteney, viz., the 3rd, 11th, 13th, 28th, 32nd, 33rd, and 34th,* received orders to return to England. The 6000 Dutch were, on the 7th of September, ordered to embark at Wilhelmstadt for Scotland, under Maurice of Nassau. Five British regiments were

Sept. 24
despatched from the camp at Vilvorde on the 24th, and the Brigade of Guards, under Brigadier Churchill, with the other two regiments, quitted it the following day, *en route* for Wilhelmstadt, which they reached after some delay on the 1st of October. Here they embarked in the most perfect order and regularity, eliciting from Sir John Ligonier the highest encomiums, and, sailing at once for England, they

Oct. 3.
reached Gravesend on the 3rd of October, and marched with all haste to London, where, on arrival, the first battalion First Guards was sent into quarters in Westminster, the second and third battalions of the regiment being respectively in Kensington and in the Holborn district.

It was the end of September before the late Ostend garrison, under Brigadier Mordaunt, including the combined battalion of Guards, reached the camp at Vilvorde. This corps,

---

* Howard's, Sowle's, Pulteney's, Bragg's, Douglas', J. Johnson's, and Cholmondely's.

together with some more British troops, had in the mean time been ordered to proceed to Wilhelmstadt *en route* for England, under the command of Lord Albemarle. The appearance of the combined battalion, composed, as we have seen, of many worn-out soldiers, did not meet with the approbation of this officer, who was himself a Guardsman, having just been appointed to the colonelcy of the Coldstream Guards, and, doubtless, their long march from Ostend to Mons, under the circumstances, and thence to Vilvorde and Wilhelmstadt, had not improved their original deficiencies in that respect. They embarked at Wilhelmstadt towards the end of October, and on landing in the river on Friday, the 5th of November, proceeded at once to London, to join their respective companies.

The whole of the British infantry had now been withdrawn from Flanders, and the Duke of Cumberland received leave also to return to England, where the alarm consequent on the progress of Prince Charles was intense. The companies of the Guards were, on the 15th of October, increased by thirty rank and file to 100 men each, thus augmenting the establishment of the First Regiment to 2800 privates, and the total number of all ranks to 3183 men and officers.

In the month of November, the state of affairs in England was most alarming. Prince Charles Edward had landed in Scotland in the last days of July; and being joined by large numbers of Highlanders, had outmanœuvred Lieutenant-General Cope, the commander-in-chief of the few royal troops in Scotland; taken possession of Edinburgh in the middle of September; and defeated the royal army at Preston Pans on the 21st of the same month. Upon the prince marching southwards with a powerful body of men, Field-Marshal Wade was sent to take command of an army assembled at Newcastle. The Dutch, Danes, and Hessians were hurried to the north, and upon the Duke of Cumberland's return from Flanders at the beginning of November, the popular voice was in favour of sending him in command of the additional troops about to be despatched against the northern invaders.

On the 16th of November, O. S., the king ordered five regiments of cavalry and fifteen of foot to be despatched towards Lancaster, under Sir John Ligonier, while the Duke of Cumberland was sent to Litchfield, where more regiments were to assemble from different parts. Amongst them were the first battalions of the three regiments of Guards just arrived from Flanders,* who were placed under the orders of Colonel Braddock of the Coldstreams, an officer destined nine years later to a melancholy fate in America.

Nov. 15.
The following were the general officers, the staff, and troops, in and around London on the 15th of November, previous to the departure of more troops for the north :†

Field-Marshal the Earl of Stair, Commanding-in-Chief.

Lieut.-Generals.—Folliott, Lieut.-Col. of 1st Guards, James Sinclair, Earl of Albemarle.

Maj.-Generals.—Read, Earl of Rothes, Onslow, Pulteney, Churchill.

Brig.-Generals.—Sir Charles Paulet, John Jeffries, Byng, and Daniel Houghton.

Brigadiers of the Guards.—Colonel Rowland Reynolds of the Third Guards, and Colonel Braddock of the Coldstreams.

Commanding the Life and Horse Guards.—J. Earl of Delawarr.

Brigade Majors.—Parker and Dean to the Guards; Sneyde, the Horse Guards; Fowke, to Houghton's command.

---

* The following scene is described by Wraxall as having occurred at a military levee held by the king previous to the Guards marching to the north. When the officers of the Guards were assembled he is said to have addressed them as follows :—

"Gentlemen, you cannot be ignorant of the present precarious situation of our country, and though I have had so many recent instances of your exertions, the necessity of the times, and the knowledge I have of your hearts, induce me to demand your services again ; so all of you that are willing to meet the rebels, hold up your right hands ; all those who may, from particular reasons, find it inconvenient hold up your left." In an instant, all the right hands in the room were held up, which so affected the king, that in attempting to thank the company, his feelings overpowered him, he burst into tears and retired.

† From a Return in the Cumberland Papers.

Troops in London.—Three squadrons of Horse Guards.   Seven battalions of Foot Guards.

At Kingston.—Cobham's Dragoons.

At the Camp at Dartford.—Royals, Royal Irish, Bragg's, Richbell's,
and Lord John Murray's regiments.

(Other regiments named, at other places at a greater distance.)

The first battalion of the First Guards, under Colonel Nov. 23.
Russell, left London on the 23rd of November, reaching
Barnet the next day, and Litchfield on the 30th, without the
loss of a man from sickness or any other accident; the
battalions of the Third and Coldstream Guards arrived in
high spirits on the two successive days. The old regiments of the line also joined in excellent condition; but
the newly raised regiments were undisciplined, undrilled,
and caused much anxiety to their officers as to how they
would behave in action. The Highland army had reached
Carlisle at the beginning of November, and summoned
the town, where Colonel Durand, a captain in the First
Guards, was deputy governor, with only a few invalids to
depend upon. He urged the inhabitants to defend the
place; but the mayor, dreading the consequences of a siege,
made good terms with the Jacobite generals, and surrendered on the 15th of November. Durand was tried by Nov. 15.
court-martial for the loss of the town, but having proved he
was helpless in the matter, was honourably acquitted.

The Duke of Cumberland still at Litchfield, having Dec. 1.
received intelligence, on the 1st of December, of the
approach of the enemy, put his troops in motion, when
the First and Third Guards, with Howard's Regiment,
marched to Stafford, and the remainder to Rugeley. The
duke was anxiously endeavouring to obtain every possible
information of the enemy's intentions, but at the same
time warned the government that they must prepare
for the defence of London in case the Highlanders should
slip past him. He sent his aide-de-camp, Lieutenant-
Colonel Conway, of the First Guards, to desire Wade to
fall upon the communications of the enemy, and directed

1745.   Colonel Cholmondeley at Chester to be prepared for an attack.   On the 2nd, the duke, in order to intercept the insurgents on their march to Chester, advanced to Stone, expecting an encounter; but Lord George Murray, the commander-in-chief of the Highland army, suddenly turned with his men to the left, gained, by a forced march, the high road to Ashbourne, and on the 4th of December reached Derby, thus placing himself between the Duke of Cumberland and the metropolis.   The greatest excitement was now caused in London, for besides the political, there was the religious element influencing the public mind, and the people were roused to the utmost in opposing the return of the Stuarts.   Lord Stair commanded in chief the troops in the southern counties; Lieutenant-General Folliott, lieutenant-colonel of the First Regiment of Guards, was placed in charge of the military in London, where Lord Delawarr, at the head of the household cavalry, and Brigadier Rowland Reynolds of the Third Guards, with the second brigade of Guards, were on constant duty.   The Londoners armed themselves, and were enrolled as soldiers; the associated regiment of Law, under Chief Justice Willes, paraded daily in Lincoln's Inn; two regiments of trained bands were on duty every night, and several wealthy citizens enlisted as volunteers in the First Regiment of Guards.   At a parade at St. James's, the city corps marched past the king, accompanied by their wives and children, as a proof that all they had was risked in the cause.

Major-General Sinclair having inspected the neighbourhood, with a view to fixing on a desirable position for establishing a camp to cover London, had reported in favour of Finchley Common, with the right resting on Colney Hatch, whereupon Lord Stair ordered the Life Guards, thirty pieces of artillery, and the grenadier companies of the battalions Dec. 18. of Guards in London, to march thither on the 18th of December.   It is possible that some irregularities may have occurred on the march, but nothing took place that could justify Hogarth in painting the celebrated picture of the march to Finchley, and the king, indignant at this libel on his Guards, refused to accept the dedication of the print, upon which Hogarth dedicated it to the King of Prussia.

Colonel Kingsley of the Third, and Captain Parslow of the First Guards, were sent into Northamptonshire and Huntingdonshire, accompanied by messengers, in order to obtain further information of the movements of the enemy, and for the purpose of reporting every possible circumstance. Prince Charles and his army had entered Derby in the highest spirits, but very few persons of any influence had joined his ranks since he had entered England, and at Derby, where a council of war was held, he met with a very cold reception. The Highland chiefs argued that as they had two powerful armies in their rear, the duke's and Wade's, as well as a strong force between them and London, and as there was an entire absence of sympathy displayed by the English people, further advance would only lead to disaster, and they therefore voted for a retreat. Prince Charles Edward protested, but in vain, and at last, compelled to submit, allowed Murray to issue orders to retire, and on the 6th of December the Highlanders were already on the march back to Scotland. When this news reached the Duke of Cumberland, who, with the Guards and rest of his army, was encamped on Meridan Common, he sent urgent orders to Wade to attack the Highlanders, and he himself, with the whole of his cavalry and 1000 volunteers from the infantry, prepared to follow with all expedition; 400 volunteers from the three battalions of Guards were accepted for this service, and placed under the orders of Lord Panmure, second major of the Third Guards. The country people furnished horses with alacrity, and the gentry gave their best assistance, amongst whom Sir Lister Holt, of Aston Hall, was remarkable for mounting 250 men. The foot soldiers on horseback, with their knapsacks and firelocks, presented a ludicrous appearance, but all were in joyful spirits, and followed up the pursuit with vigour and energy, though the winter had set in, and the high ground in Westmoreland was covered with ice and snow. Marching by Macclesfield, Lancaster, and Kendal, the duke had all his forces together on the 20th of December at Penrith, and on the 21st invested Carlisle, when Major-General Bland watched the north side, while Major Adams, Major Meriac, and Sir A. Agnew took their posts with a small force opposite the remaining gates. The Duke of Cumberland, with the Duke of Richmond as second in command, established his head-quarters at Blackhall, while the Guards were cantoned at the distance of a mile from the town, and on the 28th of December the batteries opened.   On

Dec. 30. the 30th the garrison hung out a white flag; whereupon Colonel Conway and Lord Bury were sent to ask the governor, John Hamilton, what it meant.   He replied that he offered to surrender on certain conditions, but the two officers refusing to listen to any discussion, the place was surrendered unconditionally, and Brigadier Bligh, with 1100 men, including the 400 volunteers of the Guards, took possession, when the late governor, John Hamilton, was placed under the charge of Captain Carey of the First Guards, the stores confided to the care of Captain Colleton of the same regiment, and General Hawley was appointed governor of the town.

In the meantime, a fresh alarm having been caused in the south of England by the news that an expedition was being fitted out at Dunkirk by the French, with the intention of invading the country, Sir John Ligonier, who had been left in command at Meridan camp, was directed to march at once with his army back to London, and the Guards, leaving Stafford on the 4th of December, arrived in the metropolis the day

Dec. 26. after Christmas.   Orders were promptly issued for establishing alarm posts in London in case of a disturbance being raised by the Jacobites, and every preparation was made for suppressing insurrectionary movements. The Duke of Cumberland was recalled from Carlisle, and the 400 volunteers of the Guards following a few days later, arrived in London on the 27th of January, 1746, and rejoined their battalions.

The threatened invasion from Dunkirk, however, never

took place, and as all indications of it disappeared, confidence was restored, and the volunteers returned to their civil duties. The Duke of Cumberland was sent to Scotland, where his presence became necessary, in consequence of the defeat of Hawley at Falkirk, and, after a campaign of three months, he effectually crushed the last hopes of the Stuarts at Culloden.

Amongst the orders given out by the Duke of Cumberland while in Scotland, is one concerning colours, that is interesting, as referring to a question which was brought forward again 113 years later. It says, " The union colour is the " first stand of colours in all regiments, royal or not, and " to be mounted upon the duke, except the Foot Guards ; " with them the king's colour is allowed to be the first as " a particular distinction." This is the wording of the original order, meaning that the union or first colour of every regiment of the line shall be carried by all guards furnished by those regiments that mount duty upon his royal highness, and he refers in that order to the privilege of the Guards as household troops to fly the king's colour or royal standard as their first colour, the union being their second or regimental colour.

CHAPTER XVI.

1746.   THE termination of the rebellion in Scotland was followed
by the trial of the principal persons engaged, and, after
the conviction of the rebel lords by the House of Peers,
the execution of Lords Balmerino and Kilmarnock took place
Aug. 18.   on Tower-hill on the 18th of August, 1746, on which occasion, in order to be prepared against any attempt at a
rescue, the government directed a large party of the Guards
to be present, with orders, however, not to repel force by
force unless specially required to do so.   On Friday, the
Sept. 16.   28th of November, a detachment was also made from the
three regiments of Guards, to the gaol in Southwark, to
assist in escorting the remainder of the condemned rebel
prisoners to Kennington Common, and to preserve order
during the executions.   In the following spring, Lord
Lovat was executed, on which occasion detachments of the
three regiments of Foot Guards were again present.

In consequence of the continued unsettled state of
affairs in Scotland, neither the Guards nor any other
British troops were sent over to join the confederate army
in Flanders during the year 1746, but the ministers had
for some time been preparing for an attack on Quebec,
and for that purpose had collected a body of 8000 troops

of the line under Lieutenant-General James Sinclair at 1746. Portsmouth; but when the expedition was ready, at the beginning of September, the season was too far advanced, Sept. and it was resolved to make use of the assembled troops to land on the French coast in the Bay of Biscay, and seize Port l'Orient, the French East India Company's depôt. Owing to this change of destination, it was determine that two battalions of the household troops, forming a brigade under Major-General Francis Fuller, late of the First Guards, should join the expedition; and the third battalion of the First Regiment, under Colonel Laforey, the successor of Colonel Ingoldsby, and the second battalion of Coldstreams, were ordered to hold themselves in readiness for service. These two battalions, leaving all casualties Sept. 10. and one company each in England as a depôt, forthwith embarked at the Tower wharf, in presence of the Duke of Cumberland, who spoke freely to the men as they entered the boats, bidding them do their duty against the French. The boats dropped down the river to Woolwich, where the transports awaited them, and, by the middle of September, the Guards were on their way to join the rest of the expedition. The following were the captains of companies of the third battalion First Guards at the end of 1745, most of whom, excepting General Folliott, accompanied their corps on this occasion :—

Lieut.-Gen. Folliott.	Colonel Townsend.
Lieut.-Col. Bagnal.	Lieut.-Col. Sabine.
,, Brackley.	,, Durand.
Colonel Herbert.	,, Mitchell.
Lieut.-Col. Carr.	

On the promotion, above referred to of Colonel Laforey to a battalion, Jeffrey Amherst, the future Lord Amherst, was promoted to a company in the First Guards.

The naval force of sixteen large ships and eight frigates, besides others, with about thirty transports carrying troops, originally destined for America, had in the meantime left Portsmouth for Plymouth, and on the arrival of the transports carrying the Guards at this latter port, on the 22nd of September, information was received that the expedition had sailed from Plymouth on the 14th, and landed at Port l'Orient without opposition on the 20th, where it burned and pillaged the neighbourhood. Colonel Laforey, having received orders from head-quarters, communicated them to the transports carrying the remainder of the third battalion of the First Guards, and landed his corps at Plymouth, awaiting the return of the fleet from its inglorious expedition against Port l'Orient and Quiberon, where they had only burnt some villages and plundered the country. Early in October, the Guards re-embarked, and the transports containing them were joined by the fleet on

the 8th of that month. On the 10th the whole expedition sailed again for the Bay of Biscay, but not having effected a landing, the Guards and the rest of the fleet returned to Plymouth on the 19th, when, all further attempts against the French coast being postponed to another year, the fleet was ordered to the Downs, and the ships with the brigade of Guards, under Fuller, proceeded to the Thames. As they were sailing up Channel on the 23rd, they were exposed to a very severe gale off Dungeness, which committed great havoc both amongst the ships and the arms and accoutrements of the men on board. On the arrival of the Guards in the Downs on the 27th, they sailed for the river, reaching Deptford on the 31st of October, when the third battalion disembarked, and marched to the Tower, the men attached to the second battalion during its absence at sea rejoining their respective companies.

A small change of dress is recorded as having taken place this year: the sergeants were ordered to discontinue the use of ruffles, as the duke was unable to distinguish the non-commissioned from the commissioned officers, and shortly afterwards ruffles were altogether abandoned, the duke himself setting the example.

From an inquiry made this year into the state of the army, it appears that the infantry were clothed anew annually, but that the waistcoats were made out of the

coats of the preceding year. The clothing fund arose from
the stoppages of a certain amount of the pay of the non-
commissioned officers and men above their subsistence,
which was called " off-reckonings." The colonels generally
realised thereby about 200*l.* a year, but from an examination
of the agent of the First Regiment of Guards, then under
the Duke of Cumberland, it appears that all the savings out
of the clothing fund of that corps were invariably bestowed
in gratuities and benefactions to the regiment, and that
his royal highness never applied any portion of it to his
own use. Another of the perquisites of colonels in those
days arose from the pay of vacant commissions till they
were filled up; but it appears that the duke, having the
efficiency of his regiment much at heart, always showed
much anxiety to fill them up at once.

The rebellion being crushed, and all danger of further
insurrections being over in December, 1746, the com_
panies of the Guards were reduced to ninety private
soldiers each, but at the beginning of the following year great
exertions were made to assemble a preponderating force in
Flanders, so as to terminate the war at once. Amongst
other corps the three second battalions of the Guards
were, as early as the month of January, selected for this
service. Major - General Meyrick, as first major of the
First Guards, was at the time in command of the second
battalion, but being a general officer since May, 1745, did
not accompany his battalion abroad, a duty which again fell
to Colonel Laforey, the second major. Amongst the senior
officers of the second battalion, First Guards, at this time
were,—

Colonel Laforey, commanding.

Lord Ossulston.	Colonel Fitzwilliam.
Lord George Bentinck.	,, Lord Howe.
Colonel Dury.	Captain Draper.
,, Joseph Hudson.	,, Carey.

Leaving in England one company each as a depôt,
the second battalions of the First and Third regiments,
under Colonels Laforey and Lord Panmure respectively,

proceeded on the 28th of January to Gravesend, whence, on the following day, they sailed for Wilhelmstadt. On their arrival at that port, they marched to Tilburg, near Breda, where the British, Hanoverian, and Hessian troops were assembled, and where the Duke of Cumberland, who came out about the same time, established his headquarters. The second battalion of the Coldstreams, on landing in Flanders, joined a flying column of three battalions, under General Fuller, and advanced towards East Flanders.

The Duke of Cumberland, who was again chosen to lead the confederate army, found himself at the head of about 120,000 men, but the troops, though thus early in the field, were as yet unable to commence active operations, and suffered much from the inclemency of the weather; Marshal Saxe, on the contrary, having assembled 140,000 troops, remained in his quarters till the winter was past, when, in the
April 19. middle of April, he detached to the north a force of 27,000 men, under Count Löwendahl, who penetrated into East Flanders without any difficulty, and took possession of the several towns of Sluys, Sas van Ghent, Hulst, and Sandburg, before any reinforcements from the main body at Tilburg could advance to the support of Fuller's flying column, that had for a time checked the progress of the French before the latter place.

May. In the second week of May, on the Austrians and Dutch taking the field, the duke advanced upon Antwerp, with the British and Dutch contingents, and took up a position six miles east-north-east of the town, so as to cover Breda and Bois le Duc from any attacks of the French. The camp extended from Scoten on the right, where the Austrians under Marshal Bathyany were posted, to near Sandhoven and Hal on the left, in front of which the Duke of Cumberland fixed his headquarters at the Château de Schild. In the neighbourhood of this château, amongst the shady avenues of the park, the battalions of First and Third Guards under Laforey and Lord Panmure were encamped in attendance

upon the duke, till the 26th of May, when, in consequence
of the movements of the enemy, the duke found it necessary
to move towards the Meuse.

Louis XV., who had arrived at Brussels in May, had June.
determined to make a bold stroke and lay siege to Maestricht
before his resources should be expended, and in June was
assembling his forces at Tongres, within ten miles west-
south-west of that fortress. As soon as the allies perceived
the object of the French movement, they hurried towards
Maestricht, to interpose themselves between that town
and the enemy,—a movement which eventually brought
about the battle of Laufelt. They succeeded in reaching the Meuse before the French, by the end of June,
and in taking up a position, with the Austrians on their
right, at Belsen, their left extending towards Tongres,
but they were unable to prevent the French occupying the
heights of Herdeeren, between Tongres and the fortress.
On the 29th of June, the British Guards, who had joined June 29.
in the advance from Antwerp, encamped at Hasselt,
about fifteen miles from Maestricht, where the duke's head-
quarters were that day established. On the 30th, the two
armies approached within sight of each other, the allies advancing to Lonaken, close to Maestricht, where the duke fixed
his head-quarters with the British Guards, while a brigade,
consisting of the 3rd, 8th, and 18th Regiments, were advanced
to Val, the French being this day in front of Tongres.
On the 1st of July, the Austrians were reinforced at Spawe, July 1.
on the right, and the Dutch at Wirle, on the extreme left,
where they entrenched themselves, while the British,
Hessians, and Hanoverians occupied the centre of the line,
as follows, viz., the Hessians the left centre at Laufelt, the
British and Hanoverians the centre and right centre, while
the British Guards, the second battalion of the First
Regiment being still under the command of Colonel Laforey,
took up their ground to the right of the Hessians, and
occupied a post at the village of Vlitingen in the centre of
the allied line. On the same day the enemy was concentrating a large force in rear of the heights of Herdeeren,

and contented himself with a distant cannonade on the allied movements.

At daybreak on the 2nd of July, the French cavalry advanced so as to cover the movement of a very heavy column of infantry marching on Laufelt, where a desperate struggle took place with the Hessians, and the village was taken and retaken several times; but owing to the passive attitude of the Austrians on the right, the French were enabled to increase their efforts against the centre, though their right wing was forced by the allies to give way. Later in the day, however, the French cavalry made so determined an attack upon the Dutch as almost to cut the allied army in two, and a total defeat was only saved by a brilliant charge of the British cavalry under Sir John Ligonier and Colonel Conway, when they took five standards from the enemy. These officers were taken prisoners, but they saved the army, and enabled the several regiments to retire steadily and unbroken.

The brigade of Guards was posted with some Dutch infantry in front line in defence of the village of Vlitingen, on the extreme right of the Duke of Cumberland's troops, the Austrian army being on their right, between the villages of Elcht and Great Spawe. During the attack of the French columns on the centre of the allied position at Laufelt, the British Guards had been actively engaged in maintaining their post in the village; and having set fire to it, they took up a second position on its left flank, where they were continuing successfully to maintain themselves, when, in consequence of events in other parts of the field, they received orders to retire, and the whole army took up another position so as effectually to cover the town and fortress of Maestricht, the Guards taking up their ground at Herr. Notwithstanding the unfortunate result of the day, the Duke of Cumberland succeeded in throwing four battalions into the town, and in forcing the enemy to abandon his intention of besieging it.

When Sir John Ligonier was brought before Louis XV., who had witnessed the action from the heights of Her-

BATTLE OF
LAUFELDT
21ST JUNE 1747

Allies marked ——
French ——

Scale of Miles

Compiled from an original drawing of the Row Guards, and the Belgian Government Survey.

deeren, the king assured him of his admiration of the conduct of the English, who, he added, " not only paid, but fought for all." Biggs, in his military history, relates that when Sir John Ligonier's horse was shot, Sir John was taken prisoner by a French carabineer, to whom he presented his purse and ring, which the carabineer refused, demanding only his sword. When Sir John was conducted to the French king he was graciously received by him, and on being asked whether he was ill used, replied that he could not have been better treated, and praised the carabineer, who was subsequently rewarded by the king for his conduct.

Though the duke was not satisfied with the behaviour of some of the corps engaged in the late action, he spoke highly of the conduct of the British and Hanoverian troops, and in writing to the king, said, there was not a squadron or battalion of his majesty's royal or electoral troops that had not charged the enemy two or three times. The despatch containing a hurried account of the action was taken home by Captain George Townshend, one of the duke's aides-de-camp, who, in the month of February of the following year, was gazetted to a company in the First Guards, vice Roger Townshend. The captured standards and the official despatches were forwarded a few days later in charge of Lord Ancrum, also of the First Guards.

No important military events resulted from the battle; but while the allies continued to cover Maestricht and negotiations were opened by the French through the instrumentality of Sir John Ligonier with the view to obtaining peace, Marshal Saxe continued his operations, and sent Löwendahl with 86,000 men against Bergen-op-Zoom, defended by 3000 Dutch. He opened the trenches on the 16th of July, and for nine weeks the siege was carried on with the utmost vigour, at a vast sacrifice of life to the besiegers, who received reinforcements from their army, while the besieged also received considerable reinforcements from the allied army. The second battalion First Guards was eventually sent to assist in the defence of the fortress,

1747.
Sept. 16.

which, however, fell on the 16th of September, after a tremendous slaughter, the French losing many thousand men. This was the concluding act of the campaign, for the troops shortly afterwards dispersed for the winter, the Guards taking up their quarters at Eyndhoven, about twenty miles south of Bois-le-duc.

Oct. 5.

Major-General Meyrick, who for the last nine years had been first major of the First Guards, quitted it after this campaign, and, on the 5th of October, Colonel Laforey succeeded him in the command of the second battalion; Alexander Dury succeeding as second major to that of the third; the command of the first battalion being always entrusted to the lieutenant-colonel of the regiment. Colonel

Dec. 1.

Laforey retired before the end of the year, when Colonel Dury became first, and Charles Fitzroy second major, Lieutenant-General Frampton retaining for some time longer the lieutenant-colonelcy of the regiment.

1748.
April.

A descent upon the French coast being projected in the spring of 1748, a combined battalion of Foot Guards was sent down in the month of April to the Isle of Wight to join a force of 7000 men assembling there, but after some delay the project was abandoned and the troops dispersed, the Guards returning to London, when a draft of fifty-seven men of the First Regiment and of seventy-one of the Coldstream was made, to reinforce the service battalions in Brabant; they marched to Harwich for embarkation, sailed for Helvoetsluys, and soon joined their battalions at Eyndhoven.

The French, under Löwendahl, invested Maestricht with 45,000 men early in April, before the Dutch and Hanoverians had reached the rendezvous at Eyndhoven, where the Guards were awaiting their arrival, and the allies were advancing to the relief of that fortress, when news was received that the preliminaries of peace had been signed; the garrison of Maestricht, however, consisting of twenty-four Dutch and

May 3.

Austrian battalions, was forced to surrender on the 3rd of May; the armies encamping in sight of each other, but no offensive movements took place on either side during the

remainder of the summer, and on the 18th of October peace
was definitely signed at Aix-la-Chapelle; and though by the
terms of the treaty Great Britain gained but few possessions, the French engaged no longer to support the exiled
Stuarts, whose cause excited so much trouble and disaffection in the country.

In December the Guards marched to Wilhelmstadt for
embarkation, whence the second battalion First Guards,
now under Colonel Dury, sailed on the 16th of the month;
they met with severe storms, which dispersed the transports,
but most of them arrived in the river on the 20th, and the
First Guards proceeded to their quarters in the Tower.
Some transports put in to Yarmouth, and the men of the
three regiments who were landed there, were ordered, on
the 25th, to march up to London and join their respective
corps. On their return, the several companies of the Guards
were reduced to sixty private men each, and the whole
army was much decreased in numbers; the hale old men
were drafted into invalid corps for garrison duty, and
among the officers appointed to these regiments was Sergeant Silk of the First Guards, who had much distinguished
himself at Fontenoy, and who was now made a lieutenant
of invalids at Portsmouth.

Thus ended a series of campaigns in the Low Countries,
which did not reflect much credit upon the strategy or
tactics of the allied commanders, though the Guards, as
well as the rest of the British troops, not only maintained,
but, as at Fontenoy, even raised their character for bravery
and coolness under fire; the want of a Marlborough had
been much felt, in influencing the allied governments to
the utmost exertions in maintaining a sufficient force in the
field to cope with the enemy, and his coolness and judgment at the critical moments in the hour of battle were
much missed, on emergencies, in his successors.

Colonel Alexander Dury succeeded on the 27th of April,
1749, to the lieutenant-colonelcy of the regiment, on the
resignation of Charles Frampton, and at the same time
Samuel Gumley and Edward Carr were promoted to the com-

1749. mand of the second and third battalions on the resignation of Charles Fitzroy.

The following are the captains of companies of the regiment in May, 1749. The numbers represent their relative seniority :—

FIRST BATTALION.

King's, Lord Chas. Hay, Capt.-Lt.		13	Jeffrey Amherst.
2	Alex. Dury, Lieut.-Col.	22	Robert Colleton.
6	— Hemington.	24	John Sebright.
9	Francis Hildesley.	25	George Carey.
12	John Parker.	27	William Keppel.

SECOND BATTALION.

Capt.-Lieut. Studholme Hodgson.		15	Armiger.
3	Samuel Gumley, 1st Maj.	17	Parslow.
7	Lord George Bentinck.	18	Sandford.
10	John FitzWilliams.	19	Brown.
14	Joseph Hudson.		

THIRD BATTALION.

4	Edward Carr, 2nd Maj.	21	George Boscawen.
8	James Durand.	23	George Visct. Howe.
11	Samuel Michell.	26	Maurice Johnson.
16	Studholm Hodgson.	28	George Wilson.
20	Wynne.		

This list shows clearly the practice that had long obtained, of the command of the first battalion being entrusted to the lieutenant-colonel of the regiment, while the first and second majors commanded the second and third battalions respectively; but the system had always been found an inconvenient one, and, ten years later, a third major was permanently appointed to the regiment, and continued till the year 1869.*

June.   In June of this year some uneasiness was felt at the prospect of disturbances in London from the assemblage of tumultuous persons dressed as sailors, when the three regiments of Foot Guards were ordered to find detachments when-

---

* William Barrell, who had been adjutant of the battalion of First Guards during Marlborough's campaigns, and who had risen to be lieutenant-general in the army and colonel of the 4th regiment of the line, died in the year 1749.

ever required by the civil magistrates to put them down and restore peace, but they were to have no recourse to extreme measures unless absolutely required, and, on a repetition of these disturbances in July, similar orders were repeated. The Guards continued to be often called upon to furnish escorts for civil prisoners, smugglers, and highwaymen, as well as to keep the peace at public executions, and, in August of this year, detachments of the three regiments were on one occasion present at the execution of sixteen criminals. In November, 1750, the three regiments were required to find detachments to be in readiness to assist the civil magistrates in resisting any attempts to rescue some outlawed smugglers then prisoners in Newgate, as intelligence had been received by the government that a number of desperate men, also smugglers, had set out from Norfolk and Suffolk with the view to releasing their comrades.

The next few years were uneventful in connection with the movements of the First Guards, nor were their services required abroad, but this was only the calm preceding the storm of another continental war. During this interval of peace, the three battalions of the regiment remained in London, alternating their quarters between the west end, Westminster, the Tower, and other metropolitan districts as formerly, furnishing detachments periodically to Windsor or Hampton Court, or wherever the sovereign might be residing; and during the temporary absences of the king at Hanover, the lords justices were empowered to sign warrants when required for raising the requisite number of recruits to maintain the regiment at its present low establishment of fifty men per company.

Colonel Dury, who had commanded the regiment ever since the peace in 1749, continued in that post till the year 1758, but on the retirement of Colonel Samuel Gumley, in December, 1753, Colonel Edward Carr succeeded to the first, and Colonel James Durand to the second, regimental majority, commanding respectively the second

1749.

July.

1750.
Nov. 22.

1751.

1753.

1753. and third battalions of the regiment, and these two officers also retained their posts till the year 1758.

We come now to the causes that gradually involved England in the long contest known as the " Seven years' war," in which all the great European powers took a part, the First Guards coming in for their share, whether in defence of the seaport towns, in the frequent descents made on the coasts of France, or in the campaigns carried on for the defence of the Electoral dominions of their king in Germany.

1754. The French in Canada had for some time been making encroachments on the British possessions in North America, and on the 14th of November, 1754, on the assembling of Parliament, the king demanded the necessary supplies to enable him successfully to defend British rights in that country, in the event of the negotiations then being
1755. carried on proving unsuccessful. In March, 1755, it was announced to the Houses, by the ministers, that war was inevitable, and Parliament acquiescing, voted one million of money for the defence of the American possessions. A fleet was equipped under Admiral Boscawen to intercept all reinforcements to Quebec, and on the French complaining of these acts, the British Government justified itself on the score of their previous conduct. War was soon declared on both sides, and the whole army was ordered to be
March 31. increased; the companies of the Guards being augmented to seventy effectives each, besides officers and non-commissioned officers.

George II., being apprehensive of an invasion from France, could not for the present spare any of his troops for the Continent, but with the view to securing his electorate of Hanover, the most exposed part of his continental dominions to attacks from the enemy, he entered into treaties to subsidize the Empress of Russia, the King of Prussia, and the Landgrave of Hesse Cassel, to furnish troops for its defence. The treaty with the Empress of Russia fell through, and Russia during the remainder of the empress's life coalesced with Austria,

France, and Sweden against Prussia and Great Britain, so that we see this latter power, with Prussia and some of the small North German states all subsidized by England and assisted by her fleets, standing out against the united forces of the then three largest continental powers.

The attention of the government during this and the succeeding year was directed more to naval expeditions and to the protection of the country from threatened invasions, than to dispatching an armed force to the Continent. A year or more elapsed before a British army was organised to take the field, but towards the end of 1755 Nov. 28. three battalions of Guards, one from each of the three regiments, including the first battalion of the First Regiment, 792 strong, under Lieutenant-Colonel Alexander Dury, were ordered to hold themselves in readiness to proceed abroad, the requisite camp equipage being supplied to them,* and at the same time volunteers were allowed to exchange from the second and third battalions to the battalion under orders for service.

In the spring of the following year, 1756, volunteers 1756. from the three regiments of Foot Guards were invited to offer themselves to serve in a regiment then being raised for service in America, called the " Royal America."

FIRST YEAR OF THE SEVEN YEARS' WAR.

During the winter of 1755–6 and the early spring there being many rumours of a projected French invasion, Parliament voted an army of 35,000 men for the defence of the country. Several regiments were sent to the coast to be prepared for all eventualities ; and amongst other troops, March 16. a detachment of Guards, 350 strong, consisting of four companies, of which two of the First Regiment, drawn

---

* For 1st Battalion, 1st Regiment of Foot Guards :—

12 Bell Tents.	792 Haversacks.
12 Camp Colours.	792 Knapsacks.
20 Drum Cases.	205 Hand hatchets.
205 Tin Kettles.	10 Powder bags.
792 Water Flasks.	

from the four battalions in London,* was sent to Dover Castle on the 16th of March, commanded by Lieu-tenant-Colonel Hudson of the First Guards, to be placed under the orders of the Engineer officer in charge of the works there. The companies arrived, according to their route, on the 20th, and remained there till the middle of April, when being relieved by Lieutenant-Colonel Aber-crombie's regiment of foot, they returned to London. Two more detachments of the brigade, 120 † and 130 strong, were also about the same time sent down to Portsmouth, to escort artillery stores to that garrison from the Tower of London, and to convoy some field-pieces back to town.

The Houses had petitioned and empowered the king, notwithstanding the remonstrances of Pitt, to call over some of his foreign troops to assist in the defence of the country. Accordingly 8000 Hanoverians and Hessians came over in the month of May, and detachments of the brigade of Guards were employed on two or three occasions during the first week of June, in escorting large quantities of artillery stores and ammunition to Canterbury, Dartford, and Rochester, for the use of the Hanoverians, and some more to Farnham ‡ and Winchester for the Hessian troops, who were being assembled in those towns.

In the meantime a fleet was equipped in May, the com-mand of which was given to Admiral Byng, to sail to the Mediterranean to protect Minorca from the French; but the tardiness of the government in sending it, the ineffi-ciency of the Admiralty in fitting it out, and the want of spirit in the admiral when at the island, resulted in the brave General Blakeney, who commanded in the Castle, being eventually in July forced by famine to capitulate to the French, and Minorca was lost to the British empire.

---

* Return of a detachment of First Guards for Dover Castle, 16th March, 1756 :—

1st Regt.	Capt.	Lieut.	Ens.	Serg.	Cor.	Drm.	Senti.
Lt.-Col. Hudson.	Capt. Brereton.	Ens. Cox.					
,, Winn.	,, Wilson.	,, Meadows.		6	6	4	174

† Lieut.-Col. Mitchell commanded one of the detachments to Portsmouth.
‡ Captain Marlow commanded the detachment to Farnham.

One result of this untoward expedition was the resignation of the Duke of Newcastle's ministry with Fox, and the
appointment of Pitt as secretary-of-state, as the only man
likely in the existing state of affairs to raise the country
from its present desponding state. The whole of the
brigade of Guards was retained in England during this
naval expedition, and those battalions which had been
ordered to hold themselves in readiness for service were
encamped during the summer in Hyde Park. On the 10th
of July they were ordered to be ready to march at a
moment's warning, under the command of Colonel Dury,
but they remained encamped (being excused all country
detachments) till the 23rd of October, when there being no
immediate prospect this year of their services being required, the camp was broken up, and the battalions resumed
their usual turn of duty.

The custom at this time still prevailed in the Guards
for companies to parade, that the officers lately appointed
to them might be presented. On the 13th of October
Lieutenant-Colonel the Earl of Pembroke's company was
assembled at Somerset House, that that officer, who had
been gazetted to it on the previous 8th of September, might
be presented in the usual manner.

It appears that at this time the duties of officers
of the Guards were not confined to the command of
their own men. Such was the demand for recruits to
augment the army, that recourse was very generally
had to the system of impressment, and the Guards
were frequently employed in securing those who were impressed. On the 16th of December four lieutenants of the
Foot Guards were ordered into Southwark to attend upon
the commissioners entrusted with the duties of impressing
men for the line, to receive from them the men so impressed, and lodge them in the Savoy. Detachments of
First Guards were also at times employed in escorting impressed men in boats to East Indiamen, to be conveyed in
due course to that country, where Clive was at the time
laying the foundation of the future Indian empire.

1757.

Pitt was anxious to make use of several Highland corps to serve in the ranks of the army that was eventually destined for service on the Continent. These troops, who proved themselves equal to the best in the British army before the enemy, appear to have been wanting in certain educational qualifications to fit them for the posts of non-commissioned officers, and being deficient in the number of sergeants and corporals, the secretary-at-war issued an order to the commanding officers of the three regiments of Foot Guards to call for volunteers who could speak the Highland language, and who, being qualified, were willing to serve as non-commissioned officers in those corps. These regiments soon proved themselves, with their new organization, worthy of being ranked amongst the best of the sovereign's troops, a position which they have ever steadily maintained, and the non-commissioned officers of the Guards may feel an interest in hearing that some of their predecessors were among the first to assist in making them what they are.

April 2.   A new exercise was introduced into the brigade this year. The company of Lieutenant-Colonel Keppel of the First Guards was put through the drill, in the presence of the Duke of Cumberland, in the month of April, and being approved of by his royal highness, it was ordered by him to be forthwith adopted in the three regiments.

April 29.   Towards the end of the same month the services of the Guards were required by the Lords of the Admiralty to put down some disturbances that were taking place in the Woolwich dockyards. The three battalions in cantonments were immediately called out, when a detachment of 300 men was selected from them to proceed there without delay, under the command of Colonel A'Court, and having accomplished this duty it returned to London.

During the first year of the war, as we have seen, it had not been considered expedient to maintain a British force in ·Germany for the protection of the king's Electoral dominions, and the same policy was still pursued, except that the Duke of Cumberland, now thirty-eight years of age, was in 1757 sent over to take command of the king's foreign troops, including Hanoverians, Hessians, Brunswickers, and others, while, in consequence of the continued apprehension of a French invasion, the British troops were distributed in camps near different parts of the English coast. On the 8th of June orders were issued for the several regiments to assemble at their respective camps on the 27th of the same month, viz., four at Chatham, three at Amersham, three at Salisbury, and four at Dorchester, while the Horse and Foot Guards in London and its neighbourhood were ordered to hold themselves in readiness, under Lord Tyrawley, Lord Delawarr, and Major-General Dury, for any services they might be called upon to perform, and the camp at Barham Downs and Chatham was placed under the Duke of Marlborough. Previous to the departure of the Guards to their camp, Major-General Dury reviewed the three battalions of the First Guards in June, viz., the second battalion in the Tower on the 27th, and the first and third battalions on the 28th and 30th, in St. James's Park, when he expressed himself well pleased with their appearance.

While these troops remained in England for the defence of the coasts, the Duke of Cumberland found himself in Germany at the head of an army of 50,000 Germans all in the king's pay; but he was not in a condition to compete with his adversary, for having been driven from the banks of the Rhine and from Hanover by the French, under Marshal d'Estrés, and after an unsuccessful engagement on the 26th of July at Hartenbeck, near Hameln, he was obliged to retreat across the Lunebourg Moors to Stade. Göttingen, Hanover, Bremen, and Verden were successively occupied by the French, and on the 7th of September the duke found himself obliged to sign the convention of Closter Seven, according to the terms of which, the several foreign troops were to be sent to their homes, under an obligation not to serve again during the war. The French were, however, the first to break the terms of this convention, which was therefore not carried out in all its details ; but Hanover remained in possession of the French during the following year.

The King of Prussia, in the same year, was defeated by the Austrians, under Marshal Daun, at the battle of Kolin, but he in his turn drove 100,000 Russians at Yägerndorf out of Prussia, and the Swedes out of Pomerania.

October. The Duke of Cumberland after his failure returned to England in October, and in November resigned his post of Captain-General of the Army, as well as the colonelcy of the First Guards, and other military employments ; he lived a retired life for the next eight years, and died in 1765, in the forty-sixth year of his age. During the remainder of the war the king entrusted the command of all his troops in Germany, both English and foreign, to Prince Ferdinand of Brunswick, who proved himself a first-rate officer, and well deserving of the king's choice.

Nov. 30. On the retirement of the Duke of Cumberland, the regiment was, on the 2nd of December, given to Field-Marshal Sir John Ligonier, who, on the 22nd of the same month, was raised to the dignity of an Irish viscount Sir John was of French extraction, and had served, as we have seen, with great distinction in all the wars in the middle of the century. At Dettingen he had been created a knight banneret on the field ; at Fontenoy he had commanded the infantry, and at Laufelt he had headed a desperate charge of cavalry, when he was taken prisoner. The appointment was thus notified to the regiment :—

"Regimental Orders.　　*December 2, 1757.*

Dec. 2. " The king has been pleased to appoint the Right Honourable Sir John Ligonier, Field-Marshal and Commander-in-Chief of his Majesty's Forces, to be Colonel of the First Regiment of Foot Guards."

Lieutenant-Colonel Sebright, of the First Guards, was appointed his aide-de-camp on the 11th of January following.

The new laws made this year relative to the militia

FIELD-MARSHAL JOHN VISCOUNT LIGONIER, K.B.

Commander in Chief of His Majesty's Forces. Master General of the Ordnance.
12th Colonel of the First Regiment of Foot Guards
1757 - 1770

caused great discomfort and some disturbances. Every   1757.
man, rich or poor, was bound to serve, under penalty of
paying 10*l.* for a substitute, which, after all, absolved him
from service only for three years. Regiments, both of
cavalry and infantry of the regular army, were called out to
suppress the disturbances, and the curious paradox was
observed of the standing army enforcing upon a constitu-
tional force obedience to the laws of the country.

Ill-success, similar to that which befell the Duke of
Cumberland, also attended the fleet under Hawke. The
intention had been to land Generals Mordaunt and Conway Sept.
with an army on the coast of France, near Rochefort, and
to burn and destroy to the utmost all the docks, magazines,
and shipping to be found there. Reaching Oleron on the
20th September, they at once made a successful attack on
the island of Aix, but no attempt on Rochefort itself was
undertaken, and, on the 5th of October, the whole fleet
returned to England, where much dissatisfaction being
created at this want of success, a court of inquiry was
appointed in November to inquire into the cause of failure,
the Duke of Marlborough, Lord George Sackville, and November.
Major-General John Waldegrave being appointed members.
It does not appear that the Guards were employed on this
expedition.

H.R.H. the Princess Carolina died at the end of this Jan. 2.
year, and on the occasion of her funeral, on the 2nd of
January following, each battalion of the brigade was directed
to furnish 100 men, with the usual complement of officers
and non-commissioned officers, to attend the ceremony.

1758.

Undaunted by the ill-success at Rochefort in 1757, Pitt 1758.
and his ministry now planned a descent with a larger
force upon another part of the coast of France; and
at the beginning of May an army of 13,000 men, consisting
of three battalions of Foot Guards, thirteen regiments of
the line,* nine troops of light Cavalry, and 6000 marines,

---

* The 5th, 20th, 23rd, 24th, 25th, 30th, 33rd, 34th, 36th, 67th, 68th, and
72nd.

the whole under the Duke of Marlborough, was assembled in the Isle of Wight for embarkation. The brigade of Guards, consisting of the first battalions of the three regiments, to be placed under the command of Major-General Alexander Dury, the Lieutenent-Colonel of the First Regiment, was ordered, on the 17th of April, to hold itself in readiness. Two days later the 2nd battalions were directed to prepare for foreign service in their place, but on the 25th this last order was rescinded, and the three first battalions were finally sent abroad. The reason of this uncertainty does not appear, unless it were that three months previously complaints had been made by the commanding officers of the 2nd battalions of the 2nd and 3rd Regiments against the suspected practices of the Lieutenant-Colonels of their regiments, of posting the best recruits to the 1st battalion, a practice that Lord Ligonier, in his capacity of colonel of the senior regiment, desired

might be discontinued for the future. Major-General Carr, the first major of the First Guards, was left in command of the two home battalions during General Dury's absence, and the command of the 1st battalion devolved on Colonel Cary, the second senior officer commanding a company, Colonel Hudson being the senior.

The general officers and others appointed on the Staff to command this expedition under the Duke of Marlborough were,—

Lieut.-Generals.—Lord George Sackville and the Earl of Ancrum.

Major-Generals commanding Brigades.—Dury, Mostyn, Waldegrave, Boscawen, and Elliot.

Lieut.-Colonel Hotham, Deputy Adjutant-General.

Lieut.-Colonel Watson, Deputy Quartermaster-General ; while

Major-General Durand, the 2nd Major of the First Guards, was sent to command the troops at Plymouth.

The general officers left to command in London, besides Viscount Ligonier as Commander-in-Chief, were Lieutenant-Generals Lord Tyrawley and Lord Delawarr.

In the regimental orders issued on the 5th of May, previous to the march of the Guards, Major-General Dury expressed himself to the effect, that as the brigade was the first in rank, he expected it would likewise claim that

honour by its example in the expedition it was about to
join.   Previous to its departure the brigade was reviewed
by the king in Hyde Park, and it finally left London on
the 9th of May, encamping on successive nights on the   May 9.
commons at Esher, Ripley, Godalming, Petersfield, and
Southsea.   On the 15th the Guards crossed over to the Isle
of Wight, and the whole force was embarked by the latter
end of May.   The fleet, under the command of Admiral
Howe, after encountering some rough weather in the Channel,
anchored on the 4th of June in the bay of St. Malo, within
three miles of the town; but the Admiral, seeing that no
direct attack could be made from the sea, stood along the
coast eastwards to the bay of Cancale, where, in the afternoon of the 5th, ten Grenadier companies under General
Montagu, forming the advance, disembarked without much
opposition, and the rest of the army landed the following   June 6.
day, the General making the village of Cancale his head-
quarters.

At break of day on the 7th, the army advanced in two
columns by their left across the country leading to St. Malo.
The first column, under Lord George Sackville, was composed of the brigade of Guards, two battalions of Grenadiers,
and the First Brigade.   In consequence of the difficulties
of the road these troops did not reach their new camp, only
six miles distant, till the evening, when they took up a
position facing St. Malo, with their right resting on their
head-quarters, near the village of Parama, their left
extending towards St. Servan.   The brigade of Guards was
ordered to file off two miles to the left of this encampment,
and pitch their tents there, covering the left of the army,
as it was from that quarter that an attack from the enemy
was most to be expected.

From the camp the enemy's shipping at St. Malo could
be seen collected in a large basin behind the town,
and Marlborough determined at once to set fire to it, for
which purpose, as soon as it was night, the Cavalry was
ordered forward, each trooper having a foot-soldier mounted
behind him supplied with hand-grenades.   They passed

unobserved under the enemy's cannon, set fire to and destroyed two men of war, thirty-three privateers, and seventy merchant ships, and reduced all the naval stores to ashes.

While the rest of the army remained before St. Malo, a battalion of Guards, under General Cæsar, was detached twelve miles up the country in a south-easterly direction to reconnoitre as far as Doll; but, meeting no enemy, they remained there only one night, returning the following day to camp without committing any act of hostility, the officers and men having been well received by the townspeople at Doll during their short stay. The Duke finding St. Malo too strongly fortified to be taken by a *coup de main*, and being satisfied that he had inflicted sufficient losses on the enemy, hearing also a report that a superior force was moving down to the coast to intercept his return to the ships, resolved to re-embark. He returned with his army to the bay of Cancale, and the embarkation of the troops having been effected without impediment, the fleet shortly put to sea. After encountering some tempestuous weather, it visited Cherbourg on the 29th of June, but, owing to the continuance of the storm, the Admiral forbore attacking it, and finally arrived at St. Helen's on the 1st of July, when the troops were put on shore on the Isle of Wight, to give them rest, and to await further orders.

The government having now determined to send a British contingent to Germany, a considerable portion of the troops lately engaged in the naval expedition, with others, were named for that service, and proceeded to their destination under the Duke of Marlborough. Lord George Sackville accompanied the Duke, preferring a command with the armies on the Continent, to what he was pleased to call this system of buccaneering; the Guards, however, remained some time longer in the Isle of Wight.

Considerable damage had been done to the French shipping at St. Malo, and the apprehensions caused to the French government by the expedition had effectually pre-

vented them from sending additional reinforcements to their
armies in Germany; but the results were far from commensurate with the sums so great an armament had cost,
or with the hopes it had excited; the Government therefore
resolved upon a fresh enterprise against Cherbourg. The
command of the fleet was again given to Admiral Howe, July 29.
that of the army to Lieutenant-General Bligh; and Prince
Edward, subsequently Duke of York, with other volunteers,
accompanied it.

The first battalion First Guards under Colonel Carey,
together with the rest' of the expeditionary force, now
much reduced in numbers, owing to so many troops being
sent to Germany, re-embarked, after a month's rest on
shore, and the fleet, sailing on the 1st of August, anchored Aug. 1.
off Cherbourg on the 6th. The next morning the disembarcation commenced, in the Bay of Marais, west of
that town, where about 3000 of the enemy appeared
ready to oppose them. The first landing party consisted of the brigade of Guards, and of the battalion of
Grenadiers of the army, all under General Dury; they
reached the shore in flat-bottomed boats under cover of
a heavy fire from the fleet about two o'clock in the afternoon, when the Guards and Grenadiers having formed line,
were at once led by General Dury against the enemy,
who poured in three volleys as they advanced, without
their fire being at first returned. The attack of the leading
troops was so spirited, that the French were eventually
driven off the ground with the loss of three brass field pieces.
The English loss, amongst the Guards and Grenadiers
of the army, was about twenty killed and wounded.

Mr. Jenkinson addressed the following letter* to Mr.
Grenville, on receipt of the news of this successful landing
on the coast of France :—

LONDON, August 10th, 1758.

DEAR SIR,—We have this day the agreeable news that our troops
under General Bligh are landed at Cherbourg, and have by a vigorous
action repulsed a body of 3000 horse and foot who opposed their land-

---

* Grenville Correspondence, Stow MSS., vol. i. p. 253.

1758.   ing. This service was done by the Guards and Grenadiers of the army who received three fires before they returned it, but then made their attack with so much vigour that the enemy after a considerable loss retreated. We had ourselves but about twenty men either killed or wounded; we have also taken two cannon and one pair of colours. This happened on Monday, and on Tuesday morning the whole force began their march towards the town.

I have, &c.,

R. JENKINSON.

The cavalry and artillery landed the following day, when an immediate advance was made in two columns on Cherbourg, which the enemy abandoned, and the English entered without opposition. These successes, which should have caused extra vigilance on the march and in camp, were, with one bright exception, unfortunately succeeded by great relaxation of discipline; the soldiers generally indulged in riot and licentiousness, that would well nigh have proved fatal to themselves had it not been for the " strict discipline and sobriety of which the Foot Guards set a laudable example to the rest of the army." [*]

Aug. 8.

General Bligh, having possession of the town and of the several forts to the westward, viz., Querqueville, Homet, and Galet, proceeded according to his instructions to destroy all the batteries, forts, and magazines. He burnt twenty-seven ships that were found in the harbour; destroyed 173 pieces of iron ordnance and some mortars, and captured twenty-four brass cannons and mortars, which were sent to England with the colours taken in the first attack. The harbour was at the same time demolished, and the cavalry sent out to scour the country in various directions. Having thus complied with his orders, Bligh re-embarked his troops on the 16th August, and, after waiting two days in the harbour, the fleet put to sea on the 18th, with the intention of making a descent on another part of the French coast. The success of this last expedition gave new life and spirit to the people, who, almost for the first time in this generation, were gratified with the spectacle

Aug. 16.

---

[*] History of the late War, vol. iii.

EXPEDITION to St MALO
········ AFFAIR at St CAS
12th Sept. 1758.

Scale of English miles

Road to Dinant

French approaching

St Lunaire

St Briac

St Malo

Troops lighting to protect the point

Point of Stone

BAY of St CAS

Isle

Matignon

Guards

CAMP OF GUARDS

CAMP OF VOL

FRENCH POSITION

St Laurent

Argueuon River

Breille R.

St Jacut

of cannon, colours, and trophies taken from the enemy,
being carried in triumph through the metropolis of the
kingdom.

After much boisterous weather and contrary winds the   Sept. 5.
fleet came to anchor on the 5th September in the Bay of
St. Lunaire, four miles west of St. Malo, and on the 7th the   See plan.
troops landed without opposition, taking three days' provisions with them. The French ships at St. Brieux were
burnt by some of the Grenadiers of the army, and five
barks destroyed the following day by a detachment of   Sept. 8.
Grenadiers of the Guards. The country appearing unprepared for defence, a council of war was held as to the practicability of attacking St. Malo, but the weather continuing
stormy, the admiral declared it was impossible for him to
give assistance to the troops by bombarding the town from
the fleet, as he would run the risk of losing all his ships,
and that owing to the westerly gales, the fleet could no
longer remain where it was, to enable the troops to re-
embark. He proposed, therefore, to sail to the Bay of St.
Cas, which was more protected from those winds, to which
the troops could easily march overland, and whence, if
found necessary, they could reach the ships. This plan was   Sept. 9.
agreed to, and early on the morning of the 9th of September
the army was in motion towards Matignon, three miles
distant from St. Cas. On reaching the Arguenon river in
the afternoon, opposite Le Guildo, within five miles of Matignon, the state of the tide rendered the fords impassable,
and any further advance that day was impracticable. The
following afternoon at low water, while the Grenadiers of
the line crossed the ford opposite Le Guildo, the Grenadiers   Sept. 10.
of the Guards, with two guns, that were brought into action
several times during the advance, crossed the river at a ford
lower down, opposite the wood of Val, which was occupied
by armed peasants and militia. As soon as the Guards
entered the channel, the enemy opened fire upon them from
windows and garden walls, wounding several men, amongst
them Lord Frederick Cavendish in the thigh, and Captain
David Jones in the foot. The Grenadiers of the Guards at

M 2

1758. length got across and took possession of the village, driving its garrison before them. Colonel Cæsar, commanding the brigade of Guards that was following, finding a more convenient ford still lower down, not so much exposed to the fire of the enemy from the opposite wood, led his men more to the right to gain it, and succeeded in crossing to the opposite bank without difficulty. The rest of the army followed, and encamped that night between St. Jeguhel and the wood of Val. The French were all this time quietly collecting their forces in the neighbourhood, to resist the invader.

Sept. 10. The following day the army reached Matignon, where information was received that at least fourteen battalions of the enemy, with four squadrons, twelve guns and several mortars, were advancing from Brieuc, and assembling six miles off, between Lamballe and Matignon, and that another body of 3000 men under D'Aubigny and La Chartre were advancing from St. Malo. On reaching Matignon, the Coldstreams were detached to St. Cas to convoy provisions from the fleet to the army on the following day, but before the day came, General Bligh, with the concurrence of most of the general officers, had resolved to seek safety on board the fleet.

St. Cas. The general here committed a fatal mistake. If he intended to embark his troops he should have moved off at once quietly to the Bay of St. Cas, and commenced the embarcation before the French were aware of his movement; if he meant to await the attack he should have disembarked the remainder of his forces : he did neither ; he remained some hours on the ground, and gave orders for the troops to march early the following morning to St. Cas, to embark, selecting four companies of the first battalion of the First Guards with the Grenadier companies of the Line to form the rear-guard. These intentions Sept. 11. were, however, too soon made known to the French by the *reveillé*, which was beat in the British camp. General Bligh marched off at daybreak on the 11th, meeting no enemy attempting to intercept his march to the ships ; a few shots only being exchanged between the rear-guard and the most advanced parties of the French. The troops began to embark about nine o'clock, and by eleven the three brigades of the Line, half the Guards, and the wounded, had got on board without opposition, when the French made their appearance in force, and formed on the heights above, but they would not advance until, by the continued embarcation of the troops, they found themselves in vastly superior numbers to the covering force of the British. They then descended from the heights above, occupied St. Cas, and attempted to gain a wood where they might form and extend along the front of the English, but in doing this they suffered severely from the fire of the British fleet, which broke their line, and threw them into confusion; they thereupon extended along a hill to their left and advanced by a hollow way, from whence they suddenly rushed out to the attack. By this time the only British troops remaining on shore were the four companies of the First Guards under Carey, and the Grenadier companies of the army, in all about 1500 men, under Major-General Dury, who, as the enemy advanced, ordered the Guards and Grenadiers to march out from behind the breastwork that covered them, and attack him before he could form on the plain. At first the French gave way, but successive reinforcements arriving, they in turn drove the English back, when General Dury saw, but too late, the error of having drawn his men from behind the cover, for the second division of his force could not get over the breastwork in time to succour the first, which was broken. The French having now got possession of the dyke that had formed the breastwork of the English, Dury ordered the men to make for the boats as fast as possible; some got on board, but a battery knocked many of the boats to pieces; and the French, now much superior in numbers, perceiving that the Grenadiers had no means of retreat, drove them into the sea, the greatest part being either drowned or cut to pieces. General Dury was shot in the breast, and in attempting to swim to a boat was drowned. The English loss on this

1758.   occasion was nearly 1000 men, 600 being killed or drowned and 400 taken prisoners. The officers of the First Guards killed were Major-General Dury, lieutenant-colonel; Lieutenant and Captain James Walker; Lieutenant and Captain Thomas Rolt; and Ensign James Cocks. Amongst the wounded of the First Guards were Lord Frederick Cavendish, and Sir Charles Gilmore, who were sent to Dinant. The main body of the troops having succeeded in reaching the ships, the fleet shortly afterwards sailed from the French

Sept. 18. coast, and reached Spithead on the 18th of September, where the troops disembarked. On the 26th, the remainder of the first battalion First Guards commenced its march to London, and three officers of the home battalions, Captains Haselar and De Salis, and Ensign Evelyn, were sent down on the 25th from London to join it on the road, apparently to fill the vacancies caused by casualties during the cam-

Sept. 29. paign. It arrived in London on the 29th, and was at once sent into quarters in Somerset House, the second battalion being in Holborn and Finsbury, the third in the Savoy barracks, while the wounded and disabled men of the service battalion that returned, were left for a time in the Isle of Wight, and came up to London in November.

Lord Frederick Cavendish and Sir Charles Gilmore, who, as we have seen, had taken part in and been made prisoners during the late operations on the French coast, returned to England on parole in October, to settle the exchange of prisoners taken at St. Cas. These eventually arrived at Dover at the beginning of December, and on the 31st, all officers having been released from their parole, Lord Ligonier ordered the two above-mentioned to rejoin their regiment.

The feeling against General Bligh for the disaster of St. Cas was so strong on his return to England, that he resigned both his regiment and his government.

Oct. 3.   Many promotions took place in consequence of the late casualties, all dated the 30th September, 1758. Major-General Carr to be Lieutenant-Colonel of the regiment, vice Major-General Dury, killed; Colonel Durand to be first major, vice Carr; Colonel Hudson to be second major, vice Durand, besides others to succeed Lieutenant - Colonel Winne, retired, and Captains Rolt and Walker, and Ensign James Cocks, killed.

A question arose out of the expedition to St. Cas that led to a misunderstanding between two of the senior officers of the regiment, Lieutenant-Colonel Cary and Lieutenant-Colonel Lambert, who both contested the honour of heading the troops that were left at St. Cas after the death of General Dury; the question was eventually referred in February of the following year to the opinion of a general court-martial, of which Major-General Noel of the Coldstreams was president, when it took the form of a charge against Colonel Lambert for traducing the character of Colonel Cary. The affair appears to have ended honourably to both parties, for on the 25th of March following, the king approved of the opinion of the general court-martial in acquitting Lieutenant-Colonel Lambert of the charge brought against him, and Lieutenant-Colonel Cary was shortly afterwards, viz., on the 18th June, 1759, appointed as a third major, to the command of the third battalion of the regiment.

This appointment of a third major to the First Guards, now made for the first time, appears to have been consequent upon the necessity that was found to exist that each battalion should be commanded by an officer distinct from the lieutenant-colonel of the regiment, and that this latter officer should only exercise a general supervision equally over the three battalions, a system which has prevailed till within the last few years, when in 1869, in deference to the economic spirit of the age, but at the risk of the future efficiency of the regiment, recurrence was had to the practice of combining the command of the regiment with that of one of the battalions, a system which above a hundred years before had, as we see here, been found after a long trial incompatible with the discipline of the corps, the good of the service, and the due administration of justice.

The English had met with better success this year

against the French in America by the capture of Louisburg, Cape Breton, and St. John's, and the people of London were again gladdened by the sight of eleven colours, taken from the enemy, carried in procession, and deposited in triumph in St. Paul's Cathedral amidst a salute of cannon and other public demonstrations. This procession took place on the

6th of September from Kensington Palace. Four grenadier companies of the Foot Guards under a field officer were ordered to Kensington to take part in it, as well as eleven sergeants from the four home battalions, each to carry one of the French colours. The procession was thus marshalled: sixty Horse Grenadiers, eighty Life Guards, then one sergeant and twelve Grenadiers of Foot Guards, eleven sergeants of the Foot Guards carrying the French colours, and the four companies of Grenadiers of the Foot Guards closed the rear.

The Guards, as we have seen, had taken no part this year in the war in Germany. The King of Prussia defeated the Russians in the severely contested battle of Custrin, and was himself defeated by the Austrians at Hochkirchen, but eventually forced the Austrians to evacuate Saxony, Silesia, and Pomerania. Prince Ferdinand of Brunswick who, with his Hanoverians and Hessians, was defending the Electorate, had been successful on the Rhine, and was manœuvring against the French under Soubise, when on the 14th of August the Duke of Marlborough joined him with his 12,000 English auxiliaries; but these had scarcely taken the field when an epidemic broke out amongst them which carried off their commander, the Duke of Marlborough. He was succeeded by Lord George Sackville, who soon fell out with the Prince, notwithstanding the attempts of Lord Granby to moderate his pride. The campaign, however, was a success, and the French were driven out of Hesse.

1759.

Both the ministers and parliament being anxious to carry on the war the next year with vigour, an army of 95,000 British and 7000 foreign troops was voted for the

service of 1759, with twelve millions to cover the necessary
expenditure.

A considerable number of British regiments of the line had
been sent to Germany under Lord George Sackville, to act as
a contingent in the army of Prince Ferdinand for the defence
of the Electoral dominions, but the Guards were still retained
in England, owing to the prevailing reports of French threats
of an invasion. All officers were consequently ordered to
be present by the 5th of April, and the four battalions that
were not on service in the preceding year were ordered to April 10.
complete their camp equipage, to supply themselves with
bât and forage horses, and to hold themselves in immediate
readiness during the whole summer to march at any time.
They were particularly cautioned not to encumber themselves with baggage, as no waggons or carts would be
allowed, and as the lieutenant-colonel of the First Guards
had commanded the brigade on service last year, it was
ruled by Lord Ligonier that Major-General Noel of the
Coldstreams should command the brigade this year if called
out. In July the companies were increased to eighty men July 18.
each, and on the 20th of that month the whole seven
battalions were ordered to hold themselves in readiness
to be reviewed by Lord Tyrawley, and three months later October.
the companies were still further increased to ninety men.

For purposes of defence the country had been for some
time divided into military districts, each under a lieutenant-
general. This year these were—

For Kent and the coast of Sussex, Lieut.-Gen. Campbell.
For Middlesex, Berks, and Surrey,   ,,   ,,   Earl of Ancrum.
For Essex, Suffolk, and Norfolk,   ,,   ,,   Earl of Albemarle.
For Portsmouth . . . . Maj.-Gen. H. Holmes.
For the West . . . . ,,   ,,   Onslow.
For the North . . . . ,,   ,,   W. Whitmore.

In London, Lieutenant-General Lord Tyrawley had
the chief command, with Lieutenant-General Lord Delawarr under him, besides Major-Generals Carr and Noel,
commanding respectively the First and Second Guards;

1759.   the troops in this latter district consisted of two troops of Horse Guards, two troops of Grenadier Guards, and seven battalions of Foot Guards. There were besides these, in England, thirty-four regiments of the line, seven of dragoons, and thirty-two independent companies. Viscount Ligonier, a Field-marshal in the army, was, as Colonel of the First Guards, another military authority in the London district.

Sept. 14.   Princess Elizabeth dying in the autumn, detachments from each battalion of the Guards, under command of Colonel Hudson, were present at the funeral of her Royal Highness, which took place on the 14th of September.

In consequence of the completion of the new Horse Guards building this year, a long correspondence ensued between the colonels of regiments of Foot Guards, the Secretary at War, the Board of Works, and others, with reference to the appropriation of the several apartments; as some of the field officers of the Guards had acquired the

Oct. 31.   privilege of occupying rooms in the old building. Lord Ligonier referred the question to the King for his pleasure thereon; the King's decision was signified to the colonels by Lord Barrington, confirming the said privilege, and Major-General Noel ordered it to be registered in the orderly books of the three regiments of Guards as a confirmed privilege accorded by the king. Mr. Fox, then paymaster of the forces, made representations to the Treasury against a coffee-house and sutling-house being allowed in the new building, but upon an explanation by Colonel Julius Cæsar, then field officer in brigade waiting, that the Guards had even less accommodation now than in the old building, and less than the Duke of Cumberland thought absolutely necessary for their accommodation, the question was allowed to rest, and the sutling-house remained in the Horse Guards for nearly one hundred years longer. When the apartments at the Horse Guards which the first major of the First Guards had always occupied, were at a later period given up for offices, that officer received and continued to receive 100*l.* a year com-

HORSE GUARDS,

pensation. A representation of the Horse Guards building as projected in 1753 is here given, showing the guard
mounting of the brigade of Guards at that period.

Several orders had been given out lately against a practice
which had become very prevalent in the brigade, of men
when off duty hiring themselves out in the coal-heaving
business, in unloading ships on the Thames, and some had
formed themselves into a club for their mutual protection.
An Act had been passed the previous year regulating the
coal-heaving trade, and as it was considered that the
soldiers were acting in contravention of that Act, Lord
Tyrawley gave stringent orders for the discontinuance of
the practice.

While all danger of a French invasion was removed
by Sir Edward Hawke's great victory over the French
fleet in Quiberon Bay, on the 20th of November, varying fortunes had befallen the belligerents on the Continent, the details of which we do not propose to follow,
as the brigade of Guards was not employed. Reference,
however, may be made to the army under Prince Ferdinand
of Brunswick, in which Lord George Sackville commanded
the British contingent of cavalry, infantry, and artillery.
The Prince took post near Minden on the 31st of July, and
was attacked by the French, who were completely defeated,
but not with so great a loss, as if Lord George Sackville
had properly understood the orders sent to him by the
Prince to charge with his cavalry when the enemy were
already in confusion. His dilatoriness was the cause of the
English and Hanoverian cavalry not coming up till the
action was over, while the British infantry and artillery very
greatly distinguished themselves in the battle. Lord George
wrote home to resign his command and demand a Court
Martial. After some difficulty, owing to Lord George
having in the mean time retired from the army, this was
granted to him, and a General Court Martial was held in
April, 1760, before which Lord George was arraigned on a
charge of having, when Lieutenant-General Commanding-in-
Chief the British forces, serving under the command of

1759.   Prince Ferdinand of Brunswick, disobeyed the orders of
that Prince.   Twelve Lieutenant-Generals and four Major-
Generals were upon this Court Martial; amongst the latter
were the Earl of Effingham, and Carr of the First, and
Julius Cæsar of the Second, Guards.   Amongst the Lieutenant-Generals were the Earls of Panmure, Harrington,
Albemarle, and Ancrum, and Lord George, being found
Guilty, was adjudged to be unfit to serve His Majesty in
any military capacity whatever, which sentence the King
was pleased to confirm.

CHAPTER XVII.

CONSIDERABLE reinforcements of the line* were sent over   1760.
to Germany in the spring of the next year, 1760, from
which time to the end of the Seven Years' War, the brigade
of Guards also took their share of service on the continent, their companies being increased to 100 men each,
but before their departure the services of part of the bri-   April 14.
gade were required on a special duty at home. Lord
Ferrers, who was to be tried by his peers in the House of
Lords for the murder of his servant, Johnson, was at the
time confined in the Tower, and the King ordered that
a detachment of the Guards should be present on each day
of the trial. Accordingly, the four battalions at the West-
end and the one at the Tower furnished daily during the
three days, 16th, 17th, and 18th of April, a detachment of
seven complete companies, of 100 men each, with officers
and non-commissioned officers, under the command successively of Colonel Gore, Major-Generals Robinson and
Joseph Hudson. The following is the account of the
trial in the Annual Register :—" The prisoner in his own
coach, attended by the Major of the Tower and some
other gentlemen, and guarded by a party of Foot Guards
and Warders of the Tower, arrived at half-past 10 o'clock,

---

* Consisting of the 5th, 8th, 11th, 24th, 33rd, and 50th.

1760.   at Westminster Hall, followed by the Lord High Steward
(Lord-Keeper Henley). On the 18th, sentence was passed
that he be hanged. The whole trial was conducted with
great order and regularity, and the grandeur, solemnity, and
awfulness of the Court exceeded all imagination."

July 23.   Orders were at length issued, on the 23rd of July, to the
2nd battalions of the three regiments of Foot Guards to
prepare for embarcation for Germany,* and drafts from the
other battalions were at once made to complete them. Major-
General Julius Cæsar, lieutenant-colonel of the Coldstream
Guards, was appointed to command the brigade, and Colonel
Pierson to command the 2nd battalion of the First Guards,
while all men who had enlisted for the limited period of
three years were to have their option to go abroad or not.

Major-General Carr retired from the lieutenant-colonelcy
of the regiment on the 21st of July, 1760, when James
Durand, a major-general since June, 1759, succeeded to the
lieutenant-colonelcy ; and Colonel George Carey having also
retired, Major-General Hudson, Lieutenant-Colonel Hon.
William Keppel, and Lieutenant-Colonel Pierson, became
respectively 1st, 2nd, and 3rd majors, succeeding to the
command of the 1st, 2nd, and 3rd battalions.

July 25.   The three service battalions left London on Friday, the
25th of July, the first regiment proceeding to Gravesend,
the others to Dartford, whence they embarked for Germany,
to which country no less than 10,000 men, cavalry and
infantry, had now been sent as a reinforcement, thus
raising the number of troops under the Marquis of
Granby to 32,000 men. The three battalions of Guards
under General Cæsar, 3,000 strong, arrived at Bremen
July 30.   on the Weser on the 30th of July, and marched at

---

* It is his Majesty's pleasure that you cause the second battalions of the
three regiments of Foot Guards under your command to march at such times
and to such place or places as you shall think most convenient for their embarcation for Germany. Wherein, &c.

Given at the War Office this 23rd day of July, 1760.

                                        By his Majesty's command.

˙ To Major-General Julius Cæsar.   (Signed) BARRINGTON.

THEATRE of WAR in GERMANY.
from 1760 to 1762.

Scale of English Miles

once to join the British contingent, which it overtook on 1760.
the 25th of August at the village of Buhne, near Warburg Aug. 25.
on the Diemel, the head-quarters at that time of Prince
Ferdinand of Brunswick.

·The British troops commanded by the Marquis of Granby,
were disposed in the following year as follows, in corps and
brigades :—

LIEUT.-GEN. HON. HENRY SEYMOUR CONWAY'S CORPS.

1st Brigade, Brig.-Gen. Cæsar.	2nd Brigade, Brig.-Gen. Towns-
Grenadiers of the Guards.	hend.
2nd battalion First Guards.	Barrington 40th.
,, Coldstream Guards.	Erskine 67th.
,, Third Guards.	Carr 50th.
	Kingsley 20th.

Cavalry Brigade, Brigadier-General Douglas.
Bland's, 1st Dragoon Guards, 3 squadrons; Howard's, 2 squadrons;
and Waldegrave's, 5th Dragoon Guards, 2 squadrons.

LIEUT.-GEN. HON. SIR CHARLES HOWARD'S CORPS.

1st Brigade, Ld. Fredk. Cavendish.	Earl of Pembroke, Cavalry Brig.
Bockland 11th.	The Blues, 3 squadrons.
Griffin 33rd.	Honeywood, 7th Dragoon Guards,
Brudenel 51st.	2 squadrons.
Welsh Fusiliers, 23rd.	Carabineers, 6th, 2 squadrons.

MARQUIS OF GRANBY'S CORPS.

1st Brigade, Beckwith.	2nd Brigade, Waldegrave.
Walding.	Hodgson 5th.
Maxwell.	Cornwallis, 24th.
Campbell.	Stuart 37th.
Keith.	Napier 12th.

Cavalry Brigade.

Greys 2 squadrons.
Ancrum 2 ,, 11th Dragoons } Besides Artillery.
Mostyn 2 ,, 7th ,, }

During the earlier part of the campaign of 1760, Prince
Ferdinand had successfully resisted the French armies under
the Duc de Broglie and Soubise in their attempts to penetrate further into the Electoral dominions of Hanover, particularly at Warburg on the 31st of July, when the enemy
lost ten pieces of artillery and 1,500 men, a success mainly
owing to the gallantry of Lord Granby, and a charge of the

British cavalry. The British troops had throughout maintained their high renown, and being, it is said, always put forward in the posts of honour, and consequently of greatest danger, their losses were proportionately severe. The French were still in possession of Göttingen and Cassel. The Prince, who was posted on the northern bank of the Diemel, did not think it prudent to attempt to force the French out of their position; but being secure in his own, he sent some strong detachments under his son, the Hereditary Prince, to the south of Hesse, to threaten the enemy's communication with the Rhine and Maine, whence they procured their supplies, and the grenadiers of the army, under Maxwell, accompanied this detachment.

August 9. Before the Guards reached the scene of action, great discontent had appeared in some quarters as to the manner in which the English in the Allied army were treated. The chief complaints were, " that no English General had a separate command; that there was much animosity between the officers and privates of the different nations; that the British troops were always placed in the warmest part of every action; there were also complaints of the scarcity of provisions, and that the English had to pay double for everything; there were even complaints of a derogatory nature against the General himself." In answer to these assertions it was averred that, from the Generals not being able to converse with spies, it would be imprudent to give them separate commands; that the English had perhaps begun by despising the German officers for not being so rich as they were; that the English had requested always to have the post of honour; that the purveyors, not the General, were to be blamed for their provisions; that the English, wherever they went, were known always to spoil the market; and the complaints against the General himself were shown to be unfounded.

Sept. 9.

Zierenberg. The Hereditary Prince was again despatched, on the 9th of September, with a portion of the army to surprise the French in and around Zierenberg, lying about 12 miles north-north-west of Cassel. The arrangements for this surprise were admirably planned, and as successfully carried out. Besides ten squadrons of cavalry under Major-General Bock, there were, of infantry, under Major-General Griffin—

British { The Grenadiers of the army under Maxwell.
{ 150 Highlanders and Kingsley's regiment.

Foreign { Three battalions of Grenadiers under Blocke, Mirback,
{ and Redecke.

The British regiments were to make the attack, while the cavalry and foreign Grenadiers were posted so as to cover the assault. The troops arrived at their stations, and the surprise was eminently successful, Maxwell with his Grenadiers gaining an entrance by the Dürenberg gate, the other columns by the gates allotted to them. They entered about two in the morning; by three had taken the whole Sept. 10. French garrison prisoners to the number of 428 men, of whom 36 were officers; and were back in camp by ten in the morning, having lost only five men, with very few wounded.

The other British officers of rank present with the Hereditary Prince on this occasion, were Colonel Boyd, Colonel Beckwith, and Lord George Lenox.

Göttingen being still in possession of the French, Prince Ferdinand moved his army during the autumn in that direction, with the view to forcing the enemy to abandon it; but as the season advanced, the severity of the weather and badness of the roads rendered it impossible for the troops to keep the field, and the Prince, finding himself obliged to Dec. 11. abandon his design, retired to Eimbech and Uslar, and sent them, in December, into winter quarters. The troops that were on the right bank of the Diemel and in the wood of See plan. Sababourg were recalled to the north or left bank, and the brigade of Guards was sent to Paderborn; Lord Granby fixing his head-quarters at Corvey, near Hoxter.

While Prince Ferdinand and Lord Granby were thus October. successfully defending Hanover, one of the home battalions of the First Guards was called upon for another and a secret service abroad. Active preparations were making in October to equip a large fleet at Portsmouth, and to put on board a considerable number of troops destined for this expedition. Amongst those ordered to take part in it, were the third battalion First Guards, under Colonel Hon. William Keppel, the 19th, the 21st Scots Fusiliers, 36th, 37th, and 39th Regiments of the line, some dragoons and volunteers, and two regiments from Ireland. Major-General Kingsley was appointed to command the expedition, and Colonel Crawfurd, and Colonel Keppel of the First Guards, were named the two brigadiers. The third battalion received notice on the 8th of October to hold itself in readiness, and after a fortnight's delay it left London for Portsmouth on the 23rd of October, 900 strong, in three divisions. The old king, George II., always full of zeal in regard to military matters, had placed himself in his portico at Kensington, to see the battalion march past, little dreaming that this would be the last opportunity he would have of seeing any of his

Oct. 25. Guards, for he died suddenly two days later, in the seventy-seventh year of his age. Before, however, giving an account of his funeral we will refer to the fate of the secret expedition. The battalion of First Guards on leaving London marched through Kingston and Godalming to Petersfield, thence was proceeding to Hilsea Barracks to embark, when it received counter orders, as the fleet was not ready to receive the troops, and returned to Petersfield, remaining in cantonments there for two days; it then proceeded to Southsea Common for about ten days more, when, on the 27th of November, both the Guards and the rest of the troops, with General Kingsley and Colonel Keppel, were all embarked, and after waiting a short time for a fair wind, the fleet sailed from Spithead. On the 12th of December, however, the whole expedition was countermanded, the fleet returned to Spithead on the 15th, the troops disembarked, and the third battalion, proceeding to London, arrived there on the 20th of the same month.

Nov. 11. In the meantime the funeral of the late king took place, at which the three first battalions of the brigade, all that then remained in England, were present, Previously, however, to the ceremony, the late king's bowels were, on

the 9th November, privately interred in Henry VIII.'s 1760.
Chapel, when a procession was formed, escorted by Horse Nov. 9.
Guards and Yeomen of the Guard, while a party of Foot
Guards was posted in the Abbey, through ·which the procession passed to deposit the coffin in the royal vault. The
body lay in state in the Prince's Chamber, near the House
of Lords, the following day, and on the 11th the funeral Nov. 11.
took place with regal splendour. A covered way was made
from the Prince's Chamber leading to the Abbey, the whole
of which, and the Abbey itself, as far as the steps leading
to Henry VIII.'s Chapel, was lined on each side by the
Foot Guards. Horace Walpole describes the procession :—
" Passing through a line of Foot Guards, every seventh
man bearing a torch, the Horse Guards lining the outside,
their officers with drawn swords and crape sashes on horseback, the drums muffled, the fifes, bell-tolling, and minute
guns. All this," he says, " was very solemn."

The following are the names of the officers of the First Oct. 27.
Guards as they stood on the occasion of the renewal of
commissions, 27th of October, 1760, at the accession of
George III.*

Field-Marshal John, Viscount Ligonier, Colonel.

James Durand, Lt.-Colonel. | Hon. Willm. Keppel, 2nd Major.
Joseph Hudson, 1st Major. | Sir Richard Pierson, 3rd Major.

CAPTS. AND LIEUT.-COLONELS.	LIEUTENANTS AND CAPTAINS.	ENSIGNS.
Edward Urmston,	William Miles,	William Wilson,
John Salter,	Edmd. Knyvet Wilson,	John Powis,
Philip Sherard,	Richd. Pownell,	Mordaunt Martin,
George Lane Parker,	Edward Craig,	Thomas Middleton,
Neville Tatton,	William Thornton,	Thomas Edmonds,
Richd. Lambert, after-	Thos. Howard,	Gerard Lake,
wards 6th Earl of	William Castle,	John Bartlett Allen,
Cavan,	William Hudson,	Edward Goat,
Alexander Maitland,	Henry Wickham,	Michael Cox,
Nathaniel Manlove.	Charles Dering,	Charles Cotterell,

* W. O. Com. Book, 1282.

1760. CAPTS. AND LIEUT.-COLONELS.	LIEUTENANTS AND CAPTAINS.	ENSIGNS.
Launcelot Baugh,	Rich. Schuckburgh,	William Sleigh,
Rowland Alston,	George Bridgeman,	James Stuart,
William Style, ·	John Jones,	John Rule,
Charles Hotham,	Robert Huselar,	Ben. Bathurst Keith,
Henry Clinton,	William Amherst,	George Hotham,
Charles Fitzroy,	John Johnson,	Edward Devereux,
Arthur Graham,	Samuel Wolleston,	Frederick Madan,
George H. Treby,	West Hyde,	Napier,
William Tryon,	Thomas Cox,	Percival,
David Lindsay,	William Fauquier,	Broderick.
Thomas Dickens,	William Fielding,	
George Onslow,	Philip de Salis,	
Edward Ligonier,	Charles Farnaby,	
George West,	Anthony David,	
Ch. Lewis Mordaunt,	George Garth,	
Robert Boyde,	Robert Jenkinson,	
Spencer Cowper.	George Evelyn,	
	Ridgeway O. Meyrick,	
	Sir Alexr. Gilmour,	
	John Edwards,	
	John Howard.	

STAFF.

Richard Brickenden,	Chaplain.	Rice Williams,	Quartermaster.
William Hudson,	Adjutant.	Robert Jenkinson,	,,
Richard Pownell,	,,	Lewis Davis,	Surgeon.
William Amherst,	,,	William Luard,	Solicitor.
		Fncis. Mathews. Bk. Mas. to Savoy.	

CAMPAIGN OF 1761.

The troops did not remain long in their winter quarters, as Prince Ferdinand determined, if possible, to surprise the enemy, under the Duc de Broglie, by an early and simultaneous attack with all his army along their whole line, and for this purpose he assembled his several corps as early and as secretly as possible. The Brigade of Guards, under General Cæsar, forming part of General Conway's corps, quitted Paderborn in the middle of February, and joined

Feb. 21. · Lord Granby on the 21st. The army then advanced in three columns, Lord Granby, with the Guards, and the rest of the British troops, taking the lead, and proceeding rapidly to Treysa, in Hesse-Cassel, east of Marburg, which the enemy immediately evacuated, retiring upon Ziegenhain. The Prussian king, with a view to assisting this movement of Prince Ferdinand, detached 7000 Prussians to the assistance of the Hanoverians, and they together drove back the French from Langensalza. The allies continued their advance, which was so well organized that the French were driven back at all points, first to Fulda, then upon Frankfort-on-the-Main, and the magazines and stores of the enemy, collected for the ensuing campaign, were nearly all destroyed. The Prince then undertook the siege of Cassel; but owing to a vigorous defence, to the severity of the weather, and to the French, who were gradually recovering from their surprise, advancing to its relief, he found himself obliged, after a month's open trenches, to raise the siege, and towards the end of March the armies resumed their former position.

While these events were occurring in Germany, steps were taken in England to reinforce the several regiments on service. On the 1st of March the two home battalions of the First Guards were called upon for volunteers to fill the ranks of the 2nd battalion abroad. This draft, amounting to 178 men, proceeded on the 3rd of April from the Savoy barracks by companies, under their respective non-commissioned officers, to the Tower, whence they were taken down the river, embarked on board the "Goodwill," 337 tons, and despatched to Germany. The home battalions were at the same time directed to complete themselves at once in field equipage and camp necessaries, so as to be ready to take the field at twelve hours' notice. In June these four battalions were again ordered to be kept in readiness to take the field if required, and in August the Guards in the Savoy were called upon to quell a serious mutiny that had broken out amongst the prisoners confined in that building; it was only subdued with difficulty after several shots were fired, and much blood had been spilt. Lord Ligonier still retained his post as Field-Marshal Commanding-in-Chief, with Lord Tyrawley, Earl Delawarr,

1761.
March 1.
and Lieutenant-General Noel in command of the London District.*

On the 21st of July, William Keppel, the second major, resigned his appointment, to which Richard Pierson succeeded, and Edward Urmston became major of the third battalion. William Keppel was third son of William-Anne, 2nd Earl of Albemarle; he became a major-general in the following year, and lieutenant-general in 1772. He was commander-in-chief in Ireland in 1773, and died in 1782.

Sept. 22.
The coronation of George III. took place on the 22nd of September, on which occasion all the Guards were called out, and the first regiment was drawn up three deep, with its right resting on Westminster Hall Gate, and its left extending to Parliament Street; the remainder were in single rank on the opposite side of the platform that was erected in front of the Horse Guards; and when the ceremony was over the King was pleased to signify to Lord Ligonier his high approbation of the diligence of both officers and men of the Foot Guards during the procession.

After the coronation several of the battalions of Guards were encamped for a month in Hyde Park, and on the 20th of October returned to their quarters.

Reverting now to the proceedings in Germany, where all the movements of Prince Ferdinand's army were made with regard to the safety of the Electorate of Hanover, and the Principality of Hesse-Cassel, it is to be observed, that successful as had been the Prince's operations against the French in his early campaign this year, they had no permanent beneficial results, and he was obliged in June, with his 95,000 men, to look to the safety of his own position, as when the enemy were prepared to take the field, he found himself opposed to 160,000 Frenchmen, under Soubise and De Broglie, and it was fortunate for the allies that the jealousy existing between these two French marshals prevented their always acting in concert.

Soubise was advancing from the Rhine, and De Broglie

---

* There were some alterations in the uniform this year, and all officers were requested to supply themselves with the new pattern before the coronation.

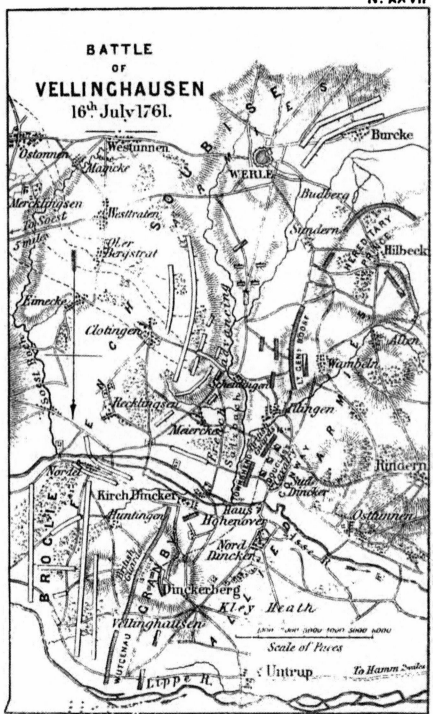

BATTLE
OF
VELLINCHAUSEN
16th July 1761.

Scale of Paces

To Hamm

from the south, when Prince Ferdinand, far from wishing to   1761.
prevent the junction of these two corps, moved so as to July.
turn the left of Soubise's army, and force him down towards
his brother-marshal, and, on the 6th of July, the French July 6.
effected a junction at Soest. Prince Ferdinand had, early
in the same month, taken up a position behind the Salzbach,
with his left resting on the south bank of the Lippe river,
to the east of Hamm, near the small villages of Vellingshausen and Illingen, and he determined to await there
the attack of the enemy. The French lost ten days in
reconnoitring the Prince's position, which time was occupied
by the allies in strengthening themselves. The Prince's extreme left was composed of Wutgenau's corps of Germans.
To his right, on and about the wooded heights of Vellingshausen, the Prince had posted the British troops under
Granby, with orders to maintain that post to the last; and
amongst these troops were Conway's three brigades,
viz., the brigade of Guards of four battalions under Brigadier-General Cæsar, Townshend's brigade of Infantry, and
Douglas's brigade of Cavalry. In the centre were the
Prince of Anhalt's corps, near Illingen, and that of Boose,
near Wambeln, while the right, under the Hereditary
Prince, occupied the high ground above the village of
Bourke. After much discussion and uncertainty as to their
plans, Soubise and De Broglie resolved to attack the allies
on the 15th of July; but, when the time arrived, the former July 15.
remained in camp, while De Broglie, after most of the day
had been spent in reconnoitring, advanced alone at six
o'clock against the left of the allies; he drove in their outposts, but could not reach Vellingshausen and its wooded
heights, where the Prince had posted Lord Granby and his
British troops, and after four hours' very severe fighting on
the part of the English till ten at night, with, as remarked,
" unbeschreiblicher Tapferkeit," * De Broglie found his
attempt unavailing and withdrew his troops. On the following morning the attack was resumed by the whole French July 16.
army, and upon the advance of the troops under De Broglie,

---

* With indescribable bravery.

the Prince ordered Conway, with his corps, including Cæsar's British Guards, to replace the Prince of Anhalt between Illingen and Hohenover. Everywhere the attack was received with such steadiness that, after five hours' continued firing, the French being observed to waver, Prince Ferdinand ordered a general advance, which turned the French retreat into a flight, when the Hereditary Prince was directed to follow Soubise towards the Rhine.

Prince Ferdinand now returned to his camp, remaining some days in the position of Hohenover, to the successful defence of which the Guards had much contributed.

The total losses of the allies in the late action of Vellingshausen were 311 killed, 1011 wounded, and 192 prisoners, while the losses of the French in their abortive attempts against the allied position were estimated at 5000 men, besides nine guns and six colours taken.

Several small affairs took place with the enemy during the next few weeks, and on one occasion the Prince advanced across the Diemel with the view to surprising the French near Cassel, but not succeeding, he recrossed the river and encamped at Buhne and Corbeke.

The Hereditary Prince having driven Soubise back to the Rhine, returned about the middle of August to Warburg on the Diemel; and, on the 16th of that month, the British Guards, under General Cæsar, rejoined the main army with Prince Ferdinand, when the whole force crossed the Diemel in several columns—Granby and his troops crossing at Liebenau—and drove the French from a strong position at Immerhausen back to their entrenchments round Cassel, whereupon the allies encamped at Ober Wielmar.

In November, Prince Ferdinand endeavoured again to surprise De Broglie in his camp at Eimbeck, and for that purpose ordered the army to concentrate in its neighbourhood on the 5th of that month. Lord Granby was directed to force a post at Cappellenhagen on the 4th, and proceed the next day to Wiedensee to block up a defile on the road from Eschershausen to Eimbeck, which orders were carried out by the British Grenadiers and the Highlanders. General Hardenburg had been ordered to secure the road

to Eimbeck, but the overturning of some pontoons, and the
consequent delay, caused the plan to fail. Prince Ferdinand
advanced towards the French camp, but finding it too strong
to attack in front, turned their left flank, and by cutting off
their communications with Göttingen forced them to retire.
This was the last expedition of the year, and on the 28th **Nov. 28.**
November the British Guards and Highlanders moved
by Bielfeldt into winter quarters in the bishoprick of
Osnaburg ; the remainder of the allies moved off on the 4th
of December to their respective cantonments, and the
French withdrew at the beginning of December to Eisenach,
Gotha, Mulhausen, and Fulda.

The following is the state of the regiment at the end of
this year, showing a large proportion of sick in the service
battalion, consequent on the fatigues of the campaign and
wounds :—

	Officers.	Non-Commissioned Officers.	Rank and File.		Total Officers and Men.	Wanting to complete.	Contingent Men.	Establishment.
			Fit for Duty.	Sick.				
1st & 3rd battalions in London . . .	68	120	1688	100	1976	112	76	2164
2nd battalion in Germany . . .	33	56	589	265	947	46	36	1025
								3189

An expedition had been set on foot by the British **April.**
government in the spring of this year with the view to
diverting the attention of the French government from the
war in Germany, to the defence of their own coast. Ten
ships under Admiral Keppel, with 9000 troops on board,
under Major-General Hodgson, were despatched in April to
Quiberon Bay, between L'Orient and the mouth of the Loire,
to take possession of Belleisle. After some difficulties,
a landing was effected on the 22nd, and the troops drove the
garrison into the citadel, of which they made themselves
masters after a six weeks' siege, with the loss, however, of
2000 men. The news of this success was received with great

1762. joy in England, although it did not effect the object in view, of inducing the French to withdraw any part of their troops from Germany.

Towards the end of the year 1761, a quarrel arose between England and Spain, caused partly by the interference of the latter country in the affairs of England, but principally by its entering into the "Family Compact" or defensive alliance of the several members of the Bourbon family, in France, Spain, and Italy; and as Spain refused to give any explanation of her conduct, war was declared between the two countries at the beginning of the following year, 1762. Spain considered an attack on Portugal, the ancient ally of the English, as the easiest mode of undermining the interests of England, and after vainly endeavouring to induce the King of Portugal to side with her, she invaded that country, little prepared for defence. The Spaniards had not, however, calculated on the vast resources of England, for though her hands were at the time full with the wars she was carrying on in Germany, America, and the East Indies, George III. immediately sent out a powerful fleet with 8000 men to the assistance of his ally, and speedily drove the Spaniards out of Portugal. An English fleet with troops on board was also dispatched to the West Indies, where the English soon captured Fort Royal, in Martinique, St. Lucia, St. Vincent, and other places from the French, and Havannah from the Spaniards, while in India they took the Spanish possessions of Manilla. All these successes, combined with the fortunate issue of the campaign in Germany, to which we must now revert, soon induced the enemies of England to make proposals for a peace.

April 3.   Drafts were sent out in the spring of 1762 to complete the various service battalions. The draft of 187 men for the second battalion First Guards was dispatched from London on the 3rd of April under command of officers of the battalion returning to Germany; they embarked on board the "Thomas and Jane," lying at Gravesend, and immediately sailed for their destination, arriving at the head-quarters of their battalion in the bishoprick of Osna-

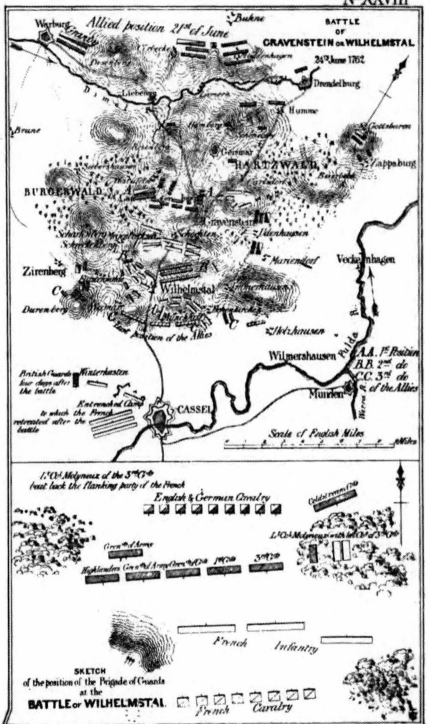

burg before the opening of the campaign. The position of
Prince Ferdinand was not essentially different from that
which he occupied at the commencement of the previous
campaign, and his nephew, the Hereditary Prince, was at
Wesel, watching the Prince of Condé on the Lower Rhine.

. The first object of the Prince, when active operations began
in the month of June, was to advance suddenly and surprise
the French camp at Gravenstein, near Cassel, where
D'Estrés and Soubise were posted in fancied security. For
this purpose, the British left their cantonments on the 4th of June 4.
June, and joined the Hanoverian corps under General
Sporken, near Blomberg, whence they advanced on the 18th
to Brackel, where the allied army was concentrating, and
as soon as the cavalry arrived, it advanced on the 20th
towards the Diemel, reaching Buhne on the 21st. Lord June 21.
Granby's corps of English troops on the extreme right
moved at the same time and occupied Warburg, lying
also on the Diemel. On the 22nd the general advance
of the allied army to surprise the enemy commenced. Lord
Granby crossed the river in three columns, one of which
consisted of• two battalions of British Grenadiers, two of
Highlanders, some Hanoverian infantry and cavalry, with
some batteries of Hessian artillery ; he was to unite his
forces at seven in the morning of the 24th on the heights June 24.
opposite Fürstenwalde, and fall on the left wing of the Battle of
enemy. The main body, under the Prince himself, crossed Graven-
the Diemel in seven columns ; the Prince personally leading stein.
five of them, amongst which were twelve battalions of English, including the British Guards ; eleven battalions of
Brunswickers ; and eight Hessian regiments, with the
English cavalry. All of these marching by various routes,
Lord Frederick Cavendish leading the advance with the light
infantry of the British army, took up their respective positions on the heights of Langenberg, opposite the enemy. At
the same time, General Sporken on the left, with his
Hanoverians, advanced in two columns by Humme and
Baverbek, and took up a position so as to turn the right
flank of the French army. The advance was so well com-

bined that it succeeded at all points; the French, who were taken by surprise, stood to their arms, but after a short resistance left their camp equipage at Gravenstein, and commenced a retreat, covered by De Stainville's corps, whose gallant resistance against Lord Granby's equally gallant attack saved the French army from annihilation. The position of the several battalions of Guards in this action is represented in the accompanying sketch. Two guns, six colours, and one standard were taken. .The total loss of the allies was 796 killed, wounded, and missing. Of the battalion of First Guards, Lieutenant-Colonel Henry Townshend,* one non-commissioned officer and seven men were killed; one officer, Captain Middleton, and twenty-eight men wounded, and one officer, Ensign Maden, one non-commissioned officer, and thirty men missing. In the battalion of Grenadiers of the Guards, there were eight killed, twenty-five wounded, and thirty-seven prisoners or missing, while the enemy's loss in prisoners alone was 162 officers and 2750 men. The other two battalions of the brigade suffered. proportionately, but the third regiment more than the Coldstreams. All the troops are reported to have behaved extremely well, and to have shown great zeal and willingness. The enemy retired towards the river Fulda, under the walls of Cassel.

Four days after the battle, the British Guards moved forward to Winter Hasten, Lord Granby remaining at Dürenberg and Prince Ferdinand at Wilhelmstal. On the 6th of July, while the main body remained near Cassel, the brigade of Guards with Bland's and Waldegrave's dragoons (1st and 2nd Dragoon Guards) advanced to Hoff; whereupon the French sent a detachment of 15,000 men between Melsungen and Homberg to preserve their communications with their base at Frankfort. On the 11th

---

* Colonel Townshend's death was regretted by the whole army. He was second son to the Hon. Thomas Townshend, and had distinguished himself on several occasions. In the previous campaign in Germany, he was shot through the arm, and in this engagement he lost his life, seeking the post of honour that his duty did not require: he was the only officer of rank killed in the action.—*Annual Register.*

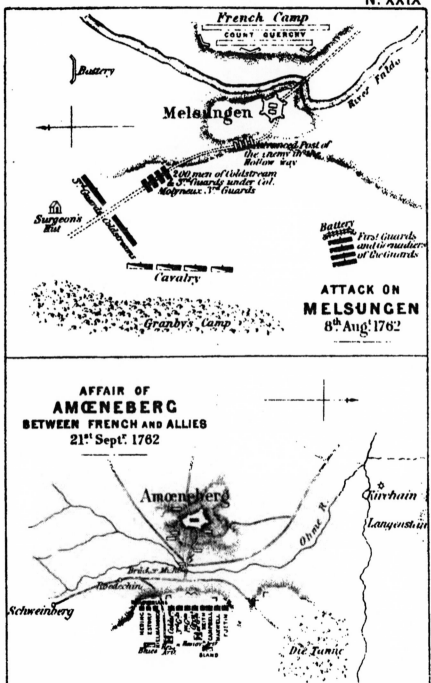

Battery

French Camp
COUNT GUERCHY

River Fulda

Melsungen

Wooded Post of the enemy in the Hollow way

200 men of Coldstream & 3ᵈ Guards under Col. Molyneux, 3ᵈ Guards

3ᵈ Guards Coldstream

Surgeon's Hut

Battery

First Guards and Grenadiers of the Guards

Cavalry

Granby's Camp

ATTACK ON MELSUNGEN
8ᵗʰ Augᵗ 1762

AFFAIR OF AMŒNEBERG
BETWEEN FRENCH AND ALLIES
21ˢᵗ Septʳ 1762

Amœneberg

Ohme R.

Kirchain

Langenshin

Brücker M.

Rodeshin

Schweinberg

Blues

Die Tunne

the Castle of Waldec surrendered to General Conway after   1762.
two days' bombardment, and on the 13th General Cæsar   July 13.
advanced with his corps and the Guards from Hoff to
Gudensberg, where the whole of the English troops were
now assembled under Lord Granby. They continued to
press upon the French, and on the 24th July, Lord Granby   July 24.
ordered the second battalion of First Guards, under
Sherrard, one battalion of Hanoverians, and 100 men from
each of the other regiments, to attack the enemy posted on
the heights of Homberg: this they successfully carried out,
encamping that night on the ground they had won, thus
cutting off the line of communication of the French. The
army remained some days in this neighbourhood, and while
here, General Julius Cæsar met with an accidental fall
from his horse, which resulted in his death, at his quarters   August.
in Elfershausen, a small village three miles south-west of
Melsungen, at a time when his brigade of Guards was
in the full career of success, pursuing the French towards
the Rhine, and when a short time longer would have
enabled him to witness the successful result of the last
campaign of the war.

The Coldstream and Third Guards were in their turn en-   Aug. 8.
gaged with the enemy on the 8th of August, while the first
regiment and Grenadiers of the Guards were kept in reserve   Melsungen.
on the right, watching the progress of the attack. The
French near Melsungen had been making several attempts
to dislodge the English, when Lieutenant-Colonel Molyneux
was sent forward with the above battalions to take possession
of the town. They succeeded in their advance in cutting
down the chevaux-de-frise, but were at first unable to force
the gates; the town, however, soon after surrendered.

On the 26th of August the French were compelled to   Aug. 26.
evacuate Göttingen, but they still held Cassel for a time;
finding themselves, however, gradually forced to retire, they
called to their assistance the army now under Condé from
the Rhine, which was being watched by the Hereditary
Prince of Brunswick. The latter, with the view of preventing the junction, attacked Condé on the 30th of   Aug. 30.
August, at Johannisberg, on the Wetter, twenty miles

north of Frankfort, but was defeated with considerable loss after receiving a wound in the action. The French, however, derived no advantage from their success, owing to Prince Ferdinand, who had that day reached the camp at Nidda, arriving with a considerable force of the allies, and checking the enemy in their pursuit.

Colonel H. Clinton, of the First Guards, who acted as aide-de-camp to the Hereditary Prince, was also severely wounded on this occasion, and was eventually obliged to leave the field.

The French continued to make a vigorous resistance, but the allies during the next three weeks were gradually gaining ground, and early on the morning of the 21st of September the Guards, with Beckwith's brigade, reached the heights of Langenstein, behind Kirchain, on the Ohm river, across which the French retired. The allies had already possession of the old castle of Amöneberg on the further side, holding it with 500 men, and Prince Ferdinand now secured all the passes over the river, of which the principal one was the bridge at the Brücken Mühle, protected by a redoubt into which the allies threw 100 Hanoverians.

The French had already determined, if possible, to repossess themselves both of the pass and of the castle, and as the mist cleared, about five o'clock in the morning of the 21st September, they commenced a heavy cannonade, which was replied to by the allies; reinforcements of Hanoverians, under Zastrow, coming up at eight o'clock, supported and eventually relieved the garrison in the redoubt, who had hitherto been very much exposed to the enemy's fire. As the day advanced more guns arrived, and the artillery fire redoubled, the men in the redoubt who survived being relieved every hour. At length Prince Ferdinand came up, and seeing how hotly the bridge was contested, and how determined the French appeared to get possession of it, he resolved to maintain it at all hazards, and sent for the brigade of Guards. Zastrow had been defending the bridge for eight hours, when Granby with the Guards and other English regiments arrived on the spot. This succour came

up most opportunely, as the Hanoverians had not only
been suffering much, but had expended all their ammunition, and the enemy's battalions were not above 300 paces
from the redoubt. The Grenadier battalion of the Guards
was the first ordered into the work, and to line the banks
of the river, both above and below the bridge, to relieve the
Hanoverians, an operation which was effected with the
greatest coolness and bravery, though the men were obliged
to march nearly 400 paces exposed to a murderous fire of
musketry and grape. More artillery continued to be brought
up on both sides, and the cannonading became more determined than ever. After a time the second battalion First
Guards relieved the Grenadier battalion in the redoubt, and
these, in turn, were relieved by the other two battalions of
the brigade of Guards, and so on alternately as the ammunition of each was expended. The Hessians then came
forward, and relieved the brigade of Guards. The cannonading continued uninterruptedly till darkness set in and
put an end to the duel, in which seventeen battalions of the
allies had taken part, though neither party had attempted
to cross the bridge. Seldom has a post been so long or
obstinately contested, for the affair lasted for fourteen
hours. The advantage, however, remained to the allies,
who retained possession of the post from which the enemy
had in vain endeavoured to drive them. The casualties of
the allies were about 800, while those of the French were
300 killed and 800 wounded.

As the French retired, Prince Ferdinand invested Cassel,
and the siege operations were carried on so vigorously
that the town capitulated on the 10th of October. These
were the last operations of the Seven Years' War, as far as
the French and English were concerned, for though occasional skirmishes took place between the two armies, the
French were unable to recover the lost ground. Preliminaries of peace were signed at Paris at the beginning of
November, whereby the Electorate of Hanover was secured
to the British Crown, and mutual restitutions were made
on both sides.

1763.   Before the allied army separated, Prince Ferdinand
addressed the troops, declaring he would ever preserve the
most flattering remembrance of having fought successfully
at the head of such an army, composed of different nations,
and which had exerted itself so vigorously for their own
and their country's honour. There were great rejoicings
in England at the successful termination of the war, and
Parliament voted the thanks of both Houses to the officers
and men of the army for the meritorious and eminent
services which they had done their king and country during
its continuance—thanks which were communicated to them
Jan. 13. in a general order issued on the 13th of January, 1763, by
General Conway, who had commanded the British contingent. General Conway was detained by illness at Warburg,
but he also issued a parting address to the troops, thanking
them for their services during the late campaigns.

The first division of the British army began its march home-
wards through Holland on the 25th of January, proceeding
through Guelderland, Nimeguen, and Breda, to Wilhelmstadt, whence the troops were conveyed in transports to
England. Each of the three battalions of Guards on its
return averaged fifteen officers and 730 men, besides above
100 horses. The total number returning home was near 700
officers, 17,000 men, and 7400 horses. According to orders
of the 3rd of January, the second battalion First Guards,
on its arrival at Harwich and Ipswich, marched to London
by Sudbury, Chelmsford, and Rumford ; the two battalions
of the Coldstream and Third Guards arrived in England
at the end of February, and in London on the 13th of
March ; and the treaty having been finally signed, peace was
March 22. proclaimed on the 22nd of that month.

No sooner was the war over than the services of part of
the brigade were required to put a stop to some tumultuous
assemblies in the metropolis, and the field-officer in
brigade waiting was directed to send detachments of the
Foot Guards to quell any disturbances, upon a requisition
from the magistrates. At a review of the Foot Guards
held this year in Hyde Park, at which the King, the Duke

of York, and Prince William Henry, were present, the King
was received by Lord Ligonier and the Marquis of Granby,
and the men who had been in Germany were all decorated
with laurel and oak sprigs. The Master-Generalship of
the Ordnance was this year conferred upon Lord Granby,
and it was made up to Lord Ligonier, who had held that
post since the year 1657, by his being created a British
peer; but many thought it an indignity to the old Field-
Marshal to be deprived of his military appointment. In the
month of October the services of the Guards were again
required in consequence of disorders breaking out among
the weavers, who were committing great outrages, many of
them going about, both by day and night, disguised as
sailors, and armed with cutlasses. On receipt of notice
of these disturbances, a detachment of the Third Guards
was sent from the Tower to be quartered in the disturbed
districts, where it remained till the 26th of the same month,
and then returned to its former quarters.

Detachments of 700 men of the brigade, drawn from the
four battalions at the West-end, and from the one at the
Tower, were ordered, on the 16th and 17th of April, 1764,
to attend the trial of Lord Byron before the House of
Lords, who was apprehended for killing his adversary,
a Mr. Chaworth, in a duel. The Guards were placed
under the command of Major-General Gore, and an
additional detachment was told off to escort Lord Byron
each day from the Tower to the Houses of Parliament;
he was found guilty of manslaughter, but dismissed on
payment of the fees. An order was issued on the 19th
by the field-officer to the whole brigade relative to the
good conduct of the men employed during the above trial,
intimating that the Duke of Ancaster had acquainted
the King with their good behaviour, and that the Duke
desired to thank them all for their exertions on the
occasion.

Colonel Richard Pierson, the second major of the First
Regiment, left the corps in September, 1764, and on the
5th of that month was succeeded by Edward Urmston; and

1764.   Colonel John Salter was promoted to third major, and to the command of the third battalion.

1765.

1765.   Considerable disturbances again took place in London in May, 1765, amongst the weavers, who assembled in threatening crowds, breaking the windows of the houses of master weavers and others, who had incurred their resentment by giving extensive orders for foreign manufactures; and a detachment of Guards was sent from the Tower, on the

May 16.   16th of May, to be quartered in Spitalfields, as in 1763, to assist in keeping the peace. The next day, a large body of people assembled in a very tumultuous and disorderly manner in the neighbourhood of the Houses of Parliament, and fears being entertained that they would proceed to extremities that could only be checked by the troops, detachments of the Foot Guards were again called out to assist the civil magistrates. Another detachment was sent on the 18th of May to Moorfields to repress the disturbances there; and the Duke of Bedford's house, in Bloomsbury-square, being threatened by the mob, another detachment of fifty men of the Guards was directed to proceed in that direction, while picquets of the several regiments were ordered to hold themselves in readiness to march to any threatened points, as it was expected that these disturbances would continue. Some picquets were sent to Whitehall and the Savoy, and all the troops were served out with six rounds of ball cartridge. The above detachments remained for ten or eleven days at their several posts, and were not recalled till the 29th of May, when all fear of further disturbances was over.

     Lieutenant-General Durand, the lieutenant-colonel of the

June 23.   regiment was, on the 23rd of June this year, appointed to the colonelcy of a regiment of the Line, and Lieutenant-General Hudson succeeded to the Lieutenant-Colonelcy of the First Guards, Urmston, Salter, and Hon. Phil. Sherrard, to the three battalions.

     The seven battalions of the brigade continued in town,

one in the Tower, six at the West-end, and on the 28th of
June, Lord Ligonier inspected the three battalions of the
. First Regiment, previous to their being reviewed the
following week by the King. On the 10th of September,
1766, Viscount Ligonier was raised in the British Peerage
to the dignity of an Earl.

The Duke of Cumberland, formerly Colonel of the First
Guards, died suddenly in London on the 31st of October, Oct. 31.
1765, at the comparatively early age of forty-six. His
funeral, which took place on the 9th of November, was Nov. 9.
attended by three battalions of the Guards, one from each
regiment, and by a combined corps of 500 men with
officers, from the remaining four battalions of the brigade.
The three battalions were drawn up in St. Martin's churchyard, and fired volleys on a signal being given that the body
was deposited in its final resting-place.

Several orders relative to dress and conduct were given
out this year to the regiment by Lord Ligonier. The
officers were required to wear Hussar boots, and half black
gaiters of leather or canvas. The non-commissioned officers,
drummers, and private men, when under arms, were to wear
their hair boxed up under their hats, and were to provide
themselves with half black gaiters: and as to saluting, all
soldiers off duty were to pull off their hats to officers, but
if on duty, they were only to raise their hand and bow.

1767.

Some modifications were made in the year 1767 both in   1767.
the exercise and dress of the brigade. In March, the
. Coldstream and Third Regiments were ordered to conform
in their exercise to the time observed by the First Regiment,
and the accoutrements, which had hitherto been yellow,
were now ordered to be white; the pouches also were no
longer to be varnished.

On the 8th of May, the eight Grenadier companies of May 8.
the brigade, were ordered to be formed into a battalion
under the command of Major-General Thornton, to be
exercised as a separate corps. This order appears to have

1767.
May.
    been preparatory to the inevitable forthcoming struggle with the American colonists. Lord Ligonier inspected the brigade in Hyde Park on Friday, the 19th of June, and the

June 22.
    King reviewed all the seven battalions on the 22nd, on which occasion Major-General Gore received the King's commands to acquaint them that their appearance and conduct gave his Majesty great satisfaction. The seven battalions changed their quarters on the 25th of August.

Sept. 17.
    The Duke of York, next brother to George III., dying at Monaco, from the effects of a cold, on the 17th of September this year, his body was brought to England; and, at his funeral, which took place at the beginning of November, there was present a Guard of Honour of 500 men of the Foot Guards, with officers and non-commissioned officers in proportion.

1768.
    The services of the Guards were again frequently called into request in the following year, 1768, to suppress disturbances in the metropolis, caused either by a general cry for a rise of wages amongst the workmen, particularly the weavers, or by other trade quarrels. More especially were they called upon to quell the popular commotions and riots consequent upon the election of Wilkes to serve as member of Parliament for Middlesex, of which some instances will be given.

Jan. 4.
    In consequence of great disturbances amongst the weavers in Spitalfields, on the 4th of January, a party of Foot Guards was detached from the Tower to that part of the town to preserve the peace. They were opposed by the rioters with old swords, sticks, and bludgeons, with which they struck some of the soldiers, who were obliged to return the blows, without, however, having recourse to their firearms. Several were hurt on both sides, and some of the rioters were apprehended by the troops and handed over to the civil power. The mob of weavers during the subsequent examination of the culprits was, however, so great, that the magistrates were forced again to send for a party of the Guards to preserve order.

    The mob also behaved in a very outrageous manner

in Hyde Park, on the occasion of the re-election of Wilkes,
who at the time was under sentence of outlawry. At
night they paraded the streets, forcing people to illuminate,
and committed many depredations, and the Guards on duty
at St. James's, as well as the battalion of Foot Guards
in the Savoy barracks, were ordered to hold themselves in
immediate readiness, on a requisition from the magistrates,
to march and suppress any riots that might ensue.

Their services were again required on the 20th of April,
on the occasion of Wilkes surrendering to take his trial
before the King's Bench on two charges, for the publication
of the " North Briton," No. 45, and for the publication of a
certain poem, when great crowds assembled, and preparations were made both by the civil and military authorities
in the event of riots.   Two battalions of the Guards lay on
their arms in St. James's Park, others in St. George's Fields ;
and those at St. James's, the Savoy, and the Tower, were all
kept in readiness to march at a minute's warning.   They
were called upon again the same day to quell another
serious disturbance that had arisen in Wapping between
the coalheavers and others of that trade.   Many shots were
fired on both sides as the disturbers of the public peace
were attacking the house of a Mr. Green, and three of the
assailants were killed, others dangerously wounded, while
several were taken prisoners by the Guards and conducted
to Newgate.   The culprits were eventually found guilty of
shooting at Mr. Green, and in July a detachment of 300 of
the Guards was on duty at the execution of seven of the
ringleaders who were sentenced to be hanged.   These riots
recommenced on the 25th of April, the men complaining
that their masters oppressed them by curtailing their wages,
and not paying them in money, but in liquor and goods of
a bad quality.

Wilkes was committed to the King's Bench on the
27th of April, and on the following morning many people
assembled in a riotous manner around the prison, pulling
up the wooden rails, and obliging the inhabitants of the
borough to illuminate, but a Captain's detachment of 100

1768.   men of the Foot Guards arriving about twelve o'clock, they all quietly dispersed.

There was, in short, discontent among all classes.   The sailors were clamorous for a rise of wages, and on the

May 3.   3rd of May collected in large numbers in Stepney Fields; others boarded some ships at Deptford, and on the 5th they assembled in St. George's Fields to present a petition to the King.   The watermen assembled on the 9th to lay their complaints before the Lord Mayor.   The hatters struck for wages.   On the 10th a large body of sawyers assembled and pulled down a saw-mill lately erected at Limehouse; and the coalheavers again assembled, but were persuaded to disperse without coming to blows.   On

May 10.   the meeting of Parliament on the 10th of May, serious disturbances took place in the neighbourhood of the King's Bench prison, where large bodies of rioters assembled in anticipation of seeing Wilkes carried thence to the House of Commons, and with the intention of accompanying him thither.   Brickbats and stones were thrown, the Riot Act read, and one man, Allen, was shot by a soldier of the 3rd Guards.   The crowd increasing, more detachments of the Guards, 100 strong each, were sent for, as well as some Horse Grenadiers.   One detachment of the Guards was under the command of Lieutenant-Colonel Style of the First Guards; another, under Lieutenant-Colonel Hon. W. Hervey, of the same regiment.   The rioting continuing, the troops fired on the mob, and five or six were killed and fifteen wounded, when the tumult was at last quelled; but the troops did not escape scatheless, several being struck and wounded by stones.   These detachments, relieved daily by others, continued to be furnished till the beginning of June, when the guard at the King's Bench prison was reduced to one officer and twenty-five men; this guard was not finally removed till the 9th of September. An inquest was held on the body of Allen, the first man killed, when a verdict of wilful murder was given against the soldier who shot him, with a verdict also against Ensign Alexander Murray, the commanding officer, for aiding and abetting, but on the soldier being brought to trial, both he and the magistrate who ordered the firing were honourably acquitted.

A company of Foot Guards was also sent to the Mansion House for the protection of the Lord Mayor Harley, a younger son of the third Earl of Oxford, who had made himself obnoxious to the mob, partly for having caused the May. burning of Wilkes' paper, the " North Briton," No. 45, in 1763, and partly because he had lately defeated Wilkes at the election of a member for London.

In the afternoon of the day that these last disturbances occurred, the Privy Council assembled, at which many of the principal officers of State were present, to take into consideration the existing state of affairs. It was considered but justice that the government should stand forward and protect the troops who were protecting the King's peaceful subjects; the more so, that repeated attempts had been made by handbills to seduce them, and many individuals had come up to tempt the soldiers to take the side of the mob. All these attempts, however, failed; and May 11. the very next morning after the tumults, Lord Barrington, Secretary at War, conveyed, by the King's commands, both to officers and men of the Foot Guards, in the following letter addressed to the Field Officer in brigade waiting, his Majesty's gracious approbation of their conduct, under the late trying circumstances.

" War Office, *May* 11, 1768.

"Sir,—Having this day had the honour of mentioning to the King, the behaviour of the detachments from the several battalions of Foot Guards which have been lately employed in assisting the civil magistrates and preserving the public peace, I have great pleasure in informing you that his Majesty highly approves of the conduct of both the officers and men, and means that his gracious approbation should be communicated to them through you. Employing the troops in so disagreeable a service always gives me pain, but the circumstances of the times make it necessary. I am persuaded they see that necessity, and will continue as they have done to perform their duty with alacrity. I beg you will be pleased to assure them, that every possible regard will be shown to them, their zeal and good behaviour upon this occasion deserve it; and in case any dis-

1768.   agreeable circumstances should happen in the execution of their
duty, they shall have every defence and protection that the law can
authorise and this office can give.

> " I have the honour to be, Sir,
>
> " Your most obedient,
>
> " and most humble servant,
>
> " BARRINGTON.

" To the Field Officer in Staff waiting for the three
" regiments of Foot Guards."

The following was the strength of the First Regiment of
Guards at this period :—

Off.	N.-Com. Officers.	Rank and File. Present.	Sick.	Total.	Wanting to Complete.	Estab.
96	153	1312	60	1621	28	1649.

On the 9th of May, Joseph Hudson, who had been
Lieutenant-General since January, 1761, resigned the Lieu-
tenant-Colonelcy of the First Guards, to which Edward
Urmston, a Major-General since 1762, succeeded ; Colonels
John Salter, Hon. Philip Sherrard, and Hon. George Lane
Parker, succeeded to the three regimental majorities.* The
eight Grenadier companies of the several regiments of the
May 14.   brigade were again this year, by the King's order of May 14th,
formed into a separate battalion, and put under the com-
mand of Colonel Salter, the senior major of the First
Guards. This Grenadier battalion under Colonel Salter, as
well as the seven battalions of the brigade, marched on
Monday, the 27th of June, to Richmond, the Star and Garter,
Petersham, and neighbouring villages, to be reviewed by
the King in Richmond Park on the following day; after
Oct. 7.   which they all returned to London. On the 7th of October,
the battalion of Grenadiers of the Guards again proceeded

---

* The Hon. Philip Sherrard was the fifth son of the second Earl of Harborough ;
he became a full general in the army, and died unmarried after 1793. The
Hon. George Lane Parker was second son of the second Earl of Macclesfield,
and married a connection of the late Major-General Cæsar. He was M.P. for
Tregony, and died a full general in the army, without issue, after 1793.

to Wimbledon and Wandsworth, to be reviewed by the King, 1769.
and during the winter a detachment of the three regiments
of Guards was ordered to do duty at the lodge in Richmond
Park, being periodically relieved by a similar detachment.

Wilkes had been again returned to Parliament, and was
again expelled from the House of Commons on the 3rd Feb. 3.
of February of the following year, 1769, and on the news
of his expulsion becoming known, a number of persons
assembled in a very riotous manner near Drury-lane,
pulling down some houses in the neighbourhood. The
peace officers in vain attempted to stop their proceedings, when a party of Guards being sent for, they took
several of the rioters into custody, and dispersed the rest.

The three regiments of Foot Guards were in this year
reviewed by the King separately instead of in brigade. The
three battalions of the First Guards were, in June, ordered
down to all the neighbouring villages of Wimbledon, to be
reviewed by the King on the 19th of June, and again on
the 28th. They marched on Saturday morning, the 17th, to
Richmond, Fulham, Kingston, Putney, and Wandsworth,
and returned to town after the review on the 19th. The June 19.
King was pleased to signify to Lord Ligonier, the Colonel,
his entire approbation of the appearance and performances
of the regiment; and he desired him to thank in his name,
not only the officers of every rank, but the private soldiers
also. Lord Ligonier had much satisfaction in communicating this pleasing testimony of Royal favour to the whole
corps, being confident, as he added, that as it had been the
generous incentive, so it would be esteemed the most grate-
ful reward, of their zeal and attention.

Detachments of the brigade continued to be daily sent to
Spitalfields during the whole of this year, to check the disturbances that were constantly threatening. In August the
weavers turned out and cut the work out of fifty looms, and
on the 30th of September, a detachment of Guards under Sept. 30.
an officer was ordered to invest a public-house in Spitalfields, where a number of riotous weavers were assembling,
to collect contributions from their fellow-workmen towards

1769.

September. supporting them in idleness, and to force their masters t advance their wages. On the arrival of the Guards th rioters took the alarm, armed themselves with guns, pistols and other offensive weapons, and immediately began a attack upon the soldiers who, in their own defence, fire upon and killed two of them. One soldier was also killed and four of the principal rioters were eventually taken pri soners. Another detachment of Guards was sent to Spital

Oct. 5. fields from the Savoy on the 5th of October, to protect th inhabitants from the outrages of the mob; and two day later a serious collision took place in the same quarter o the town, between the military and the cutters, in which fiv of the latter were killed, and many wounded. The rioter were all tried, and two of the ringleaders were condemned

December. and executed on the 6th of December, and more toward the end of the month.

Though the riots were for a time suppressed, the Guard were again called out on the 18th of December to prevent meeting of the weavers who were assembling at a public house in Moorfields with the intention of petitioning the King in favour of their condemned brethren, and precaution were also taken to prevent their assembling near the Queen' palace. The services of the Guards on this occasion, how ever, were not required; and as the mob appeared peaceabl disposed, the Lord Mayor dispensed with their further pre sence, relying upon the civil power for the preservation o peace.

1770.

1770. The Earl Ligonier, who had been colonel of the First Regiment of Foot Guards for nearly thirteen years, died in April of the following year, 1770. He had held that post throughout the Seven Years' War, during which period part of the regiment was constantly employed abroad, but for the last seven years their duties had been of a different and, as we have seen, of a far less agreeable character, being constantly called upon to suppress disturbances in the metropolis amongst a population with whom they were living in daily intercourse; but whether in fighting the

WILLIAM HENRY, DUKE OF GLOUCESTER AND EDINBURGH,
K.G.
13ᵗʰ Colonel of the First Regiment of Foot Guards.
1770 - 1805.

foreign enemy abroad or in putting a stop to domestic dis- 1770.
turbances, their conduct on every occasion had elicited the
approval of their superiors.

The title of Viscount Ligonier became extinct in his person, but the earldom was continued in the person of his
nephew, Edward Ligonier, who was now serving as a captain
and lieutenant-colonel in the First Guards, and who became
a major-general in 1775. The first earl, the late colonel of
the First Guards, was a French Protestant, and had been,
some years before, elected governor of the French Protestant
Hospital in London, in the board-room of which establishment is to be seen to this day a portrait of this renowned
general of the eighteenth century. He was succeeded in the
colonelcy of the regiment by his royal highness William,
Duke of Gloucester, brother to the King, who was born in,
1743, and was now in his 27th year. The Duke was gazetted
to the colonelcy of the First Guards on the 30th of April,
1770, and on Friday, the 4th of May, the whole regiment was May 4.
assembled in Hyde Park for his royal highness's inspection,
on the occasion of his appointment. The Duke turned his
attention immediately to the dress of the officers of the
regiment, and on the same day ordered several modifications therein, amongst others, that the coat and regimental frock be lined with white; the waistcoat to be of
white cloth lined with white, the breeches also to be of white
cloth.

The whole regiment was reviewed by the King at Black- June 5.
heath on the 5th of the following month, when he was
graciously pleased to express his approbation of its appearance.

On the 21st of June the King again reviewed the First June 21.
Regiment of Foot Guards, and "thanked the several officers
in every company of the regiment, as well as the private
soldiers, for their masterly performance on the occasion, of
which his Majesty was pleased to signify his entire approbation."

Major-General Gansell of the Coldstreams, having been
arrested for debt in the vicinity of the Horse Guards,

1770.   persuaded the bailiff to take him near the guard, and when there, an officer of his regiment called on the guard to rescue him. Lieutenant Garth, of the First Regiment, who commanded the Tylt guard, seems to have taken no part in the proceedings, but to have permitted his men to interfere, for Sergeant Bacon and two file stepped out on being called for by Lieutenant Dodd, and released General Gansell. This matter naturally caused much commotion, and on the 26th of September, Captain Cox, adjutant of the First Guards, appeared before the Court of Aldermen to state that the lieutenant and men were confined. General Gansell was at the same time committed to gaol, and on

April 21. the 21st of April, 1770, the following brigade order was promulgated :—

Parole. Hounslow.

His Majesty has signified to the field officer in waiting that he has been acquainted that Sergt. Bacon, of the First Guards, and Sergt. Parks of the Coldstream, William Powell, William Hart, Samuel Potter, and Joseph Collins, private soldiers in the First Regiment of Foot Guards, were more or less concerned in the rescue of Major-General Gansell in September last. The King hopes and is willing to believe they did not know the Major-General was arrested, and only thought they were delivering an officer in distress; however, his Majesty commands that they should be severely reprimanded for acting in this business as they have done, and strictly orders for the future that no non-commissioned officer or soldier do presume to interfere with bailiffs or arrest on any account or pretence whatever, the crime being of a very atrocious nature, &c. &c.

A general change again took place this year in the command of the regiment and battalions. Edward Urmston retired from the lieutenant-colonelcy, and on the 10th of November, 1770, Colonel John Salter, who had become a major-general in April of that year, succeeded to the lieutenant-colonelcy, and Colonel Nevil Tatton became the third major. Some disturbances ensued early in the following year, when the Guards were again called upon to keep the peace in the metropolis. These originated in the

1771.   Lord Mayor and aldermen, amongst whom was Wilkes, refusing to put in force the press warrants, and they were called to the bar of the House for their contumely. Wilkes refused to appear, but on the Lord Mayor attending, all the Guards, both horse and foot, were ordered to hold themselves in readiness in case of a disturbance. The Lord Mayor was sent to the Tower by a majority of 202 to 39, and remained confined there till the prorogation on the 8th of May following.

A custom had hitherto prevailed of one shilling in the pound being deducted by the paymaster-general from the pay of the whole army, but on the 20th of April this year, in what were then considered dear times, the King, by royal warrant, exempted the private soldiers of the Foot Guards from this deduction, thus adding between fifteen and sixteen shillings to their pay.

The three battalions of the regiment were assembled at Blackheath on the 6th of June, to be reviewed in Greenwich Park by the King. The field officer in brigade waiting had hitherto attended in that capacity all reviews held by the sovereign, but on this occasion George III. ordered the discontinuance of the practice. After the review the Duke of Gloucester signified to the regiment the King's entire approbation of its appearance.

An installation of Knights of the Garter took place at Windsor on the 23rd July, on which occasion the King ordered two combined battalions to be formed out of the brigade of Guards in London. The first was a battalion of Grenadiers, consisting of five captains, eight lieutenants, with non-commissioned officers and 300 men; the second consisted of the same number of officers and 500 men. This second battalion was in all the orders of the day called the hat battalion, as wearing hats, while the other battalion wore the Grenadier cap; on this occasion the First regiment furnished 150 Grenadiers and 250 hats, half the required number. They marched from London early on the morning of the 23rd of July with tents and camp equipage complete, all under the command of Colonel William Hudson, the field officer in waiting; the caps by Colnbrook, and the hats by Staines. On their arrival at Windsor, both

1772. battalions encamped in the Little Park, and returned to town after the ceremony.

1772.

Feb. 15.   On the occasion of the interment of the Princess Dowager of Wales on the 15th of February, 1772, whose death had taken place on the 6th of the same month, the Foot Guards were called out, when they lined each side of the path along which the procession moved, from the Old Palace Yard to the south-east door of Westminster Abbey.

A warrant was issued this year fixing more definitively the position of the captain-lieutenants of cavalry and of line May 25. regiments, namely, that from the 25th May, 1772, they should bear the rank of captain, and rank from the date of their future commission as captain-lieutenants. Similar orders were issued on the same subject with reference to June. the artillery and engineers. On the 4th of June, orders were issued for the three battalions of the First Regiment to march to Blackheath to be reviewed by the King on the 6th of the month, when his Majesty expressed himself well satisfied with their appearance. The Coldstream and Third Regiments were reviewed on the 18th and 19th of June respectively, and on the 15th, detachments from the brigade attended the ceremony of the installation of Knights of the Bath. It had been the practice during the late disturbed times in the metropolis for the troops to mount duty with Nov. 30. loaded firelocks, but the practice was discontinued towards the end of this year.

1773.

Nothing particular occurred during the subsequent year, 1773, in the movement of the brigade, but some changes took place in battalion commands. The honourable George Lane Parker resigned the command of the second battalion on the 3rd of May, when Nevil Tatton, a major-general since 1770, succeeded to that battalion, and Richard Lambert, now Earl of Cavan, who had been promoted to major-general on the 25th of May, 1772, and who in the same year inherited the earldom from his cousin, succeeded to the third regimental majority. The Earl, however, did not retain this post in the First Guards above fifteen months, and was succeeded on the 5th of August, 1774, by Colonel Launcelot Baugh. The practice of out-duties being furnished by detachments from each regiment, was discontinued in 1774, and in future they were to be found by regiments. The officers also were ordered by Major-General Salter, now the lieutenant-colonel of the regiment, to do duty by battalions instead of regimentally, in order that each battalion might be as complete as possible in the field. Company order books were now for the first time introduced, and the dress of officers of Grenadiers was more assimilated to that of other battalion officers by their being directed to wear the same sort of epaulettes.

We must now refer shortly to the causes which for the last twelve years had been threatening a rupture between Great Britain and her North American colonies, and which in 1775 produced open war between the two countries, during which, a portion of the brigade of Guards was throughout actively employed.

CHAPTER XVIII.

1773—1778.

CAUSES OF AMERICAN WAR—GUARDS SENT TO NORTH AMERICA—FLATBUSH, NEW YORK, WHITEPLAINS, FORT WASHINGTON, TRENTON—CAMPAIGN OF 1777—WESTFIELD—BRANDYWINE—BURGOYNE'S SURRENDER—ALLIANCE OF FRANCE WITH BRITISH NORTH AMERICANS—CAMPAIGN OF 1778—SIR WILLIAM HOWE RESIGNS—SIR HENRY CLINTON—MARCH FROM PHILADELPHIA TO SANDYCREEK — FRESHFIELD — FRENCH FLEET THREATENS NEW YORK—PREPARATIONS FOR DEFENCE—GUARDS IN NEW YORK.

1773.   THE Seven Years' War had much impoverished the British exchequer, increasing the funded debt to one hundred millions; and notwithstanding the great reductions made during the first year of the peace in 1763, the expenditure of the country still exceeded the revenue. Mr. Grenville, then prime minister, with the view to increasing the sources of supply, proposed that the North American colonies should share the burdens entailed by the late war. These colonies, thirteen in number, which subsequently became the United States of North America, contained at this time, besides half a million of other castes, a population of two million Europeans, all at that time well disposed towards the mother country. Much irritation was, however, now caused amongst them by the new duties, and in 1765 that irritation was still more increased by the passing of the Stamp Act, the estimated revenue from which did not exceed 100,000*l.* a year. This Stamp Act was received with indignation by the colonists, and a congress of representatives from the provincial assemblies met at New York, which denied the right of the mother country to tax them without their consent. After some violent debates in Parliament, the Act was repealed in 1766, and the public mind in America was for a time tranquillized. An Act was, however, subsequently

Map of the
BRITISH COLONIES
of
NORTH AMERICA
AT THE TIME OF THE BREAKINGOUT
of the
AMERICAN WAR
1776.

passed, imposing on the Americans import duties on tea, 1775. and in 1768 this fatal measure aroused such a spirit of resistance amongst the colonists, particularly in Massachusetts and its capital of Boston, that a military force was sent for, which still further exasperated the population, 'and in New York the Assembly refused to provide barracks, fuel, and other articles for the British troops quartered in the city. Unsuccessful attempts were made in the House of Commons to repeal these obnoxious duties, and in 1778, Lord North added to the irritation by introducing a further tax upon the direct importation of tea to America. The colonists refused to be thus burdened without their consent, and the Port of Boston was by order from the British government closed against commerce.

General Gage, who had six regiments under his command 1775. in America, was in 1775 appointed governor of Massachusetts, but his authority was confined almost exclusively to Boston, where his troops were quartered. A conference of delegates again met, this time in Philadelphia, at which though the members acknowledged the sovereignty of Great Britain, they declared the proceedings of the government to be oppressive, and resolved to prevent their being carried into effect, for which purpose they called out their militia, and commenced collecting warlike stores. A vain attempt was made by Lord Chatham to induce the Commons to renounce the right of taxing the Americans without their consent, and Franklin's prayer to be heard at the bar of the House of Commons was also rejected.

A hitherto loyal dependency thus became alienated from the Crown, and with such smothered feelings rankling in their minds a mere accident sufficed to kindle the flames of civil war, and it was not long before a collision took place. General Gage hearing that military stores were being collected at Concord, about twenty miles from Boston, dispatched a April. secret expedition of 800 men, under Colonel Smith, to destroy them. On the march he met with some opposition from the militia, who were assembling at Lexington, but he reached Concord, and succeeded in his object,—on his

1775. return, however, the opposition at Lexington was renewed; and the militia, concealed behind houses, ditches, and woods, inflicted considerable losses upon his detachment, till he was reinforced by Lord Percy, and eventually found security under the guns of Charlestown, opposite Boston. Thus was the first blood shed, and the War of Independence commenced. Further reinforcements were sent out from England to General Gage, thus increasing his force to 10,000 men, and he proceeded to fortify Boston, whereupon the Americans, under Washington, invested it with 20,000 troops, and seized the heights of Bunker's Hill, commanding the town. General William Howe, brother to the Admiral Lord Howe, was sent by Gage to dislodge them,

June 17. and after a very serious encounter, in which the British were twice repulsed, they eventually succeeded in driving the Americans from the field, but with a loss of above 1000 men, while the loss of the Americans was very much smaller. The contest had now commenced in earnest. General Gage was recalled, and in the month of August, 1775, General William Howe, who was on the spot, was appointed commander-in-chief, with Generals Clinton and Burgoyne under him.

George Washington, who had been appointed to command

June 19.. the American armies, commenced, on the 19th of June, by blockading General Howe in Boston, and sending an expedition to Canada, in hopes that upon the appearance of the Americans in that now British colony, the old French colonists would rise against their new masters. Two expeditions were dispatched by Washington, of which one of 3000 men against Montreal, obliged the British Governor-General Carleton to evacuate that town, but the other of 1500 against Quebec, failed in its object. The American forces that had formed these expeditions having subsequently united, made another unsuccessful attempt against Quebec at the end of the year 1775, and shortly afterwards, General Carleton, receiving reinforcements from England, compelled the enemy to a precipitate retreat, and drove them out of Canada.

The news of the battle of Bunker's Hill, followed by the invasion of Canada, aroused the British Government to a sense of the formidable foe they had to encounter. Already in the autumn of 1775 they had dispatched several regiments to America* under the command of Major-General the Earl of Cavan, late of the First Guards. More active measures were now taken to recruit the army generally, and with the view to increasing the establishment of the three regiments of Foot Guards, several sergeants were detached to Ireland to raise recruits in that country. Nine sergeants of the first, and seven of each of the other two regiments were dispatched from London on the 21st, 22nd, and 23rd of August respectively, and proceeding by Chester reached their destination early in September, when they reported their arrival to the adjutant-general.

Upon the retirement of Major-General Salter from the command of the First Regiment, after holding that post for five years, he was succeeded on the 8th of August by Major-General Honourable Philip Sherrard, son of the Earl of Harborough, who, however, held it but one month, being appointed to the colonelcy of the 69th Regiment in September, when Colonel Francis Craig, from the Coldstream Guards, was gazetted on the 8th of September, 1775, to the lieutenant-colonelcy of the First Regiment. Colonels Launcelot Baugh, William Style, and William Tryon had become the majors commanding the three battalions, on the 8th of August, on the retirement of General Salter, and no alterations took place in these commands upon the appointment of Colonel Craig, nor do the circumstances under which such an appointment was made from the Coldstreams appear on record.

When Parliament assembled on the 26th of October, the King announced that his subjects in some of the American provinces were aiming at the establishment of a separate government and an independent empire, and that he had therefore seen fit to increase the naval and military establishments of the country, as it was absolutely necessary to adopt some decisive measures. After a stormy debate the ministry carried their point by a majority of 170, whereupon

* The 17th, 27th, 28th, 46th, 55th, and 56th.

1776.

February.

it was resolved to maintain 25,000 troops in North America, and that the navy should be increased to 28,000 men and eighty ships. The ministry, after some opposition in both Houses, early in the following year, 1776, carried also the question of the employment of foreign troops, and active steps were taken to send out a powerful reinforcement to the colonies. Regiments were ordered to assemble there from the West Indies, and the Mediterranean, as well as from England, and treaties were concluded with the Hessians and other German princes for the hire of their troops.

The following are the names of the officers of the First Guards in January, 1776, at the commencement of the war with the British North American colonies :—

Francis Craig, Lieut.-Col. Maj.-Gen. 8th Sep., 1775.
Launcelot Baugh, 1st Major, Col., 8th August, 1775, retired 19th February, 1776.
William Style, 2nd Major, Col., 8th August, 1775, to 1st Major, 19th February, 1776.
William Tryon, 3rd Major, Col., 8th June, 1775, to 2nd Major, 19th February, 1776.

CAPTAINS AND LIEU-TENANT COLONELS.	LIEUTENANTS AND CAPTAINS.	ENSIGNS.
Wm. Miles,	Gerard Lake,	Kingsmill Evans,
Wm. Thornton, 3rd Major, Feb., 1776,	Hon. John Byng,	Walter Strickland,
Thos. Howard,	Mich. Cox,	H. Fanshawe,
Wm. Hudson,	Thomas Gordon,	Colin Campbell,
West-Hyde,	Robt. Keith,	Arch. Edmonstone,
Sir John Wrottesley, Bart.	Fred. Madan,	Hon. G. Hanger,
Saml. Wollaston,	John Woodford,	Will. Heywood,
Robt. Haseler,	W. C. Farrell Skeffington,	John Milbanke,
Th. Cox,	Samuel Hulse,	John Turner,
G. Garth,	John Horton,	Ch. Whitworth,
John Deaken,	Alb. Bertie,	Hon. F. Finch,
Will. Fielding,	Hon. I. T. De Burgh,	Th. Dowdeswell,
John Howard,	Nicholas Bayly,	Hon. W. K. Nassau,
Temple West,	G. Dewar,	Th. Glyn,
Hon. Sl. Digby,	Robt. Hampden Pye,	Willm. Colquhoun,
John Leland,	Isaac Pratveil,	A. J. Drummond,
Wm. Fleming,	Will. Leeves,	E. Satchwell Fraser,
John Dodd,	G. Ascough,	Hon. G. Parker,
	Ch. Frederick,	John Jones,
		F. Dundas,

Chap. XVIII.] *under H.R.H. Wm. Duke of Gloucester.* 213

1776.

Captains and Lieu-tenant Colonels.	Lieutenants and Captains.	Ensigns.
Sam. Stewart,	Hon. R. Fitzpatrick,	J. Bridges Townshend,
Lord T. P. Clinton,	Patrick Bellew,	Thos. Hussey,
Hon. Robert Seymour Conway,	Fred. Thomas,	Hon. H. Phipps,
G. Hotham,	Thos. Colins,	— Dury.
Th. Edmondes,	Rd. Steynor Jones,	
	John Scawen,	
	F. D'Oyly,	
	Hon. Rt. Fulke Greville,	
	Jas. Duffe,	
	Rich. Nugent,	
	Ch. Talbot,	
	Jacob Whittington.	

STAFF.

Chaplain.—John Fox.

Adjutants.—John Woodford, Henry Fanshawe, and Fran. Richardson.

Quarter-masters.—Rees Williams, and Thomas Gordon.

Surgeon.—Lewis Davis.

Solicitor.—Rowland Maltby.

Colonel Launcelot Baugh, as well as Colonel William Miles, retired on the 19th of February following, when Colonels William Style, William Tryon, and William Thornton, became the first, second, and third majors, and Gerard Lake, the future Lord Lake, was promoted to a company in the regiment.

Amongst the corps to be sent from England was a com- Feb. 13. bined battalion of 1000 men of the Guards, composed of drafts from the three regiments, the command of which was given to Colonel William Mathew of the Coldstreams with the rank of brigadier. The detachment of the First Guards, according to brigade orders of the 13th of February, 1776, consisted of thirteen officers and 465 non-commissioned officers and men.* One combined Grenadier, and one combined light infantry company were also formed from the

* Four captains, five lieutenants, and four ensigns, eighteen sergeants, eighteen corporals, seven drummers, two fifers, and 420 privates, or fifteen men drafted from each of the twenty-eight companies.

several drafts for foreign service, in the following proportions
for each company :—

	Sergt.	Corpl.	Men.
1st regt. Foot Guards	2	2	42
Coldstream Guards	1	1	27
3rd regt. Foot Guards	1	1	27
Total	4	4	96

The officers of the First Guards selected for this duty,
on the 13th of March, were taken from the three battalions
as follows :—

From the 1st Battalion.

Lieut.-Col. Thos. Howard.
Lieut.-Col. Thomas Cox.
Captain Michael Cox (Adjt.).
Captain Robert Keith.
Ensign Charles Whitworth.

From the 2nd Battalion.

Lieut.-Col. Sir John Wrottesley.
Captain I. T. de Burgh.
Ensign John Turner.
Ensign Finch.

From the 3rd Battalion.

Lieut.-Col. West Hyde.
Captain Albert Bertie.

Captain Thomas Gordon.
Ensign Thomas Dowdeswell.

They were ordered to supply themselves with a uniform with white lace, and to discontinue carrying spontoons
and halberts, so as to assimilate their appearance more to that
of the men, a report being current that the Americans were
in the habit of picking off the officers, who were too easily
distinguished from the rank and file. The Secretary-at-War
wrote at the same time to General Howe, announcing to him
that it was the King's pleasure to send the above battalion of
Guards, under Colonel Mathew, to Portsmouth, with their
camp equipage and tents, to embark in the course of the
month for North America. The following detail of the
detachment was enclosed in the above letter :—

10 Captains and Lieut.-Cols.
11 Lieut. and Captains.
9 Ensigns.
42 Sergeants.
40 Corporals.
20 Drummers.
960 Private men.

1 Brigadier.
1 Major of Brigade.
1 Chaplain.
1 Adjutant.
1 Quarter-master.
1 Surgeon.
3 Mates.

Captain Cox of the First Guards was appointed adjutant   1776.
of this battalion; Captain Stevens, the brigade-major, and
Captain Lister, the quarter-master, were from the two other
regiments.

This combined battalion of thirty officers and 1062 men
of all ranks left London in three divisions on Friday, the March 15.
15th of March, to be quartered for a time in the neighbouring villages west of London, as follows:—

1. The Grenadier company,   at Hammersmith.
2. The Light Infantry comp.   at Turnham-green.
3. 1st company 1st Regt.
   Lieut.-Col. Thos. Howard,   at Putney.
4. 2nd company 1st Regt.
   Lieut.-Col. Wrottesley,   at Fulham.
5. 3rd company 1st Regt.
   Lieut.-Col. Hyde,   at Parsons and Walham Green.
6. Brigade company, 1st Regt.
   Lieut.-Col. Cox,   at Clapham, and the Common.
7. 1st company 3rd Regt.,
   Lieut.-Col. Ogilvie,   at Wandsworth.
8. 2nd company 3rd Regt.,
   Lieut.-Col. Twistleton,   at Wimbledon and Roehampton.
9. 1st company Coldstreams,
   Lieut.-Col. Trelawney,   at Mitcham and Tooting.
10. 2nd company Coldstreams,
    Lieut.-Col. Wyndham,   at Merton.

On the 19th of March the King reviewed this battalion on March 19
Wimbledon Common, and on the 1st of April it proceeded in
two divisions of five companies each—one to Chichester, the
other to Guildford and Godalming, with orders to remain
there till the transports were ready to convey them to
America. They eventually embarked on the 29th of April, April 29.
and the officers of the First Guards who finally sailed with
their companies on this service were—

CAPTAINS AND LIEUT.-COLONELS.	LIEUTENANTS AND CAPTAINS.	ENSIGNS.
Thomas Howard.	Thomas Gordon.	Charles Whitworth.
West Hyde.	Robert Keith.	Hon. J. Finch.
Sir J. Wrottesley.	Frederick Madan.	T. Dowdeswell.
John Cox.	Hon. J. T. de Burgh.	Hon. W. K. Nassau.
	Nicholas Bayly.	Thomas Glyn.

Lieut.-Colonels Garth and Bayly joined them during the summer.

1776.

After a further delay of a fortnight, the fleet and transports, under Admirals Lord Howe and Parker, carrying the Guards and other large reinforcements to support their comrades in America, sailed from Spithead on the 12th of May.

In the meantime, Washington having, at the end of February, 1776, gained possession of Dorchester heights, from whence he could bombard Boston, the British army in garrison there was placed in a very critical position, and General Howe resolved upon evacuating the town. He embarked his army, without molestation, on the 6th of March,

March 6.

and sailing out of Massachusetts Bay, directed his course to Halifax, but hearing while there, that there was to be a general concentration of British troops on Staten Island, with the view to attacking New York, he left Halifax on the

June 12.

12th of June, and landed his forces on that island on the 3rd of July, where he awaited the reinforcements from England.

The fleet, under Lord Howe, with part of these, arrived off Boston, in Massachusetts Bay, in the middle of June, and the admiral, after following General Howe to Halifax, directed his course thence to Staten Island, which he

July 12.

reached on the 12th of July. The Foot Guards and the Hessians, under the convoy of Commodore Hotham, in the " Preston," of 50 guns, did not reach Staten Island

Aug. 12.

till the 12th of August, and two days later the Commodore, Sir Peter Parker, arrived from the south with three thousand more troops, under Lieutenant-General Clinton, when the British forces assembled on Staten Island amounted to 30,000 men, including a considerable number of German mercenaries, and were at once organized as follows, in brigades and divisions :—

General commanding, General William Howe.

Lieut.-Generals.—H. Clinton, Earl Percy, Earl of Cornwallis.

The Brigade of Foot Guards under Brigadier Mathew.

1st Brigade Maj.-General Robert Pigott, 4th, 27th, 45th, 15th.
2nd   ,,   Brig.-General James Agnew, 5th, 35th, 49th, 28th.
3rd   ,,   Maj.-General Valentine Jones, 10th, 38th, 52nd, 37th.
4th   ,,   Maj.-General James Grant,   17th, 46th, 55th, 40th.

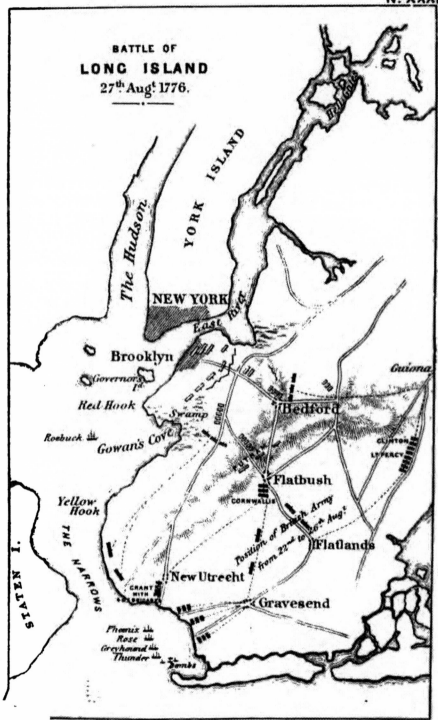

BATTLE OF
LONG ISLAND
27th Augt 1776.

5th Brigade	Brig.-General Francis Smith,	22nd, 54th, 63rd, 43rd.	
6th ,,	J. Robertson,	23rd, 57th, 64th, 44th.	
7th ,,	Sir William Erskine,	71st, 2 bat. 17th Lt. Cav.	
8th ,,	the reserve, Maj.-General Vaughan, 33rd, 42nd, and		
		4 bat. of Grenadiers.	
9th ,,	Leslie, 4 Light Infantry battalions.		

And two battalions of Marines and some Artillery.

There were also about twenty battalions of Hessian troops, under Lieut.-General Baron de Knyphausen and Maj.-General Leopold de Heister.

General Clinton commanded the First Division, consisting of the 1st, 2nd, 5th, and 6th brigades.

Lieut.-General Earl Percy the Second Division, consisting of the 3rd, 4th, and Vaughan's four battalions of Grenadiers.

Lord Cornwallis commanded in chief the reserve, consisting, besides the Hessians, of some of the remaining corps.

On the arrival of the Guards, who appear at once to have been formed into a brigade of two battalions, they were welcomed by the governor of New York, their brother officer, Colonel William Tryon, second major of the First Guards, who since May, 1775, had been employed in Carolina, and had only lately received his appointment at New York ; but he had scarcely entered upon his duties, when he found himself forced to seek refuge on board a British vessel, from whence he in vain issued proclamations urging on the people to return to their allegiance.

It was much to be regretted that many of the reinforcements had not arrived two months earlier, when Washington had not above 9000 men fit for duty, of which 2000 were still unarmed ; but the troops being now all assembled, General Howe was enabled to assume the offensive, and with the view of attacking New York, resolved to transport the army across the Narrows to Long Island. Accordingly, on the 22nd of August he sent a division of Aug. 22. 4000 men across in boats, which effected a landing without much opposition at Gravesend Bay, the rest of the troops following in ships or boats. The Guards landed near Utrecht, under cover of the fire of Commodore Hotham's squadron, experiencing very little resistance, and immediately marched to Flatlands, with the second division under Earl Percy, and a brigade of Hessians, under the gallant old officer, Major-General Heister.

The main body of the enemy was at Brooklyn, round which and along the river-side they had constructed a line of entrenchments secured by abattis, and it was partly covered by a swamp. As soon as the British landed, the Americans withdrew their troops within the above lines, burning or otherwise destroying all houses or granaries on the road, but leaving an advanced body of 10,000 men, under General Putnam, to occupy the wooded heights in their front which separated the two armies, and to defend them against any attempts of the British. General Howe was not long in deciding on his plan of attack. The American centre was posted in rear of the village of Flatbush, to which the Hessians, under De Heister, were sent to attract the enemy's attention, while Clinton was directed to turn the American left with the right wing of the British, supported by Lord Percy and the brigade of Guards. Upon the army advancing on the 26th of August, Clinton gained the pass of Guiona, in front of the extreme left of the enemy, which

they had failed to occupy, and at nine o'clock the following morning, he effected the passage of the hills and reached Bedford, when the enemy, after a short fight, fell back in confusion to their lines near Brooklyn, which the British were eager to assault, but were prevented by Lord Howe, who repeatedly sent orders that they should desist.

During the attack of the right wing, De Heister, who commanded the centre at Flatbush, under Cornwallis, opened a heavy cannonade on the enemy, and sent forward Colonel Donop's Hessian corps, supported by the light infantry battalions, while a considerable detachment of the Foot Guards was sent forward to join in the affair. These troops were very warmly engaged with superior numbers in the woods, took three pieces of cannon, and on the approach of the Hessians completely routed the enemy. General Grant, commanding the fourth brigade on the left,

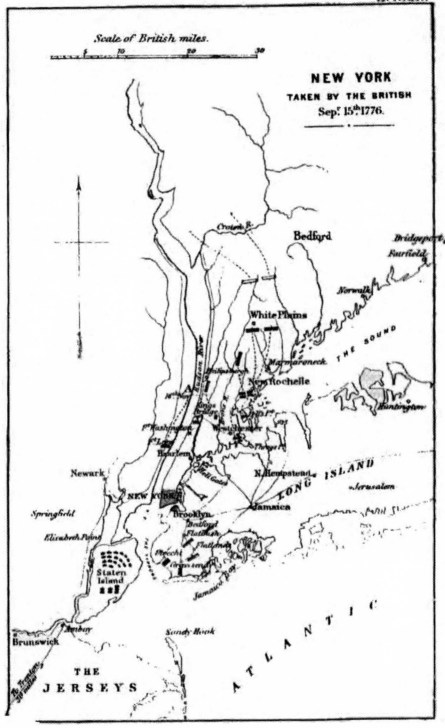

Scale of British miles.

NEW YORK
TAKEN BY THE BRITISH
Sep.ʳ 15ᵗʰ 1776.

advanced against the enemy's right. A heavy cannonade 1776. ensued, which lasted till the enemy, hearing of the retreat of their left wing, became apprehensive of being cut off from their lines, and suddenly retired across a morass, or mill creek, which covered the right of their works. General Howe, knowing that the position of the enemy in Brooklyn was untenable, desisted from further pursuit, in order to avoid unnecessary bloodshed, and, in fact, the Americans evacuated Brooklyn two days later under cover of a fog, and crossed over to New York. Their loss in the action had been great, amounting to 2000 killed in the field, drowned, Aug. 29. or taken prisoners; amongst the latter were Generals Sullivan, Hall, and Lord Sterling; they also lost six brass field-pieces. The English loss did not exceed sixty or seventy killed, and about 230 wounded. The British troops displayed on this occasion great activity and valour, and it was not without difficulty that they were restrained from attacking the American lines.

After some fruitless attempts to negotiate, General Howe Sept. 15. resolved on the 15th of September to attack New York itself, situated on the southern extremity of York Island, from which he was only separated by the East river, 1300 yards broad. Washington's army, now increased to 23,000 men, was advantageously posted in York Island, but most of the men were raw and undisciplined recruits; 4500 were in the town itself, 6500 at Haerlem, ten miles off, and 12,000 at Kingsbridge, which place was fortified so as to secure a retreat from the island, if necessary. The troops in New York could not long withstand the furious cannonade opened upon them from the five men-of-war that were stationed to cover the embarcation of the army, and they eventually evacuated the town, retiring to Haerlem. The British troops then crossed over without further opposition, and took possession on the same day. The Guards were at first quartered in New York, while the leading divisions of the British army were encamped immediately outside the town, across the island of Manhattan, protected on each flank by ships of war lying in the Hudson and in the East

1776. river. Subsequently the Guards joined the rest of the army in the camp; but were very shortly ordered again into New York, in consequence of a great fire which some unprincipled zealots had kindled on the night of the

Sept. 21. 20th–21st of September, with the view to destroying it, rather than it should become a place of refuge for the British army. The flames spread considerably, and but for the exertions of the Guards and the troops in garrison, more of the town would have suffered; about one-fourth of it, however, was consumed, and ten days later the equestrian statue of George III. was pulled down by the rebels, to the great indignation of the Guards at such an insult being offered to their Sovereign. New York remained in possession of the King's forces during the whole progress of the war, till the final evacuation on the 25th of November, 1783, and formed the principal base on which all minor operations turned.

Oct. 12. With the view to forcing the Americans from their strong position at Haerlem without having recourse to a direct attack on their lines, General Howe, leaving four brigades in New York, under Lord Percy, embarked the Guards and the rest of the army on the 12th of October, and passing up East River through the passage called Hell Gates, landed his troops at Frog's Neck, from whence if he had advanced rapidly he might have surrounded the American army before they could retire by Kingsbridge. General Washington had proposed to await the conflict on York Island, but upon the advice of General Lee, withdrew all his troops, and posted them behind entrenchments extending from Kingsbridge to Whiteplains, facing the east, having the Brunx, a deep river, in their front. General Howe determined to pursue, in the hope of still bringing the enemy to action, and the British troops accordingly re-

Oct. 18. embarking at Frog's Neck on the 18th, landed a little further eastward at Pell's Point, with but slight opposition, and with the loss of thirty-two men killed and wounded. On the 21st the main body reached New Rochelle, whence it advanced towards Whiteplains, where the American army was concentrating, and on the approach of the British on the morning of the 28th of October, the Americans hastily struck their tents and prepared for action. The British army formed at once in two lines behind some rising ground ; Sir Henry Clinton's division, to which the brigade of Guards was now attached, forming the right wing, while General Howe placed himself at the head of the left wing, and as the Americans continued to strengthen their position, the British attacked and drove them from their advanced posts into their intrenchments.

1776.
Oct. 28.

Battle of White-plains.

Further reinforcements, under Lord Percy, from York Island, reached the royal army on the 30th, and Howe prepared to attack the enemy the following day; but the weather proved unpropitious, and on the morning of the 1st of November, the Americans abandoned their position and retired across the Croton river. Howe, instead of pursuing, directed his attention to the reduction of Kingsbridge and Fort Washington, for which purpose he turned south, dividing his army into four columns of attack—the first, under Knyphausen, was sent against Kingsbridge ; the second, under Cornwallis, including the brigade of Guards and light infantry under Brigadier Mathew, two battalions of Grenadiers, and the 33rd Regiment, was conveyed in flat-bottomed boats to Haerlem Creek ; the two other columns advanced in other directions. The second column with the Guards, on landing, marched straight up the hill on which stands Fort Washington; and after passing with great labour a thick wood, the passage of which was rendered all the more difficult by the erection of abattis, they established themselves on the summit. The other columns were equally successful, when the garrison, finding it impossible to hold out, surrendered prisoners of war. The royal army lost about 800 killed and wounded; the loss of the American garrison was about 3000, including the prisoners. Two days later, General Howe dispatched Cornwallis with his troops across the Hudson, to capture Fort Lee. The troops engaged in this operation were, the brigade of Guards, five battalions of Grenadiers, including

Oct. 30.

Nov. 16.

Nov. 18.

the Hessians and four other regiments. No sooner had Cornwallis crossed the Hudson on the 18th of November, and landed on its western bank, than with great secrecy he moved off in a southerly direction towards the fort; but the garrison, having timely notice of his approach, abandoned it, and retreated in the utmost confusion towards Brunswick, leaving their tents, provisions, and military stores behind them, and the fort was taken possession of. The Guards and the rest of Cornwallis's troops pursued towards Brunswick, and the Americans, continuing their retreat, left the Jerseys in possession of the royal army. On the 24th Cornwallis was ordered to discontinue the pursuit and remain at Brunswick, an order which saved the Americans from total destruction, and the troops remained accordingly at Brunswick till
the beginning of December. On the 7th of that month they again advanced, when the Americans retired across the Delaware. Shortly afterwards the cold weather setting in, the troops went into winter quarters; the Guards, the Grenadiers, and light infantry of the army, and the second and fourth brigades remaining at Brunswick. The first brigade returned to New York, the sixth to Haerlem, the third to Amboy, the fifth to Rhode Island, while the Hessians occupied Trenton and Bordenton to the south on the Delaware, as the most advanced posts of the royal army.

General (now Sir William) Howe in his report of the late proceedings, says: "I cannot too much commend Lord Cornwallis's services, and particularly the ability he displayed in the pursuit of the enemy from Fort Lee to Trenton, a distance of eighty miles, on which occasion he was well supported by the ardour of his corps, who cheerfully quitted their tents and heavy baggage as impediments to their march."

Though the British army had been so far successful, the advantages they had gained over the colonists, at Long Island, New York, Whiteplains, as well as at Forts Washington and Lee, were not commensurate with the great superiority of the royal army over the half-drilled and badly

equipped raw levies of the colonists, and Sir William   1776.
Howe has been much criticised for his want of vigour in
following up his successes, as well as for the too extended
line of eighty miles, along which he placed his troops in
winter quarters. The Americans were, however, much dispirited by the result of the campaign,—the men who had
enlisted only for one year claimed their discharge, while
others returned to their allegiance, whereby their army was
for a time reduced to little more than 3000 or 4000 men;
but the severest blow in a military point of view to their
cause, was the capture of Lee, their best General, which was
effected by Colonel Harcourt and a detachment of light
horse; and Howe refused to release him on exchange, on
the plea that he was a deserter from the British service.

While things appeared at their worst for the cause of the   Dec. 26.
colonists, Washington took advantage of the fancied security
of the Hessian advanced post at Trenton, and collecting
4000 or 5000 men at Philadelphia, succeeded, by a combined movement, in capturing upwards of 1000 Hessian
cavalry and some artillery, with which he retired across the
Delaware to Philadelphia, as he felt he was not yet in a
position to maintain himself north of that river in the
event of the approach of any British troops.

As soon as the report of the defeat of the Hessians at
Trenton reached General Grant at Brunswick, he ordered
the assembly of the British forces in his neighbourhood,
and proceeded to Princetown, where he was shortly joined
by Cornwallis from New York, who took the command and
advanced towards the enemy. Thereupon Washington again
crossed the Delaware, taking up a strong position at
Trenton, and Lord Cornwallis found the place so well fortified that, after cannonading it for a few hours, he took
post in the neighbourhood, and on the 3rd of January, found
that Washington had withdrawn his troops unperceived.

Sir William Howe commenced a mid-winter campaign   1777.
early in 1777, with an attempt to remedy the cause of his
late check, by concentrating some of his outlying detachments. He abandoned for the time any further intentions of

1777.   reoccupying Trenton, and withdrew all the troops from the Delaware, sending Lord Cornwallis with reinforcements, to assist in protecting the magazines that were established at Brunswick, where the Guards remained under Brigadier Mathew. Washington, meanwhile, having given the slip to the royal army, advanced to Princetown, retook possession of nearly all the Jerseys, and continuing his advance, threatened Brunswick itself and its magazines, whereupon Brigadier Mathew, commanding the garrison, took the precaution of sending away immense quantities of stores, and posted himself with his small force, including the Guards, on some high ground commanding the town, with the view to covering the retreat of the store waggons. This disposition of his forces and the opportune arrival of Cornwallis saved the town, and forced Washington to desist from any further attempts against it. Washington was however enabled to establish himself for the rest of the winter on the shore opposite Staten Island, near Middleton, in the county of Monmouth. Lord Percy returned to England shortly afterwards, and during the whole winter Sir William Howe was occupied in organizing battalions of loyalists, to assist the army in the ensuing campaign.

Several skirmishes took place during the remainder of the winter between the foraging parties of the enemy and the escorts of provisions for the British army, and Howe organized also several expeditions against the enemy's magazines to the north of New York, which were carried out with success, and without serious loss. The enemy, however, made a successful reprisal towards the end of May, in surprising the troops protecting large stores of hay, grain, and rum, which were being collected at the east end of Long Island for the use of the royal army, and destroying the vessels that contained the provisions.

Several exchanges were allowed amongst the officers of the Guards before the opening of the ensuing campaign. In the First Guards seven, in the Coldstream six, and in the Third Regiment five officers were ordered out in the month of February to replace a similar number then in

America. Lord Barrington, writing to Sir William Howe
on the 3rd of February, announced to him the approaching
arrival of these officers, requesting that, on their arrival,
the relieved officers might be sent home on promotion.

The officers of the First Regiment of Foot Guards thus
ordered for the American service were

Capt. Robt. Hampden Pye,		Capt. Charles Whitworth,
G. Ayscough,		,, Hon. J. Finch,
Hon. R. Fitz-		,, J. Dowdeswell,
patrick,	to replace	,, Hon. W. K.
Ensigns E. S. Fraser,		Nassau,
G. Parker,		,, Thos. Glyn,
John Jones,		,, Will. Colquhoun,
Fredk. Dundas,		,, A. J. Drummond.

A draft of thirty men was also sent out from the home
companies in March, and a second draft of thirty-two men
in May.

Sir William Howe was delayed in opening the campaign in
the spring of 1777 by the want of tents. The troops in the
Jerseys, under Lord Cornwallis, were however assembled in
camp on the hills near Brunswick towards the end of May. May 26.
Washington had succeeded at that time in collecting and
arming about 7000 men, with whom he advanced to the hilly
country around Middlebrook, within a few miles of Brunswick,
where he took up so strong a position that Howe, who was
enabled at last by the 13th of June to take the field, and June 13.
whose object was to penetrate across the Delaware to Philadelphia, hesitated to attack him in front. He determined to
feign a retreat, ordered his army to fall back through
Amboy, constructed bridges as if to bring it all over into
Staten Island, and himself retired to New York. This
device succeeded ; Washington quitted his stronghold and
made a forward movement, whereupon Howe returned to
Amboy, advanced on the 26th with his army to meet the June 26.
enemy, and detached Cornwallis with the British Guards
and Hessians by a circuitous road to the right to turn his left
flank. Cornwallis soon fell in with a corps of Washington's
army, under Lord Sterling and General Maxwell, which

1777.

June 26.   was strongly posted in a woody country near Westfield. The brigade of Guards and the Hessians advanced to the attack, and during the action, so great was the emulation between these troops that they not only routed the Americans but captured from them three field-pieces, occupied Westfield, and advanced the following day to Samplow. Captain Honourable John Finch, of the light infantry of the First Guards, was wounded on this occasion, and died at Amboy on the 29th of June following. The Americans lost 200 men. In consequence of this defeat Washington retired to his former strong position among the hills, and Sir William Howe, finding that he could not induce him again to come to action, resolved to withdraw from the Jerseys, with the view of reaching Philadelphia

June 28.   from the south, and quitting Amboy on the 28th of June, he crossed over on the following day to Staten Island.

Sir William's plan was, while leaving Sir Henry Clinton in command of some troops for the defence of New York, to embark the rest of the army, sail round to the head of the Delaware Bay, and march thence overland to Philadelphia, a movement which would turn Washington's position, and force him to move south for the defence of that town. The expedition consisted of the two battalions of the brigade of Guards commanded respectively by Colonel Trelawney of the Coldstreams, and Lieutenant-Colonel Ogilvie of the Third Guards: of five other British brigades under Cornwallis; and two Hessian brigades under Knyphausen, with some cavalry and artillery—total infantry, twenty-three British and eleven foreign battalions, all under Sir William Howe himself.

The fleet of 267 sail, under Lord Howe, on board of which this expedition was embarked early in the month of

July 23.   July, put to sea on the 23rd, but owing to contrary winds, did not reach the Delaware till the 29th, when the navigation of that river being found to be obstructed, the fleet sailed to the Chesapeak, which it entered on the 15th of August, and with the assistance of pilots, proceeded to an anchorage between the mouths of the Sasafras and Elk

BATTLE
of
BRANDYWINE
11th Sept. 1777.

rivers, at the head of Chesapeak Bay, reaching it on the
22nd of that month. Washington was long left in doubt
as to the destination of this large force; but as soon
as he heard from trustworthy sources that the fleet was
sailing up the Chesapeak, he divined the intention of
the British commander, and, after sending detachments
to Connecticut and Saratoga, withdrew the bulk of his
army from the Jerseys, crossed the Delaware, and repaired
to Philadelphia, directing his army of 20,000 men to take
up a position at Brandywine Creek, about twenty miles
beyond Philadelphia. Lords Howe and Cornwallis landed
on the 25th of August on the northern shore, opposite Cecil
Court House, six miles from Turkey Point, and about sixty
miles south-west of Philadelphia. On the 28th the troops
moved to the head of the Elk river, and on the 3rd of Sept. 3.
September five miles further to Iron Hill, whence they could
command a view of the Delaware. Here General Howe,
hearing that the American army was in position at Brandywine Creek, ready to dispute with him the passage of that
river, gradually moved his forces towards the enemy, and on
the 11th of September advanced in two columns, detaching Sept. 11.
one under Cornwallis, with the Guards and other regiments, Battle of
to cross the river more to the left, and the other under Brandy-
Knyphausen towards Chad's Ford; whereupon Washington wine Creek.
detached 10,000 men to his right, under General Sullivan,
who took up a strong position on commanding ground
above Birmingham Church, with his left near Brandywine
Creek, both flanks being covered by thick woods, and his
artillery advantageously posted. As soon as Howe observed See Plan.
this movement he directed the King's troops to advance. On
approaching the enemy Cornwallis formed his line of battle
with the right towards Brandywine, the Guards being on
the extreme right, with the British Grenadiers on their left,
supported by the Hessian Grenadiers in second line. To
the left were the two battalions of light infantry, with the
Hessian and Anspach chasseurs, supported by the fourth
brigade; the third brigade forming the reserve. The
light infantry and Chasseurs began the attack; the Guards

and Grenadiers instantly advanced from the right, the whole under a heavy fire of artillery and musketry, and the attack was made with such impetuosity, that the enemy could not withstand it; they fell back into the woods in their rear, pursued for nearly two miles by the King's troops, who entered with them. The Guards and a battalion of Grenadiers, with some Hessians, got entangled in the woods for a time during the pursuit, and lost sight of the enemy; later in the day, however, the Guards appeared again on the right flank, when the retreat of the enemy became general, but darkness coming on before Knyphausen's corps could reach the heights, checked the pursuit. Part of the enemy retired that night to Chester, the remainder to Philadelphia; their loss in officers, both killed and wounded, was considerable, and of men they lost 300 killed, 600 wounded, and nearly 400 prisoners. The British loss was much slighter—80 killed, and 400 wounded. In the brigade of Guards one man only was killed, five wounded, and one missing.

The royal troops lay that night on the field of battle. On the following day the pursuit of the enemy continued, and small affairs were constantly occurring between the two armies till, on the 21st of September, the British army encamped on the banks of the Schuylkill river, which runs into the Delaware below Philadelphia. This position extended from Fatland Fort to French Creek. The following day the Grenadiers and light infantry of the Guards were sent across the Schuylkill at Fatland Fort, while some Chasseurs crossed it at Gordon's Ford. During the night the whole army followed, and on the 25th of September marched in two columns to occupy Germantown, about six miles from Philadelphia. On the 26th Lord Cornwallis with the British Grenadiers and two battalions of Hessians, took possession of Philadelphia, and at once proceeded to place it in a posture of defence, during which an attack of the Americans by water was defeated. Sir William Howe having thus succeeded in carrying out the first part of his plan of operations, the admiral, Lord

Sept. 21.

Sept. 25.

BATTLE OF
GERMANTOWN
October 4th 1777.

AA. *Outposts of the British Army*
B. *Advance of Left Wing under Knyphausen to 2nd Position.*
C. *Original Position of Brigade of Guards under Mather*
D. *British Guards covering Head Quarters*
E. *Advance of Right Wing with Guards to 2nd Position.*
F. *Advance of Right Wing of Enemy to Germantown*
G. *General Grant's Right Wing attacking Washington and forcing him to retreat.*

Scale of miles

Howe, with part of his fleet, came round from the Chesapeak to the Delaware, with stores for the army, three regiments being detached down the river from Philadelphia to Chester and Billing's Point, to convoy them to head-quarters.

Washington immediately endeavoured to take advantage of this weakening of the British force at Philadelphia, and advanced on the 3rd of October ·towards Germantown, still occupied by the royal troops. Lieutenant-General Knyphausen held the ground to the left of Village, extending his left to the Schuylkill. Major-General Grant and Brigadier-General Mathew, with the British and Hessian Guards, six other battalions, and two squadrons, formed the right of the line. Early on the 4th of October Oct. 4. the enemy was observed approaching, and the royal troops were immediately ordered under arms. The advanced posts of the British were at first driven in, but the enemy's attack ultimately failed on all points, though not without some serious fighting. Two columns of Americans, which Battle of Germantown. advanced against the Guards and the 27th and 28th Regiments, on the right of the line, were driven back; and Lord Cornwallis coming up from Philadelphia with reinforcements, joined in the pursuit of the enemy, who retired nearly twenty miles from the field of battle toward Parkyomy Creek. The Americans lost 200 killed, 600 wounded, and 400 prisoners. The total British loss was 4 officers, 64 men killed, amongst whom was Brigadier Agnew, 30 officers and 390 men wounded, 1 officer and 13 men missing. The brigade of Guards lost 3 men, wounded; no casualties amongst the officers.

The conduct of officers and men during the late operations elicited from Sir William Howe very high encomiums in his despatch of the 10th of October, to the effect that the late Oct. 10. successes of the army were the best vouchers of the conduct of the general officers, and of the bravery of all other ranks; and that the manner in which they had borne the fatigues of the late marches was a proof of the noble spirit of emulation prevailing in the army to promote the King's service.

1777. It was now decided to attack, both by land and sea, Fort
Island, immediately below Philadelphia, at the mouth of
the Schuylkill.   This operation was successfully carried
Oct. 15. out on the night of the 15th of October, and the Grenadiers
of the Guards took possession of the fort on the following day, when Sir William Howe again expressed
himself with great satisfaction at the behaviour of the
troops engaged.   The British loss was thirteen killed,
thirty wounded; that of the Americans, 400 killed and
wounded.

About this time the news of the unfortunate result of the
operations of Lieutenant-General Burgoyne, and of his surrender at Saratoga, was received, and all thoughts of co-
operation with that army being at an end, Sir William
Howe turned his attention to securing the free navigation of
the Delaware, and to reducing the fort at Red Bank before
General Washington could receive any of the reinforcements now disposable.   All the necessary preparations were
made, and Lord Cornwallis was detached for the purpose
Oct. 19. on the 19th of October to Chester, where, being joined
by other troops, he moved forward to the attack, but the
Americans did not await the assault; they spiked their
guns and evacuated the fort, leaving considerable stores
behind them, and Lord Cornwallis, having demolished the
works on the island, returned by Gloucester to Philadelphia
before the end of the month.   The enemy having now lost
all his strongholds on the Delaware, endeavoured to convey
his ships up that river past Philadelphia.   A few succeeded in passing up, but being detected, the remainder,
seventeen in number, were set on fire.

In consequence of its becoming now known that the
French were entering into an alliance with the so-called
United States, it became necessary for the British to concen-
trate both their fleet and army; but in the meantime their
troops continued at Philadelphia till, at the end of the month
November. of November, Washington, having received a reinforce-
ment of 4000 men, advanced to Whitemarsh, whereupon
Howe moved out with his army, and took up a position

on the 5th of December on Chesnut Hill, in front of the right of the enemy, whom he in vain attempted to draw out. On the 7th he moved to his own right, and took post at Edgehill, in front of the enemy's left, where he attacked with Cornwallis's corps, defeating the troops opposed to him with loss; but being still unable to bring on a general engagement he returned to camp. Another skirmish on a foraging expedition took place on the 11th of December, in neither of which does it appear that the Guards were engaged. After this the Guards and the rest of the army, with the exception of the 71st Regiment, which returned to New York, went into winter quarters in Philadelphia. The Americans, under Washington, remained during the winter, in huts, near Valley Forge, upon the Schuylkill, twenty-six miles distant from the British head-quarters; during the whole of which period no attempts were made by Sir William Howe to dislodge them from the position they had taken up, and the British army remained undisturbed at Philadelphia till June, 1778.

Lieutenant-Colonels Thomas Howard and West Hyde, the two senior officers of the First Guards in America, were both promoted to brevet-colonels in 1777, for their services in that country, as were also Lieutenant-Colonels Twisselton and Stevens, of the 2nd Regiment, and O'Hara and Trelawney, of the Third Guards.

1778.

Major-General Tryon, the nominal second major of the First Guards, who had been serving some time in North America, quitted the regiment on the ·14th of May, 1778, on appointment to the colonelcy of the 70th Regiment, and in September the same year he was appointed to act as major-general on the staff with the forces under Sir William Howe. Colonel William Thornton and Colonel Thomas Howard succeeded to the 2nd and 3rd Regimental majorities, Colonel Thomas Howard continuing in command of the companies of the First Guards in America till the end of this year's campaign.

Many remarks were made even in those days on the want

1777.

Dec. 7.

Dec. 11.

1778.

1778.

of energy and determination shown by Sir William Howe, in not following up the various successes he so often obtained over the rebel army. At Long Island, in the Jerseys, at Brandywine, at Whitemarsh, and at Valley Forge, the enemy was ever within his grasp, but he failed to take advantage of the opportunities offered, and his supineness, according to the present ideas of carrying on war, is not consistent with the idea of his being a great strategist.

Sir William Howe having, at the end of the previous year, applied for leave to resign, received permission on the 14th of April to return to England. He appears most unjustly to have given as a reason for his wish to resign, the little support he received from his superiors at home, but for this there was no ground, as he had under his command many thousand men more than he had declared would be sufficient to overcome the enemy. Sir William, after participating with his brother in a magnificent triumphal fête, got up in their honour by the officers of the army at Philadelphia, returned to England, leaving the command of the army to Sir Henry Clinton, who received his appoint-

May.

ment on the 8th of May following.

Several attempts at negociation were made in the course of the spring, but the Americans would listen to no proposals that did not recognise their absolute independence. In the month of June the negociations were consequently broken off, and as the French had declared themselves friendly to the American cause, it became necessary to concentrate the army at a point not so distant from the sea as Philadelphia; the first operation therefore that Sir Henry Clinton found himself under the necessity of carrying out, was the evacuation of that town, and a march through the Jerseys to New York. He crossed over to the New Jersey side of the Delaware on the 18th of June, and proceeded northwards towards Sandy Hook, followed at a distance by Washington's army. He was much incommoded by a very large amount of transport, which he sent before him under the charge of Lieutenant-General

Knyphausen; he himself keeping a day's march in rear 1778. with all the British troops under Cornwallis. On the 27th of June, Clinton arrived at his encampment at Freehold Court House, where he was posted on advantageous ground, and the next day resumed his march, but no sooner had June 28. he descended into the plain than the Americans appeared on the ground he had left. Leaving Knyphausen to pursue his route with the baggage, he ordered.Lord Cornwallis to halt and drive the enemy back, which was successfully accomplished. The corps of Grenadiers and the brigade of Guards posted on the right of the village of Freefield, commenced the attack with such spirit that the first line of the. enemy gave way immediately; and after a more stubborn resistance the second line gave way also. This attack was followed up by the rest of the army, and the Americans were driven off the field. The British loss was 4 officers and 60 men killed, 15 officers and 144 men wounded; Colonel Trelawney of the Third Guards and Captain Bellew of the First Guards were amongst the wounded. Sir Henry Clinton then continued his march unmolested to Sandy Hook, whence the troops were conveyed over to New York on the 5th of July. July 5. No sooner had the British fleet and army concentrated at Sandy Creek near New York, than the French fleet, of vastly superior strength, with 11,000 men on board, recently equipped in France, on the French Government taking up the cause of the British American Colonies, arrived in America, and, after visiting the Delaware on the chance of ·some of the British fleet being still detained there, appeared off New York on the 11th of July. The British fleet was much inferior in numbers and weight of metal, but volunteers to man it came forward from every quarter, and a noble enthusiasm was created which redounded much to the credit of the nation. This feeling existed equally in the army, men vieing with each other to be employed as marines on board. Every preparation was made to give the French a warm reception should they attempt to advance towards Sandy Hook. Batteries were erected, and Colonel O'Hara was ordered there with four regiments, to

1778.

prevent the enemy attempting to take possession of it. On the 22nd of July, everything denoted the intention of the French to sail up to attack the British position, but at the last moment the Admiral changed his mind, put to sea,

July 29.

and on the 29th of July appeared off Rhode Island, where there was a British garrison of four English and four Hessian regiments, under Sir Robert Pigot. Sir William Clinton, hearing that Washington was detaching some troops to co-operate with the French navy in their attack on Rhode Island, also detached five more regiments to reinforce Sir Robert Pigot. The French fleet advanced up the harbour

Aug. 8.

and attacked the land batteries on the 8th of August, but the British fleet under Lord Howe hove in sight the following day, and the French retired from the harbour. Both fleets manœuvred for several days to get the advantage over the other, but a storm arose by which they were separated before either was prepared for an engagement. Isolated actions then occurred between several ships, and towards the end of August the two fleets put into port,—the French at Boston, the British at New York, and the latter being shortly reinforced, proceeded in a few days to attack the French at Boston, where it arrived on the 30th of August, but finding the enemy well secured, it sailed again to Rhode Island. As the Americans, however, had withdrawn from that post, the British fleet returned in the middle of September to New York, and the Guards remained quartered in that town during the whole of the subsequent winter.

Several changes took place amongst the officers of the First Guards serving in America this year.

Colonel Thomas Howard, as before mentioned, having been promoted to third major in the spring, embarked for England in September, but on his passage home on board the "Eagle Packet," was killed in an action with an American privateer, and Colonel West Hyde succeeded him both as third major of the regiment, and in the command of the detachment of First Guards in America, which latter post he retained till June, 1779.

The following officers of the First Guards were in America at the commencement of the ensuing campaign in May, 1779 :—

CAPTAINS AND LIEUT.-COLONELS.	LIEUTENANTS AND CAPTAINS.	ENSIGNS.
West Hyde.	Thomas.	St. George.
G. Garth.	Colins.	Per. Maitland.
J. Howard.	Hon. Geo. Lane	Goodricke.
J. Leland.	Parker.*	
James Stewart.	J. Jones.	
Lord Thos. Clinton, afterwards Earl of Lincoln.	F. Dundas. Cochrane. Richardson.	
F. Madan.		
R. H. Pye.		

* Second son of 2nd Earl of Macclesfield.

CHAPTER XIX.

1779—1789.

1779.
Feb. 23.

BRIGADIER MATHEW, who continued in command of the brigade of Guards in America, was promoted to Major-General in the early part of 1779, and Colonel Garth of the First Guards was promoted at the same time to be Major-General, and appointed a king's aide-de-camp. On the 23rd of April, Colonel William Stile retired from the command of the first battalion of the regiment, to which Colonel William Thornton succeeded, Colonel West Hyde and Colonel Sir John Wrottesley, Bart., becoming second and third majors.

The usual drafts were sent out in the spring to complete the battalions.

An expedition was set on foot in the year 1779, to Virginia, in which a portion of the brigade of Guards took part. It had come to the knowledge of Sir Henry Clinton, that the Americans had established a marine-yard at Gosport, within the mouths of the Chesapeak on its southern bank, where they had collected a quantity of timber for ship-building, and other stores, and it was resolved to send some troops from New York to destroy it. The expedition con-

May.

sisted of the Grenadier and light infantry companies of
the Guards, commanded by Colonel Garth, now Major-
General,—the 42nd,—a Hessian regiment, and other troops,
amounting in all to 2,500 men, under Major-General
Mathew. They sailed from New York on the 5th of May,
entered the Chesapeak on the 8th, and the Elizabeth
river on the 10th, but the morning being calm the ships
were prevented coming within five or six miles of their
destination; whereupon General Mathew transferred the
first division of his troops into flat-bottomed boats, and
proceeding up the river, landed at three in the afternoon
at the *Glebe,* on the western shore of Elizabeth river,
three miles below Portsmouth, and out of cannon shot of
Fort Nelson. The rest of the troops soon following,
were landed, and as General Mathew advanced with the
view of investing the fort, the garrison, afraid of their
retreat being cut off, evacuated it, the British at once
taking possession both of the fort and town of Portsmouth. On the following day General Garth pushed for- May 11.
ward two corps, of which the flank companies of the Guards
formed the right, about ten miles towards Suffolk. On the
12th, the Guards made a night march of eighteen miles, May 12.
arriving at Suffolk at daybreak on the 13th, where they
destroyed some vessels, a large quantity of provisions, some
naval stores, and two cannon. Fort Nelson, and the town
of Norfolk, lying opposite Portsmouth, were also taken
possession of, and large quantities of stores as well as
provisions were found there; some of which were taken,
the rest destroyed. Other expeditions were organised up
the Elizabeth and the Chesapeak rivers, which were all
successful either in destroying the enemy's ships or in
harassing the enemy himself; and General Mathew having
thus fulfilled all his instructions, destroyed the Fort of
Portsmouth, burnt the barracks and storehouses, as well
as the buildings in the dockyard, re-embarked his men
on the 24th of May, and returned to New York on the
29th. The loss of property inflicted on the Americans by May 29.
this expedition was computed at half a million, and

the number of vessels taken or destroyed amounted to 137.

Previous to the return of General Mathew with his troops from Virginia, Sir Henry Clinton had been preparing to send a force under General Vaughan to attack the enemy, now occupying two forts on the Hudson river, about sixty miles above New York,—Fort La Fayette, and Verplanks, near Stoney Point. The two battalions of the Guards, with other detachments of the army, were on the point of sailing, when the above expedition, arriving at New York, was ordered at once to join this new service, and the flank companies of the Guards joined their battalions. The

May 30. whole force sailed up the river on the 30th of May, landing the next day a few miles below Verplank's Point. General Vaughan with the Guards and his other troops invested Fort La Fayette, while General Pattison with the rest of the British landed on the east bank of the river, and drove the enemy from a post opposite La Fayette Fort. On the 1st of June preparations were made for the attack, by

June 2. landing guns, erecting batteries, &c., and on the 2nd, the fire from the ships and batteries opened so effectively that the American garrison surrendered prisoners of war. A British garrison was left there, as well as at Stoney Point, by which means Sir Henry Clinton became master of King's Ferry, a serious loss to the enemy; and the rest of the troops, including the Guards, returned to New York.

July. In July the flank companies of the Guards, under Major-General Garth, again formed part of an expedition into the East Sound, designed by Sir Henry Clinton, with the view partly to destroying a number of privateers, which the Americans were fitting out, to the great detriment of the British commerce; and partly to land on the north coast of the Sound, in hopes of inducing Washington to abandon his strong post in the mountains, and come down and accept battle. The troops, 2600 strong, under Major-Generals Tryon and Garth, both First Guards men, embarked on transports which joined Sir George Collier's squadron, on the 3rd of July, when they all put to sea; and on the 5th the fleet was off Newhaven, above 100 miles from New York. The same day the first division of the troops under General Garth, consisting of the flank companies of the Guards, the 7th and 34th British regiments, and a detachment of Yägers, with two guns, was landed at a place a mile south of West- Westhaven. haven, and immediately advanced, making a circuit of above seven miles to get round a creek on the west side of the town, while the rest of the troops, under Tryon, were disembarked to the east of the harbour, and proceeded direct on Newhaven. The Americans offered considerable opposition, and General Garth had to fight his way for the greater part of his march from Westhaven, but the British armed vessels were enabled to draw near the scene of action, and the two columns of attack effected a junction within the town, when the public stores, some vessels, and guns were destroyed, and a privateer ready for sea was carried off. On this occasion, Adjutant Campbell of the Guards was killed, Captain Parker of the Guards wounded, one sergeant and nine rank and file wounded, and fourteen missing. The troops re-embarked on the 6th of July, and July 6. landed again on the 8th near Fairfield, where they experienced some opposition from the militia and others who had assembled there. They continued their march on the town, which was set on fire by some loyalist refugees, whereby many whale-boats and a large part of the town itself were destroyed. On the 9th, the troops re-embarked, and were carried across the sound to Huntingdon, in Long Island, where provisions were taken on board. The loss here was four rank and file killed, one sergeant and ten rank and file wounded, and two missing. The expedition then returned to the north coast of the Sound, and on the 11th anchored five miles from the bay of Norwalk. The July 11. troops, who were landed in three divisions, marched straight to the town, and the inhabitants having fired upon them from windows and tops of houses, the General ordered his men to set the place on fire. It was entirely consumed, and several vessels and whale-boats burnt. On the 12th the troops re-embarked, and were conveyed to Huntingdon Bay in

Long Island, to be ready for any further service. They were then ordered to return to New York, and no sooner had they arrived there, than information was received that the Americans had surprised the garrison left at Stoney Point, to the east of the River Hudson, whence they commenced a furious cannonade against the British position at Verplank's Point, under Colonel Webster. Sir Henry Clinton immediately organised an expedition of as many troops as he could spare to proceed northwards to the assistance of Colonel Webster. He marched on the 19th, drove back the Americans, and left five battalions at Stoney Point under Brigadier-General Stirling. The two battalions of Guards remained in garrison in New York during the remainder of the year 1779, and on the 3rd of November their brigadier, Major-General Mathew, returned to England on being appointed Colonel of the 62nd Regiment of Foot.

While great preparations were still making in England for carrying on the war with vigour, Sir Henry Clinton, finding that, with the reinforcements from home, he would have sufficient troops both to protect New York, in case of an attack either by sea or land, and at the same time to make an expedition against another part of the coast, resolved to proceed to Charlestown in South Carolina. Leaving a considerable garrison in New York, under Lieutenant-General Knyphausen, consisting of the two battalions of Guards, the 17th, 26th, 37th, and 38th regiments of the line, 1500 Hessians, the 17th Dragoons, besides several other corps, he sailed at the end of December, 1779, with above 8000 men, and was successful in speedily reducing Charlestown, with a loss of 76 killed and 189 wounded, while the American loss was above 6000 prisoners, 400 guns, and a vast quantity of stores.

In the meantime, General Knyphausen, who was left in command at New York, was very active in taking all necessary measures for its security; and a body of 360 Americans, having established themselves during the winter of 1779-80 (which was one of the coldest on record), at a place called Young's House, near White Plains, about twenty miles in front of the outposts of the British army, and thirty from New York, it was resolved if possible to dislodge them. This service was entrusted to Lieutenant-Colonel Hon. Chapel Norton, of the Coldstreams, who took with him the four flank companies of the Guards, two companies of Hessians, and some Yägers, together with two light 3-pounder field pieces. The detachment left New York on the evening of the 2nd of February, and proceeding by unfrequented tracts to avoid the enemy's patrols, arrived at daybreak on the 3rd within seven miles of Young's House. As the guns could not be brought on, the detachment had nothing with them but some axes and an iron crow-bar to force the doors. The men had been marching all night in snow two feet deep, and were much fatigued, but, nothing daunted, they continued their advance, notwithstanding that a reinforcement of the enemy was observed coming up to strengthen the post. The Guards, on approaching the house, were warmly received by a party of the enemy stationed in an orchard, but the Grenadiers of the Guards leading the way, succeeded in forcing an entrance: forty of the Americans were found dead, and ninety were made prisoners; the flank companies of the Guards losing two killed and twenty-five wounded.

On the 5th the following order was issued as a recognition of the gallant services of this detachment:—

"Head-quarters, New York, *Feb. 5*, 1780.

"His Excellency Lieutenant-General Knyphausen desires his thanks may be given in public orders to Lieutenant-Colonel Norton, of the Guards, for his good conduct and gallant behaviour in attacking and forcing a considerable body of rebels, advantageously posted at Young's House, in the neighbourhood of White Plains, on the morning of the 3rd instant. His Excellency returns thanks to the officers and private soldiers of the different detachments employed on this service; and the General is particularly obliged to the officers and men of the West Chester Refugees for their

1780. very determined behaviour upon this as well as former
occasions."

Colonel O'Hara, of the Coldstream Guards, who had
lately been in command of an African corps, was appointed
in April, 1780, to serve as brigadier in North America,
May 12. and on the 12th of May received the command of the brigade
of Foot Guards then serving in that country, in the place of
General Mathew, who had returned to England.   The same
officers of the First Guards were present with the service
battalion this campaign as during the last, except Colonels
West Hyde and Garth, who had returned to England.

During the spring and summer of 1780, occasional skirmishes with the enemy's outposts took place in the neighbourhood of New York, in which the Guards took their full
June. share; and in the month of June General Knyphausen advanced
into the Jerseys, crossing over to Staten Island with about 5000
men, and thence to Elizabeth Point.   The two battalions of
Guards formed part of this expedition, the first battalion being
under the command of Lieutenant-Colonel Honourable Cosmo
Gordon of the Third Guards; the second battalion under
Lieutenant-Colonel Schutz of the Coldstream; but beyond
the destruction of Springfield, lying some miles above
Elizabeth Point, little was effected, and General Knyphausen
returned to New York early in July, where he was soon
joined by Sir Henry Clinton, who, after his successful expedition against Charlestown, had left the Earl of Cornwallis to operate with the British troops under his command in South Carolina.   Sir Henry, on his arrival at
New York, pushed forward a large corps of his army some
miles beyond Kingsbridge, towards White Plains.

The field of operations of the brigade of Guards was now
about to change.   Lord Cornwallis had driven several
bodies of the enemy out of South Carolina, and having left
Lord Rawdon with some troops in the neighbourhood of
Camden on the Catawba, he returned to Charlestown; but
no sooner had he arrived there than he heard that the
Aug. 9. enemy, 5000 strong, under General Gates, were marching
upon Camden, to cut off the British communications, and

EXPEDITION
TO
SOUTH CAROLINA
AND
VIRGINIA
under
Lord Cornwallis
in
1781.

Lord Rawdon had not above 1400 regulars to oppose to them; whereupon Lord Cornwallis hurried back to Camden, advanced with this small force, and meeting the enemy on the morning of the 14th of August on a ground where they could not deploy all their troops, gained a complete victory over them. 1780.
Aug. 14.

With the view to forcing Congress to withdraw some of the troops they were sending against Lord Cornwallis in South Carolina, Sir Henry Clinton resolved to send an expedition from New York to Virginia, under Major-General Leslie, who was to act in conformity to orders that he might receive from Lord Cornwallis. This force, consisting of the two battalions of Guards, now temporarily under Brigadier-General J. Howard of the First Guards, of detachments from the 17th, 82nd, and 84th Regiments, 1000 Hessians and Yägers, and some Provincials, sailed from Sandy Hook on the 16th of October, and entering the Chesapeak, which forms the eastern boundary of Virginia, landed and took post at Portsmouth, near the mouth of the James river. Here the troops threw up some works, while awaiting further orders from Lord Cornwallis, who was advancing northwards through the Carolinas towards the frontiers of Virginia. The orders at length arrived, to the effect, that as the distance was too great to form a junction with him by land from the north, General Leslie should sail to Charlestown, whence he could move up the country; the Guards were therefore re-embarked, and General Leslie, leaving Virginia, reached Charlestown with 2000 men about the 13th of December, where Brigadier-General O'Hara joined them. He had been dispatched from New York, on the 10th of November, by Sir Henry Clinton, to take command of the Guards, under Major-General Leslie, and brought with him further instructions. Having devoted a few days to organising the transport of provisions, Leslie quitted Charlestown on the 19th of December, and after a month's march up the country, effected a junction with Lord Cornwallis on the 18th of January, 1781, near the Catawba river. Lord Cornwallis, when Oct. 16. November. December. 1781.
See Plan.

R 2

writing to Sir Henry Clinton, on the 22nd December, informed him that, with the exception of the Guards and Bose's regiment, the recent reinforcements were exceedingly bad ; he considered it but justice to the troops serving in that district to state the fact, lest the services performed by the army in South Carolina should appear inadequate to what might be expected from the numbers of which it was composed. Previous to the arrival of the brigade of Guards and other reinforcements under Leslie, Cornwallis had been much affected by the defeat of Colonel Tarleton's light cavalry at "Cowpens," on the 7th of January ; but upon this accession to his strength he no longer hesitated to continue his advance into North Carolina towards Salisbury, as the only means of maintaining the British interests in the Southern colonies ; trusting to overtake the Americans, encumbered as they were with their prisoners, between Broad river and the Catawba.

Lord Cornwallis's object, after moving up the right or western bank of the Catawba, to within two days' march of Salisbury, was to advance upon and force a passage across it, with his whole army. All the fords were occupied by the Americans ; but Lord Cornwallis, in hopes of deceiving the enemy as to which ford he would attempt, eventually resolved to cross on the 1st of February at a private ford, near M'Gowan's. For this purpose he detached
Jan. 31.
part of the army on the previous day to make a demonstration at Beattie's Ford, six miles higher up the river, while he himself marched, at one A.M. on the 1st of February, with the brigade of Guards, Bose's regiment,
See Plan.
the 23rd, and 200 cavalry, with two guns, to the ford in question. The morning was dark and rainy, and as the leading companies of the Guards arrived at the ford at dawn of day, fires were observed on the opposite bank, showing that some opposition might be expected ; but as the rains were likely to increase the difficulty of crossing, and the enemy were known to be expecting reinforcements, Lord Cornwallis, full of confidence in the zeal and gallantry of Brigadier-General O'Hara, and of the brigade of

Plan of
PASSAGE or CATAWBA RIVER
BY THE BRITISH TROOPS
Feb⁄ 1ˢᵗ 1781.

CATAWBA RIVER

AMERICAN ARMY

THIRD POSITION AND RETREAT

AMERICAN
Guildford
Court Hou

AMERICAN 3ʳᵈ LINE

2ⁿᵈ POSITION AFTER AMERICAN
FRONT LINE RETIRED

AMERICAN 1ˢᵗ LINE

ORDER OF BATTLE
1ˢᵗ POSITION

The whole country
was woods

BATTLE OF
GUILDFORD COURT HOUSE
15ᵗʰ of March 1781.

Scale of 1 English mile

Guards under his command, ordered them to advance; but,
to prevent confusion, not to fire till they gained the opposite
bank. Their behaviour justified his high opinion of them.
Neither the rocky bottom of the ford, the strong current,
its length of 500 yards, nor its depth, often up to the waist,
made any impression on their cool and determined valour,
nor did the constant fire of the enemy in any way check
their progress. As soon as the light company entered the
water, supported by the Grenadiers and the two battalions,
the enemy commenced a galling and constant fire, which
was steadily received; but upon reaching the opposite banks,
the light and Grenadier companies of the Guards advanced to
the attack, and killed or dispersed all that appeared before
them; the rest of the troops forming in succession as they
crossed. Lieutenant-Colonel Hall, of the Third Guards,
commanding the light company of the brigade, was killed,
and of the same company three men were killed and thirty-
six wounded. The Americans lost their leader killed on
the field, and forty men killed and wounded. Lord
Cornwallis, in writing to Lord Rawdon from Salisbury,
February 4th, says, " We passed the Catawba on the 1st of
February. The Guards behaved gallantly, and although
they were fired upon during the whole time of their passing,
by some militiamen under General Davidson, never returned a shot until they got out of the river and formed."
This success caused the Americans to withdraw from all
their posts on the river, and Colonel Tarleton, with his
cavalry, following the retreating enemy to Tarrant Tavern,
where they were re-assembling, charged and dispersed them
again, killing fifty on the spot. The gallant action of the
Guards in the morning, followed by Colonel Tarleton's
success, enabled the whole force to continue their progress
through the most hostile part of North Carolina without
any further impediment.

The army advanced the next day, the 2nd, in hopes of
intercepting the enemy between the Catawba and Yadkin
rivers, and the Guards, who were in advance, came up with

their rearguard on the 3rd and routed it. On the 4th the British troops reached Salisbury, and Lord Cornwallis, hearing that the enemy were still at Trading Ford on the south side of the Yadkin, dispatched the Guards, with Bose's regiment and the cavalry, all under General O'Hara, to intercept them; but owing to the bad roads, the Guards did not reach the Yadkin till midnight, when it was found that the enemy had crossed in the evening, leaving some waggons, which were captured. General O'Hara endeavoured to procure some boats to cross the river, but in vain, upon

Feb. 5.

which he posted the Guards and Bose's regiment in a position commanding the ford and ferry, and sent the cavalry back to Salisbury. As there were no means of crossing the river at Trading Ford, Lord Cornwallis moved westward, crossed the Yadkin higher up, where the fords were shallower, and entered the Moravian district, intending to push forward in a north-easterly direction as rapidly as possible, and bring the enemy to bay before he could reach the Dan and Roanoke rivers, forming the boundary between North Carolina and Virginia. Cornwallis in his despatch says nothing could exceed the patience and alacrity of his officers and soldiers under every species of hardship and fatigue in endeavouring to overtake the fugitives. The Guards and the rest of the royal troops reached Boyd's

Feb. 12.

Ferry, on the Dan, on the 12th of February, but the Americans had been too nimble in their flight, and had crossed the day before.

This was the furthest point northward to which Lord Cornwallis advanced. He hesitated to enter the powerful province of Virginia with his comparatively small force; but having cleared North Carolina of all armed troops, he determined to favour the assembling of the loyalists in that country, and moved southward again to Hillsborough, where he erected the King's standard, and issued a proclamation, to which many responded, but still hesitated to join in active measures, from fear of the return of the American troops. During this period the Guards and the rest of the

army gradually recovered from the fatigues they had undergone on their late march northwards, which they had borne
with so much patience.

As soon as Lord Cornwallis retired from the Dan to
Hillsborough, the Americans made preparations to recross
it and follow in his steps; but finding forage scarce, and **Feb. 26.**
Hillsborough too far distant to afford efficient protection
to those loyalists who were assembling between the Haw
and Deep River, Lord Cornwallis crossed the Haw on the
26th of February, and on the following day encamped near
Allamance, detaching Lieutenant-Colonel Tarleton with his
cavalry, the light company of the Guards, and 150 of
Colonel Webster's men, towards Deep River, so as to afford
more protection to the country people.

General Green, with his Americans, advanced from the **March.**
Dan, with the view to giving support to the waverers in
the national cause, as well as to defeat Lord Cornwallis's
wishes of forming a loyalist body in North Carolina, and
the American army being now increased to 5000, General
Green advanced to Guildford Court House, within twelve
miles of the British, with the apparent intention of bringing
on an action. Lord Cornwallis was rejoiced at the opportunity thus afforded him, and after making preparations
on the evening of the 14th of March for the safety of
his baggage, marched at dawn the next morning against the **March 15.**
enemy. When within four miles of Guildford Court House,
the advance of the British army, under Colonel Tarleton,
consisting of some cavalry, the light infantry of the Guards,
and some Yägers, came upon the enemy, and a sharp conflict
ensued, till the British being further supported by the 23rd
Regiment, the Americans were forced to retire. In the meantime, the main body of the enemy, under General Green, **See Plan.**
had taken up a strong position in three lines on very commanding ground, with their two flanks protected by woods.
The right of the British was formed of the 71st and Bose's
regiment of Hessians, under Leslie, supported by the first
battalion of Guards, under Colonel Norton. The left was
formed of the 23rd and 33rd, under Lieutenant-Colonel

Webster, supported by the Grenadiers and second battalion of the Guards, under Lieutenant-Colonel Stuart, all commanded by Brigadier-General O'Hara. The light infantry of the Guards, with the Yägers, were on the left of the artillery, and the cavalry in rear.

Battle of Guildford Court House.

The attack of the British commenced along the whole line, and the advance, without firing, was executed with the most determined coolness, unchecked by the fire of the enemy, who opened upon them at a distance of 140 yards. On approaching the Americans, the British poured in a volley and charged down upon the enemy, who did not await the shock, but retired beyond their second line. Owing to the extent of the American position, the first battalion of Guards was brought up and formed on the extreme right, while the 33rd, which was on the extreme left, supported by the Yägers and light company of the Guards, finding itself outflanked, moved still more to the left, so as to enable the second battalion of Guards under Lieutenant-Colonel Stuart, and the Yägers to move up from the rear into the first line to the left of the 23rd. The line continued its advance through woods and other obstructions, meeting at times with an obstinate resistance. The second battalion of the Guards was the first to gain the open space at Guildford Court House, when, observing a corps of the enemy's infantry much superior in numbers, they instantly attacked and defeated them, taking two six-pounders; but pursuing too far into the woods, they were temporarily put in confusion and lost many men. Here Lieutenant-Colonel Stuart was killed, but General O'Hara, though wounded, quickly rallied the battalion, and returned to the attack, recapturing two field-pieces which they had taken at an earlier period, and had been forced to abandon during their temporary discomfiture; while the 23rd regiment coming up at the same moment joined in the movement, and the defeat of the right and centre of the Americans was complete.

While success was thus attending the left of the royal army, Webster, on the right of the line, with the first battalion of Guards, under Norton, and the 71st Regiment, continued his advance, overcoming all opposition, and driving the enemy before him. This first battalion of the Guards had also met with some check in the middle of the action, and suffered much after ascending the wooded height while attacking the second line of the enemy, strongly posted on the top, who after discharging a volley retired behind the brow of the hill, returning again as soon as loaded. No sooner, however, had the First Guards reached the summit, and put that part of the American line to flight, than other corps of the enemy appeared on the ground, one of which on the extreme right threatened to turn their flank. The Guards had already lost several officers, their ranks had been thinned in ascending the height, and Captain Maitland, who was wounded, was forced to retire, rejoining his corps, however, as soon as his wound was dressed. The fire of the third American line in front, as well as that of the regiments on the flank, put this battalion of Guards for a time in a state of confusion; but, nothing daunted, they were soon rallied again by Colonel Norton, under cover of Bose's Hessian regiment, which opportunely arrived on the ground. The Guards and Hessians then again renewed the attack against the enemy's third line, and eventually defeated it; but no sooner was this effected than they had to return to attack some more troops who appeared in their rear, and who were also finally driven off the field.

The British showed great courage in this encounter; their numbers were only 1445 against from 5000 to 7000 of the enemy, strongly posted; and it says much for the discipline of the Guards, that though on two separate occasions the two battalions were for a time thrown into confusion by an overpowering fire and superior numbers of the enemy, they were both rallied on the field of battle without retiring, and continued the attack till the enemy was finally defeated. The British lost nearly one-third of their numbers, the total being 532, of which 93 killed, 413 wounded, 26 missing.

The casualties in the two battalions of Guards were—

KILLED.	WOUNDED.	MISSING.
1 Lieut. Col.	2 Brig.-Gen.	22 R. and F.
8 Sergeants.	6 Captains.	
28 R. and F.	1 Ensign.	
	1 Staff officer.	
	2 Sergeants.	
	2 Drummers.	
	143 R. & F.	

Amongst the officers of the brigade of Guards there were—

KILLED.	WOUNDED,
Lieut.-Colonel Hon. James Stuart,* 1st Guards.	Brig.-Gen. O'Hara,
Capt. and Lieut.-Col. Schutz,	„ Thos. Howard,† 1st Guards,
Capt. and Lieut.-Col. Maynard, — Died of wounds.	Capt. Swanton,
	„ Lord Douglas,
Capt. and Lieut.-Col. Goodricke, 1st Guards,	„ Maitland, 1st Guards,
	Ens. Stewart,
	Adj. Colquhoun.

Lord Cornwallis in his despatch says : "The gallantry of Brigadier-General O'Hara merits my highest commendation, for after receiving two dangerous wounds, he continued on the field while the action lasted, and by his earnest attention on all occasions, seconded the officers and soldiers of his Majesty's Guards, who are no less distinguished by their order and discipline than by their spirit and valour."

After the great wars of the present century, this action of Guildford Court House may not be considered of great

---

* The Hon. James Stuart was fifth son of Robert Lord Blantyre. His son, Lieut.-Colonel John Stuart, commenced his military life in India, in the 72nd Regt. Infantry. On his return to England, was promoted to a company in 52nd Foot, in which regiment he became successively Major and Lieut.-Colonel. Sir John Moore having been requested by Lieut.-General Brownrigg to recommend an officer to make and form his regiment, the 9th Foot—consisting of young recruits—recommended Lieut.-Colonel Stuart, who was given the command of that regiment. Its state of discipline was evinced by its conduct against the enemy at the battle of Roleia in Portugal—where Lieut.-Colonel Stuart fell at its head, in the 32nd year of his age, 1808. His brother officers have put up a monument with an inscription testifying to his worth and excellence, in the cathedral church of Canterbury.

† Future Earl of Suffolk.

importance. An eye-witness, however, makes the following
observations :—

" History perhaps does not furnish an instance of a battle gained
under all the disadvantages which the British troops, assisted by a
regiment of Hessians and some Yägers, had to contend against at
Guildford Court House. Nor is there perhaps on the record of history
an instance of a battle fought with more determined perseverance than
was shown by the British troops on that memorable day. The battles
of Cressy, of Poictiers, and of Agincourt, the glory of our own country,
and the admiration of ages, had in each of them, either from particular
local situation or other fortunate and favourable circumstances, something in a degree to counterbalance the disparity of numbers. Here
time, place, and numbers, all united against the British. The American general had chosen his ground, which was strong, commanding,
and advantageous; he had time, not only to make his disposition, but
to send away his baggage and every incumbrance. His cannon, and
his troops, in numbers far exceeding the British, were drawn out in
readiness to commence the action, when Lord Cornwallis approached
to attack him."

Though this victory was highly honourable and glorious to
the troops engaged, it was in its consequences of no real
advantage to the general cause, for Lord Cornwallis had lost
one-third of the troops that were in action, and the army was
so destitute of provisions that a retreat towards a country
where supplies could be obtained became necessary. The
sick and wounded of the brigade of Guards, about seventy
in number, were left behind, under a flag of truce,
in charge of Captain J. Colquhoun, the adjutant of the
second battalion, himself wounded, and they appear to have
escaped the eventual fate of their comrades, and to have
remained in the Carolinas till December of the following
year, when they embarked for England under his command,
and reached London in February, 1783. Lord Cornwallis
commenced his march on the third day after the action
through Cross Creek to Wilmington, at the entrance of
Cape Fear River, in the south-eastern corner of North
Carolina, and reached this latter place after three weeks'
march on the 7th of April; and it was during this period
that Colonel Webster, as well as Captains Schutz and
Maynard, of the Guards, and other officers, died of the

1781.   wounds received in the late action.   Captain Richard
St. George of the First Guards was, on the 3rd of January,
1781, appointed deputy adjutant-general to the forces in
America, with the rank of major in the army.

The following officers of the First Guards, who all
entered the corps since the commencement of the American
war, were sent out this spring from England with the usual
drafts :—

Cols. Conway,	Lieuts.	Charles Asgil,	Ens. Perryn.
Gerard Lake,*	& Capts.	George Ludlow.†	
Woodford.			

After resting his troops eighteen days at Wilmington,
Lord Cornwallis, finding he was not joined by the loyalists,
and that he would be unable to reach Camden, in South
Carolina, in time to succour Lord Rawdon and his troops,
determined on continuing his march, and proceeding northwards into Virginia, he left Wilmington with that object

April 25.   on the 25th of April, 1781, with the two battalions of
Guards, now much reduced in numbers, and the other
regiments of his division.

While Lord Rawdon was successfully defending himself
at Camden in South Carolina, and Generals Philips and
Arnold were maintaining themselves in Virginia, Lord
Cornwallis continued his march almost uninterruptedly
through North Carolina, till he reached Halifax, on the
banks of Roanoke, within sixty miles of Petersburg.   Here
the light cavalry was sent forward, and Cornwallis, following with the Guards and the rest of his infantry,
effected a junction with Arnold's troops at Petersburg on

May 20.   the 20th of May.   Cornwallis, having received still further
reinforcements, determined to cross the James River
and attack the Americans under La Fayette, who were
near Richmond ; but on the approach of the British,
La Fayette retreated, and Cornwallis, finding it in vain to
follow, made small detachments in different directions to
annoy the enemy.   On the 6th of July he attacked
the American position near Williamsburg, on the James

* The future Lord Lake.   † The future Earl Ludlow.

River, and drove them off the field, but the Guards do not appear to have been engaged on this occasion; the brunt of the action falling on the 76th and 80th Regiments. After this, Lord Cornwallis crossed the James River and proceeded partly by land, partly by water, to Portsmouth, where he received fresh instructions from Sir Henry Clinton, directing him to return and occupy Yorktown and its neighbourhood, on the peninsula between the James and York rivers, for the better protection of the fleet. The army accordingly evacuated Portsmouth and returned in transports and boats up the Chesapeak, and took possession of Yorktown and Gloucester, on the 22nd of August, where the whole of Lord Cornwallis's forces were now concentrated, consisting, besides the Guards under O'Hara, of the 33rd, 43rd, 71st, 76th, and 80th regiments of the Line, 1st and 2nd battalions of Light Infantry, De Bose's regiment, and two battalions of Anspach. The Guards, under General O'Hara, with others, were from the first continually occupied in throwing up works to strengthen the defences. The French and Americans now laid a plan to surround the British forces, in which the French fleet was to co-operate. They commenced to assemble as large a land force as possible at Williamsburg, south of the James River, and at other places, near Yorktown, so as to invest it on all sides. At the same time, Washington, who was then near White Plains, watching New York, dispatched part of his forces towards Kingsbridge, as if with the intention of attacking the base of operations of the British army, thus preventing Sir Henry Clinton sending any reinforcements from the garrison to Lord Cornwallis; and collecting the rest of the troops at his disposal, he was enabled, early in September, with the assistance of the French fleet, to concentrate within a few miles of Yorktown a force of about 19,000 men, while the united garrisons of Yorktown and Gloucester, under Cornwallis, did not much exceed 5000. Information was at once sent to New York to inform Sir Henry Clinton of the critical position of the British at Yorktown. Sir Henry promised to send 5000 troops as soon as transports were ready to receive them, and the 5th of October was named as the day they would sail; but, as will be seen, these reinforcements were delayed for several weeks, and then were too late to be of any use. The combined French and Americans advanced upon Yorktown on the 28th of September and invested it; the garrison retiring from the outer line of detached works to the inner line.

October. On the 6th October, the enemy commenced their first parallel, and on the 9th opened fire with an incessant cannonade. On the 11th, the second parallel was opened, when it became necessary for the besieged to make an attempt to impede the construction of more of the enemy's batteries, and on the morning of the 16th, two sorties of 350 men each were made against them; one detachment consisted of the Guards and a company of Grenadiers, under Lieutenant-Colonel Lake of the Guards, the other of some light infantry under Major Armstrong. Both sorties were successful, and after killing or wounding many of the enemy, and spiking eleven of their guns, the troops returned within their lines with very little loss: but, though successful, these sorties had but little influence on the progress of the siege; the bombardment was incessant, and the garrison beginning to fail in ammunition, Lord Cornwallis foresaw the necessity either of a surrender or of an attempt to cross over to the Gloucester side of the river and thence effect a retreat through Virginia to New York. With the view of carrying out this latter alternative, most of the two battalions of Guards, now still further reduced in numbers, the light infantry, and the 23rd Regiment were transported the same evening to, and landed on, the Gloucester side of the river, when a storm arose which prevented the return of the boats for the rest of the garrison. The batteries opened again at daybreak, and Lord Cornwallis finding his plan impracticable, directed the boats which had now returned, to bring back to Yorktown the Guards and other troops they had conveyed over the

Oct. 17. night before. At the same time, finding the town no longer tenable, and being unwilling to expose the remains of his gallant army to the danger of an assault, which from the great superiority in numbers of the enemy could not fail to

be successful, he made proposals on the 17th for a capitulation, according to which both Yorktown and Gloucester
were surrendered to Washington on the 19th, the garrison
remaining prisoners in America, and being allowed the same
honours which the American garrison of Charlestown was
allowed when it surrendered to Sir Henry Clinton. The
reinforcements of 7000 men sent from New York did not
sail till the 19th of October, the day of the surrender,
and upon the commanders arriving off the capes of Virginia and hearing the disastrous news, both the fleet
and troops returned to New York, the sole object of the
expedition having been the relief of those towns. The
officers were allowed to retain their private property and
subsequently to proceed on parole to Europe. During the
siege, which lasted from September 28th to October 19th,
the loss of the Guards was 1 sergt., 3 R. and F., killed;
1 sergt., 21 R. and F., wounded, and the Hon. Major
Cochrane, late of the First Guards, acting aide-de-camp
to Lord Cornwallis, was also wounded.

The number of Guardsmen made prisoners were, three
lieutenant-colonels, twelve captains, one ensign, two adjutants, one quarter-master, one surgeon, three mates,
twenty-five sergeants, twelve drummers, and 465 rank and
file, who were all sent to Lancaster in Pennsylvania. A few
men of the brigade of Guards, who escaped captivity at
Yorktown, joined Major-General Leslie in South Carolina,
under Captain Swanton of the Third Guards, and were
afterwards sent by Sir Henry Clinton's orders from
Charlestown to New York. The officers of the First
Guards made prisoners were Lieutenant-Colonel Lake,
and Captains Dundas, Richardson, Maitland, Asgill,
Perryn, and Ludlow, and they remained prisoners till
May, 1783.

Amongst these officers of the Guards made prisoners
was Captain Asgill of the First Regiment, who had only
come out to America in the spring of the year 1781; and
in consequence of the subsequent execution of a Captain
Huddy, an American officer, in the spring of 1782, the life
of one of the British officers, then prisoners of war, was

1782. demanded in retaliation. One officer from each regiment was first selected, and on drawing lots between Captains Eld, Finch, and Asgill, of the Guards, Coote of the 47th, and Hathorn of the 80th regiments, the chance fell upon Captain Asgill, who on the 27th May was closely imprisoned, removed from Lancaster to Chatham, loaded with chains and threatened with death. A gallows of unusual height was erected in sight of his prison-window, placarded with these words : "For the execution of Captain Asgill." He continued in confinement till the 13th of November, 1782, when he was released by the authority of the American Congress, as explained in the following letter addressed to him by General Washington :—

Nov. 13. Letter from General Washington to Captain Asgill, First Guards, enclosing a resolution of a Committee of Congress to the following effect:—"That the Commander-in-Chief be directed, &c., to set Captain Asgill at liberty."

"HEAD QUARTERS, *Nov.* 13*th*, 1782.

"IT affords me singular pleasure to have it in my power to transmit you the enclosed copy of an Act of Congress of the 7th inst. by which you are released from the disagreeable circumstances in which you have so long been. Supposing you would wish to go into New York as soon as possible, I enclose a passport for that purpose.

"Your letter of the 18th of October came regularly to my hands. I beg you to believe that my not answering it sooner did not proceed from inattention to you, or a want of feeling for your situation. I daily expected a determination in your case, and I thought it better to await that, than to feed you with hopes that might in the end prove fruitless. You will attribute my detention of the inclosed letters, which have been in my hands about a fortnight, to the same cause.

"I cannot take leave of you, sir, without assuring you that in whatever light my agency in this unpleasing affair may be received, I never was influenced through the whole of it by sanguinary motives, but by what I conceived a sense of my duty, which loudly called upon me to take measures, however disagreeable, to prevent a repetition of those enormities which have been the subject of discussion ; and that this important end is likely to be answered without the effusion of the blood of an innocent person is not a greater relief to you, than it is to, sir,

"Your most obedient,
"And humble servant,
"G. WASHINGTON."

Captain Asgill at once made his way to New York, and returned by the earliest opportunity to England. The Guards remained in America during the whole of the year 1782, during which period their numbers were from various causes considerably reduced. A return, dated New York, 4th December, 1782, signed by Lieutenant-Colonel J. W. T. Walton, commanding the brigade, gives the following numbers of the Guards prisoners with the enemy:—

	Serg.	Drms.	R. & F.	Total.
First Regiment,	8	3	152	163
Coldstream Regiment,	4	3	108	115
Third Regiment,	2	2	103	107
	14	8	363	385

Various incidents connected with the closing acts of the American war took place during the year 1782, particularly with the fleet in the West Indies; but as all serious attempts by land to coerce the Americans into returning under the flag of Great Britain, ceased with the surrender of Lord Cornwallis's army, it will be unnecessary to follow its details further. Conditional articles of peace were ratified in November, 1782, between Great Britain, France, Spain and America, when the thirteen provinces were declared independent, and on the 20th of January, 1783, upon the preliminary articles of peace being signed, that part of the brigade of Guards that still held New York returned to England on board the " Adamant," while the other portion which had been in captivity, including four staff officers, twelve sergeants, six drummers, and 254 rank and file, returned to New York between the 8th and 27th May. Of this number, there were of the First Regiment of Guards one staff officer, eight sergeants, four drummers, and 108 rank and file, who, with the women and children belonging to the detachment, embarked on board the " Chatham " and "Jason " at New York on the 6th of June, and landing in England early in July, the men were ordered to rejoin their respective battalions. On the 18th of July they were inspected by Major-General West Hyde, who now resumed the duties of lieutenant-colonel of the First Guards, to which he had been

Nov. 30.

1783.

May 27.

July 18.

1782.
July 18.
appointed on the 18th March, 1782, after which the combined service battalions were completely broken up, and the
establishment of the regiment reduced to fifty rank and file
per company. The standard of the Grenadier companies
was raised to 5ft. 10¾ in., and all men under 5ft. 6in. were
discharged.

During the war, from the 3rd of July, 1779, the colonel
of the First Guards had allowed the captains to recruit for
their respective companies, but as the immediate cause of
that order no longer existed, the regimental order of
October, 1775, that all recruiting should be general, was,
in December, 1783, again enforced.

The usual change of quarters of the several battalions of
the brigade at home took place during the several years of the
1779. American war, and in 1779, from the 12th of June to the 24th
of November, several regiments were assembled and encamped on Warley Common, under the command of Lieutenant-General Hon. George Lane Parker, who, after serving
many years in the First Guards, had quitted them in 1773.

Beyond the drafts that were sent out annually from the
home battalions to the service companies in America, but
little occurred in England during the war with reference to
1780. the brigade of Guards, excepting that, in June, 1780, they
were called upon to suppress some serious disturbances
in London, known by the name of the Gordon riots,
from the name of the person who incited the mob to
deeds of violence. Lord George Gordon, son of the
duke of that name, born in 1750, had been in the
navy, but left it during the American war and entered
Parliament; he was eccentric, but not wanting in talents.
A Bill was introduced this session into Parliament for
the relief of Roman Catholics from certain penalties and
disabilities, which much irritated the Protestant party; and
Lord George Gordon, who strongly shared this feeling,
collected a mob, at the head of which, in the beginning of
June, he marched to the House of Commons to present a
petition against the proposed measure. Dreadful riots
ensued, during which many chapels, dwellings, prisons, and

other buildings were destroyed. The rioters proceeded to
the Roman Catholic chapels in Duke Street, Lincoln's Inn
Fields, and Warwick Street, and gutted them, before the
Guards, who were sent for, could arrive. On Sunday and
Monday, the 4th and 5th of June, fresh outrages were perpetrated against the Roman Catholics, but no steps were taken
to prevent them, till Tuesday, the 6th, when all the troops
were called out. One battalion and a regiment of cavalry were
placed at the Houses of Parliament, the Third Guards at
St. James's, and the third battalion of the First Guards at
St. George's Fields, under Colonel De Burgh. The mob,
however, instead of menacing the West End, stormed the
prisons, released their friends who had been confined
on previous days, and attacked Lord Mansfield's house in
Bloomsbury Square, and on a party of Guards arriving there,
the officer commanding refused to act without the orders
of a magistrate; the depredation continued, and the house
was destroyed. At last a magistrate arrived and gave the
order to fire, and a few rioters fell, while the rest were put
to flight by the approach of the Life Guards. More
serious disturbances were anticipated, and additional troops
were hurried up from the country. Twenty guns and six
Militia regiments, besides the Guards, were established
in St. James's Park, others in Lincoln's Inn; and the
Yeomen of the Guard mounted at St. James's Palace.
The King, with several general officers, was in the Queen's
Riding House, or walked about among the soldiers in St.
James's, giving strict orders to the men not to fire.

A cabinet council was held on the morning of Wednesday, the 7th, when it was debated whether persons riotously
collected together and committing outrages might be legally
fired on by the military without staying previously to read
the Riot Act; but no minister would take on himself to
advise this step, till Wedderburn, the attorney-general,
said that any such assemblage might be dispersed by
military force without waiting for form. He then drew
up an order, which the King signed, and Lord Amherst,
the commander-in-chief, issued and acted on the same day.

The riots had now reached their height, notwithstanding the appearance of the military. Great Russell Street and Hart Street were full of bonfires of furniture taken from the houses of obnoxious persons, and it was not till the Horse and Foot Guards appeared that the mob dispersed. The King's Bench Prison was in flames. Colonel de Burgh, who was again with the Third Regiment in St. George's Fields, was now sent for, when the populace tried to seduce the soldiers by calling upon them as Protestants not to fire, and doubts were expressed as to their fidelity; but the colonel replied he knew his men, and could rely on their prompt obedience. He reached the King's Bench in a few minutes after he had been sent for, and gave the order to fire, when the men levelling their firelocks, gave a deadly volley. The rioters dispersed immediately, carrying the dead and wounded with them.

The toll-house on Blackfriars Bridge was also burnt, the house of a Roman Catholic distiller on Holborn Hill, and scores of other fires were raging everywhere, in the midst of which the mob made for the Bank, preceded by a man on horseback laden with the chains of Newgate. Lieutenant-Colonel Rodney, afterwards Lord Rodney, of the Third Guards, commanded here, in company with Colonel Holroyd and his militia, and Lord G. Gordon being there also, told Rodney he would stand by him, but this officer ordered him at once to join the mob, and endeavour to persuade them to retire. As they would not do so, it became necessary to fire again, when numbers were killed.

The troops were ordered to hold the bridges, and all communication between the Southwark and the City rioters was thus interrupted. On the 8th the rioting terminated, and all was quiet; but London presented the appearance of a town that had suffered from a siege. The fault of the tardy call for military assistance was attributed to the Lord Mayor, who certainly showed a total want of capacity for the very difficult business he had to deal with. Lord Amherst was also blamed for forbidding the citizens to arm, but it seems that his prohibition was against the irresponsible nature of the volunteers thus called out by themselves, who, being under no control, might have committed many illegal acts. 1780.

Three hundred people are said to have lost their lives in these riots, but the bodies were carried off, and no trace of killed or wounded appeared on Thursday. On Friday, the 9th, Lord George Gordon was arrested and taken to the Tower, under a strong military escort. He was afterwards released, when he went to Birmingham and turned Jew, complying with all the ceremonies required, and some years later was imprisoned for a libel on Marie Antoinette. That he was mad no man can doubt.

The whole brigade of Guards, from Monday, 5th, to Monday, 12th of June, were thus continuously employed in checking the rioters and making prisoners, who were confined in the Tilt-yard Guard. In consequence of the extra picquets and detachments, and the harassing duty required from the brigade during the continuance of those tumults in various parts of London and its neighbourhood, extra subsistence was issued to the men, and it was deemed advisable, with the view to having the brigade more available for service, that the troops in London should be encamped. The three battalions of the First Guards went into camp in St. James's Park on the 7th of June, Lieutenant-Colonel Sir James Duffe acting as brigade-major till relieved six weeks later by Lieutenant-Colonel Sir Charles Rooke. This camp did not break up till the month of August. Other camps were formed in the neighbourhood of London, at Blackheath, and Finchley Common. June.

The Guards were again encamped in Hyde Park in the summer of 1782 till the 15th of August.

Francis Craig, a lieutenant-general since the year 1777, who was transferred from the Coldstreams to the lieutenant-colonelcy of the First Guards in 1775, retired from that lieutenant-colonelcy on the 22nd of February, 1781, when he was succeeded by Colonel William Thornton, a major-general since 1779, and Colonel Thomas Cox was promoted to a regimental majority.

In the following year, 18th March, 1782, General Thornton retired, and Colonel West Hyde, who had gone out to
America with the first detachment in 1776, and, after the
return of Colonel Howard in 1777, was for two years senior
officer of the First Guards on service, succeeded to the
command of the regiment.   Colonels Sir John Wrottesley,
Thomas Cox, and George Garth succeeded at the same
time to that of the three battalions respectively.

Lieutenant-Colonel Thomas and Major St. George, both
of the First Guards, though they remained in America for
some months after the capitulation of Yorktown, were not
included in the list of prisoners of war.   Major St. George
returned to England in June, 1782, and Lieutenant-Colonel
Thomas, whose melancholy fate will now be referred to,
returned in November of the same year; Captain Richardson, who was one of those constituted prisoners of war,
returned early in 1783, while the remaining officers, Colonel
Lake, and Captains Dundas. Maitland, Asgill, Perryn, and
Ludlow, continued prisoners on parole till May, 1783.

As far back as the month of June, 1780, at the Battle
of Springfield, an accusation was made by one officer of the
Guards against another, which in the year 1783 terminated
in a fatal duel.   Lieutenant-Colonel Thomas, of the First
Guards, had stated on that occasion that Colonel Cosmo
Gordon had been wanting in his duty; and, when called
upon to affirm his accusation, he did so before a court-
martial.   Colonel Gordon was honourably acquitted, and
Lieutenant-Colonel Thomas was then arraigned for making
a frivolous charge, but was also acquitted.

Colonel Gordon, however, on his return home, not satisfied
with the result of the trial, called out Colonel Thomas, who
refused; but Gordon insisting thereon, in consequence, it is
said, of an expression of surprise, made at a meeting of the
officers of the Third Guards, at his taking no further steps,
Thomas complied, and, attended by Captain Hill, of the
First Regiment, went out in Hyde Park.   It was decided by
the seconds that each should fire when they chose; and at
the first fire no harm was done, but a second shot being in-

sisted on, they again fired; Gordon was wounded in
the hip, and Thomas shot through the body, dying
shortly afterwards. His will, on being opened, was found
to contain a paragraph expressive of his horror at the
barbarous custom of duelling, which the habit of society
rendered it imperative he should follow.. Gordon was tried
for murder, but acquitted on a legal quibble suggested
by the judge, who in those days did not consider duelling
anything but a necessary evil.

Several alterations were made in the dress of the
British soldier at this time, and a warrant was issued on
the 21st of July, 1784,* regulating various details, viz.,
Each soldier was to carry fifty-six rounds of ammunition,
thirty-two rounds in a pouch on the right side, and twenty-
four rounds in a cartridge box, by way of magazine, to be
worn occasionally on the left side. The cartridge box to be
fixed to the bayonet belt. The cross-belts to be two inches
broad. The gaiters to be of black woollen cloth (instead of
linen), with white metal buttons, and without stiff tops.
The Grenadier swords, as also their matches and match
cases, were in future to be laid aside ; and the light infantry
were to have a small priming horn, to contain two ounces,
instead of the horn and bullet bag hitherto in use ; the
horn and hatchet, however, were not to be fixed to the accoutrements, but to be carried either with knapsack or as the
commanding officer might think proper. The spontoons,
also, which had hitherto been carried by officers, were discontinued in 1786, and, on the 16th of April, the officers
mounted guard at St. James's, and all other guards, with
their swords.

During these, and several subsequent years, the battalions of the brigade continued the uniform change of
quarters in the several districts of London, the Grenadier
company of one battalion being always quartered at the
Savoy, as forming *parcel of the royal duchy of Lancaster.*
They also furnished detachments at times to Deptford
Richmond, and Windsor.

* Dress. W. O. Mis. Bk., 539.

George Garth, a major-general since 1782, had succeeded on the 20th of October, 1784, to the second majority of the regiment, and Colonel Gerard Lake, the future Lord Lake, to the third majority. No further changes took place amongst the commanding officers of battalions till the year 1789.

The following were the captains of companies by seniority in the year 1786 :—

H.R.H. Duke of Gloucester, Col.	Lt.-Col. Charles Talbot.
Maj.-Gen. West Hyde, Lt.-Col.	„ Kingsmill Evans.*
„ Thomas Cox, 1st Maj.	„ Walter Strickland.
„ George Garth, 2nd Major.	„ Fothringham.
	„ Thomas Glyn.
Colonel Gerard Lake, 3rd Major.	„ William Colquhon.
„ Samuel Hulse.	„ Andrew J. Drummond.
„ Albemarle Bertie.	„ John Jones.
„ Sir John Dyer, Bart.	„ Hon. Francis Needham.
„ Edmund Stevens.	„ Sir Hew Dalrymple, Knt.
„ Patrick Bellew.	„ Hon. Henry Phipps.
„ Richard Steynor Jones.	„ Hon. H. Fitzr. Stanhope.
Lt.-Col. Francis D'Oyley.	„ Hon. John Douglas.
„ Hon. R. Fulke Greville.	
„ Sir James Duff, Bart.	Capt.-Lt. Alexander Dury.

The companies of the regiment were ordered to be increased by one corporal and ten men each in September, 1787, but they were reduced again on the 8th of November following.

The two troops of Horse Grenadier Guards, under the command respectively of Lord Howard and the Duke of Northumberland, were ordered, in May, 1788, to be disbanded, as the third and fourth troops had been in 1746 ; and the two troops of Horse Guards under the command respectively of the Marquis of Lothian and Jeffrey Lord Amherst, were by warrant, dated 18th of June, 1788, formed into two regiments of Life Guards, to commence as such from the 25th of June, 1788. The rank of these two corps was to continue as formerly, but with the title of First and Second Regiments of Life Guards.

* Died of wounds received at Lincelles, 1793.

The brigade of Guards was called out on the 25th of April, 1789, on the occasion of the King going in state to St. Paul's, to return thanks for his recovery, when the streets were lined by the Household troops as far as Temple Bar, the Grenadier companies being posted in St. Paul's Church and Churchyard.

CHAPTER XX.

1789.

1789.
French
Revolution.

THE French Revolution, brought about by the general discontent existing at the excessive privileges of the nobles, the unequal taxation, the corruption of the court, and the mal-administration of justice, all of which gradually alienated the affections of the people from the government, broke out in 1789. The fidelity of the army had been much weakened by various abuses in its administration. The finances were seriously embarrassed, and Louis XVI. by his irresolution had lost the confidence of all parties. A general cry being raised for the assembly of the States-General, they were convoked, and the King himself opened

May 5.

them, on the 5th of May of this year. The entire power was thus by degrees thrown into the hands of the representatives of the people, and notwithstanding the attempt of the King to close the Chamber, the members re-assembled in another locality, and took an oath not to submit; the French Guards revolted, the Bastile was stormed, and revolutionary clubs under the names of Jacobins and Girondins were formed, which afterwards exercised much influence through-out the country; and in the course of the following year, 1790, the National Assembly repealed many old laws, voted

the abolition of titles, and confiscated church property.   1790.
General anarchy prevailed, the nobles and landed gentry fled
the country, and the King remained a prisoner in his own
palace.

Little was done in England towards increasing the army
in the first years of the French Revolution. In May, 1790, **May 9.**
in consequence of the uncertainty prevailing as to the effect
of the late events in Paris, a slight augmentation was made.
The First Guards were increased by about 300 men, and on
the 28th of June the regiment was informed by General
Garth, the lieutenant-colonel, that its services might soon
be required ; but the autumn arrived before any serious
preparations were made, when, on the 19th of October, the
first battalion of the First Guards, and one battalion of
each of the two other regiments, were ordered for foreign
service ; the companies of the first battalion were completed
from the others ; sea stock was provided ; camp equipage
issued, and sent down to Portsmouth, and everything was in
readiness for embarkation, when the expedition was counter-
manded, all transfers were directed to return to their
respective companies, and the regiment was reduced to its
former establishment of fifty rank and file per company.
Upon the occasion of this intended expedition, four officers
of the First Guards, viz., Ensigns Lawley, Harvey, Bathurst
and Bligh, were taken off duty to raise independent companies.

In 1791, Louis XVI., while endeavouring to escape and join   **1791.**
the French emigrants, who were assembling at Coblentz, **June.**
was arrested and brought back a prisoner to Paris, when a
still more democratic Assembly was formed. Early in 1792,
the French Royal Guards, who had previously been set
aside in favour of foreign mercenaries, were disbanded, as
one of the surest modes of undermining the power of the
sovereign, many of the clergy were exiled, the mob broke
into the palace, and the life of the King was with difficulty
for the time saved ; but the revolution made rapid progress,
marked by excesses unparalleled in history.

The German powers, fearing the rapid spread of demo-

1792.

War
between
France
and
Austria.

cratic principles, placed their armies on a war footing, and war was declared between France and the Imperialists, in April, 1792. The command of the allied forces was given to the Duke of Brunswick, who, in August, advanced into France, but in the following month was forced to retire, taking up a defensive position behind the Meuse, and before the end of the year the towns of Mons, Tournay, Brussels, Namur, and Antwerp, all fell into the hands of the French under Dumourier.

The Republic was declared in September, 1792, and three months later Louis XVI., who had long been a prisoner in the Temple, was brought to trial, condemned to death, and perished on the scaffold on the 21st of January, 1793.

Since the commencement of the French Revolution Great Britain had pursued a policy of strict neutrality, and all solicitations to join the Confederation of the allies had been steadily resisted; but the recent events in Paris had excited a feeling of horror throughout the country, and when the Convention announced that it would grant assistance to the people of any country who wished to recover their liberty, and that it would treat as enemies those who desired to preserve their ancient traditions, society was endangered, and further neutrality rendered almost impossible.

Nov. 16.

The French had also committed aggressions on the Dutch, by opening the Scheldt; British remonstrances not only had no effect, but a circular was issued by the French Minister of Marine, with the view to spreading revolutionary principles in England. The execution of the King brought

1793.

matters to a crisis; the French ambassador received notice to leave the British dominions within eight days; and on

Feb. 3.

the 3rd of February, 1793, the French Republic declared war against Great Britain.

Ever since the resignation of General the Honourable Henry Seymour Conway, in December, 1783, no general officer had been appointed to the head of the British army; but under present circumstances the necessity of such an appointment became apparent, and on the 21st of January,

1793, Jeffrey Lord Amherst, formerly an officer of the First Guards, who had held an appointment at the head of the British army, from 1778 to 1782, previous to Conway, was again appointed a general on the staff, and the King directed that all military matters to be transacted at home, excepting those relating to the Foot Guards, should be referred to him. The King thus specially retained in his own person the command of his Foot Guards, the field officer in brigade waiting receiving orders direct from his Majesty or from his adjutant-general.

The absence of a general commanding in chief to watch over the organisation and discipline of the British army had been very prejudicial to its efficiency. It was at this time weak in numbers, there being only 32,000 men in the United Kingdom; and the unfortunate result of the American war had temporarily dimmed its reputation. Its state is thus described by a military writer:—" Our army was lax in discipline, entirely without system; each colonel of a regiment managed it according to his own notions, or neglected it altogether; there was no uniformity in drill or movement; professional pride was rare, professional knowledge still more so; never was a kingdom less prepared for a stern and arduous conflict."

This opinion was many years afterwards, in 1828, corroborated by Lieutenant-General Sir Herbert Taylor; he states: " I went abroad, and saw what had been the result of the total neglect of every military establishment in the country. Nothing could be more disgraceful, and we were the objects of ridicule to every other service; I saw the state in which the army at times joined head-quarters, which, with the exception of the Foot Guards and a few other corps, was most disgraceful."

Though the British Government still hoped to avoid hostilities, they had already, in December, 1792, taken the precaution of calling out the militia, and increasing the strength of the army. Orders were also issued to the brigade of Guards that all officers on leave were to rejoin their regiments immediately, and an augmentation of ten men per company was made throughout the army. Major-

1793. General Gerard Lake had been appointed lieutenant-colonel of the First Guards, on the 1st of August, 1792, on the retirement from the regiment of Major-General Garth.

In the spring of the year, 1793, Henry Phipps, who had lately succeeded to the title of Lord Mulgrave * by the death of his brother, retired from the regiment on being appointed Colonel of the third regiment of the line; and in his place H.R.H. Prince William, son to the Duke of Gloucester, now just commencing his 18th year, received a commission of Captain and Lieutenant-Colonel in the First Guards. The appointment was notified to the corps by the following order of the same date:—

"Friday, *8th February*, 1793, Parole, Banbury.

"His Majesty has been pleased to appoint His Royal Highness Prince William of Gloucester, to be Captain of a company in the First Regiment of Foot Guards (*vice*) Lord Mulgrave, promoted to the command of the 31st Regiment of Foot.

"His Royal Highness's Commission is to bear date from the 11th March, 1789. His Royal Highness the Duke of Gloucester orders His Royal Highness Lieutenant-Colonel Prince William to be posted to the Grenadier Company of the 3rd Battalion."

The antedating of His Royal Highness's commission to the 11th of March, 1789 (when he was little more than 13 years old), placed him next after Lieutenant-Colonel Coussmaker and before George Richardson, by which he gained seven steps in the regiment. His Royal Highness was in the following year sent out on service to join the first battalion in Holland; and shortly afterwards was appointed Colonel of the 115th regiment, but that corps being disbanded in 1795, H.R.H. was transferred on the 4th of November of that year to the colonelcy of the sixth regiment of the line.

The French having followed up their declaration of war against Great Britain by ordering Dumourier, who com-

* Lord Mulgrave subsequently in 1812, became 1st Earl of Normanby.

manded their northern army, to invade Holland, that officer 1793. crossed the frontier on the 17th February, 1793, with 18,000 men. The Dutch were then not only unprepared, but were even disaffected towards their own Government : the frozen waters enabled the French general to advance rapidly with his artillery through their country, and Breda, Klundelt, and Gertruydenberg, three towns in North Brabant, lying south of Dordrecht, soon fell into the hands of the invaders. The British Government saw that no time was to be lost if they meant to succour their ally, and oppose Dumourier's advance. On the first notice of the invasion, on the 20th Feb. 20, of February, a brigade of Guards was ordered to hold itself Guards dispatched in readiness for immediate foreign service. The Duke of to Holland. York assembled the Guards on the Horse Guards' Parade, and called for volunteers to serve under him, when every man stepped forth. The first battalions of the three regiments, all under the command of Major-General Lake, were the three battalions selected, that of the First Regiment being placed under Colonel Samuel Hulse, Captain Hill being appointed major of brigade. Captain Hon. — Hope of the First Regiment was also appointed brigade major when the Guards were formed into two brigades. The two Grenadier companies of the battalion of the First Guards and one of each of the two other battalions were formed into a Grenadier battalion, the command of which was given to Colonel Leigh of the Third Guards.

The following are the officers of the first battalion First Guards now about to proceed on foreign service :—

Maj.-Gen. G. Lake, Lieutenant-Colonel, Commanding Brigade.

Colonel Samuel Hulse, 1st Major, Commanding Battalion.

CAPTAINS AND LIEUT.-COLONELS.	LIEUTENANTS AND CAPTAINS.	ENSIGNS.
Major-Gen. Lake, Lt.-Col.	G. Fitzgerald.	G. D. Drummond.
Col. S. Hulse, 1st Maj.*	Hon. J. Leslie.	E. G. Ruddock.
	H. Wynyard.	H. F. Campbell.

* Colonel Samuel Hulse was a younger son of Sir Edward Hulse, of Breamont House, Hants, and was born the 27th March, 1746 ; was appointed ensign in the First Guards, 14th Dec. 1761, and lieutenant in August, 1769,

1793.	CAPTAINS AND LIEUT.-COLONELS.	LIEUTENANTS AND CAPTAINS.	ENSIGNS.
	P. Bellew.	J. Smith.	D. Onslow.
	F. D'Oyly.	W. C. Archer.	G. Bruhl.
	Sir J. Duffe.	G. Bristow.	Wm. Wheatley.
	Ch. Talbot.	Hon. C. Fitzroy.	J. D. Burnaby.
	Kingsmill Evans.*	H. Chayter.	
	Colin Campbell.	R. Williams.	
	Sir How Dalrymple.	H. Warde.	ADJUTANT.
	J. Perryn.	W. H. Clinton.	J. Smith.
		J. Andrews.	

Feb. 25. On the morning of the 25th of February, 1793, the Guards, 1539 strong, were reviewed by the King and Prince of Wales in St. James's Park, whence they marched to Greenwich, where they embarked in boats in presence of the King and Queen, and of the Dukes of Gloucester and York, and were thence conveyed to the ships by Greenwich pensioners. As each boat full of soldiers left the shore, the King took off his hat, while the Queen and princesses waved their handkerchiefs in response to the cheering of the men. The Duke of York, who was appointed to command all the King's forces in Holland and Flanders, proceeded at once to the Hague, where he arrived on the 27th of February; and the transports, after anchoring at the Nore on the 27th, put to sea, and arrived off Helvoetsluys on the

Mar. 1. 1st of March. Seven companies of the Third Guards and

captain and lieut.-colonel in April, 1776, and major, commanding a battalion, on 12th March, 1789. He embarked in command of the first battalion in February, 1793, at the commencement of the war, and served with it, till he became major-general in December of the same year. He was appointed to command the brigade of Guards in Flanders, vice Lake, in May, 1794; and in May, 1795, became colonel of the 56th regiment. He served on the home staff from 1795 to 1798, when he was employed in Ireland during the Rebellion, having become lieut.-general in January, 1798. He accompanied the expedition to St. Hilda's in 1799, and on his return, commanded the south-west district. On the 25th of September he rose to the rank of general; was appointed lieut.-governor of Chelsea in February, 1806, and governor in 1820, an appointment which he held till his death; and in 1830, he received the field-marshal's baton, after 76 years' service.

Sir Samuel also held the position of equerry to the Prince of Wales, and governor and treasurer to the household, which he held for twetny-five years; he died unmarried, 1st January, 1837.

* Died of wounds received at Lincelles.

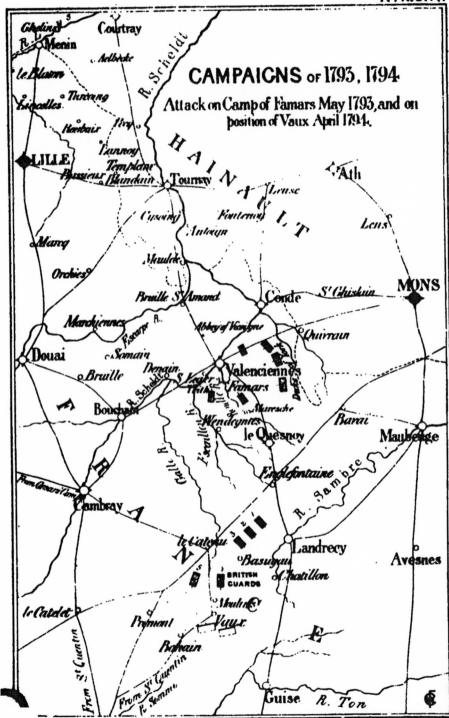

CAMPAIGNS of 1793, 1794

Attack on Camp of Famars May 1793, and on position of Vaux April 1794.

five of the Coldstreams landed on the 4th, the former marched   1793.
to Brill, below Rotterdam, and the latter for a time occu-   Arrival in
pied Helvoetsluys.   The First Guards and the remainder   Holland.
of the brigade under General Lake disembarked on the 5th   March.
of March, and proceeded in boats up the river towards
Dordrecht, but in consequence of the slowness of this
means of transport they landed and marched to their destination, where they were rejoined by the other detachments
of the brigade on the 7th of the month.   The brigade of
Guards were thus the first troops of the British army to
commence that series of operations in a long, arduous
struggle which, with alternating success, was ever carried
on by Great Britain with much tenacity of purpose, drew
forth the inexhaustible resources of the country, and finally
terminated in triumph, with great credit and glory to the
British arms.

When the campaign of 1793 opened, the allies mustered
altogether about 140,000 men—viz., 70,000 Imperialists,
with 38,000 English, Dutch, and others, under the Prince
of Coburg, on the frontiers of France and on the Lower
Rhine ; and 33,400 more Imperialists between the Meuse
and the Moselle.   The French Republic, on the other
hand, could place 30,000 men in line on the frontiers of
the Netherlands, 70,000 towards Maestricht, and 25,000
on the Moselle, making a total of 125,000 men.

When the British Guards landed early in March, part of
the left wing of the French republican army was laying siege
to Wilhelmstadt, on the southern bank of the Meuse, near its
mouth, in hopes of forcing its way thence to Amsterdam ;
but the Dutch commandant, emboldened by the assistance
that was arriving for the defence of his country, resisted
with great determination, and Dumourier was baffled in
his plan of penetrating further north, before the British
appeared in the field.   The siege was consequently raised   March 15.
on the 15th of March, and the French retired.   The right   Retreat of
wing of the French army near Liege was equally unsuc-   the French
cessful ; it was driven across the Meuse by the Imperialists,   armies.
and in an attempt to recross that river and attack the

1793.　Austrians it was completely routed, and shortly afterwards both the French armies retired within their own frontier, when Dumourier, being summoned to Paris to answer for his non-success, deserted the service of the Republic, and went over to the Austrian camp. He was

April 5.　succeeded by General Dampierre, who at first threw the remnants of the French army into the frontier towns, and then concentrating them near Valenciennes, formed an entrenched camp at Famars, south of that town, where he proceeded to reorganise his troops. The Prince of Coburg, with the Imperialists, advanced towards him, and the British contingent—still very small, owing to the difficulty of providing transport for the embarcation of the remainder from England—was ordered to move south and assemble at Tournay, where the principal magazine for the British army was established, on account of the easy navigation of the Scheldt.

March.　The use of light infantry troops had for some time been established in continental armies, and during the stay of the Guards at Dordrecht, towards the end of March, one light infantry company was formed, composed of picked men from the three battalions of the brigade, each battalion furnishing twenty-seven men; the officers were also selected from the service battalions, and the command of this company, which was attached to the Grenadier battalion of four companies, was conferred on Lieutenant-Colonel Perryn of the First Guards, who had already seen service in America, his place and those of the other officers being filled up by officers of corresponding rank from the battalions at home.

As the value of the use of light infantry in the field has from the year 1793 to the present time risen more and more in the estimation of the best judges of military tactics, till it is now considered by some to be almost the only mode of attack to be employed against the new long range weapons, it will be interesting to record what steps were taken in the First Guards for its introduction. Nearly simultaneously with the formation of the above temporary brigade company while on active service, an order was issued in England, on the 16th of April, by the King's command, for raising four light infantry companies for the First Regiment of Guards, each of one captain, two lieutenants, two buglers, and 100 rank and file, and two of like strength for each of the other two regiments. As many of the officers who were to receive commissions in those companies were then with their battalions abroad, the Duke of York ordered them to be relieved by others upon the first opportunity, and return home.

The following were the officers selected in April for the four light infantry companies of the First Guards :—

CAPTAINS AND LIEUT.-COLONELS.	LIEUTENANTS AND CAPTAINS.
Lt.-Colonel Thos. Glyn.	Capts. Rob.Cheney, Denzil Onslow
,, Hon. G. J. Ludlow.	,, H. Clinton, Hon. A. Hope.
,, Will. Thornton.	,, Jn.Gosling, Hon. Jn.Broderick
,, Duncan Campbell.	,, M. Disney, H. F. Campbell.

These companies were actively trained for their new duties under proper instruction at home, and in July two of those of the First Guards, and one from each of the two other regiments, were sent out to Holland.

In accordance with their orders to join the main army near Tournay, the brigade of Guards embarked on the 1st of April from Dordrecht, and proceeded to Bergen-Op-Zoom; where they remained till the 9th of April, when, moving by canal and the Scheldt to a place opposite Antwerp, they landed and marched to Beveren, being there joined by a brigade of the line, consisting of the 14th, 37th, and 53rd Regiments, under Major-General Ralph Abercrombie. On the 13th and 14th of April, these two brigades, moved by Lockeren to Ghent, where they were warmly welcomed, and after two days' halt proceeded by canal to Bruges, whence they moved by Thieldt to Courtray, and on the 23rd of April arrived at Tournay. The next evening the flank battalion of the Guards advanced as far as Orchies, twelve miles S.S.W. of Tournay, and being joined on the following day by the other battalions, they all took up a position on the right of the allied line.

1793.   The town of Condé, fifteen miles east of Orchies, was at
this time blockaded by the Austrians. Dampierre attempted
May 1.   its relief, and attacked the allies on the 1st of May, between
Condé and St. Amand, but was repulsed with loss. The
French general determined, however, to make another
attempt to save the place, and in consequence of his
movements, the Duke of York was ordered to march with
May 8.   his British contingent at midnight on the 8th of May to the
support of the Prussians under Knobelsdorff. He arrived at
the camp of Maulde at six o'clock in the morning with the
brigade of Guards and a battalion of Hanoverians; soon after
which the action commenced, when the efforts of the enemy,
who had been considerably reinforced, were at first mainly
directed to forcing the position between St. Amand and the
Abbey of Vicogne. The Prussian general Knobelsdorff
having sent a considerable part of his troops to support the
Action at   Austrians at the Abbey, the Duke of York was ordered in the
St. Amand. afternoon to reinforce him with three battalions, viz., the
Grenadier battalion, the Coldstreams, and Third Guards, all
under Major-General Lake, leaving the First Guards and
the Hanoverians in reserve. While the Grenadier companies of the Guards were detached to the right front, the
Coldstreams advanced into a wood, driving the French
before them, until they came upon a line of the enemy
strongly entrenched, and protected by a battery, which
obliged the battalion, after suffering severely, to re-occupy
the wood, where it maintained itself till reinforced by the
Third Guards, when they drove the French from their
posts. The importance of the British attack was acknowledged by the general-in-chief, while the Duke of York,
in his despatch, states, " that nothing could exceed the
spirit and bravery displayed by the Coldstreams, nor is less
praise due to the activity and intrepidity with which the
other battalions went into action." The French General
Dampierre was killed, and his troops returned to their
entrenched camp at Famars.

The following orders were issued on the occasion to the
troops serving under Major-General Lake :—

" Tournay, *May* 10.

" His Royal Highness the Duke of York returns his warmest thanks to the officers and private men of the troops who were engaged on the 8th instant, and particularly to those of the Coldstream Regiment, who bore the brunt of the attack. The Hanoverians are to relieve the brigade of Guards in all their posts to-morrow, in order to ease those troops who have undergone so much fatigue.

" His Majesty has been pleased to order that his Grace's approbation should be expressed to Major-General Lake, and the rest of the officers and men who have so masterly contributed to the late success."

On the 9th it was observed that the enemy had com- May 9. menced to entrench themselves, whereupon, while the Duke of York held the camp at Maulde with his contingent, the Austrians and Prussians were ordered to attack the enemy's batteries early the following morning before they were completed. The French, however, withdrawing during the night, their entrenchments were taken possession of by the allies, and the brigade of Guards returned to Tournay.

The British contingent was reinforced on the 15th of May by a brigade of cavalry ; on the 18th the Prince of Orange joined the Duke with ten battalions of Dutch infantry, and 2000 cavalry, and the Prince of Coburg, having now 80,000 men under his command, determined to dislodge the enemy from their camp at Famars and besiege Valenciennes ; the camp was defended by redoubts and abattis in rear of the Ronelle. The Duke of York's corps, May 19. about 12,000 strong, with the flank battalion of Guards in advance, proceeded on the 19th to Bruille, and the next day defiled past the commander-in-chief as they moved to take up their ground near Quievren, on the frontiers between Mons and Valenciennes.

At midnight, between the 22nd–23rd of May, the column May 22-23. placed under the Duke of York's command, composed of Storming the British Guards, the Hanoverian and Austrian troops, at Famars. in all sixteen battalions, passed through the Austrian camp

1793.

May 23.

to turn the enemy's right; the fog was thick, and when it cleared off about half-past five in the morning, the allied army was seen advancing with the utmost regularity. Another column of nearly equal force, under General Ferraris, in which was Abercrombie's British brigade, was ordered, after carrying the enemy's works on the right bank of the Ronelle, to second the operations of the Duke of York's column as circumstances might direct; there were two other columns, one of which observed Valenciennes, and another masked Quesnoy, while at the same time threatening the French right.

On discovering the advance of the Duke's column, the enemy opened a heavy cannonade, but at too great a distance: they were answered by the Austrian and Hanoverian artillery, under cover of which two divisions of Hussars passed the river at a ford opposite Maresche. The Duke ordered the Guards and two battalions of Austrian infantry with some cavalry to pass the ford, take the batteries in flank, and secure a passage for the rest of the troops; this being effected, the enemy was driven from wood to wood, and fell back upon a redoubt on the heights behind Famars. The soldiers having now been thirty hours under arms with only two hours' rest, and with nothing to eat, and the Duke observing from the dispositions of the enemy, that the redoubts behind Famars could not be carried without a loss disproportionate to the benefit that could arise, determined to turn the position in the night and attack it at daybreak; the enemy, however, apprehensive of such a movement, abandoned the works after dark, and retired into Valen-

May 24.

ciennes. The next morning this important post was occupied by the Duke of York, and the camp of Famars fell into the hands of the allies, the remainder of the French army retiring on the same day across the Scheldt to Denain. The First Guards suffered no loss during these operations.

Siege of Valen- ciennes.

Valenciennes, garrisoned by 13,000 men under General Ferrand, was now invested, the conduct of the siege being entrusted to the Duke of York, who established his head-

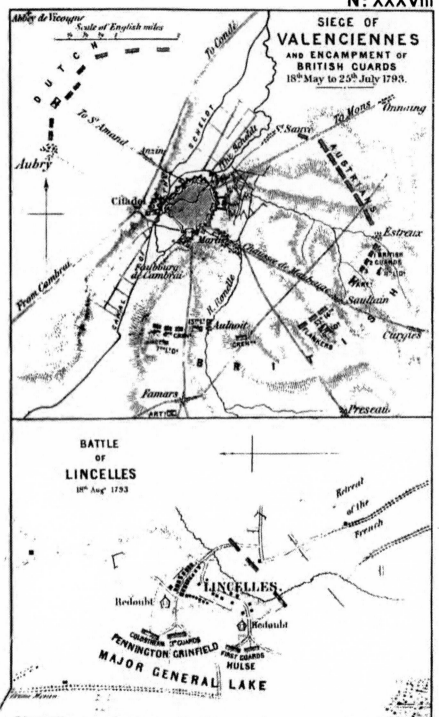

SIEGE OF
VALENCIENNES
AND ENCAMPMENT OF
BRITISH GUARDS
18ᵗʰ May to 25ᵗʰ July 1793.

BATTLE
OF
LINCELLES
18ᵗʰ Augᵗ 1793

quarters at Estreux, while a corps of 30,000 men watched
the enemy on the side of Bouchain and Douay. The attack
was made on the south-east, between the river on the right
and the suburb of Marlis on the left, out of which the
enemy were driven on the 26th of May. The Guards took
up a position between the Mons road and Estreux, taking
their share in the several duties of the siege, during which
they distinguished themselves by their superior work, arising,
it was said, from many of the men being accustomed to coal-
heaving in London, a common employment, both then and at
a still later period, among those soldiers who were permitted
to work when off duty. The first parallel being completed by
the 14th of June, the town was summoned, but the veteran
commander refused to surrender. The batteries of the second
parallel were completed by the 8th of July, during the whole
of which time an unremitting fire of shot and shell was
poured into the devoted city. The batteries of the third
parallel opened fire on the 23rd of July, soon completely
silencing the enemy's guns. It was resolved, therefore, on
the night of the 25th, to make three attacks on the town, of
900 men each ; on the ravelin of the hornwork, on the half
bastion on the right, and on the Flêche ; the two latter
were attacked by the Austrians ; the former by the British,
Hanoverians, and Hessians, under General Abercrombie.
Of this column 150 men of the Guards, under the command
of Colonel Leigh of the First regiment, formed the advanced
party, followed by 150 men of the brigade of the line,
and an equal number of Hanoverians, under Colonel
Doyle : 150 Hanoverians and 300 Hessians composed the
rest of the column in support.

Upon the signal being given about nine o'clock, Colonel
Leigh and his party, rushing out from the sap, advanced
with the utmost alacrity. The enemy was almost instantly
driven from the covered-way, abandoning the hornwork and
all the outworks ; and the Guards entered it by the gorge.
The first intention had been to spike the guns and
retire ; but an underground passage being discovered from
the ditch, and no enemy appearing in the counter-guard,

Margin notes:

1793.

May 26.

June 14.

July 25.
Assault.

1793.
July 25.
•

the Duke of York directed that a lodgement should be made and a battery at once erected.

The Duke expressed himself in general orders as follows, with regard to the gallantry and good conduct of the troops in this attack:—" His Royal Highness the Commander-in-Chief returns his thanks to Major-General Abercrombie, Colonel Leigh, Colonel Doyle, and the officers and soldiers under their command, for the gallantry they showed in the attack last night."

Ensign Tollemache, of the First Guards, was killed by a shell in the third parallel, during the attack, and the Duke, in his despatches, expressed his regret at the loss of this brave officer; Captain Henry Warde,* of the First Guards, who subsequently rose high in the army, was wounded.

Capitula-
tion.

Aug. 1.

The Duke of York, anxious now to spare the town the horrors of an assault, sent the governor a summons to surrender, and after some discussion, a capitulation was agreed to on the 28th, when the advanced works were given up, and on the 1st of August, 7000 Frenchmen, after a siege which had lasted forty-five days, laid down their arms on the glacis as they marched out of the Cambray gate,

---

* Captain H. Warde was appointed ensign in the First Guards in 1783, and lieutenant in July, 1790. He was so severely wounded at Valenciennes, that he was compelled to return to England, and on his recovery rejoined the battalion in July, 1794, as adjutant. He obtained his company as captain and lieut.-colonel on the 15th Oct. of the same year, when he was ordered home. He commanded the light infantry companies of the First Guards in the expedition to Ostend in 1798, and was present in all the actions in the campaign at the Helder in 1799. In 1807, as brigadier-general, he commanded a brigade in the expedition to Copenhagen, and he was included in the thanks of Parliament. In 1808, he became major-general and commanded the first brigade of Guards under Sir David Baird, and was in the retreat to, and battle of, Corunna, under Sir John Moore; for this service he again received the thanks of Parliament. In 1809, General Warde proceeded to India, was second in command at the capture of the Mauritius in 1810, and afterwards acted as governor, and commanded the forces. He again received the thanks of Parliament. Major-general Warde was appointed to the colonelcy of the 68th regiment in 1813, in which year he became lieut.-general, and general in 1830. Sir Henry Warde was one of those selected " for eminent service during the late war," on the augmentation of the Order of the Bath, receiving the distinctions of K.C.B. and G.C.B. in due course. Sir Henry died on 1st October, 1834.

between two lines of the allies. The flank battalion of the 1793.
Guards and the men who stormed the outworks on the 25th Aug. 1.
of July, under the command of Sir James Duffe of the
First Guards, were specially selected to be stationed near
the Cambray gate on this occasion.

The losses sustained by the brigade of Guards during this
siege were :—

	Killed or died of wounds.		Wounded.		
	Offs.	R. & F.	Offs.	Sgts.	R. & F.
1st batt. First Guards,	1	9	1	1	12
Flank battalion,	...	7	...	2	15
1st batt. Coldstreams,	...	3	1	1	14
1st batt. 3rd Guards,	...	8	...	...	17
Total	1	27	2	4	58

The Duke issued the following order on the termination Aug. 2.
of the siege:—"His Royal Highness the Commander-in-
Chief returns his thanks to the troops for the steadiness
and gallantry with which they have conducted themselves
during the siege, and he is happy to inform them that
it has insured them the respect and esteem of the troops
with whom they are serving."

The King's approval of the conduct of the troops on the
occasion was communicated to them in the following
order :—

"ORCHIES. His Majesty has been most graciously pleased Aug. 14.
to approve in the fullest manner of Major-General
Abercrombie, Colonel Leigh, and Captain Doyle, and the
rest of the officers and men who had the good fortune to be
most actively engaged in the reduction of Valenciennes."

While the siege of Valenciennes was progressing, Condé
capitulated to the allies, and shortly afterwards Mayence
also fell into their hands.

The practice of employing light infantry becoming much
more general in all the continental armies, the Duke of
Gloucester, as colonel of the First Guards, had, as we
have seen, received authority in the spring to raise four April 9.
companies of light infantry of one hundred rank and file
each, which increased the establishment of the regiment

from twenty-eight to thirty-two companies; and on the day previous to the capitulation of Valenciennes two of these companies belonging to the First Guards arrived in camp, under the command of Lieutenant-Colonel Hon. George Ludlow, as also one company from each of the Coldstream and Third Guards. At the same time there arrived a reinforcement of ten men per company for each battalion, the whole under the command of Colonel Watson, of the Third Guards. The light companies were now added to the flank battalion, which for some time therefore consisted of four Grenadier and four light infantry companies.

The French army under General Kilmaine, the successor of Custine, who had been summoned to Paris and guillotined, having been forced back from their own frontier, now occupied the position of the camp of Cæsar and the heights of

Aug. 6.
Capture of
the camp of
Cæsar and
Bourbon.
Bourbon, west of Cambray, and on the 6th of August the allies advanced for the purpose of attacking these positions. The Duke of York's corps, about 22,000 strong, marched in three columns to Villers-en-Courtrie, and passed the Scheldt at Manières and Crèvecœur, to the south of, and above Cambray, the flank battalion of Guards forming part of the advanced guard. Here he made the necessary dis-

Aug. 8.
positions to attack the camp of Bourbon on the 8th, by turning the enemy's right flank; but the French general would not compromise the safety of his army against such superior forces, and though his works were strong and complete, he retreated at daybreak, pursued by the British cavalry as far as Arras. Cambray was then summoned, and was only saved by the alteration that was now taking place in the policy of the allied governments.

The Republican forces had not only been driven out of Holland and West Flanders, but the allies had succeeded in capturing two important frontier fortresses, and were firmly established on French territory; from Lille to Basle, in Switzerland, they had 280,000 men in the field. The French were disorganised and weak in numbers; the road to Paris was open, and there was now an opportunity, by a simultaneous advance from the north and east, of crushing

the Reign of Terror in Paris, and dictating terms that
would satisfy all the legitimate objects for which the war
had been commenced. But ambitious projects divided the
councils of the allies. Instead of the fleur-de-lys, the
Austrians had hoisted the eagle over Valenciennes and
Condé, in token of conquest, ignoring the royalty of
France, on behalf of which they had been fighting. The
British · Cabinet was anxious to obtain the fort of Dunkirk, while the Prussians, jealous of the aggrandisement of
their Austrian allies, had interests to secure in Poland.
The armies consequently, when on the point of securing
the original object of the war, separated to pursue each
their own selfish policy, and France was thus saved when
at the mercy of her enemies. Each nation suffered before
this error was redeemed, and twenty years of warfare added
hundreds of millions to the debt of Great Britain, while
Austria and Prussia were in turn humbled to the dust by
the legions of France.

That country was now roused with patriotic energy by the
invasion of her soil, and the National Convention decreed a
levy *en masse* of the population, when a million of soldiers
were embodied. At a council of war of the allied generals
they decided, notwithstanding the remonstrances and advice
of the Prince of Coburg, to form two armies to act inde-
pendently of each other, whereupon the Imperialists returned to Valenciennes, and laid siege to Quesnoy, while
the Duke of York on the 10th of August commenced a
movement towards Dunkirk, with the view to assisting in the
siege of that town. His army, about 35,000 strong,
marched in two columns, the First Guards and the flank
battalion forming part of the rear guard, under General
Lake. The line of march was through Villers-en-Ferté,
Somain, and Marchiennes, back to Orchies, near which a
detachment of 14,000 Austrians joined the Duke of York
on the 14th, raising his forces to 50,000 men. On the 15th
of August the Duke continued his march through Baisieux,
lying half-way between Tournay and Lille, the British
troops forming his right column, and reached Tourcoing

Marginal notes:

1793.

Alteration
of policy of
the allies.

Aug. 10.

Aug. 15.

1793. on the 16th. The next day the flank battalion of Guards marched through Menin, on the frontier, to Ghelins, Aug. 18. followed on the 18th by the rest of the brigade of Guards, when they encamped in the neighbourhood. No sooner Action at Lincelles. had the Guards taken up their position than they had an opportunity, which they did not allow to escape, of highly distinguishing themselves. The Prince of Orange with his Dutch troops, while covering the left of the Duke of York's army, had attacked the French in an intrenched position at Lincelles and Blaton, on the morning of the 18th of August; in this he had succeeded with some difficulty ; but about one o'clock in the afternoon, the French being reinforced, returned and attacked the position with 5000 men, driving out the Dutch and capturing their·guns and ammunition, upon which the Prince of Orange sent at once to Menin to request assistance. The British troops had scarcely pitched their tents when a Dutch aide-de-camp galloped up to head-quarters. and delivered his message. The Duke, knowing that the Guards were the " first turn-out boys," directed General Lake, without loss of time, to march with his three battalions, which were nearest to the scene of action, to support the Prince, ˙accompanied by some guns, under Major Wright. The brigade, consisting of 378 men of the First Guards, under Colonel Hulse, 346 of the Coldstreams, under Colonel Pennington, and 398 of the Third Guards, under Colonel Greenfield, left their encampment at 2 P.M., and arrived in front of Lincelles at 6 o'clock, when they moved into a large bean field, where the crop was so high they could hardly see in front. Here they found that the Dutch could not be induced to rally; General Lake thereupon, while he sent a message to the Duke explaining his isolated position, embraced a resolution, which, according to the Duke's report, was worthy of the troops he commanded, and at once determined to attack, notwithstanding the superiority in numbers of the enemy, who acknowledged to having twelve battalions in the field, and who occupied two redoubts of great size and strength in front of the village ; the road was also defended by other

works, strongly palisaded, while woods and ditches covered
their flanks. The First Guards being at the head of the
column began the attack, and the other battalions formed
on their left with the utmost celerity. After firing three or
four rounds, the line advanced with fixed bayonets, under a
heavy fire of grape, with an order and intrepidity for which
no praise could be too high, and stormed the redoubts. The
French having been accustomed to the spiritless attacks of
the Dutch, were amazed at the impetuosity of the British,
and gave way. They re-formed, however, behind the village,
when the Guards, moving round it, again attacked them,
and drove them off the field with the loss of twelve
pieces of cannon, of which five 6-pounders were taken in
the redoubt attacked by the First Guards, and four
9-pounders in the other redoubt; one stand of colours was
captured by a sergeant of the First Guards, and seventy
prisoners fell into the hands of the brigade; but the want of
cavalry was much felt to follow up this victory, which,
however, was in itself complete. The pursuit ceased about
10 P.M., when, the 14th and 53rd Regiments and two battalions of Hessians having arrived, the Guards marched
back to Menin, which they did not reach till three o'clock in
the morning.

The French prisoners admitted the presence of twelve
battalions. In physique there is no doubt that at this time
the French troops were inferior, for the better part of the
population had not yet been drawn into the ranks. The
Guards, instead of killing them when they got into the
redoubt, rather treated them as a mob in London, striking
them with their fists, and frequently calling out, " Let him
alone, the little animal can't do much harm."

The Dutch were so much ashamed of their conduct and
so crest-fallen, that they slunk about, avoiding the British
soldiers as much as possible; but the Prince of Waldeck,
who commanded at Menin, the next morning, in a noble
manner, caught the first officer of the Guards he met with
by the hand, and in presence of his own officers extolled
the gallantry of the British soldiers, exclaiming, " Your
glory is our shame." An historian of the time speaks of

1793.
August.

Lincelles.

the action as "the most brilliant exploit which happened in the course of the campaign," and praises the judgment and decision of the commander, afterwards so distinguished.

Five officers of the First Guards were wounded—Lieutenant-Colonel Kingsmill Evans (died of his wounds), Lieutenant-Colonel Francis D'Oyly, Captains A. Whetham, G. Bristow, and W. C. Archer; two sergeants and nineteen rank and file were killed; two sergeants and forty-two rank and file wounded, and the Duke reported, "It can only be imputed to the ability of the commander and the extraordinary valour of the officers and men that the loss was not greater." The Coldstreams had one officer and eight men killed, and two officers and forty-five men wounded. The Third Guards had eight men killed, and two officers and forty-five men wounded.

On the 19th the Duke, while at Menin, issued the following order, thanking the troops engaged:—"His Royal Highness the Commander-in-Chief returns his warmest thanks to Major-General Lake, Colonels Greenfield, Hulse, and Pennington, and the officers and men belonging to the brigade of Guards, to Major Wright, and the artillery under his command, for the gallantry and intrepidity they so frequently showed in the attack of the French redoubts, &c., at the village of Lincelles, yesterday evening."

The King was also pleased to express his approbation of their services, in the following words:—

"Dunkirk. His Majesty has been graciously pleased to express the strongest approbation of the spirited and judicious conduct of Major-General Lake, and of the gallant behaviour of Colonels Greenfield, Hulse, Pennington, and Major Wright, and of the rest of the officers and men who were engaged at the fort of Lincelles on the 18th instant. His Majesty very much laments the loss of Lieutenant-Colonel Bosville,* Lieutenant de Piesti, R.A., and the non-commissioned officers and men who fell on that occasion, and it will afford sincere satisfaction to his Majesty to be informed that those brave officers and men

---

* Of the Coldstream Guards.

who had the misfortune to be wounded in the conflict, are 1793.
now in a fair way of recovery."

A graphic description of this action is also given in a
letter from Sergeant Darby, of the First Guards, dated a
week later, from the camp before Dunkirk. The writer
was one of the first to enter the village of Lincelles. The
rewards to the three regiments of Guards for their conduct
on this occasion were not confined to the thanks of their own
sovereign; for, in consequence of their distinguished gallantry,
they were subsequently authorised to emblazon the word
LINCELLES on their colours, which they retain to this day.

After a day's rest in camp, the brigade continued their
march on the 20th of August, through Ypres, towards Dunkirk, encamping the first night at Boesinghen, and reaching Furnes on the 21st. To the Hanoverian Marshal
Freytag had been assigned the duty of covering the attack
on Dunkirk. On the 22nd of August he drove the enemy
from their posts near Hondschoote, and on the same day
the Duke advanced against the enemy's camp at Gyveldt,
near the sea, which they abandoned. The next morning
the British army took up its ground about a league and a
half from Dunkirk, and on the arrival of the Guards, who
marched along the Dyke by the Furnes Canal, their flank
battalion encamped on the right or northern, and the other
three battalions on the southern bank.

In reply to a summons to surrender, the governor
declared he would defend the town to the last, and immediately followed up his answer on the 24th of August
by a vigorous sortie with 9000 men; fortunately the Duke
had, at the same time, resolved to advance in force and
attack the enemy, who were still outside the town. General
D'Allon's column, and the flank battalion of Guards,
which had formed throughout the advanced guard, were
on the extreme right near the sea, and though they
were exposed to a severe fire both from the troops in
front, from the ramparts, as well as from the gun-
boats, during their attack, they drove the French before
them in a most gallant manner; the line of advance of

1793.

the flank battalion was through gardens and inclosures surrounded by deep ditches full of water and double hedges, notwithstanding which impediments, the enemy did not stand, but kept firing and retiring till they reached the glacis of the fortress, suffering considerably in their retreat. Captain Williams of the First Guards was severely wounded in this affair, which took place on the same ground as that occupied by the Royal Regiment of Guards, 135 years before, on the 15th of June, 1658, at the battle of the Downs.

Aug. 26.

The flank battalion of the Guards joined the rest of the brigade, on the 26th of August, at Zeteghem, where they commenced to entrench themselves; but Dunkirk being only partially invested, the French, on receiving considerable stores and reinforcements from the side of Wenox

Sept. 6.

Bergues, advanced on the 6th of September, from Cassel, and made a simultaneous attack on the Hanoverian covering army, and on the besiegers. After a severe contest, they succeeded in driving in Marshal Freytag's advanced posts and getting possession of Bambeke and Rossbrugge, lying south of Hondschoote. On the same afternoon a sortie was made from the city against the allied right, where the Guards were entrenched, but though the enemy were much assisted by their gun-boats, they were beaten back to the covered way of the town before sunset. The Duke, however, on hearing of Marshal Freytag's partial defeat stopped all further disembarcation of guns on the canal, and sent the heavy baggage back to Furnes.

Sept. 7.

The next morning the French again attacked the Hanoverians at Hondschoote, carrying the entrenchment, whereupon Walmoden, who was in immediate command, retired over the Loo Canal; and later in the day the garrison, led on by Hoche, sallied out and attacked the allied right, but were a third time driven back to their works with considerable loss. Though the British troops had thus proved their superiority whenever they came in contact with the enemy, the effect of the defeat of the covering army of Hanoverians, under Freytag, proved fatal to the successful progress of the siege, which was consequently abandoned, and the British army retired on the morning of the 9th of September to Furnes, leaving behind several guns and some ammunition which could not be destroyed, as well as some baggage, amongst which were the tents of the First Guards. The duke had no sooner taken up a position behind the Loo, with the Guards and the rest of his troops, than the French, under Houchard, marched against the Prince of Orange at Menin, a movement which threatened the British left, whereupon the duke, 'leaving General Abercrombie at Furnes with 4000 men, moved on the 12th through Dixmuyde towards Rousselaer to form a junction with the prince. Menin itself was captured by the Republicans on the 13th, when, in order to check their further progress, the British army advanced on the 15th beyond Rousselaer and encamped on the Menin road.

During the recent operations, though the men had been continuously under arms and much harassed, the greatest cheerfulness prevailed amongst them, and the force was now increased by the arrival of three regiments from England, the 19th, 57th, and part of the 42nd. The duke was, therefore, enabled to continue his advance upon Menin, which had been pillaged by the French while in their temporary possession, but was subsequently recovered by the Austrians serving in the duke's corps, and the Guards again occupied the position they held on the 15th of August near Menin, from which they had advanced to Lincelles. On the 15th of September, the brigade had to regret the temporary loss of the general who had commanded them with so much ability during the campaign; for General Lake fell dangerously ill, and Colonel Greenfield of the Third Guards, being the next senior officer, was directed to take command. The general had sufficiently recovered in October to return to England, but the loss of his presence was much felt by all, as he was universally respected and beloved.

The Duke of York issued the following order, giving the soldiers great credit for their endurance and discipline during their late arduous marches :—

1793.

Sept. 9.

Sept. 15.

Sept. 17.

MENIN, 17*th September*, 1793.

H.R.H. the Commander-in-Chief returns his thanks to the troops for the spirit with which they have gone through their late fatigues, and the soldierlike manner in which they have borne the distresses occasioned by so long and rapid marches. They may depend upon his utmost care and attention to have them supplied with every comfort to which their conduct so justly entitles them.

Sickness, however, had now much increased in the camps, and one-third of the force was in hospital; part of the brigade was consequently moved, on the 23rd September, to higher ground, but the First Guards having no tents, were quartered in a village behind Menin. Colonel Leigh, who had commanded the flank battalion during the campaign, received at this time orders to proceed to Ireland, and was succeeded in his command by Colonel Sir James Duffe of the First Guards.

After the capitulation of Quesnoy to the Austrians on the 11th of September, the Prince of Coburg resolved to besiege Maubeuge on the Sambre; Houchard endeavoured to interrupt the investment, but was repulsed, and although he had been successful at Dunkirk, he was arrested, and eventually guillotined, the command in the north being conferred upon General Jourdain. The French had now 100,000 men, in six strongly entrenched camps, extending from Lille to Dunkirk, where they were busily employed in disciplining their raw levies, and whence they frequently made desultory attacks upon the advanced posts of the allies, without, however, obtaining much success. The allied army was still superior in numbers, but their line was too extended, and their right near the sea was being constantly threatened by feigned attacks; for the new French general, with the view to deceiving his opponents, was gradually drawing off the troops from opposite that flank and concentrating them at Guise, to the south of Landrecy, in order to relieve Maubeuge, against which the besiegers opened their batteries on the 14th of October.

Weak as the Duke of York was in British troops, he was ordered at the beginning of October to send home four regiments. Under the existing circumstances he was

naturally very unwilling to do so, for at the same time, the
Prince of Coburg, considering the force he had with him
too weak to storm Maubeuge, had, upon the refusal of a
Dutch corps of 14,000 men to cross the Sambre, directed
the Duke of York with his army to move down to his assistance.   The duke accordingly left Menin on the 10th of   Oct. 10.
October, marching by Courtrai, Pecq, and Tournay to
Cysoing, whence he was forced to dispatch the four
English regiments to Ostend, retaining with him of English
troops only the four battalions of Foot Guards, 1400
strong, and the 37th Regiment. The duke, however, continued his march on the 14th, to join the grand army before
Maubeuge, and that night the Guards occupied the monas-
tery of St. Amand ; thence moving round Valenciennes,
they encamped on the 16th at Englefontaine, between Ques-   Oct. 16.
noy and Landrecy, where the duke received the news, not
only that the Prince of Coburg had been obliged to raise
the siege of Maubeuge and recross the Sambre, but that Jourdain had made a general attack upon the right of the allied
line between Menin and Furnes, that Furnes had been abandoned on the approach of General Vandamme from Dunkirk, and that this latter general was about to attack
Nieuport, when the opportune arrival of eight English
regiments under Sir Charles Grey obliged the French to
raise the siege, leaving three guns behind them. Upon the
receipt of this intelligence, the Duke of York retraced his
steps with the Guards and other troops northwards, through
Maulde, to Tournay, where he arrived on the night of the
25th of October ; and while here, the news arrived of the   Oct. 25.
execution of the unfortunate Queen of France, the intelligence of which was communicated to the troops in the
following order :—

" H.R.H. the Commander-in-Chief, in informing the   Oct. 26.
troops of the unparalleled and cruel murder of the Queen of
France, which took place on the 15th instant (after a mock
trial), by a common hangman, is very certain that every
soldier will join with him in feeling the strongest indignation
and horror at the atrocity of such a crime."

The duke having now resolved to attack the enemy at

1793.   Menin, the execution of the design was entrusted to General Walmoden, while, to favour the enterprise, the army moved from Tournay southwards to Cysoing, whence General Abercrombie was detached with the flank battalion and Third Guards, with cavalry and two guns, to attack Lannoy ; and in this they were completely successful, the French retiring in disorder, after a slight resistance, many being taken prisoners. The enemy having evacuated Menin the previous evening, in consequence of the position taken up by the duke, and having failed in all their other undertakings, were now completely driven out of Flanders, on which occasion H.R.H. promulgated the failure of the enemy's combinations in the following general order :—

Oct. 31.   H.R.H. the Commander-in-Chief has the pleasure of acquainting the army, that in consequence of the gallant behaviour of the British and allied troops under his command at their different posts, the enemy has been completely beaten, foiled in all his undertakings, and been driven out of Flanders.

November.   The Austrian general in vain endeavoured during the month of November to bring the French to action ; and Jourdain, who failed in driving the allies out of France, was, notwithstanding his representations, ordered back to Paris, and deprived of his command, which was subsequently given to General Pichegru.

Although the allies had been successful during this campaign in keeping the enemy out of Flanders, and in occupying part of the French territory as well as some of their fortresses, they had failed in the great object of the war, that of marching upon Paris and striking at the root of the revolutionary system. The campaign was, however, honourable to the British regiments engaged ; in no instance had they experienced a reverse, and the First Guards, both in action and on the march, had supported its ancient reputation.

Dec. 13.   Before ordering the army into winter quarters, the duke, on the 13th of December, issued the following address to the troops :—

TOURNAY, 13*th December.*

H.R.H. the Commander-in-Chief cannot suffer the troops to go into winter quarters without expressing to them, previous to their separation, the sense he entertains of the intrepidity, patience, and perseverance they have displayed, so much to their own honour and to his satisfaction, in the course of the campaign. H.R.H. desires the officers and men will accept his warmest acknowledgments, and be assured their meritorious exertions have made an impression on his mind that will never be effaced. He is persuaded that the good conduct of the troops in quarters will equal their gallantry in the field. H.R.H. desires the officers will explain to their men the good consequences which must naturally result from their conciliating by their behaviour the affection of our allies, the subjects of his Imperial Majesty; and H.R.H. is perfectly assured that every officer, feeling the importance of this object, will take every opportunity of giving it the weight it so justly deserves, both by precept and example.

The order continues to enjoin respect to religious ceremonies, and thus concludes :—

H.R.H. is confident that the troops will bear in mind, that, though we differ in some of the ceremonies of religion, we unite with our gallant allies, and it is our glory to do so, in every sentiment of duty to our Creator, and of attachment, affection, and loyalty to our sovereign.

The brigade of Guards moved by Oudenarde to their winter quarters in Ghent on the 14th of December, where Dec. 14. the First regiment, now under the command of Lieutenant-Colonel Glyn, in the absence of Col. Hulse, together with the flank battalion, were quartered in a large nunnery, that had lately been converted into temporary barracks.

Colonel Albemarle Bertie, the commanding officer of the second battalion, retired from the Guards on the 25th of December, 1793, being succeeded by Colonel Patrick Bellew. Colonel Bertie was promoted to major-general in the following month, and rose in 1803 to be a full general in the service.

1794.

Early in the ensuing year a complete change took place in the command of the regiment and battalions by the appointment of the lieutenant-colonel of the regiment, General Lake, to the colonelcy of the 53rd Regiment of the line ; Colonel Hulse, the future Sir Samuel, succeeded, on the 30th of April, 1794, as lieutenant-colonel, and Edmund Stevens, Patrick Bellew, and Francis D'Oyly as the three regimental majors.

The British army was considerably increased at the end of the year 1793, in anticipation of the ensuing campaign. Each of the thirty-two companies of the First Guards was increased to 100 rank and file, the total strength of the regiment being raised to 3546 men of all ranks. During their stay in Ghent the Guards were not sorry to find themselves in good barracks, where rest and food restored them to health ; and they were warmly welcomed by the aristocracy of the town, who looked upon them as their protectors from the republicans, whose opinions were daily gaining ground among the lower classes in Flanders and Holland. The Guardsmen were invited by all to splendid entertainments, the Bishop of Ghent, once a soldier, being among the most hospitable. Anxious to return civilities, the army gave a ball to the Ghentois, but unaware of the great jealousy that existed between the noblesse and the bourgeoisie, many of the latter, who had been civil to the Guardsmen and others, were included in the invitation. One of these, a well-known tradesman, was requested to leave the ball, at the repeated instance of the nobles, and the consequent indignation of the middle class drove many of them into the ranks of the republican sympathisers.

At a meeting of the confederate commanders in England, in February, at which the Duke of York was present, as well as General Mack on the part of the imperialists, it was arranged that the principal object of the ensuing campaign, in which the Prussians agreed to co-operate, should be a general advance upon Paris. How far the allies were enabled to carry out their plans will be seen hereafter.

It was while the authorities were under a full belief of a triumphant termination to the ensuing campaign, that

Prince William of Gloucester was directed, on the 24th of February, to join the first battalion of the First Guards on foreign service, and he left England with some drafts on the last day of the month. He was, however, now only attached to the regiment, as Captain Dowdeswell had been gazetted to a company in his place on the 8th of February

previous. The following were the officers of the first battalion at the period of the commencement of this campaign :—

Major-Gen. GERARD LAKE, Lieut.-Col. of the regiment.
,,   SAMUEL HULSE, 1st Major.

CAPTS. AND LIEUT.-COLONELS.	LIEUTENANTS AND CAPTAINS.	ENSIGNS.
F. D'Oyly, Comg.,	Duncan Campbell,	Lord F. Montagu,
Sir Jas. Duffe, Knt.,	W. Dowdeswell,	M. C. Darby,
A. J. Drummond, L.I.,	A. Whetham,	Per. Maitland,
Hon. H. F. Stanhope,	G. Bristow,	Hon. W. Townshend,
Alexander Dury,	F. C. White, Adj.,	Hew Dalrymple,
John St. Leger,	R. Williams,	Hon. H. G. Bennet,
G. K. Coussmaker,	Hon. J. Brodrick,	J. Ashley Sturt,
His Roy. High. Prince	H. Warde,	Hon. Edward Capel.
William (attached),	T. Boone,	
James Perryn,	M. Disney,	
Hon. George Ludlow.	R. Cheney,	
	G. Cooke,	
	Jos. Andrews,	
	F. G. Ruddock, Adj.	

Many officers of the First Guards were at this time
serving on the staff. Captain Hope was acting as major of brigade on foreign service, but was shortly afterwards appointed
A.D.C. to Major-General Abercrombie. Captain Dyer was
adjutant of the first battalion, and Captain Wheatley of
the light company battalion, when it was formed ; Captain
Henry Clinton was acting as A.D.C. to H.R.H. the Duke
of York, Captain F. G. Lake as A.D.C. to Major-General
Lake, and Ensign Rainsford A.D.C. to Lieutenant-General
Rainsford. Colonel Needham was all this year Adjutant-
General to the Earl of Moira, and Colonel Sir Hew
Dalrymple commandant at Chatham barracks.

During the duke's absence reports were rife that the
enemy were concentrating their troops on the frontier, upon
which a detachment of 800 men of the Brigade of Guards
(the First Regiment furnishing 200 men), under the command
of Colonel A. Drummond (First Guards), marched, on the
16th of February, to reinforce the garrison of Courtrai ;
200 men of the light companies of the Guards, under

Lieutenant-Colonel Perryn, of the First Regiment, were also sent to relieve the Austrians at Marke and Aelbecke, two advanced villages nearer the frontier ; and on the 24th, the remainder of the brigade marched from Ghent to Courtrai, where they were stationed for a month, and in the event of an attack, or a move towards the enemy, the flank battalion of the Guards was to form the advanced guard. A draft of 800 men joined the brigade from England on the 9th of March, raising its strength to 3200 rank and file, or 100 men per company ; and Major-General Lake, being restored to health, resumed the command of the brigade on the 13th of March, while it was still at Courtrai.

At this time the allied army on the French frontier was estimated at 180,000 men, and in consequence of the difficulties and jealousies that had arisen in the previous campaign, it was agreed that the emperor should take the supreme command in person. The Duke of York had under his immediate command about 40,000 of these troops, of which at the commencement of the campaign only seven battalions and twenty-nine squadrons were English.

The French government had made such strenuous efforts to hold their own against the allies, that their two armies of the north and of the Ardennes amounted together to no less than 280,000 men, their principal force being concentrated near Cambrai and at Guise, about thirty miles south of Valenciennes.

Towards the end of March, Prince Coburg, having reason to expect an attack, directed the Duke of York to march, on the 26th, by Pecq and Tournay, to St. Amand, where, on the 27th, the First Guards took up their quarters in the convent, and here the soldiers of the brigade who had fought at Lincelles received, on the 30th of the same month, an acknowledgment of their gallantry in that action.* On the 9th of April the duke moved with his contingent towards the Escaillon river, the Guards halting at S. Leger,

---

* Each sergeant, corporal, and private received respectively £1 1s., 14s. 3d., and 9s. 9d.

five miles south-west of Valenciennes, and the next day at
Wendegnies. The Emperor of Germany arrived at Valenciennes on the 15th of April, and assumed the command of
the allied forces, when a grand review of all the troops
was announced for the 16th.   On that day the duke's
army, including the Brigade of Guards, removed to Cateau,
where they were inspected by the emperor, encamping
afterwards beyond that town. The review was said to be a
pretence for assembling a large force, in order to attack the
enemy's entrenched position at Vaux, about ten miles south-
west of Landrecy, between that town and Premont, the
ultimate object being the investment of Landrecy.

The attack on Vaux was made in eight columns; three
columns of imperialists moved to their left towards Landrecy,
and the fourth and fifth columns, under the orders of the Duke
of York, advanced on Vaux, which was strongly entrenched.
The Guards were at the head of the fourth column, and as
soon as they appeared in sight, the enemy opened fire on
them. A hollow way, or ravine, ran parallel to the front of
the French position; on the left, it led up towards the
village of Vaux, and to the rear of a redoubt; under cover
of this the brigade formed four lines, the flank battalion
with O'Donnell's corps in front, while some guns were sent
to the edge of the wood on the right. Two companies
of O'Donnell's corps and two grenadier companies of
the First Guards, under Colonel Stanhope, followed by
the other battalions of Guards, marched to their left and
turned the redoubt, the French abandoning it without
resistance. The flank battalion and First Guards then
advanced to the right, in the direction of Bohain, and
captured four pieces of artillery, while the other battalions
remained at Vaux. The fifth column, under Sir William
Erskine, on the right of the Guards, attacked and carried
Premont; the three first columns of imperialists, on the left,
also carried the enemy's positions at Chatillon and Basuyau,
and invested Landrecy. The Duke of York thus expressed
himself as to the manner in which the operations were
carried out by the columns under his command :—

" H.R.H. the Duke of York takes the earliest opportunity of testifying the sense he entertains of the bravery and conduct of the troops, which compose the two columns under his immediate command, in the very extensive operations of the 17th instant. His personal observations of the spirit and steadiness with which the officers and men of the column which attacked the enemy's entrenchments on the heights above the village of Vaux, and in the wood of Bohain, supported a very severe cannonade; and the report made to him by Sir W. Erskine that the same qualities were equally displayed by the column at the attack of the enemy's works at Premont, calls upon him to express to them his warmest approbation."

Captain Henry Clinton of the First Guards, aide-de-camp to the duke, was dispatched to England with the news of this success. The siege of Landrecy was now entrusted to the Prince of Orange, while the emperor covered it on the south side towards Guise, and the duke on the west towards Cambrai.

On the day after the action the flank and First Guards battalions, with cavalry, continued their advance against Bohain, but as the French fled with precipitation, the two battalions returned to Vaux, and on the 19th of April proceeded through Cateau, encamping on the road leading to Cambrai, and, after being joined by the rest of the army, a line of redoubts was commenced to strengthen the position now taken up to cover the siege of Landrecy.

While at Cateau on the 18th of April, the duke had occasion to find fault with the system of pillaging and burning of houses, which was very prevalent in some of the foreign regiments of his corps. It would appear there was less of this irregularity in the brigade of Guards, for on that day he directed a detachment of one officer and forty men of the Guards to proceed immediately to the neighbouring village of Baseaux to enforce the duke's orders on the subject, the officer being ordered to report himself on his arrival to General Otto, who was in command there.

The enemy having made a demonstration towards Valenciennes, the duke sent a force of cavalry to interrupt their
movements, and upon their coming up with him at Villers
en Cauchie, a brilliant affair of cavalry took place, in which
the 15th Light Dragoons were so distinguished, that the
emperor recorded it by conferring a gold medal on the
officer engaged.   The French now determined not only
to attempt the relief of Landrecy, but to attack West
Flanders, and for this purpose the army of the Ardennes
was directed to join General Pichegru.

Two French columns accordingly advanced on the 26th
of April against the entrenched camp at Le Cateau, but as
they approached the British right, they got into confusion,
whereupon the duke sent his cavalry to turn their left,
which service they performed in " a manner beyond all
praise," attacking column after column with great success.
The Guards were on the scene of action, but the enemy
were so quickly dispersed by the cavalry that they found no
opportunity of taking any active part in the affair.   The
Austrians were also successful on the left in repelling the
French attacks, and the attempt to relieve Landrecy having
thus failed, that town surrendered on the 30th of April.
This was the last of a series of fruitless triumphs of the
allies, for upon receiving information from General
Chapuis, who had been taken prisoner on the 26th instant,
of the serious attack with which West Flanders was
menaced, all their plans were changed, and instead of
marching triumphantly on Paris, they had now to look to
the security of their own frontiers.   It appears that Pichegru,
who was at Lille directing the movements of the French
army against the right of the allies under the Austrian
General Clairfait, in West Flanders, had by a succession of
manœuvres, on the 26th and 29th of April, defeated his
opponent, and got possession of Menin and Courtrai, thereby
threatening to cut off the Duke of York's communication
with the coast.   The duke immediately ordered the whole
Brigade of Guards, three other battalions, and a brigade of
cavalry, to turn out, and moved off with them at twelve

1791.

May 1.

May 2.

May 6.

o'clock on the night of the 30th, the Guards heading the column; his object being to gain St. Amand by forced marches, and to oppose the enemy's progress in that quarter. At ten o'clock on the 1st of May the weary troops halted at Famars for a few hours, resuming their route in the afternoon, and passing the Scheldt at Trith, arrived at last on the road leading from Valenciennes to St. Amand. The rain fell in torrents, accompanied by thunderstorms; the night was so dark that no one could perceive whether man, horse, or waggon was next to him; men and horses got into the ditches, and the drivers of the guns were obliged to grope their way before the horses. In this way the brigade arrived at a village not far from Vicogne, half way between Valenciennes and St. Amand, when worn out by fatigue every one shifted as well as he could for himself; General Lake, with his horse, fell into a dangerous hole, and was much bruised. The column arrived at St. Amand on the 2nd of May, and on the 3rd, after another harassing march of eleven hours, took up a position between Marquain and Blandain, to the west of Tournay, where, on the following day, General Lake issued an order laying down concise rules for the regulation of discipline, which during the late harassing marches had become somewhat relaxed. The more serious the nature of the difficulties, the greater the necessity for the preservation of the military code, without which soldiers soon become inefficient and more injurious to their friends than their foes. The tactics of the enemy since the commencement of the campaign had been to harass the allies by a constant repetition of attacks on the outposts, keeping them constantly under arms in expectation of some serious movement; the marches had also been very severe. The order reminded the soldiers of their duty, and the principles then laid down, were in future years carried to a perfection seldom exceeded.

In the midst of these operations the Guards lost the chief under whom they had hitherto so successfully served; Major-General Lake, being appointed to the colonelcy of the

WEST   FLANDERS

Becelaere   Dadizeh

To Ypres

Menin   L y s   Marcke

COURTRA

Werwick

Comminex   Linselles   Scutam   Neuville   Aelbecke   Bessul

Le Quesnoy   Turcoign   St Leger   Expieres   Helchin

Mouscron

Moevaux   Watrelos

Brigade   Leers   Pecq

Marcq   Roubaix   Lennoy   2   Nechin   2

Beauvere   Saillly   Willem   Templeux

Tressin   Blandin

Pont d'Tressin   Baisseux   Marquain   TOURNAY

Pourines   Kinsky   Antoing

Cyseing

Pont a Marcy   Bruielle

Sedin

Maulde

The Archduke   Orchies   Bruille

Nortean   St Amand

F R A N C E   Vicogne

Scarpe   R.

Marchiennes

DOUAI

To Arras   Aulenhicourt   Denain   Trith   Famars

VALENCIENNES

PLAN or OPERATIONS
16ᵀᴴ 17ᵀᴴ & 18ᵀᴴ May 1794
ATTACK or GUARDS on ROUBAIX and MOUVEAUX
and retreat from Mouveaux

Scale of English Miles

Scheldt R.

53rd Regiment, returned to England, and Major-General 1794.
Samuel Hulse, of the First Guards, who was at the time on
duty in England, succeeded to the command of the brigade.
About the same time Lieutenant-Colonels Richardson and
H. Burrard received orders to join the first battalion,
in place of Colonels D'Oyly and H.R.H. Prince William May 4.
of Gloucester, the latter having been ordered home on
being appointed to the colonelcy of the 115th Regiment,
which being shortly reduced, his royal highness received the
colonelcy of the 6th regiment of the line. Lieutenant-
Colonel Dowdeswell had, as before stated, been gazetted,
on the 11th of February this year, to a company in the
First Guards in Prince William's place, and on several
other occasions during this campaign officers of all ranks
were ordered out to relieve those in the service battalion, on
promotion or otherwise.

The duke having arrived at Tournay, General Clairfait. May 8.
was enabled on the 8th of May to resume the offensive, and
advanced on Courtrai, but he was attacked on the 11th by May 11.
General Souham, and though he maintained his ground
yet he thought it prudent to draw off at night, and retire
to Thieldt, eighteen miles west of Ghent, whereby his
communications with the Duke of York were again
interrupted. During the progress of these movements,
Pichegru, with 30,000 men, attacked the Duke of York's
corps, near Tournay, attempting to turn his right, but was
repulsed by Kaunitz's Austrians; while the British cavalry,
under Lieutenant-General Harcourt, charged the enemy's
left with so much resolution that he retreated in confusion
across the Marque, with the loss of thirteen guns. Major
Clinton, First Guards, aide-de-camp to the Duke of York,
was wounded in the thigh on this occasion.

Such was the position of the rival armies in West Flanders,
when a most intricate combined movement was devised by
General Mack to recover this important district, which led
to the battle of Turcoign. Hitherto in every instance the
British troops had engaged the enemy with success, and
they went into every encounter with confidence in their own

prowess; and although they were now to experience a reverse, it was under circumstances which reflected much credit on their discipline.

The emperor, after securing his left, moved his Austrian troops on the 15th of May to St. Amand, at the same time occupying Orchies, where a new plan of operations, afterwards sarcastically called " le plan de destruction," was arranged, by which it was intended to cut off the French army, now advanced into West Flanders, from its base at Lille. The operation was to be effected by a combined advance of the whole army in six columns, extending along a front of sixty miles from St. Amand on the left, to Thieldt on the right. The operation was a hazardous one, as its success depended upon the simultaneous, as well as successful, carrying out of their instructions, by each and every column. The troops were to move on the evening of the 16th of May, so as to arrive in such a position as would enable them to advance upon the several points of attack, and concentrate on the 17th at Turcoign. General Clairfait, with his Austrians at Thieldt, now separated from the rest of the allies, was to cross the Lys at Warweck, with twenty-five battalions and twenty-eight squadrons, then move on Lincelles and co-operate with the left column as circumstances would admit, and envelop the enemy.

Of the other five columns the first or northernmost and right column (Hanoverians under Busche), was to advance by Dottignies to Moescron, the second (Austrians under Otto), to advance by Nechin and Leers to Watrelos and Turcoign; the third (British and Austrians under the Duke of York), from Blandain by Willem and Sailly, on Lannoy, Roubaix, and Mouveaux; the fourth (Austrians under Kinsky), to cross the Marque at Bouvines; and the fifth (Austrians under the Archduke), to cross the same river at Pont-à-Marque. Clairfait experienced so much resistance in forcing the Lys, that he did not arrive at his destination till the morning of the 18th, too late to co-operate with the other columns even had they been successful. Busche, on the right, after some success at Moescron, was driven back

to Espierres. Otto drove the enemy before him as far as
Turcoign, but alarmed by Busche's failure on his right,
halted his main body at Watrelos; the two left columns
which should have acted with vigour to cover the operations
on their right, were unable to perform the duty entrusted to
them, for Kinsky, after driving the French to Tressin, was
himself attacked, and did no more than hold his ground, so
that the French general, Bonneau, leaving some battalions
to watch him, marched off in the night to his left with 16,000
men, and on the following morning, as will be shown, fell
on the Duke of York at Roubaix; and the archduke's
column, worn out by fatigue, did not arrive on the Marque
at Cherang till late on the 17th, also too late to be of any
assistance.

Had the Austrians been the sworn enemies of the British
instead of their allies, they could not have devised a series
of combinations more likely to terminate in their destruction, or have carried them out in a manner more certain to
ensure such a result, and the third column deserves all
the more credit that it was enabled to extricate itself
with so little loss from so imminent a danger. This third
column, under the Duke of York, was composed of the four
battalions of the brigade of Guards, of the first brigade of
the line, and of O'Donnell's corps, with some cavalry and
artillery, all under Major-General Abercrombie; also of five
battalions of Austrians and two of Hessians. The column
moved according to orders at eleven o'clock at night on the
16th, and halted near Templeuve. At dawn, when the morning of the 17th broke, it was so foggy that the march was not
resumed till eight o'clock, when the troops of the third
column advanced to Lannoy, which was abandoned on their
approach. The Hessians were left here as a garrison, while
the leading corps of the duke's column, consisting of the
brigade of Guards, O'Donnell's corps, and the 7th and 15th
Light Dragoons, proceeded to Roubaix, about four miles
to the front, with the light company of the First Guards
protecting their left. On the flank battalion of Guards,
which was in front, showing itself, the French opened fire,

1794.

May 17.

but retired upon the arrival of the artillery, and the British established themselves in the evening without further resistance in front of the village, thus successfully carrying out the duty entrusted to them. The Guards drew up in a field on the west side of the town, the other regiments taking up a position on the chaussée, between Roubaix and Lille. In this affair Lieutenant-Colonel Ludlow, of the First Guards, was wounded in the left arm, which was amputated.

The attacks of the first, fourth, and fifth columns had by this time entirely failed, and that of the second only partially succeeded; the third or centre column was therefore isolated, and the duke's left flank completely *en l'air*. The French general, who had received private information of the plan of the allies, now took the bold resolution of maintaining his communication with Lille, by marching on Turcoign, the intended point of the allied concentration.

Attack on
Mouveaux.

The duke, aware of his dangerous position, determined to proceed no further that night, and leaving General Abercrombie with the Guards and other troops at Roubaix, was returning to Lannoy, when he received a positive command from the emperor to attack Mouveaux, in order to assist Clairfait, who by the delay of the two left columns of Austrians was liable to be destroyed. The duke having vainly represented the state of affairs, reluctantly returned to Roubaix, and desired General Abercrombie to attack Mouveaux with the Brigade of Guards. This village was not only strong by nature, but was surrounded by palisades and entrenchments, with flanking redoubts. The flank battalion, supported by the First Guards and one other battalion, having the 7th and 15th Light Dragoons on their flanks, formed line and advanced in perfect order, while the rest of the brigade moved to the heights on the right. As soon as the flank battalion was sufficiently near, the men rushed on with the greatest impetuosity, not stopping to fire, and the French, dreading the assault, retired in the direction of Lille, leaving one gun and a howitzer behind them. The Duke remained at Roubaix this night, and thus ended the 17th of May, on which day, of all the attacks, that made by the

Guards, in conjunction with their comrades of O'Donnell's corps and the British cavalry, was alone successful.

The scene was changed on the morning of the 18th, when the duke found his column, as he had foreseen, almost surrounded by the enemy's troops. Souham was advancing with 45,000 men from the north, Thierry from Moescron on his right, and Bonneau from the south ; but so little was this fearful position understood by the emperor, that he sent a positive order for the third column to continue its advance on Lincelles, though its isolation was fully represented at head-quarters. The Guards, with their advanced guard and Congreve's battery, were at Mouveaux, the guns with their left on the village, protected on their right by four companies of the Third Guards, who were afterwards joined by the Coldstreams, with the intention of keeping up a communication to their right ; General Fox's line brigade was in rear of Roubaix, the Hessians at Lannoy, and three battalions of Austrians covering Roubaix. The other two Austrian battalions had been sent to reinforce Otto, and, contrary to orders, were retained by him.

Bonneau's column from the south showed itself early in the morning, between Mouveaux and Roubaix ; that from Moescron in the east, having forced its way through the Austrian column under Otto, attacked the Duke of York in rear of Roubaix, who on the first appearance of the enemy, attempted to go to the front for the purpose of joining the Guards at Mouveaux ; finding, however, the communication intercepted, he endeavoured to form a body of troops to support them in their retreat, but as he could not reach the line brigade, the French being already in possession of the suburbs of Roubaix, he rode off to Watrelos to obtain succours from General Otto. The French, however, were there also, and after narrowly escaping being made prisoner he had no resource but to make for Leers.

It was nine o'clock in the morning before General Abercrombie received orders to retire with the Guards, when the main body of the brigade commenced its retreat protected by skirmishers of the light companies, who kept up a running fight with the enemy, who were rapidly closing in upon them. On arriving at Roubaix they drove the French from a wood that flanked the entrance to the town on the right, and proceeded through the streets; but before their rear was clear of the town, the enemy pressed on them and inflicted some loss. The brigade, on gaining the summit of the hill in rear of the town, halted to close up, but the French came on in such superior numbers that it was vain to attempt to act on the offensive; they marched on, beset on both flanks as well as on their proper front, till, on arrival near Lannoy, they found the enemy also in their proper rear. Here the guns of the Guards, having proceeded too far without adequate support, were captured by some French cavalry that dashed out from Lannoy. The gallant column, thus surrounded and with no chance of assistance, now left the road and struck across the fields towards Leers. More guns were here lost, owing to the delay in getting them through hedges and over ditches; the 7th and 15th Light Dragoons behaved nobly, constantly rescuing the infantry prisoners, and it was owing to their exertions that so few were taken. At last the column reached Templeuve, whence they marched to their former position near Blandain. General Fox's brigade, consisting of the 14th, 37th, and 53rd Regiments, was also surrounded, and suffered more than the Guards, not having the advantage of cavalry; but they also displayed great firmness and resolution in their retreat.

The Duke of York, in his despatch, declared that the column under his command had executed to the full extent their intended part of the operations, and that the conduct of the British troops in the subsequent check had entitled them to the warmest expressions of gratitude and admiration on the part of the emperor.

The total casualties of the brigade of Guards in these two days was 196 men of all ranks, a loss small in comparison with the desperate position in which they had been placed. This may be attributed to their own discipline, to the admirable conduct of the light companies in keeping the enemy at a respectful distance, and to the support afforded to them by the Light Dragoons.

* RETURN OF KILLED AND WOUNDED AT THE BATTLE OF TURCOING, 17—18 MAY, 1794.

	Officers			Sergeants.			Drummers.			Rank and File.			Total.		
	K.	W.	M.	K.	W.	M.	K.	W.	M.	K.	W.	M.	K.	W.	M.
Flank battalion . .	3			1	1	2			3	17	54	25	18	58	30
First Guards . . .										5	7	20	5	7	20
Coldstreams . . .								1			6	9		7	9
Third Guards . . .					1					1	8	32	1	9	32
	3	.		1	2	2		1	3	23	75	86	24	81	91
														196	

LUDLOW.
DRUMMOND.

The Duke of York returned to Tournay on the 18th of May, when, though little notice was taken by the population of the emperor, the houses poured forth their inhabitants in token of joy at the duke's safe return; and next day his royal highness issued an order, of which the following is an extract, expressing his satisfaction at the conduct of the troops engaged in the late operations :—

GENERAL ORDER, HEAD QUARTERS, TOURNAY, *May 19th*, 1794.

In noticing the events of yesterday, H.R.H. the Commander-in-Chief finds little to report but the loss of brave men, which, however, appears to be less than from the nature of the action might have been anticipated.

The proximity of the enemy's garrisons and armies, the want of the complete success in other parts of the intended operations which would have secured the flank of our position, and above all, the nature of the country, so favourable to the kind of attack which the enemy undertook — these will sufficiently account for what has happened without any imputation on the conduct and bravery of our troops. With them H.R.H. has *every reason to be perfectly satisfied,* and he doubts not that the enemy will feel to their cost upon the first occasion that may present itself, to what they owe the advantage they had the good fortune to obtain yesterday, over troops as much superior to them in bravery and discipline, as is the cause we maintain to that for which they contend.

Malicious reports were spread in the allied army that the duke had been surprised on the 18th, but the emperor, who

1794.
May 25.

had with blind obstinacy done the mischief, had the justice to publish in a general order the untruth of this report, as inserted below, and by his desire Prince Coburg wrote a letter to the duke to the same effect :—

HEAD QUARTERS, TOURNAY, 25 *May*, 1794.

His Imperial Majesty has heard with the greatest displeasure that a report has been spread of the British troops having allowed themselves to be surprised on the 18th inst.

He hastens, therefore, to make it publicly known that he is perfectly convinced of the untruth of this report, and of their having behaved that day with their accustomed resolution and courage ; that they only retired from the too great superiority of the enemy's numbers, being attacked in front, flanks, and rear at the same time ; and that their retreat was performed with the utmost steadiness and order.

His Imperial Majesty takes the earliest opportunity of informing the troops of the combined powers, that since he has taken the command of the army, he has almost every day had proofs of their ardour and courage, and cannot too strongly express his satisfaction and gratitude to them on their former conduct.

Such a recognition of their services was but a just testimony to their steadiness and bravery under very trying circumstances.

Battle of
Pont-à-
Chin.

As the Duke of York's army with the brigade of Guards still continued to cover Tournay, with his right resting on Pont-à-Chin, and his left in front of Lemain, the French commanders determined to follow up their late success by

May 23.

attacking it, and at daybreak on the 23rd of May appeared with 100,000 men in front of the right and centre of his line. The Guards, with the heavy cavalry, were on the left flank, opposed to a French column of 6000 men ; but as throughout the day the enemy refused his right, the brigade was not engaged. The village of Pont-à-Chin was, however, the scene of a desperate contest, and late in the day, as the duke's right, wearied out, was beginning to give way, he ordered up General Fox's line brigade, with some Austrian battalions, to its support. As the British brigade came up the allies opened out to the right and left to let them pass, when, under a heavy fire, the British gave a volley, rushed on with the bayonet, and drove the enemy from the village,

who then gave up the contest, which had lasted fifteen hours. 1794.
The honour of this repulse rested solely with the Duke of
York, and the emperor thanked the army, while the duke
specially complimented General Fox's brigade.

At the beginning of June a sanguinary and atrocious June.
decree was promulgated by the National Convention that no
quarter should be given to any British or Hanoverian
soldier; and handbills were circulated among the French
soldiery to this effect, which gave the duke the opportunity
of issuing the following order to his army, laying down with
admirable clearness the spirit of civilized warfare :—

GENERAL ORDERS, *June* 7, 1794.

The Duke of York thinks it incumbent upon him to announce to
the British and Hanoverian troops under his command, that the
National Convention of France, pursuing that gradation of crimes and
horrors which has distinguished the periods of its Government as the
most calamitous of any that has yet occurred in the history of the
world, has just passed a decree that their soldiers shall give no
quarter to the British or Hanoverian troops. H.R.H. anticipates the
indignation and horror which has 'naturally arisen in the minds of
the brave troops whom he addresses, upon receiving this information.
H.R.H., however, desires to remind them, that mercy to the vanquished is the brightest gem in a soldier's character; and exhorts
them not to suffer their resentment to lead them to any precipitate
act of cruelty on their part, which may sully the reputation they have
acquired in the world. H.R.H. believes that it would be difficult for
brave men to conceive that any set of men, who are themselves exempt
from sharing in the dangers of war, should be so base and cowardly
as to seek to aggravate the calamities of it upon the unfortunate
people who are subject to their orders.

   •   •   •   •   •   •   •

In all the wars, which from the earliest times have existed between
the English and French nations, they have been accustomed to
consider each other in the light of generous as well as brave enemies,
while the Hanoverians, for a century the allies of the former, have
shared in this reciprocal esteem. Humanity and kindness have at all
times taken place the instant that opposition ceased, and the same
cloak has been frequently seen covering those who were wounded and
enemies, whilst indiscriminately conveyed to the hospital of the
conqueror.

The British and Hanoverian armies will not believe that the French
nation, even under their present infatuation, can so far forget their
characters as soldiers, as to pay any attention to a decree as injurious

to themselves as it is disgraceful to the persons who passed it: • • • and H.R.H. is confident that it will only be on finding, contrary to every expectation, that the French army has relinquished every title to the fair character of soldiers and of men, by submitting to and obeying so atrocious an order, that the brave troops under his command will think themselves justified, and indeed under the necessity of adopting a species of warfare, for which they will stand acquitted to their own conscience, to their country, and to the world. In such an event the French army will alone be answerable for the tenfold vengeance which will fall upon themselves, their wives, their children, and their unfortunate country, already groaning under every calamity which the accumulated crimes of unprincipled ambition and avarice can heap upon their devoted victims.

June 4.

June 19.

Pichegru, after his defeat at Pont-à-Chin, turned from the British, and on the 4th of June directed Ypres to be invested, while Bonneau at Moescron watched the Duke of York, who failed in an attempt to relieve Ypres, and it surrendered on the 19th of June.

For some time it had become evident that Austrian interests prevailed over those which had brought the allies into the field, and the Prince of Coburg, in preference to remaining where he was for the defence of Tournay, determined, on the 21st of June, to draw off the Austrian troops and attempt the relief of Charleroi, a town on the Sambre, which was being besieged by the French, and which, though of great importance to the allied cause, had been hitherto left by the Austrians nearly defenceless;—but he was too late, for Charleroi surrendered on the 25th, and on the next day, while on the march to its relief, he was himself defeated at Fleurus. About the same time the Austrians in West Flanders, under Clairfait, were driven back into Ghent; and the French, having advanced to Oudenarde, succeeded again in cutting off his communications with the Duke of York.

The French were now carrying all successfully before them, except when opposed to the British troops; but these at last were obliged to conform to the general retrograde movement of the allies. By the retreat of Clairfait, the Duke of York had lost his communication with Ostend, while that with Holland being seriously threatened, it

RETREAT
OF THE ALLIES
through
HOLLAND
to
BREMEN
1794.5

English miles

became impossible for him to remain any longer before
Tournay, and he commenced his retreat on the 24th of June
by Frasne, taking up a position at Renaix, near the Scheldt.
The Prince of Orange was soon forced to retire upon
Tubize, south of Hal; and Mons having fallen on the 2nd
of July, the British and the other troops on the Scheldt July 2.
became thereby exposed to an attack in their rear. Under
directions, therefore, from the Prince of Coburg, the duke
abandoned the line of that river, and marched on the 3rd of
July to Grammont, when Tournay also fell into the hands
of the enemy.

It became necessary now to take up a new line of defence,
and the Duke of York was directed to fall back behind the
Dyle beyond Brussels. He quitted Grammont on the 4th
of July, the Guards marching at the head of the column,
and passing by Wambeke, reached Mollen, near Brussels,
on the 6th. He crossed the Dyle at Malines on the 8th,
and encamped on the 9th between Waerlos and Contik, on July 9.
the north side of the Nette, on the road to Antwerp. While
here the outposts of the two armies were only separated by
the Nette, and in spite of the savage attempt of the Convention to render the war one of extermination, the best
feelings existed between the soldiers of the rival armies,
and the men would frequently be seen carelessly walking
about in conversation with each other. Twenty years
later similar scenes occurred in the Pyrenees. While the
army was here, a reinforcement of 7000 men, sent out
from England under Lord Moira, who had landed at Ostend
on the 26th of June, arrived in camp, and took up a position
in the first line, when the duke's army, including the Dutch,
still amounted to about 50,000 men. The reserve, consisting
of the brigade of Guards, and a brigade of Hessians, with
thirteen squadrons of cavalry, was placed under the command of Lieutenant-General Abercrombie.

The strength of the Guards was also augmented in this
month by the arrival of four additional light companies July 18.
which had sailed from England on the 5th of July, and of
which two were for the First Regiment. They were all

1794.   added to the four light companies already out, and formed into a separate light infantry battalion under Colonel Sir James Duffe, First Guards, with Captain Wheatley as adjutant, while the four grenadier companies were made into another battalion, under the command of Colonel Stanhope of the First Guards, with Captain Warde as adjutant.

July.   A conference took place in the middle of July at the Prince of Coburg's quarters, at which the Duke of York was not present, owing to indisposition, and it was not till the 20th that he learnt with surprise and indignation that a complete separation of the two armies had been agreed upon, and that the prince, without even giving him notice of it, had withdrawn all the Imperialists from the country, and marched to Maestricht. Since the commencement of the war, the duke had always acted under the orders of the prince, except during the operations at Dunkirk, and the troops under his command had ever performed their duty with signal success, for the failures at Dunkirk and Mouveaux can only be attributed to the previous defeat of the Hanoverians or Imperialists. Now, although independent of Austrian control or assistance, he found himself in the presence of superior and constantly increasing forces, for Pichegru's army, which had followed the retreat of the allies, and entered Brussels on the 10th of July, amounted to no less than 84,000 men.

By the withdrawal of the Austrians the duke's left flank was exposed to such an extent, that he found himself obliged

July 22.   to continue his retreat, and on the 22nd the First Guards moved to Wyneghem, near Antwerp; on the 23rd, they halted at West Wesel, and on the 24th reached Rosendaal, lying between Bergen-op-Zoom and Breda, where they remained about a fortnight. From here the army

Aug. 4.   moved on the 4th of August, by Breda, to Oster Hout, where, with the object of giving greater security to the neighbouring towns, they commenced forming an entrenched camp. The two hostile armies remained opposed to each other in these positions for several weeks, while the rest of the French troops were engaged in reducing the several frontier fortresses of Quesnoy, Valenciennes, Condé, and Landrecy, all of which surrendered between the 15th and 30th of August, without any attempts being made to save them.

1794.
August.

Towards the end of August, the French army, now still further strengthened by the arrival of troops relieved from the several sieges, betrayed an intention of attempting to turn the British left. The Duke of York, deserted as he was by his allies, and with the Dutch so favourable to the invaders, that it was difficult to obtain intelligence, had hitherto attempted to defend Holland, against vastly superior forces, but not deeming it prudent to risk an action in his present position, he retired at midnight on the 28th-29th to Uden, on the Aa river, the outposts being on the Dommel. On the 14th of September, Pichegru having driven the Hessians out of Boxtel, the duke directed General Abercrombie with the reserve, viz., the brigade of Guards and 3rd line brigade (12th, 33rd, 42nd, and 44th regiments), with cavalry and artillery, to march in the night and retake the village, though leaving him to act according to circumstances. These troops arrived at daylight, when the enemy's guns opened on them from a wood. Captain Bristow of the First Guards was sent with his company in advance to commence the attack, while the cavalry and the First and Third Guards, supported by the 35th and 44th Regiments, were pushed forward in support; but General Abercrombie perceiving the French artillery well protected by a large force of Chasseurs, and that he was in presence of the main body of the French army, recalled the troops. Captain Bristow, however, was so far advanced that he was unable to join the main body in time, and was taken prisoner, with his men. The retreat was covered by the flank battalion and the First Guards, a duty which they performed in such order as to call forth the following acknowledgments of the general:—

Sept. 14.

Sept. 15.

"GRAVE, 17th September.

"Lieutenant-General Abercrombie returns his thanks to the Royal Artillery and brigade of Guards for their cool and steady behaviour on the 15th inst. To the attention and exertions of officers and men is to be attributed the regularity with which the retreat was conducted."

The operations of this day bear an additional interest from their having afforded to the future Duke of Wellington the first opportunity of being engaged with the French. The Guards were at one time of the day hard pressed, and a regiment of Irish light dragoons got mixed up with them in a narrow lane, causing some confusion, of which the French hussars hastened to take advantage. Colonel Wellesley, then commanding the 33rd Regiment, observing this, formed up his men at the end of the lane, and the Guards having passed through his ranks, he wheeled up and threw in some cool and well-directed volleys, which checked the enemy, inflicting much loss upon them. The casualties of the First Guards on this occasion were five rank and file killed, one wounded, and one officer and fourteen men taken prisoners, besides seven men of the grenadier companies, and two of the light infantry, wounded.

Sept. 16.   The duke at once retired to Grave, across the Meuse, the reserve of Guards covering the retreat, and on the 21st of September took up a position at Mook and Gennep, near Nimeguen. The subsequent defeat, however, of General Clairfait and his Austrians on the 29th of September, and his retreat across the Rhine on the 2nd of October, again exposing the duke's left, forced the duke to continue his retreat into Holland. He accordingly broke up on Oct. 4.   the night of the 4th-5th of October, and after halting for a day close under the walls of Nimeguen, passed the river Whaal, and extending his line seven or eight miles down the river, occupied the Bommeler Waard; the grenadier battalion of Guards being stationed opposite Bommel, and the remainder of the reserve in the villages or on the river, where they received but indifferent treatment, for the Dutch were now openly favouring the invaders, as shown by what occurred in one of the villages through which the reserve passed. A driver went up to a

house during a temporary halt, and was shut out, fired at 1794.
from the window, and wounded; several other shots were
then fired, and a soldier of the First Guards, named Street,
fell; a crowd of the grenadier battalion assembling round
the house, an officer ordered Drill-Sergeant Malpas of the
First Guards to examine into the matter. In forcing the
door his sword broke, but seizing a firelock he rushed up
the stairs, when he was stabbed, and shot dead. The en-
raged soldiers immediately set fire to the house, when
two men jumped out of the window, one of whom escaped,
but the other was seized and forthwith hanged upon a
tree, while two women and a child who also came out were
allowed to proceed unmolested.

The grenadier battalion and two companies of light infantry of the Guards were sent to Helsdt, between Nimeguen
and Arnheim, on the 17th of October, where they remained some days, during which a change took place in the
command of the first battalion First Guards, in consequence Oct. 20.
of the promotion to major-general of its commanding officer,
Francis D'Oyly, on the 4th of October, who still, however,
retained his regimental majority; he was succeeded in the
command by Colonel A. J. Drummond, and at the same time,
Colonel Sir James Duffe, of the First Regiment, who had
hitherto commanded the light infantry battalion, having
also been promoted to the rank of major-general, was
relieved in that command by Colonel Manners, of the
Third Guards.

On the 21st of October, the Duke of York withdrew his Oct. 21.
head-quarters to Arnheim, while General Walmoden, with
twenty battalions, occupied the entrenched camp in front of
Nimeguen. On the 28th, the British outposts were driven Oct. 28.
in, and Nimeguen was invested, when the First Guards and
light infantry battalion moved to Thiel, Heeris, and Dode-
waard, along the north bank of the Whaal. Every exertion
was still made during the early part of the month of
November to defend the line of this river, and the Guards
were daily finding 400 men on fatigue to throw up entrenchments to strengthen the position; a sharp frost, however,

setting in on the 17th, which lasted about a fortnight, rendered the position on all sides more assailable, and it became necessary to concentrate the troops. On the 23rd, therefore, the grenadiers of the Guards, now reduced to about 200 men, moved into Arnheim, and the First Guards to Elden, a few miles south of that town, while their light infantry companies were stationed at Osterhoub on outpost duty. Sickness now increased with giant strides; the Guards alone had 900 sick, and a low fever prevailed in the country; the general hospital was at Rhenen, and the men sent out of it to do duty soon relapsed from exposure and cold. The duke had hitherto looked forward to establishing himself in winter quarters in Holland as soon as the cold season set in, but the Republicans with stern energy prepared to turn the elements to account; the frost broke up at the end of November, and the country was for a short time impassable from the state of the roads, but it soon set in again, and the French continued their advance with

superior and irresistible forces. At this time, however, the Duke of York having learnt that Lord Cornwallis was about to come out from England to supersede him, quitted the army, and the British troops were placed under the immediate command of Lieutenant-General Harcourt. On leaving the army, the duke issued the following general order to the troops:—

" ARNHEIM, *December* 2.

" His Royal Highness the Commander-in-Chief having received His Majesty's commands to proceed without loss of time to England, the command of the allied armies devolves on Count Walmoden, the senior officer, whose orders the troops of the several nations will follow with the same alacrity, zeal, and spirit, which they have on all occasions shown in obeying the orders of his Royal Highness.

" His Royal Highness cannot let pass this opportunity of bearing his testimony to the qualities in the troops comprising the army under his command, and of returning his best thanks to the officers and men for them."

The frost recommenced with intense severity in the middle **1794.** of the month, and Holland became one sheet of ice, inter- Dec. 15. sected by dykes and canals. In open weather and with the power of inundation, this country is a natural fortification, but in a frost these advantages disappear; every canal may be crossed or turned, the power of a small force is reduced, and its flanks are never safe; so that in addition to the defection of allies, and the more than covert hostility of the Dutch, nature appeared to be in alliance with the enemies of the overmatched British force.

In addition to the officers of the first battalion, mentioned p. 272 as serving abroad, the following officers of the light companies of the other two battalions were also on the Continent at the end of the year 1794 :—

Second Battalion, light company: Lieutenant-Colonel Bennet; Captains W. H. Clinton, Per. Maitland, and Cocks.

Third Battalion, light company: Lieutenant-Colonel Honble. Ch. Monson; Captains White, Ruddock, Knox, and Coleman.

In the first battalion, Lieutenant-Colonel Sir Charles Asgill commanded the King's company; Lieutenant-Colonels Hon. H. Stanhope and Hon. G. Ludlow the two grenadier; and Lieutenant-Colonels Coussmaker and Perryn the two light infantry companies.

At the close of the year the command of the brigade of Dec. 25. Guards devolved upon Colonel Morshead of the Third Guards, in the absence of Major-General Hulse, who received leave to return to England.

CHAPTER XXI.

1795.

1795.
Jan. 7.

THE defence of the line of the Whaal was maintained till
the commencement of the following year, when, on the 7th
of January, as the enemy were pressing their advance, all
the batteries and *matériel* collected for its defence were destroyed, and the army retired behind the Rhine, the First
Guards and light infantry battalion crossing that river at
Rhenen, at which place no less than 4000 men had been
buried within the last three months. Half the army was
now sick, the other half worn out by hard duty; and in the
brigade of Guards the men, what with night marches and
constant alarms, had enjoyed no rest for ten nights. In the
midst of this, on the 14th of January a general attack was made
by the French on the allied line, extending from Arnheim
to Amerongen, the most serious part of which was at Rhenen,
when the advanced posts fell back from the other side of the
river; these posts were, however, recovered by the brave and

Jan. 14.

spirited conduct of the Guards and of Salm's infantry; on 1795. which occasion Colonel Wheatley of the First Guards was wounded. Of the Guards, General Walmoden says, " I cannot express myself in terms of sufficient commendation." And General Harcourt reported, " that the conduct of the Guards and other corps was as steady as it was spirited." The fate of Holland, however, was decided; and at midnight on the 14th General Walmoden found himself constrained to order a retreat upon the Yssel. The brigade of Guards moved on the 15th of January by Amerongen to Schar- Jan. 15. penzaal; thence, in company with Col. Strutt's brigade, they started at 4 o'clock on the morning of the 16th, and about three in the afternoon, after marching eleven hours, they arrived upon the verge of an extensive common, called the Welaw, where they expected to rest, but were informed they had fifteen miles further to march; through this dreary waste the gallant soldiers trudged on, suffering acutely from the severity of the weather, fatigue, and want of food, many having had nothing to eat or drink that day except water. The wind was high, the snow and sand drifted, and the frost was intense; night came on—numbers exhausted lagged behind; there was no track, and if they lost the column, there was little chance of finding it again. To sit down was death; many crept into the bushes and slept their last sleep; others, knowing the danger of lying down to slumber, wandered over the pathless waste till they sank to rise no more. At last, about ten at night, Bick-borge was reached; but it was already occupied by the Hessians, who had retired upon it on the direct road from Arnheim, and who, not being very friendly, often refused the men the comfort of fire or shelter, a refuge which could only be obtained by force or stealth.

The next morning waggons were sent out to search for those absent from the ranks, when many were found dead; some so dreadfully frost-bitten that their extremities came off; while others who had straggled from the line of march were never heard of more. On the 18th of January the army, Jan. 18. continuing its retreat, passed through Deventer, and took

1795. up a position behind the Yssel, the First Guards being quartered at Vausson.

January.   All the principal towns of Holland being now in the hands of the enemy, the Prince of Orange felt that it was hopeless to continue the struggle, and abandoning all further attempts to save his country, went to the Hague and embarked for England on the 26th of January (the same day that General Pichegru entered Amsterdam), leaving orders for the Dutch to resist no longer. These had for some time, as we have seen, shown no great favour towards the British troops, to whom they afforded neither assistance nor hospitality; that feeling had now broken out into the most inveterate hostility, and a large crowd assembled on the morning of the prince's departure, insisting on his being brought to trial for the part he had taken in favour of the English, but he was protected by his guards.

Under these circumstances the British government determined to withdraw altogether from the Continent, and Bremen being selected as the port of embarcation, General Walmoden, on the 27th of January, evacuated Deventer with the advanced part of the army, for the purpose of cantoning it behind the Ems, leaving General Abercrombie with the Guards and Strutt's brigade as a rear guard to remove the sick and stores. On the 29th the Guards marched to Holten, thence to Delden, and on the 31st arrived at Oldenzaal, where they remained till the 9th of February, when, marching through Bentheim, they reached

Feb. 12. Osnabruck on the 12th of the month.

The Duke of York was created a Field Marshal on the 10th of February, and was at the same time appointed Commander-in-Chief of the British army at home; the despatches of General Walmoden and Lieutenant-General Harcourt, however, continued to be addressed to him, and were by him laid before government. He took the greatest interest in the difficult and harassing retreat of the British army, and the following extract from his letter,

Feb. 21. published in general orders at this period, shows that he was watching their movements with the greatest anxiety :—

Extract of a letter from H.R.H. the Duke of York, 21st Feb., 1795.   1795.

"The perseverance and exertions of the British troops on all occasions since I left the army, have merited my warmest commendations, and impressed with this opinion of their conduct, I cannot but sincerely regret the losses they have sustained in the different conflicts to which they have lately been so often exposed."

The light infantry battalion which formed the rear guard continued some distance from the reserve, ever on the alert in case the enemy advanced, and remained for a fortnight longer near the frontiers of Holland, when upon the French appearing in force in front of their outposts on the 26th of February, it leisurely retired to Schuttorp on the Feb. 26. Vecht, crossed the Ems at Rhenen, and reached Ippenburren on the 28th. The First Guards and the other battalions moved on the 4th of March from Osnabruck to Thuc- March 4. kenburg, where they remained stationary for about three weeks, partly waiting for the transports to be sent to Bremen, and partly owing to the bad state of the weather, which had broken up all the roads and rendered the country a complete swamp. On the expected arrival of the transports, the British army left Osnabruck and its neighbourhood on the 25th of March, and being no longer molested, retired by easy marches to Bremen, which it reached on the 28th, March 28. when the inhabitants at first objected to any troops being quartered upon them, as their town had maintained its neutrality during the war; but finding they could not help themselves, they received the Guards and two Hanoverian regiments, while the rest of the army marched through the town without halting. The grenadier companies of the brigade were at once, on their arrival, ordered to join their respective regiments, but to be considered as a separate battalion in their returns.

After waiting a fortnight for the rest of the British troops April 10. to embark, the First Guards and the light battalion marched out of Bremen on the 10th of April, accompanied by a great number of the inhabitants, who showed them every respect, and arriving at Wilderstadt, a few miles above Bremen Lake,

1795.

April 24.

May 8.

on the 13th, the First Guards, 790 strong, embarked the next morning at daybreak in three transports, while the light infantry, mustering 602 men, embarked in other vessels. The fleet sailed on the 24th of April, and after encountering contrary winds and serious storms, made the coast of England on the 30th, but did not reach Greenwich till the 8th of May. Three companies of the First Guards disembarked at once, and were inspected by the king ; the remainder of the battalion disembarked the next morning, and marched to the parade in St. James's Park. The two grenadier companies of the First Guards, under Lieutenant-Colonels Sir Charles Asgill, who had narrowly escaped the American scaffold, and Ludlow, the future Earl, together with the king's company under Lieutenant-Colonel Fitz-Gerald, arrived, on the 15th of May, at Greenwich, where they were met by the colonel of the regiment, the Duke of Gloucester, and on landing, found the king on the pier, who welcomed them back with much earnestness, and shook many of the private soldiers by the hand. They all received on their return eight days' leave of absence to visit their friends.

On its arrival, the first battalion of the First Guards was billeted in Southwark, and on the 18th of May, the first battalion, as well as the light infantry companies of the First Guards, were inspected by the lieutenant-colonel of the regiment, after which the four last-named companies, under Lieutenant-Colonels Hon. Ch. Monson, J. Perryn, Bennet, and Boone, were detached to Windsor. Lieutenant-Colonel Bristow, the captain-lieutenant of the regiment, remained a prisoner of war on the continent till the following month of October, when, on his return, he was posted to the Duke of Gloucester's company.

The four light infantry companies of the First Guards continued at Windsor during the autumn of 1795, and on the 26th of November, on being relieved by a detachment of five officers and 200 men of the same regiment, returned to London, and rejoined their respective battalions.

It will be observed, on looking back at the campaigns of

the last two years, that the First Guards, and the brigade of which it formed a part, were the first of the British troops that took the field. They had shown the most distinguished gallantry at Lincelles, the most heroic and stubborn resistance when surrounded by overwhelming numbers at Mouveaux, and upon other minor occasions had conducted themselves with firmness and due attention to discipline. They formed part of the rear guard of the army during its retreat through Holland, and were actively engaged in covering it in conjunction with the Hanoverians. They had shown patience and endurance under harassing marches and want of food, and though some plundering may have existed at times in their ranks, as it did in those of other regiments, the cause may be assigned to anger at the treachery of allies for whom they had come to shed their blood, rendering the men occasionally reckless ; yet, considering the state of the military system of that period, they were in a state of superior discipline, and exhibited general efficiency, and that their conduct had been appreciated at home was sufficiently shown by the reception their sovereign gave to them on their return.

Major-General Hulse had held the lieutenant-colonelcy of the regiment but a year, when on his retirement from that post on the 7th of March, 1795, he was succeeded by Major-General Edmund Stevens, and the vacant Third majority fell to Sir James Duffe.

A plan for forming a body of light troops was drawn up this year by Lieutenant-Colonel Perryn, of the First Guards, who had been a most active captain of the light company of the first battalion during the late campaign, and Sir W. H. Clinton, another officer of the First Guards, makes the following remarks on this subject, which may be read with interest :—

"The fact is, that we have no such thing as light troops, and all our own finest battalions are frittered away on outposts and picquets, and this must always be the case until something like Perryn's plan is adopted in our army; viz., the forming so many light battalions, clothed and armed very differently from the present way of arming light infantry, which in a regiment is of no sort of service, and is only a picked battalion company. The uniform is perfectly simple, no finery of any sort, and perhaps this is the very reason why it would be neglected in this country, where scarcely anything but elegance, not convenience, of uniform is thought of; objection there can be none to such corps. The clothing for the men would come, if anything, cheaper. The hat is one of the best imagined stamp possible; it has all the convenience of the Austrian cap, the Highland bonnet, and the hat, without the inconveniences of either, might be made nearly as cheap as the hat now worn, and I should think would last to the full as long, if not longer.

"But there is at present so much party fashion, and intrigue, that though the Duke of York approves in toto of Perryn's plan for dressing battalions, the country will, I dare say, never adopt any plan, but will continue the present unmilitary one in which clothiers and contractors are permitted to cheat government and commanding officers of regiments, to the no small distress of the private soldier. It appears to me that all the clothing of regiments should be made up by regimental tailors, and that a quantity of clothes be for that purpose kept in the regimental store, or if this should not be found practicable, every regiment should send so many men to be formed into a Board under proper military direction, when all the clothing should be made up, and no commanding officer should have any thing to do with clothing his regiment, but receive a certain pay as colonel; by this means a great deal of money would be saved to government, and most commanding officers benefited. But we are so little a military country, and have so little idea of arrangement, that these abuses, in common with a number of others, will be continued till time and universal discontent correct them."

The Duke of York was now commander-in-chief of the British army, and from this time the country began to feel the benefit of the experience he had gained in the recent campaigns. The administration of the army had been in a lamentable condition. Recruits of an inferior description had been sent, imperfectly clad, insufficiently fed, and often without arms; the commanding officers of regiments were often mere boys who had attained rank by interest, or by raising regiments by means of crimps; men and officers were all hard drinkers, discipline was loose, and some brigades were left without general officers. There was no uniform system either in interior economy or in drill, and the commissariat and medical branches of the service were absolutely inefficient. It took years to eradicate

the evils which existed, but it is not too much to say
that the campaigns of 1793–5, disclosing, as they did, to the
Duke of York and Colonel Wellesley, the total inefficiency of
the British army in all but fighting powers, laid the founda-
tions of the triumphs of the Peninsular War. The Duke of
York set to work resolutely to raise the British army from
the degradation into which the system had fallen, and to
cleanse the Augean stable. Sir Harry Calvert and Sir
David Dundas became his able coadjutors in his efforts to
remedy these lamentable defects, and to Sir David Dundas
the army is indebted for the introduction of a uniform
system of drill, and a series of evolutions and manœuvres.

One of the first acts of the Duke of York was the
establishment of camps of exercise, where the troops might
be trained in habits of discipline, and practised in uniformity
of drill; and an encampment was formed at Warley, to
which the second and third battalions of the First Guards
marched on the 29th and 30th of June, 1795. They remained
there till the 20th of October, when they returned to
London, where they were stationed throughout the years
1796 and 1797, during which time no occurrence took place
out of the ordinary routine of duty.

Shortly after the British troops had left the Continent, in
1795, a treaty of peace was ratified between Prussia and the
French Republic, by which the French were left undisturbed
to pursue their revolutionary projects; and in October of
that year, the authority of the Convention being seriously
threatened, the command of the troops in Paris was conferred
on General Bonaparte, who, after establishing order, was
continued in that command, as well as in that of the army
of Italy, till 1798, during which period, Bonaparte, by a
series of victories, had driven the Austrians out of Pied-
mont and Lombardy, overthrown the government of Venice,
and concluded the treaty of Campo Formio.

Upon Major-Generals Edmund Stevens and Patrick
Bellew retiring from the First Guards in 1797, Major-
General D'Oyly succeeded on the 11th of October to the
lieutenant-colonelcy of the regiment, and Sir James Duffe,

1798. Andrew Drummond, and the Hon. Francis Needham to the three regimental majorities respectively.

The French government had, early in the year 1798, turned its attention to the possible invasion of England and Ireland, and an army was formed, pompously called "the Army of England," the command of which was conferred on the Conqueror of Italy. Bonaparte, however, probably felt that the attempt was premature, and did not wish to risk his reputation on a project so uncertain, and the idea was for a time abandoned. The Convention then determined to attack Egypt, thus opening a way to empire in the East, and, jealous of the popularity of the young general, it was not sorry to give him a command in that distant country, for which he sailed later in the year. In consequence, however, of the threats that had been made, and of the original serious intentions entertained by the National Convention of invading England—a project which would have been facilitated by the possession of Antwerp and Ostend, now in the hands of the French — the British government resolved in April to make an attempt on the latter town, with the object of destroying the docks, and crippling thereby any armaments that might be fitting out in that port, and the light battalion of the Guards was selected to form part of the expedition. In the previous month of March the third battalion of the First Guards had been sent to Winchester with its flank companies, but upon this expedition being

April 24. determined upon, these were, on the 24th of April, ordered back, the grenadier company being directed to march to London, and the light company to Canterbury, where it

May 4. arrived on the 4th of May, and joined the light battalion of the brigade, that was being formed there, under the command of Colonel Calcraft, of the Coldstream Guards, the four light companies of the First Regiment being under Colonel Warde.* The other troops that were to take part in the expedition were the 11th Regiment, and the flank companies of

* Coldstreams. Colonel Calcraft's and Colonel Finch's companies. Third Guards. Colonel Cuninghame's and another.

the 23rd and 49th Regiments, in all 1200 men, which were 1798.
placed under the command of Lieut.-General Eyre Coote,
with Major-General Harry Burrard, of the First Guards, as
second in command. The naval armament was placed under
the command of Captain Popham, R.N., and the troops
embarked on the 13th of May, the light companies of the
First Guards, under Colonel Warde, being in the "Minerva."

It was intended that the expedition should be a surprise,
and with this view, orders were issued that the men were not
to land with their knapsacks, but to take only their canteens
and one day's cooked provisions in their havresacks, and as
much ammunition as could be stowed away in the pouches
and in an extra cartouche box, to be supplied to each man
by the captains commanding His Majesty's ships. According to the orders of the 14th of May, issued by General
Coote, from on board his ship, the "Expedition," the
Guards from that ship and from the "Ariadne" and
"Minerva," were to be the first troops to disembark.

Early on the 19th the squadron was off Ostend, with the May 19.
exception of the "Minerva," which had lost her station on
the previous day; the light infantry companies of the
First Guards that she was carrying were therefore unable to
join in the descent on the enemy's coast, or take part in
the subsequent operations. The light companies of the
Coldstream and Third Guards, and of the line, however,
landed unobserved, burnt the boats collected near Ostend,
and blew up the locks and basin gates of the Bruges Canal,
thereby frustrating the plans of the French. The soldiers
were ready to re-embark about noon, but by this time a
high surf was raging on the shore, rendering it impossible
to gain the boats, whereupon General Coote took up a
position on the beach, and prepared to defend himself.
The enemy having collected a considerable force, advanced
upon him in overwhelming numbers, and after a noble and
gallant defence, General Coote found himself obliged to
capitulate with all the troops on shore.

The "Minerva" transport, with Colonel Warde's light
companies of the First Guards on board, did not arrive

at the rendezvous till after nine on the morning of the 19th. Captain Popham thought that from the little probability already existing of his being able to re-embark the troops then on shore, it would only increase the anxiety of the general if the men of the First Guards were now landed; he therefore sent the captain of the " Minerva " ashore to report his arrival to the general. In his absence, Colonel Warde filled two boats with his men, and was zealously preparing to join his comrades on shore, without considering the danger of crossing the surf, when a naval officer advised him to return to his ship. General Coote reported that everything that brave men could attempt was done at the imminent risk of their lives to accomplish, and that the zeal and courage they manifested to partake in the dangers of their brother soldiers, would have made them ample sharers in any honour to be acquired or danger to be encountered on shore had they been able to reach it.

The prisoners of war, including Major-General Burrard and Captain Wheatley, proceeded to Lille, where they were placed under certain restrictions, but were well treated; while the light companies of the First Guards, returning in the " Minerva " to England, disembarked at Margate on
the 25th of May, and proceeded to London, probably rejoicing that they were not sharing the captivity of their comrades, which continued till the following month of November.

THE IRISH REBELLION.

No sooner had the expedition to Ostend come to this untimely end, than a new field opened for the services of the brigade, for though the intention of the French government to invade England had been postponed for the present, the state of Ireland appeared to it to present an eligible opportunity for threatening Great Britain on her weakest side.

Ireland had for years been discontented and turbulent; the country was split into political and religious factions; and while the members of the Irish Parliament fulminated patriotic sentiments, they used the legislature as a means of party aggrandisement, rather than for the improvement of their country. The difference of religion and the foreign education of the priesthood gave the people a strong leaning towards France. The presence of English forces to maintain order, galled the national pride, they eagerly sought foreign aid to relieve them from the yoke, and leagued together, for the establishment of a republic, or an alliance with France, and for a severance of the union with England.

The country was in a deplorable condition : outrages were committed by armed men, there was no security for life or property, and accredited agents from the French Directory were fomenting revolt under promise of assistance. The British Government, anxious to crush this rebellious spirit, increased the military force in the country ; but these vigorous measures only induced the leaders of the peasantry the more readily to have immediate recourse to arms, thus anticipating the promised assistance from France.

The rebellion broke out on the 24th of May, 1798, the insurgents assembling in different parts of the country at the same time. Some thousands of armed men obtained possession of Wexford on the 25th of May; on the 29th, Major-General Sir James Duffe, who was still first major in the First Guards, defeated a considerable number of the insurgents at Kildare; on the 5th of June, the rebels attacked New Ross near Waterford, but were driven back with great slaughter ; another body attacked Major-General Hon. Francis Needham, the third major of the First Guards, at Arklow, with the same result. They then established themselves at Vinegar Hill, under the command of a priest named John Murphy, upon which General Gerard Lake, who had resigned the command of the First Guards in 1794, on being appointed to the colonelcy of the 55th Foot, and was now the commander of the forces in Ireland, after concentrating his troops in the neighbourhood, attacked their position on the 21st of June, and after an obstinate resistance completely routed them.

The serious aspect of affairs in Ireland towards the end of

the month of May rendered it necessary to send over rein-forcements, which were placed under the command of Major-General Samuel Hulse, also a late lieutenant-colonel of the First Guards. Amongst the troops selected for this service was a brigade of Guards under Major-General Stannix of the Coldstreams, consisting of the third battalion of the First Regiment, and the first battalions of the two other regiments. The third battalion being ordered to march from Winchester to Fareham on the 10th of June, embarked at Gosport the next day, on board the " Russell " and the " Robust ; " while the first battalions of the Coldstreams and Third Guards were dispatched in conveyances from London, and embarked on the 12th.

June 18.   The fleet, after encountering tempestuous weather, anchored at the mouth of the Waterford river on the 18th of June, and upon the following day the third battalion First Guards disembarked and marched to Waterford, the other battalions remaining on board till the transports could ascend the river. This force arrived most oppor-tunely, for a plot had lately been discovered to burn the city and murder the chief inhabitants. Numerous arrests were made, and many were tried by courts martial.

Lord Cornwallis was now appointed Lord Lieutenant of Ireland, and Commander of the Forces, and immediately after his arrival on the 20th of June, he issued a proclamation of pardon and amnesty to the insurgents under certain conditions, and forthwith took the field in person.

June 26.   On the 26th of June, the third battalion First Guards was detached to New Ross to relieve the Cheshire Fencibles, in order that these might reinforce Major-General Sir Charles Asgill, another First Guards' man, at Kilkenny, as 5000 rebels had occupied Gore's bridge, in the neigh-bourhood of that town. Sir Charles Asgill attacked and defeated them the same day with the loss of 1000 killed and wounded. After this the battalions of the brigade of Guards were in turn detached to New Ross, where, though a poor place, the soldiers were hospitably treated by the inhabitants, and during their stay detachments were frequently sent out in search of rebels and arms.

The French Directory, now thoroughly awakened to the importance of the opening which had been afforded to their arms by the rebellion in Ireland, sent General Humbert with 1100 men to rouse the expiring spirit of revolt. He landed at Killala Bay, County Mayo, in the north-west of Ireland, on the 22nd of August, amply supplied both with *matériel* and equipment for 8000 men, and advanced towards Castlebar, where General Lake, having collected from 2000 to 8000 men, was in position to oppose his further progress. On the morning of the 27th of August, General Humbert attacked and compelled him for a time to retreat with the loss of six pieces of cannon, and established his own head-quarters in Castlebar. Upon information being received at Dublin Castle of the landing of the French, Lord Cornwallis proceeded to Athlone, and directed that the brigade of Guards should concentrate there to meet this new danger; the third battalion arrived at Birr in King's County on the 8rd of September, and on the 7th at Kil- beggan, twenty miles east of Athlone. In the meantime General Lake, notwithstanding his temporary discomfiture, had closely followed up the movements of the enemy. He came up with Humbert at Ballinamuck on the 8th, and immediately attacked him; the action lasted upwards of half-an-hour, when the French surrendered at discretion, and the rebels fled in all directions.

Lord Cornwallis had ordered the brigade of Guards to Kilbeggan that they might be available, either to assist his own operations, or arrive in a few hours in the capital in case of any serious alarm. For this purpose boats were in readiness on the canal at Philipstown, and the battalions were preparing to move to Kilbeggan, when, in consequence of the anticipated disturbances, an express arrived ordering the general to proceed without loss of time to Tullamore and Philipstown, and thence embark for Dublin. The third battalion First Guards started forthwith, but on the morning of the 9th of September, when within thirty miles of

1798.

Sept. 11.

Dublin, General Hulse overtook the flotilla, and ordered the troops to return to Tullamore, whence they proceeded to their old quarters at Birr, arriving there on the 11th of September; some of the Guards, however, continued their march to Portumna. Accounts had been received sometime previously, of Bonaparte's landing in Egypt on the 2nd of July, of the battle of the Pyramids, and of his entrance into Cairo on the 25th of that month; and now, shortly after the arrival of the Guards at Birr, news arrived of the French fleet having slipped out of Brest; upon which the brigade was ordered to proceed without loss of time to Mullingar, in case it was found necessary to act towards the north.   On the march an express arrived announcing the victory gained by Nelson at the Nile over the French fleet, upon which, according to an eye-witness, " the joy expressed by the battalion was most gratifying." The march had been a long one, twenty-two miles, and the men were jaded and beginning to fall out; in an instant every man was upon his legs rejoicing, and all those who were fatigued said they would want no further inducement to enable them to continue the march, and they did indeed perform the remainder of it with un-common spirit.

The destruction of the French fleet removed all anxiety as to any further attempt of the enemy to assist their co-religionists in Ireland, and the brigade of Guards instead of proceeding northwards was ordered to Limerick.   The third battalion First Guards proceeded there on the 19th of October, remaining in those quarters for about two months, when events occurred on the Continent which in-duced the government to equip another expedition to be despatched in the following year, to co-operate with the Russians in Holland, and the following arrangements were drawn up by the Duke of York in December, with the view to preparing a proportion of the brigade of Guards for that service. The grenadier companies of the three regiments to be completed to 120 rank and file; the third battalion First Regiment to be brought from Ire-

Oct. 19.

Dec. 7.

land, and be completed also to 120 rank and file per company. The battalions of Coldstream and Third Guards to remain for the present in Ireland, and be completed to the same establishment by drafts from their battalions in England, which drafts were to hold themselves in immediate readiness to proceed to Ireland. In obedience to these orders the third battalion First Regiment proceeded in December from Limerick to Cork, where it was, however, detained till the month of February, 1799, when it sailed, according to previous arrangements, and upon landing at Portsmouth marched to London. The Coldstreams did not leave Ireland till June, and on disembarking at Southampton, marched to Shirley Common, where the troops were assembling previous to sailing for the Continent. Major-General Harry Burrard, the future Sir Harry, was promoted to a regimental majority on the 31st of August, 1798, on the retirement of Sir James Duffe.

1798.

December.

1799.

It will be necessary now to refer to the events which caused the British government to embark once more in a campaign on the Continent.

1799.

At the close of 1798, the French republic was in possession of the resources of a military confederacy, extending from the Texel in the north of Holland, to the south of Italy. The Emperor of Russia began to feel the necessity of putting a stop to this career of conquest, and to the extension of republican opinions, and after consultation with his allies, he moved an army of 60,000 men towards Southern Europe. Austria also thought the moment opportune for recovering the provinces recently ceded to France, and Great Britain, seizing the occasion to form another European coalition, concluded a treaty on the last day of the year 1798, with Russia, to whom she granted subsidies to carry out the objects in view. The French Republic demanded that the Germanic Diet should refuse to permit the Russian forces to march through their territories, and, no answer being returned, France declared war against

Russia on the 12th of March, 1799. Since the last campaign the French army had much deteriorated, both in
numbers and in quality, and in the course of the spring and
summer of this year, Italy was overrun by the Austrian and
Russian armies under Melas and Suwarrow ; the Archduke
Charles had driven the French over the Rhine, and Switzerland was free as far as Zurich.

During these operations Great Britain, although the
leader of the Confederacy, had taken no active part on the
Continent, but now, secure from invasion, the British
government, in conjunction with Russia, resolved to make
a diversion in Holland in favour of the allies. According
to the treaty, Russia engaged to furnish 17,600 men, and
Great Britain 13,000, for service abroad. The British
troops were forthwith ordered to assemble, and the several
battalions of Foot Guards that were selected to form part
of the expedition were divided into two brigades.

The following list of the senior officers of the regiment at
the commencement of this campaign is here given :—

H.R.H. William Duke of Gloucester, Colonel.
Francis D'Oyly, Lieutenant.-Col. Maj.-Gen., commdg. 1st Brigade.
And. J. Drummond, 1st Maj.,   ,,   ,,   ,,
Hon. Franc. Needham, 2nd Maj.,   ,,   ,,
Harry Burrard, 3rd Maj.,   ,,   ,,   ,,   2nd Brigade.
Capt. Sir Chas. Asgill, ⎫ Captains ,,   ,,
Hon. Chas. Monson,   ⎪   of   ,,   ,,
Hon. George Ludlow,   ⎬ Companies ,,   ,,
Augustus Maitland,   ⎪ acting Colonel   ,,   3rd Battalion.
Hon. John Leslie,   ⎪ Majors.   ,,
Henry Wynyard,   ⎭   ,,   ,,   Gren. Battalion.
Wm. Thornton,   Captain.   ,,
W. C. Archer,   ,,   ,,

The First Brigade, under Major-General D'Oyly, consisted
of the grenadier battalion, under Colonel H. Wynyard,
formed from the several regiments, and of the 3rd battalion
1st Regiment, under Colonel Augustus Maitland, all three
officers of the First Guards, Lieut.-Col. Smollett, of the
same regiment, being appointed Brigade Major. The Second
Brigade, under the command of Major-General Harry Bur-

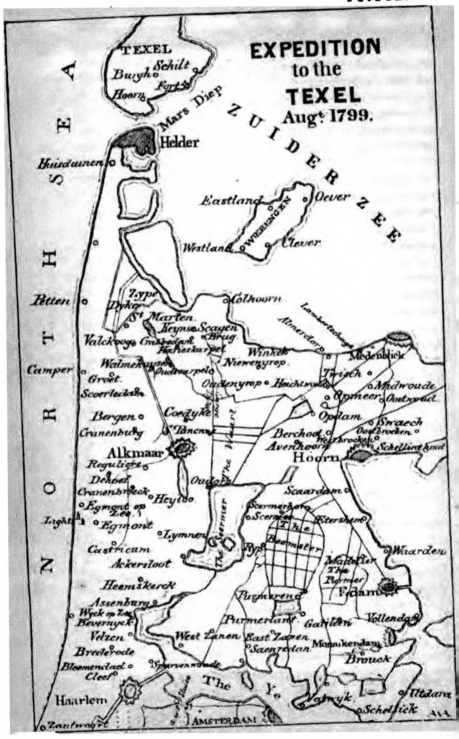

EXPEDITION
to the
TEXEL
Aug.ᵗ 1799.

rard, also of the First Regiment, was composed of the 1st
battalions of Coldstream and Third Guards, all about 900
strong. According to the above selection, it would appear
that Maitland was chosen to command the service battalion
as the senior field officer not yet promoted to major-general.

The third battalion First Regiment,* under Colonel
Maitland, which had returned from Ireland in the previous
February, marched to Shirley camp near Southampton,
at the beginning of July, and was soon joined by the two
battalions of the other regiments of Guards from Ireland,
when the grenadier companies were formed into a separate
battalion, the troops being all placed under the command
of Lieutenant-General Ralph Abercrombie. Here the first
brigade was stationed until the 18th of July, when it
marched to Barham Downs, six miles south-east of Canterbury, whence it proceeded on the 5th of August to
Ramsgate, and embarked ; and the fleet, consisting of 200
vessels, sailed on the 13th of August with the first division
of the army, amounting to nearly 12,000 men.

The first object of the expedition was to land in North Holland, on the peninsula of the Helder, where the shores are of
easy access ; seize the Dutch fleet at the Texel ; advance on
Amsterdam ; hoist the Orange colours ; and restore the
Prince of Orange as Stadtholder.

The Batavian Republic (Holland) had 20,000 troops in
the field, and the French were bound by treaty to support
them with 24,000 more. General Brun was appointed to
command their united armies. The French had 7000 men
at Haarlem, and General Daendel with 10,000 Dutch
soldiers was at Schargenberg to oppose the landing.

The British fleet, after encountering tempestuous weather
and contrary winds, anchored off the Helder Point on the
26th of August, and at three on the following morning, Sir
James Pulteney, landing with the third brigade and reserve
under Major-General Cook and Colonel Macdonald,
advanced without opposition to the sand hills, where the

---

* For names of officers First Guards accompanying this expedition, see
page 348, line 4.

Dutch attacked their right, but after a spirited resistance were driven back to Groete Kleete. The first brigade of Guards on landing formed up on the left of Sir James Pulteney's columns, upon which the Dutch made another attempt to dislodge the British troops, and while General Daendel attacked the British right, General Von Guerecke advanced against the first brigade of Guards. The action was maintained by musketry alone, as the deep ditches prevented the rival forces coming into contact, and in spite of their numerical superiority, the enemy, after a trying struggle lasting from five in the morning to three o'clock in the afternoon, retired to a position near Alkmaer Castle. The casualties of the First Guards on this occasion were Lieutenant-Colonel Smollett, brigade-major of the first brigade, killed, whose appointment was subsequently conferred on Captain Capel of the same regiment. In the third battalion First Guards were one officer, Captain Ruddock, and thirteen rank and file, wounded. In the grenadier battalion, one officer, Captain Gunthorpe, of the First Guards, wounded, one sergeant killed and two wounded, and two rank and file killed, and forty-eight wounded. The total losses were two officers and fifty-four men killed, eighteen officers and three hundred and fifty - two men wounded. Amongst the regiments of the Line principally engaged were the 2nd, 27th, 29th, 69th, and 85th, under Picton, who was wounded, and the reserve consisting of the 2nd battalion Royals and the 55th Regiment. Sir Ralph Abercrombie issued the following general order from Klein Keeling, thanking the troops engaged on the 27th for their conduct :—

"Lieut.-Gen. Sir Ralph Abercrombie desires to return his warmest thanks to the troops who were engaged yesterday, who during the course of a long contest shewed the most conspicuous proofs of gallantry and persevering intrepidity."

This was followed by the king's approval, which was communicated to the troops in the following letter from the Secretary of State :—

"Although it is impossible for me to convey to you in

adequate terms, the sense His Majesty entertains of the steady and enterprising bravery of the army under your command in the arduous and ever-memorable action of the 27th ultimo, I cannot allow H.R.H. the Duke of York to proceed to the Continent without taking the opportunity, in obedience to His Majesty's commands, to desire you will in the strongest manner signify to all officers and men under your command, His Majesty's warmest approbation of their valour and good conduct on that day. High as the character of the British army stood before that event, it is impossible that the landing at the Helder Point, preceded and attended by so many untoward difficulties, and the battle by which it was immediately followed, should not attract the admiration of Europe, and raise that character still higher in every part of the world, as it has done already in the eyes of their Sovereign and their countrymen at home."

On the following morning the second brigade of Guards under Burrard, and the fourth under Moore, were told off to attack the Helder, in which was a garrison of 2000 men, but their services were not required, as the town was evacuated immediately after the successful landing of the British, and that was followed on the 30th by the surrender of the Dutch fleet, whereby the navigation of the Zuyder Zee was secured to the British, and the right flank of the Republican army became exposed to an attack from that quarter.

On the 1st of September, the British troops took up a position in advance, with their right at Petten, on the sea-shore, and their left at Oudesluys, their front being covered by the Zuype canal and several dykes. Sir Ralph Abercrombie had determined to remain on the defensive until the arrival, either of the Russians, or of the reinforcements expected with the Duke of York, who was appointed Commander-in-Chief, as referred to in the above letter of the Secretary of State; but General Brun, with the French army, arrived at Alkmaer on the 2nd of September, with the intention of attacking Sir Ralph, and crushing him before he received any accession of strength. On the morning of the 10th of September, accordingly, the French, led by Vandamme, poured impetuously along the approaches defended by the two brigades of the British Guards, and persevered in their assault, without cover, with reckless bravery, till mown down by the steady fire of the second brigade of Guards, when they drew off after suffering enormously. The first brigade of Guards, more to the right, were not so immediately opposed to the French column, though they assisted in its overthrow and suffered some loss. The 20th Regiment held Krabbenham, which formed a salient angle of the British position, and repelled an assault with signal success. The enemy were also completely repulsed in other parts of the British line. The loss of the First Guards in this action was, six rank and file wounded; in the grenadier battalion, six rank and file killed, one officer, Captain Nevill, one sergeant, and thirteen rank and file wounded; the second brigade lost three killed and one officer and eleven men wounded. Sir Ralph Abercrombie issued the following general order on the occasion:—"This day has again afforded Sir Ralph Abercrombie an opportunity of thanking his troops for their noble and steady conduct." In his despatch he states that "the two brigades of Guards repulsed with great vigour the column of French which advanced to attack them."

Such was the position of affairs when, on the 12th of September, 7000 Russians, under General D'Hermann, appeared in the field. On the 13th, the Duke of York also came from England with large reinforcements, and assumed the command of the allied army, now amounting to 33,000 men; but the composition of the British forces was not good, the ranks being filled with many raw volunteers from the embodied militia. It was now divided into nine infantry brigades, including two of Guards, as given below, the last five, from the 5th to the 9th, being almost exclusively militiamen.*

* 1st Brigade. Major-General D'Oyly, Grenadier Battalion of Guards, under Colonel H. Wynyard; 3rd battalion First Guards, under Augustus Maitland.

The right of the line was conceded to the Russians as the post of honour.

It was clear that now, as formerly, there was no good-will towards the allies on the part of the people of North Holland, and that if Amsterdam was to be reached, it could only be by hard fighting; and at a council of war, it was decided to make a general attack on the enemy on the 19th of September. The enemy's position was short and Sept. 19 very strong: the Dutch on the right were entrenched at Oude-Scarpel, and their left was in front of Bergen, at the foot of the sand-hills, surrounded by enclosures and woods. The duke determined to turn their right and force them southward, and thus obtain the advantage of a narrow front, and with this object in view, Abercrombie, with 9000 men, Battle of was detached at dusk on the 18th of September to move round Bergen. the enemy's right to Hoorn, fourteen miles distant, with orders to push on to Purmarend, twelve miles further; and at daybreak on the 19th, the remainder of the army were to assault the position in three columns simultaneously. The right, composed of Russians, supported by the 9th or Manners' brigade, started before the other columns, and earlier than was intended; a severe contest of two hours took place near Schovel, when, the French beginning to retire, the Russians advanced in a reckless, hurried manner,

2nd Brigade. Major-General Harry Burrard, 1st battalion Coldstream Guards, 1st battalion Third Guards.
(The Battalions of these Brigades were each above 900 strong.)
3rd Brigade. Major-General Coote, in succession to Pulteney, wounded; 2nd (596 strong), 27th (863), 29th (630), 69th, and 85th Regiments.
4th Brigade. Major-General Moore; 1st Royals (596), 25th (501), 49th (461), 79th (780), and 92nd (792).
Reserve. Colonel Macdonald; 23rd (905), 55th Regiments.
5th Brigade. Major-General Don; 17th, 1st battalion (686), 2nd battalion (676), 40th, 1st battalion (684), 2nd battalion (645).
6th Brigade. Major-General Earl of Cavan; 1st battalion (774), 2nd battalion (774), 20th and 63rd (761).
7th Brigade. Major-General Earl of Chatham; 1st, 2nd, and 3rd battalions of 4th, and 31st Regiment.
8th Brigade. Major-General Prince William; 1st battalion (686), 2nd battalion (666), 5th Regiment, 1st battalion (607), 2nd battalion (614), 35th Regiment.
9th Brigade. Major-General Manners; 1st and 2nd battalions 9th and 56th (676).

driving everything before them, and took possession of Bergen, where they began plundering; but in consequence of their impetuous advance, and having no support on their flanks, they were in turn driven back with great loss, thoroughly routed, and appeared no more.

The centre column, under General Dundas, composed of the two brigades of Guards, the 8th or Prince William's brigade of militiamen, and 200 Russians, were to force Walmenhuysen and Schoveldam, and then co-operate with the right towards Bergen, while the grenadier battalion of Guards was detached to observe Schoveldam. The post of Walmenhuysen, though strongly occupied by the French, was carried in very good style; the First Guards forcing it at one extremity while the Russians entered it at the other, capturing 500 prisoners and three guns. The battalion then moved towards and carried Schoveldam with slight resistance on the part of the Dutch; Manners' brigade appeared at the same time on the side of Schovel, but after checking the French in pursuit of the Russians, he was compelled to retire, until reinforced by Prince William, when they retook the village; at this moment the Duke of York brought up the first brigade of Guards from Schoveldam, and the whole, except the Russians, who could not be induced to return to the combat, pursued the French to the sand-hills.

The Third Guards and 5th Regiment had been detached from the centre column to protect Sir J. Pulteney's right, whose column had got into some confusion from the intersected ground; he successfully carried the post of Oude-Scarpel after a determined resistance from the Dutch, and pushed on within a short distance of Alkmaer, but by this time, the total defeat of the Russians on his right, and the extreme exhaustion of the troops, compelled the duke to return to the position from which they had advanced.

The enemy followed up this retreat with great activity, shewing themselves in such strength opposite the right of the British position and the village of Krabbenham, that apprehensions were felt they would attack the lines; a great

part of the army, consisting of young soldiers, were in confusion, and the Russians, with the exception of three battalions, were dispersed. Coote's brigade was away to the
left, and there remained little to trust to but the artillery
and three battalions of Guards, which having been detached
successively to support and cover their neighbours, were
arriving separately, much jaded, and with but little ammunition left in their pouches. During this attack of the main
body, Hoorn opened its gates to Abercrombie; but the
roads being in a dreadful state, and his troops much fatigued,
he halted on the morning of the 19th, when, hearing of the
misfortune at Bergen, he retreated also, and on the 20th
reoccupied his former position at Culhaven.

The battle of Bergen lasted thirteen hours and a half;
the part assigned to the first brigade of Guards had been
successfully accomplished, and the British troops had overcome every obstacle of nature and art; they had been
throughout victorious, and no permanent reverse took
place during the day, but owing to Abercrombie's enforced
absence, with the view to turning the enemy's right, the
superiority of the enemy in numbers was decisive. The
First Guards lost on this occasion, one officer, Captain
Gunthorpe, killed, and six officers wounded, viz., Colonel
Wynyard, commanding the grenadier battalion of Guards,
Lieutenant-Colonels Cook and Dawkins, Captains Forbes
and Henry Wheatley, and Ensign D'Oyly. The first brigade, consisting of the grenadier battalion and third battalion First Guards, also lost thirteen men killed, ninety
wounded, and seventy missing.

The duke, in his despatch, expressed "his great satisfaction at the conduct of Major-Generals Prince William,
D'Oyly, Burrard (the two latter commanding the two brigades of Guards), Manners, and Don, to whose spirited exertions the credit gained by the brigades they commanded is
specially to be imputed;" and, in the general order of the
20th of September at Shagenburg, the duke acknowledged the
services of the Guards on this occasion in the following
words:—"The column of General Dundas, consisting of

first brigade of Guards, under General D'Oyly, and the Coldstreams under Major-General Burrard, and the brigades of Prince William and Manners, maintained the action on the right of Alkmaer Castle in the most spirited manner."

Incessant storms and heavy rains prevailed now for several days, forcing the duke to defer making another general attack on the enemy's position; but he determined to operate against the enemy's left along the shore, and for this purpose the disposition of the army was altered, the Russians, whose second division had recently arrived, being in the centre column. The chief duty assigned to the left column was to keep the enemy in check near Alkmaer, and prevent him from sending assistance to his left. The troops were put in motion on the 29th of September, but from the state of the roads, it being found impossible to proceed, the attempt was not resumed till the 2nd of October, when the army again advanced. The right column, destined for this operation, under the immediate command of Sir Ralph Abercrombie, was composed of the first brigade of Guards, Moore's 4th brigade, the reserve, and the 6th or Lord Cavan's brigade, with the 7th and 15th Light Dragoons under Lord Paget, and twenty pieces of artillery; these were to penetrate to Egmont-op-Zee; the covering of the extreme left flank of the column being entrusted to Colonel Macdonald and the reserve. General Abercrombie

advanced soon after 6 A.M. on the 2nd, when the reserve drove the enemy along the sand-hills, gradually losing all connection with the brigades on their right; Moore's brigade moved along the dyke on the coast, with Lord Cavan on his left, while Abercrombie himself, on the extreme right, marched on the beach with the Guards, cavalry, and artillery. The march was very severe: after advancing six miles, the sand-hills were lined with skirmishers, and Moore's brigade was gradually detached to the left flank, left uncovered through the absence of the reserve, but it was checked in an attempt to carry the sand-hills, and an obstinate contest ensued, which lasted several hours; at length, late in the afternoon, the British infantry, with D'Oyly's

first brigade of Guards in support, established themselves
on the road leading from Bergen to Egmont. While this
was going on on the right, the centre column under General
Dundas stormed the village of Schovel, which was carried
by the Russians; and Burrard's 2nd brigade of Guards drove
the enemy out of Schoveldam. Cook's and Lord Chatham's
brigades had successfully attacked the positions in their
front, and were now prepared to move to the attack of
Bergen; but the Russians who were to have made the assault
in front insisted on waiting for Abercrombie, during which
delay, the enemy, taking the opportunity of re-forming,
turned upon their assailants, but were again repulsed, and
finally gave way on all sides.

Later in the day the battalions of the reserve arrived
to the support of Abercrombie's infantry, and about seven
o'clock the enemy abandoned their well-defended position
and drew off towards Beverwyck, but as Bergen was still
in possession of the enemy, Sir Ralph Abercrombie considered he had advanced far enough, and the troops halted
until morning. The men were suffering greatly from want
of water, for the heat had been excessive, their thirst was
only increased by the rations of salt meat, and the only
relief they obtained was from a heavy shower of rain.
During the night, General Brun, regarding his position
at Bergen as no longer tenable, now that Abercrombie
had forced his left, retired, and the abandoned positions
were occupied the next day by the British and Russian
forces, while a detachment of the 18th Dragoons and of
Burrard's brigade of Guards took possession of Alkmaer,
the capital of North Holland. Sir Ralph had intended
advancing in pursuit of the enemy at daybreak, but the men
were so exhausted from want of food, that he decided to
wait until they were refreshed, and the bad state of the roads
delayed the waggons till four in the afternoon; when, however,
intelligence arrived of the retreat of the French from Egmont-
op-Zee, the troops were at once ordered under arms, and,
moving forward, occupied that village, but they were unable to
come up with the enemy in his retreat. The total loss of the

[margin notes:] 1799.
Oct. 2.
Alkmaer.

Oct. 3.

British in this action was—officers, eleven killed, sixty-four wounded; men, 226 killed, 1033 wounded. The casualties of the third battalion First Guards were three officers wounded, viz., Major Coleman, Ensign Spedding, and Ensign Campbell, five sergeants wounded, and of rank and file, six killed, forty-seven wounded and eight missing. There were also twenty casualties in the grenadier battalion, viz., one rank and file killed, one sergeant, eighteen rank and file, wounded.

The Duke of York complimented the army on the victory which they had so gallantly achieved in the following words :

Gen. Order.　　Head Quarters, Alkmaer, *Oct. 5th*, 1799.

H.R.H. the Commander-in-Chief desires to express to the army his warmest thanks for the steady and persevering gallantry of their conduct in the general action of the 2nd inst., to which alone is to be ascribed the complete victory gained over the enemy under circumstances of the greatest difficulty * * * * * H.R.H. thinks it no less his duty, to place on record the names of the following general officers and brigades of British which had an opportunity of contributing to the success of that ever-memorable and distinguished day.

Then follow their several names, amongst which are those of Major-General Francis D'Oyly's brigade, consisting of grenadiers of the Guards and third battalion First Regiment of Guards, and Major-General Burrard's brigade of Coldstreams and Third Guards.

Lord Hutchinson says:—" The Guards repulsed with great vigour the column of French which had advanced to attack them, and where the slaughter was great.

" Major-General Ludlow and the brigade of Guards will accept the thanks of his Excellency the Commander-in-Chief for the cool, steady, and soldier-like manner in which they repulsed the enemy's columns."

No plan having been concerted for the subsequent operations of the army in the event of success on the 2nd of October, Abercrombie's column on the right remained for three days unconnected with the rest of the British army.

The advantages gained by the late victory were more apparent than real; it was supposed that the enemy had retired to ·the still stronger position of Beverwyck, ten miles south of Alkmaer, to which place a reinforcement of 5000 French was marching to join them, and early on Sunday, the 6th of October, the British right was pushed forward to drive back the enemy's advanced posts, the duke intending to attack the position of Beverwyck on the following day; but the French had not retired to so great a distance as was imagined, and at Baccum the resistance to the Russians was so great, that reinforcements were gradually brought up on both sides. Upon the French taking the offensive, Abercrombie moved up to support the Russians, when the two armies engaged along the whole line, and the action became general, but as there was no plan of attack on either side, all was confusion. Abercrombie's column was engaged with the French left wing; after a severe contest, the British and Russians repulsed every attack made upon them, and when reinforced by the reserve, advanced as far as Ackersloot and Wyck-op-Zee, but it was ten at night before General Brun withdrew his troops, leaving the allies masters of the field. In the course of the day a brilliant charge was made by four companies of the Third Guards and one of the Coldstreams, under Colonel Clephane, into the village of Ackersloot, from which they drove two battalions of French, taking 200 prisoners.

The casualties in the First Guards on the 6th of September were—Colonel Augustus Maitland, commanding the third battalion, severely wounded, who, dying a few days later, was succeeded in the command by Lieutenant-Colonel Archer; Lieutenant-Colonel Lake taken prisoner, and Ensign Bourke wounded. The losses of the third battalion First Guards in rank and file were three killed, twenty-six wounded, and twenty-one missing. The total loss of the British army was about 2500 men.

This action, though it ended favourably, crushed all hopes of ultimate success; the Anglo-Russian army, six weeks earlier, numbering 35,000 men, and confident in its strength, had already lost 10,000 in maintaining a footing in the country, and from the torrents of rain that came down, pro-

1802.

Oct. 6.

1799.   visions were difficult to procure, and no shelter to be obtained on the sand-hills. A council of war decided to withdraw the army to its original position on the Zuype, where, dispirited

Oct. 8.   and out of humour, it arrived on the 8th of October. The resumption of hostilities was entirely out of the question, and the commander-in-chief had to consider whether to act on the defensive in his present position or evacuate the country. The approach of winter, with the recollection of that of 1794 before him, and the impoverished state of the country, rendered the former impossible, and the latter alternative was resolved on, upon which the following general order was issued to the army :—

SCHAGENBERG, Oct. 8, 1799.

H.R.H. the Commander-in-Chief desires the troops will accept his best thanks for the persevering bravery and good order, which have so eminently distinguished their conduct during the whole period from the 2nd to the 8th past, although suffering from the inclemency of the weather and precarious supplies, necessarily originating out of the situation of the army. From the former of these two causes H.R.H. has found it necessary to withdraw the troops from a situation where they must have been continually exposed to insupportable hardships, and which no efforts of an enemy twice beaten could have effected.

The duke also mentioned in his dispatch that the gallantry the troops had displayed, and the perseverance with which they had supported the fatigues of the day, rivalled their former exertions.

The British general could have secured his retreat by inundating the country, but as this would have been still greater ruin to the inhabitants, the duke sent a flag of truce on the 14th of October to General Brun, with whom a convention was concluded, by which the embarcation of the allied forces was to be effected without interruption, and 8000 French prisoners taken during the campaign were to be restored.

Oct. 21.   On the evening of the 21st of October the first brigade of Guards marched to the Helder, and embarked the next morning at daybreak, and landing at Yarmouth on the 29th and 30th of October, proceeded by Norwich, Stratford,

and Epping, to London, which they reached on the 8th
of November. Upon the breaking up of the first brigade
of Guards, Major-General Francis D'Oyly was ordered upon
another duty, and was thereby prevented from returning
with it to England, apparently much against his wishes, for
on quitting the brigade he issued the following order :—

"Major-General D'Oyly cannot but feel hurt at being
prevented by other duty from returning to England with his
brigade. He must consider it a great honour having commanded it, and is persuaded that the approbation he has
received from his country and the commander-in-chief is
entirely owing to the good conduct and bravery that has
been so conspicuous in the officers and soldiers composing
the first brigade, for which he begs to return them his most
sincere thanks, and trusts the same good behaviour that has
distinguished them during the campaign will be continued
after their arrival in England."

On receipt of intelligence of the action of the 6th of
October in England, the light-infantry battalion of Guards,
in which were the four companies of the 1st Regiment,
received orders on the 11th to embark at Greenwich the
next day, and sail for the Helder; but, upon the 15th, on
the decision of the generals to evacuate the country becoming known, òrders were sent to intercept them, and
they were directed to disembark again at Gravesend and
return to London.

An augmentation of the establishment of the First Guards ·
by 32 lieutenants and 992 men took place on the 25th of
November, each company being increased to 150 rank and
file. The establishment was now greater than it had ever
been raised to, viz., 140 officers, 224 sergeants, 3 staff, 75
drummers, and 4800 rank and file, making a grand total of
5242 men, at an annual charge of 158,000*l.*, but the increase
of officers was not complete till October in the following year.

Major-General Francis D'Oyly resigned his post of lieutenant-colonel of the First Guards at this time, and was
succeeded by Major-General Andrew J. Drummond; Charles
Asgill (the future Sir Charles), was promoted to the majority,

1799. but he retired in May following, and Colonel Honourable George J. Ludlow became third regimental major in his place.

The following were the officers that accompanied the third battalion First Guards in the expedition to the Helder, September, 1799 :—

Colonel Augustus Maitland, Commanding 3rd Battalion.

Capts. & Lieut.-Cols.	Lieuts. & Capts.	Ensigns.
Grenadier, H. Warde.	— Darby.	
2. H. Burrard, *s.*	Hon. D. S. Hallyburton.	Hen. D'Oyly.
3. W. C. Archer.	R. D. Forbes.	Rd. Bourke.
4. H. Chaytor.	Hen. Wheatley.	T. Congreve.
5. W. H. Clinton, *s.*	— Colman.	J. Speddings.
6. Hen. Clinton.	Evd. Buckworth.	J. R. Udny.
7. G. Cooke.	— Dyer.	Ch. Munday.
8. — Dawkins.	Jn. Lambert.	F. W. Campbell.
9. F. G. Lake.	Fran. Todd.	Samuel Townshend.
Light Infantry,—		
H. F. Campbell.	{ Hon. J. F. Moreton.	
	{ E. T. Hussey.	

Captain J. Lambert, Adjutant.

Lieutenant-Colonel Wm. Henry Clinton was A.D.C. to H.R.H. the Duke of York ; Captain Francis D'Oyly, A.D.C. to Major-General D'Oyly ; and Captain G. G. Donaldson A.D.C. to Major-General Graham.

The officers of the grenadier companies of the 1st and 2nd battalions were :—

1st Battalion : Colonels J. Smith and Hon. C. Fitzroy ; Captains Hon. F. G. Upton, Hon. Ed. Capel, E. Wm. Salisbury, and Hon. Wm. Stuart.

2nd Battalion : Colonel H. Wynyard, who commanded the Grenadier Battalion ; and Captains — Churchill and Hon. H. Townshend.

1800.

1800. January. The following were the senior officers of the regiment in the last year of the eighteenth century ; and as several of the captains of companies shortly became major-generals, the date on which they obtained that rank is inserted opposite their names :—

OFFICERS OF FIRST GUARDS, JANUARY, 1800.

Lieut.-Col. Andrew J. Drummond, Lieut.-Gen., 26th Feb., 1795.
1st Major, Hon. Francis Needham, Lieut.-Gen., 26th Feb., 1795.
2nd Major, Harry Burrard, Major-Gen., 1st Jan., 1798.
3rd Major, Hon. George James Ludlow, Maj.-Gen., 18th June, 1798.

CAPTAINS AND LIEUT.-COLONELS.

Hon. John Leslie, Maj.-Gen., 20th April, 1802.
Henry Wynyard, „ „ „ „
William Thornton „ „ „ „
Wm. C. Archer, „ „ „ „
Hon. Ed. Phipps, „ „ „ „
John Smith, „ „ 25th Sept., 1803.
Hon. Ch. Fitzroy „ „ „ „
Arthur Whetham, „ „ 1st Jan., 1805.
Henry Warde,
William Henry Clinton,
Moore Disney,
Henry Frederick Campbell,
F. Charles White.

After the failure of the expedition to Holland, Russia concluded a treaty of peace with the French Republic, while the British Government sent an expedition of 12,000 men to the Mediterranean, under Sir Ralph Abercrombie, to assist the Austrians in North Italy. They were too late to save Genoa; but arrangements were made between the British Government and the Porte for an attack on Egypt in the following year.

In the summer of 1800, the troops in England were assembled in camps with a view to perfecting their drill and discipline, as well as that they might be ready prepared in the event of the threats of an invasion being carried out. One of the camps of exercise of 14,000 men was formed at Swinley, near Windsor, under the command of General Dundas, the author of the improved system of drill. Amongst the troops assembled there on the 10th of June, June 10. was a brigade of Guards under the command of Major-General Harry Burrard, consisting of the grenadier battalion under Colonel Henry Wynyard, the light infantry battalion under Lieutenant-Colonel William Henry Clinton, and the third battalion First Guards under Lieutenant-Colonel W. Archer, Captain Hon. Edward Capel being the brigade-major. During the continuance of this camp, the greatest exertions were made to establish a uniform system in manœuvring. The Duke of York, who for some time occupied Swinley Lodge, took command of the troops;

1800.

July 17.

the king frequently came from Windsor to attend the field-days, and on the 17th of July a grand review took place in his presence on Wingfield Plain. Upon the breaking up of the camp at the end of August, a portion of the troops were ordered to Colchester; amongst others the above brigade of Guards, viz., the grenadier and light battalions, and Archer's third battalion First Guards, and upon their proceeding to those quarters in the first days of September, Major-General Burrard issued the following order to the brigade :—

" SWINLEY CAMP, *30th August*, 1800.

" Major-General Burrard is persuaded that the brigade of Guards will continue to preserve the good opinion they have deserved (which his Majesty, as expressed in general orders, was so graciously pleased to entertain of them, and of which he has again this day so fully declared his opinion), and by their good conduct and regularity on their march to Colchester, stamp a character on themselves, as soldiers, which can never be impaired."

1801.

1801.

Jan. 1.

July 10.

The Guards brigade remained at Colchester throughout the winter of 1800–1, under the divisional command of Lieu-tenant-General Garth, who had been lieutenant-colonel of the First Guards from 1789 to 1792 ; and while here, on the occasion of the union between Great Britain and Ireland on the 1st of January, 1801, the brigade and the rest of the corps in camp fired a royal salute and a *feu de joie*, when the new Union colours were for the first time displayed before the troops. The several battalions remained at Colchester till the summer of 1801, when, on the 10th.of July, the light infantry battalion, under Lieutenant-Colonel W. H. Clinton, marched to Chatham, where it encamped within the lines, and on the 11th, the grenadier battalion and third battalion First Guards proceeded to Chelmsford, whence on the 20th these also marched to Chatham, where they all remained till the following year, and were placed under the command of Lieutenant-General Samuel Hulse.

Though no battalion of the First Guards took part in 1801.
the expedition to Egypt, we must not omit mentioning
that a reinforcement of 5000 men, in which was the second
brigade of Guards, consisting of the first battalions of
the Coldstream and Third Regiments, had been sent out
in August, 1800, to reinforce Sir Ralph Abercrombie in the
Mediterranean, and assist in the proposed operations
against the French in Egypt, in which General Baird,
with 6000 men, was to co-operate by the Red Sea from
India. The above brigade was placed under Major-General
Hon. George Ludlow, third major of the First Guards.

The British troops, after remaining some time at Mar-
morice Bay, on the coast of Asia Minor, landed in Aboukir
Bay on the 8th of March, 1801, the Guards, under Ludlow,
with General Coote's and Moore's brigades, being the first
on shore, and driving the French from the position they
had occupied. On the 21st of March, General Menou March 21.
attacked the British army at Alexandria, where it was
drawn up prepared to maintain its ground, the Guards
being in the centre ; an attempt to storm the British right
was repulsed by Moore, while an attack upon the left of
Ludlow's brigade of Guards was received with so terrible
a fire that it totally failed. An attack of the enemy's
cavalry was equally unsuccessful, but in the midst of it,
Sir Ralph Abercrombie received a ball in his thigh, and
though he remained in a battery close to the Guards, he
could not mount his horse, and at the end of the battle
was carried in a litter to Lord Keith's ship, where he
died on the 28th of the same month.

The First Guards must ever recollect with pride having
served under Sir Ralph Abercrombie, for during the campaign of 1794–95, both in the affair at Mouveaux and as the
reserve in covering the retreat through Holland, they were
under his immediate command, and in 1799 at Bergen and
Alkmaer they fought under his immediate inspection.
General Hutchinson, who succeeded to the command, wrote
in his despatch that Major-General Ludlow deserved much
approbation for his conduct when the centre of the army
was attacked ; and added, " under his guidance the Guards

1801.

conducted themselves in the most cool, intrepid, and soldier-like manner."

The French garrison of Cairo surrendered on the 9th of July; Alexandria capitulated on the 2nd of September, and upon the French army, 26,000 strong, embarking on the 14th of the same month, the First Consul's ambitious projects for empire in the East were totally annihilated.

Sept. 2.

In the meantime, a coalition, called the armed neutrality of the north, which was, in effect, an act of direct hostility against Great Britain, was organised at the instigation of France by the Baltic powers, who had considerable maritime forces; and no sooner did it become known, than a squadron, under Sir Hyde Parker and Lord Nelson, was dispatched from this country to act against them. On the 2nd of April, Nelson stood in to Copenhagen and destroyed the greater part of the Danish fleet, upon which the Danes agreed to suspend all proceedings under the neutrality treaty. In France, also, great preparations had been made for the invasion of England; Boulogne was selected for the rendezvous of a flotilla of gun-boats, organised in nine divisions, but nothing was attempted this year; the British Government, however, appointed Nelson to the command of the channel squadron, to watch the proceedings of the French.

Major-General Andrew J. Drummond, the lieutenant-colonel, and the Honourable George J. Ludlow, third major, left the regiment this year, having been appointed to the colonelcies of the fifth and fity-second regiments of the line respectively; and on the 21st of August the Honourable F. Needham was promoted to the lieutenant-colonelcy; Major-General Harry Burrard became first major, and the Honourable John Leslie and Henry Wynyard succeeded to the second and third regimental majorities.

Early in this year Mr. Pitt had resigned office, and the new government opened negotiations for peace without a suspension of arms; the preliminaries were agreed to on the 1st of October, consequent upon which, there was a general reduction in the army, the companies of the Guards were reduced to 117 men each, and on the 25th of

March, 1802, the Peace of Amiens was signed, when tran- 1802.
quillity was for a time restored to Europe.

The troops being no longer required for the defence of the
coast, the brigade of Guards at Chatham moved to London
on the 29th of April, 1802 ; the battalions of grenadiers and
light infantry were broken up, the flank companies of the
First Guards joining their respective battalions at Windsor
and Winchester. In June the companies were still further
reduced to seventy-one men, and on the 25th of December,
all the lieutenants junior to Captain Clitherow, twenty in
number, were placed on half-pay.

The king and the royal family removed with the court, in
June, to the marine residence at Weymouth for the summer
months, on which occasion, Major-General Leslie, with the
second battalion of the First Guards, marched from Winchester to Weymouth, to take the duties of the palace, and
on the return of the court to Windsor the battalion proceeded to London.

1803.

There soon appeared signs portending that peace 1803.
would not be long maintained; a demand from the
First Consul that the British Government should restrain
the freedom of the press was refused in dignified terms.
An evident design upon the independence of Turkey by
Buonaparte became known at this time, it was admitted even
by himself ; and in the correspondence that ensued, the
British Government announced that they would not surrender either Malta or Alexandria, until explanations were
given as to the hostile preparations of France, when the First
Consul retorted that peace or war with Great Britain would
depend on the cession by them of Malta. The British
Parliament, supporting the Government, at once voted
10,000 additional seamen ; the militia were called out, and
war was again declared on the 12th of May, 1803. May 12.

As early as the month of March, all officers had been
ordered to join ; an augmentation of ten men per company was ordered; the standard of height of the Guards
was in June lowered to 5 feet 6 inches, and in October
the companies were further augmented to 114 men each.

It was at this time that an important improvement was introduced into the company system throughout the army ; hitherto, in the First Regiment of Guards, the lieutenant-colonel and the three majors had been at the same time actual captains of companies, by which their companies were deprived of an effective officer in the field. This system was now abolished as well as the intermediate rank of captain-lieutenant, which office was made that of a *bonâ fide* captain. The new system came into operation on the 25th of May, when the Hon. Francis Needham, the lieutenant-colonel, and the three regimental majors, Harry Burrard, Hon. John Leslie, and Henry Wynyard all lost their companies, five additional captains being added to the establishment. One of the companies was given to the Hon. John Proby, second son of the first Earl of Carysfort, who exchanged from the line ; and in the following year, on the death of his elder brother, became Lord Proby, and, eventually, succeeded to the earldom.   Three of the companies were given in the regiment to Captains J. Burnaby, Peregrine Maitland, and Hon. Edward Capel, and the fifth to Colonel Andrew Gammell, from the line.

On the declaration of war, the country was placed in a complete state of military organisation, it being considered certain that Buonaparte would attempt an invasion.   General the Earl of Harrington was placed in command of the London district, and the three regiments
of Guards, by an order of the 26th of June, were formed into three separate brigades.   The first brigade was composed of the first and third battalions of the First Guards, under Major-General H. Wynyard, third major, with Captain Sabine (First Guards) as brigade-major ; the second brigade consisted of the first battalions of the Coldstream and Third Guards, under Major-General Finch of the Coldstreams, Captain Stirling (Coldstream Guards), major of brigade ; and the three second battalions formed the third brigade, under Major-General Harry Burrard,* then

---

* Sir Harry Burrard had in early days, 11th December, 1786, risen to the rank of major in the 14th Regiment of Foot.   On the 13th March, 1789, he

first major of the First Guards, to whom Major Dalzell was attached as brigade major; these last-named battalions became virtually for a time the depôts of the two other brigades, and remained in London till the year 1810; they consisted principally of those unfit for active service and of raw recruits, who were always being drilled, which earned for the second battalion of the First Guards, in time, the nickname of the "bone-drivers," from their having always the piece of bone in place of the flint in their firelocks.

Detailed instructions were subsequently issued for the march of the troops to the points of concentration in the event of invasion, and all arms and services were placed in a complete state of efficiency for immediate action. In June, 1803, the first brigade, under General Wynyard, was ordered to Chatham, the third battalion First Guards under Colonel Hon. Charles Fitzroy arriving there from Windsor on the 1st of June, but the first battalion, under Colonel John Smith, was detained in London till the end of the month. While in these quarters the men were employed in improving and strengthening the works, and on the 29th of July the Duke of York inspected the brigade; the two grenadier companies of the first battalion, under Lieutenant-Colonel Salisbury, forming, on the occasion, the guard of honour to his Royal Highness. General Wynyard, while commanding the two First Guards' battalions at Chatham, was applied to officially in the month of July by officers of the navy to allow a party of his brigade to assist in the service of pressing men for the navy; but the general did not consider himself authorised to employ his men on such a duty. About the same time, however, a detachment of the second battalion First Guards in London was, with men of other battalions, mainly instrumental in saving Westminster Abbey from destruction

was transferred to the First Guards as capt.-lieut., and lieut.-colonel. In 1798 he became major in the Guards, and on the 16th April, 1804, he became the lieut.-colonel of the regiment, a post which he retained during all the subsequent war till his death in 1813. He attained the rank of major-general in 1798, and of lieut.-general in 1805. At the time of his transfer to the Guards he had, as a Hampshire man, the governorship of Calshot Castle, which he retained till his death.

1803.   by fire, and their exertions were duly acknowledged by the Chapter in the following letter :—

> "July 9, 1803.
>
> "The Dean and Chapter of Westminster thank Major-General Leslie, and acknowledge the great obligation they are under for the protection and assistance afforded by the officers and men, to whom, under Providence, they ascribe the preservation of the fabric."

October.   A general fast having been proclaimed on the 19th of October, the Duke of York and the brigade of Guards in London attended church at the Almonry Chapel, Westminster, several of the Guards assisting in the choir.

On the 26th and 28th of the same month the king reviewed the metropolitan volunteers. On the former day they were assembled in Hyde Park, 12,401 strong, under the command of General the Earl of Harrington ; Major-Generals Burrard and Leslie commanding two of the divisions, and the second battalion of the First Guards assisted in keeping the ground. On the latter day, 14,676 volunteers mustered under arms.

The admission of a body of German soldiers into the British army is consequent upon the following circumstances. The Hanoverian general Walmoden, having been unsuccessful during this year against the attacks of the French under General Mortier, had in June signed a convention, by which the Hanoverian troops were to retire across the Elbe and not serve till exchanged. George III. refused to ratify this treaty, and Walmoden having refused to lay down his arms, it was eventually agreed that the army should be dissolved, and the soldiers sent to their homes; they afterwards took service in the British army and became famous as the "King's German Legion."

War was at this time raging in India, and it is referred to here in order to record that in the East a great general, in after life colonel of the First Guards, was already appearing at the head of armies, conspicuous for daring, energy, and firmness, and exhibiting in administration great forethought, clearness of intellect and power of mind ; one who though he met Buonaparte but once in the field was destined on that occasion to be the instrument of his final overthrow. Major-General Wellesley had been ap- pointed to the command of 20,000 men, and marched against Scindiah; he took Ahmednugger on the 12th of August, and with 8000 men, on the 28th of September, attacked and routed 50,000 Mahrattas at Assaye. After several other successes on the part of the British, Scindiah sued for peace, which was signed on the 30th of December, 1803, but General Wellesley did not leave India for Europe till fourteen months later.

1804.

At the commencement of the year 1804 Buonaparte's preparations for the invasion of England were progressing with energy; Ostend, Dunkirk, Calais, Ambleteuse, Vime-reux, and Boulogne, were fixed on as points of concentration for his flotilla, which began to assemble in May; but while the plans of the First Consul were maturing, the patriotism and military spirit of Great Britain were roused; Pitt was recalled to the head of the government; 50,000 men were voted to increase the army to near 130,000 men, and the whole youth of the nation was in arms for its defence.

In the month of August Buonaparte was declared em-peror, and on the 6th of November the empire being estab- lished by universal suffrage, Napoleon invited the Pope to Paris to give éclat to his coronation, which took place on the 2nd of December, but though he sought the papal bene-diction, it was remarked that no other hands but his own put the crown on his head.

During the whole of this year the Guards and the rest of the troops in England were kept on the alert in anticipation of the projected invasion by the French, and the first brigade continued at Chatham until the end of July, 1804, when they marched to and encamped on Barham Downs. On the breaking up of this encampment in October, they occupied the barracks at Deal, where they remained till the month of August of the following year. So many officers of the Guards were now receiving appointments on the staff, that a regulation was made by the Duke of York, limiting their number.

Major-General Harry Burrard succeeded, on the 16th of

1804. April this year, to the lieutenant-colonelcy of the First
Guards, *vice* the Hon. Francis Needham, who was shortly
appointed colonel of the Fifth Royal Veteran Battalion.

In April of this year the rank of surgeon major was conferred upon the senior surgeon of each regiment of Guards.

1805.

1805. The emperor's plan for the invasion of England was to
obtain for a few days if possible a naval superiority in the
Channel, under cover of which 150,000 men, transported in
2,000 vessels, would effect a landing.

The French fleet from Toulon and the Rochfort squadron
having escaped the British blockade, sailed to the West
Indies, and while Nelson's fleet was searching for them in
the Mediterranean, they obtained thirty-five days' start before their destination became known, when Nelson instantly
pursued; the French Admiral Villeneuve in the meantime
was returning home to raise the blockade of Ferrol and
Brest, and form the flotilla at Boulogne, which, when
complete, would have been the largest naval force ever
known. On the 22nd of July, however, Sir Robert Calder
fell in with the French admiral and his fleet, and though
with five ships less, attacked and captured two French men-
of-war, and the next day Villeneuve sheered off to Ferrol
and thence to Cadiz, where he arrived on the 18th of August,
while the emperor, at Boulogne, was awaiting with im-
patience the signal of his approach. Nothing could exceed
his rage when he learnt that Villeneuve had retired,
whereby his deep-laid schemes were totally frustrated.
He returned to Paris on the 6th of September; and so
ended the greatest danger to which Great Britain had for
centuries been exposed.

While at all times ready to meet the enemy, should he
attempt a landing, the Guards continued to perform their
several duties at the camps and in quarters. On the occasion of an installation of Knights of the Garter at Windsor
on the 23rd of April of this year, two battalions of Guards,
the first composed of five companies of grenadiers, and the
second of five companies of light infantry, brought together

from London and Chatham, marched into Windsor barracks   1805.
on the 19th of April under the command of Major-General
Leslie; the king's colour of the First Guards carried by
the grenadiers, and that of the Coldstreams by the light
infantry. On Sunday they paraded in the castle yard when
the king and queen went to church; and on the 23rd they
lined the avenues of the castle through which the procession passed to St. George's Chapel. On the following day
the battalions were reviewed in the park.   •

The following general order was issued after the cere- April 23.
mony of the installation had taken place.

WINDSOR, April 25th.

Lieut.-General H.R.H. the Duke of Cambridge has received his
Majesty's commands to express to Major-General Leslie, commanding
the brigade of Guards on duty for the ceremony of installation, his
Majesty's approbation of their general good conduct and soldier-like
behaviour, and also, the high state of discipline displayed by them in
the performance of their several evolutions in the review of yesterday.

H.R.H. has great pleasure in communicating the above commands
of His Majesty to Major-General Leslie, and begs to add from himself
how sensible he is of the honour of having such a brigade of Guards
under his command.

A review took place at Wimbledon, before the king, on
the 14th of June, on which occasion the Duke of York
commanded the troops, consisting of artillery, cavalry, and
the second and third brigades of Guards, the light companies acting as a battalion. The first brigade—viz., first
and third battalions of First Guards, still under General
Wynyard—was at this time at Deal, but when it became
known that the French fleet had retired into Cadiz, and
that Nelson was watching it, it was no longer considered
necessary to keep the troops on the coast; and on the 30th
of August this brigade left Deal and returned to Chatham.

H.R.H. the Duke of Gloucester, colonel of the First
Guards, had been seriously ill in the summer of this year, and
some of the officers of the regiment expressed much anxiety
concerning his indisposition; he rallied however in the early
part of August, when he conveyed his thanks to the above

1805.   officers in the following regimental order of the 19th of the same month :—

August 19, 1805.

H.R.H. the Duke of Gloucester returns his thanks to the officers of the 2nd battalion for the anxiety and concern they have expressed for him during his indisposition, and how gratified he is with their attention.

Aug. 23.   His recovery, however, was only temporary, for he suffered a relapse, and breathed his last four days later, on the 23rd of August, after having held the appointment of colonel of the First Guards for above thirty-five years. He lay in state on the 3rd of September, when a guard of honour of the First Guards attended, and the funeral took place at Windsor on the 4th, on which occasion the second battalion of H.R.H.'s late regiment was formed in front of Gloucester House, in Park Lane, to receive the coffin. The procession to Windsor was accompanied by detachments of the battalions, which were stationed at Hammersmith, Hounslow, and other places, and on arrival at Windsor the grenadiers of the regiment preceded and flanked the coffin from the castle to St. George's Chapel. The following letter was afterwards addressed to Colonel White, the commanding officer of the second battalion, by his son H.R.H. Prince William, the future Duke, expressing his recognition of the respect which the officers had shown to his father's memory :—

"6th September, 1805.

" DEAR SIR,—I must request you to convey to the First Regiment of Guards my warmest thanks for the respect and attachment manifested by that most distinguished corps to my beloved father, and the assurance of my feeling perfectly sensible of their attention, which has made a deep and lasting impression upon me.

" I am convinced that had it been possible for my ever-lamented parent to have known that he would have been attended on the late melancholy occasion by a regiment to which he was so sincerely attached, and in whose welfare he always felt the truest interest, it would have been gratifying to his feelings. And having had the honour to serve in the First Regiment of Guards, an honour of which I shall ever be proud, I trust that upon this occasion I shall be allowed to add the assurance of my ever forming the most anxious and heartfelt wishes for the glory and success of that regiment.

" WILLIAM."

FREDERICK, DUKE OF YORK AND ALBANY, K.G. G.C.B.

Commander in Chief of His Majesty's Forces.

14.ᵗʰ Colonel of the First or Grenadier Regiment of Foot Guards

CHAPTER XXII.

THE Duke of Gloucester was succeeded in the Colonelcy
of the First Guards on the 5th of September, 1805, by his
Royal Highness Frederick Duke of York, born 1763, now
in his forty-second year. At the age of seventeen the Duke
of York was appointed a brevet-colonel in the British
service, and studied the military profession in Berlin. In
1784, being then of age, he was promoted to lieutenant-
general, and appointed to the colonelcy of the Coldstream
Guards. The duke's command of British troops in Holland and Flanders in 1793-4 and 1799, has already been
adverted to. He was appointed Field Marshal and Commander-in-Chief February 10th, 1795, and still held that
appointment, and after being Colonel of the Coldstreams
for twenty-one years, he was now transferred to the colonelcy
of the First Guards, a post he was destined to hold for
a still longer period throughout the long war, and during
many years of the subsequent peace.

The Duke of Cambridge, who succeeded the Duke of
York in the command of the Coldstreams, was on the 27th

1805. of November, 1805, appointed to the command of the united London and home district.

At this period, Lieutenant-General Sir Harry Burrard was in command of the regiment, Major-General Hon. John Leslie,* Henry Wynyard, and William Thornton respectively, the three regimental majors.

A third coalition had been formed this year between Russia, Austria, and Great Britain, when Napoleon, seeing that all chance of successfully invading England was over, took the initiative, and at once ordered his legions to march from Boulogne towards the Danube; he joined his army at Strasbourg on the 26th of September, forced Mack to surrender at Ulm on the 19th of October, entered Vienna on the 14th of November, defeated the allied armies at Austerlitz on the 2nd of December, and signed the treaty of Presburg on the 27th of the same month; but in the midst of the emperor's successful career he received the

Oct. 21. fatal tidings that, on the 21st of October, the united fleets of France and Spain had been almost entirely destroyed at the battle of Trafalgar, in which the heroic Admiral Nelson fell in the hour of victory.

1806.

1806.
Jan. 9. The year 1806 began with a public funeral to Lord Nelson, which took place on the 9th of January; the command of the infantry in the procession, consisting of regiments of the line, was conferred on Lieutenant-General Burrard. The second battalion of the First Guards (the other two being still at Chatham), was employed in aid of the civil power in the preservation of peace and good order; detachments of the battalion occupied Hyde Park Corner, and the King's Mews, while the head-quarters remained in Knightsbridge Barracks till dismissed in the evening.

The above ceremony was soon followed by a similar one for another of Britain's worthiest sons; the great minister,

---

* Fourth son of David, sixth Earl of Leven and Melville, died a Lieut.-General in 1824.

Mr. Pitt, died on the 23rd of January, when detachments of 1805.
the second battalion First Guards and the rest of the
brigade stationed in London were on duty at the lying-
in-state, and at Westminster Abbey ; 120 rank and file of
the Guards were also daily on duty in Westminster Hall
during the whole of the trial of Lord Melville, which
took place in April and May, when public feeling ran
very high.

EXPEDITION TO SICILY.

Since the expedition to the Helder, in 1799, no battalions
of the First Guards had been employed on foreign service,
the safety of the coast having been of paramount importance. Their services were now about to be required abroad
on the occasion of an expedition being sent out to Sicily,
under the following circumstances :

After the victory of Trafalgar, England had become complete
mistress of the Mediterranean, and on the 20th of November,
1805, a combined force of Russian and British troops, under
General Sir James Craig, was landed at Naples, when the
Neapolitan court was persuaded to declare war against
France and resist Murat, who, after the rupture of the peace
of Amiens, had been ordered by Napoleon to detach part of
his force to take possession of that kingdom. The power
of the confederacy on the continent against France was,
however, much shaken by the defeat of the Austrians at the
battle of Austerlitz, and, in the plenitude of his power,
Napoleon, on the 27th of December, 1805, after declaring
that "the dynasty of Naples had ceased to reign," placed
his brother Joseph on the throne; neither the energy of
the queen, nor the entreaties of Ferdinand for forgiveness
availed anything, and in the month of January, 1806, the Jan. 23.
court as well as the British troops withdrew to Sicily,
while the Russians embarked for the Ionian Islands, and
Joseph entered Naples as sovereign on the 15th of the
following month.

In the spring of the year, Sir James Craig resigned the 1806.
command of the army, and the defence of Sicily was

entrusted to Sir John Stuart. This general was well aware that the French were preparing to assail the island, and conceiving that he could destroy some of their preparations, and at the same time keep alive the spirit of insurrection still existing in Calabria, as well as give some encouragement to the garrison of Gaeta, which was being besieged, he crossed over to Italy, landing without resistance on the **July.** 1st of July with 4800 men in the gulf of St. Euphemia. General Regnier, with 7000 Frenchmen, was near Maida; both armies advanced upon each other; the contest was short and severe: but British firmness prevailed, and the enemy retreated in disorder. The forces were small on either side, though the French were much superior in numbers; yet from this battle, dates that renewed confidence of the British army in their own prowess, which led afterwards to the overthrow of the Imperial armies.

Notwithstanding these efforts made in favour of the Neapolitans, Gaeta was forced to surrender on the 18th of July, whereby 16,000 more Frenchmen became disposable; Sir John Stuart, therefore, established himself for a time at Scylla, and towards the end of the year withdrew his forces again to Sicily; he was shortly afterwards transferred to Malta, and was succeeded in Sicily by General Fox, brother to the minister, with whom Sir John Moore was associated as second in command. Some months, however, previous to this change of generals, the British Government had, in July, 1806, determined to reinforce largely the army in the Mediterranean, and to spare no exertions to prevent the French emperor from getting possession of Sicily.

At this the commencement of another act of the war against France, it will be well to lay before the reader the names of the senior officers at that time in the First Guards, several of whom, having superior army rank to that they enjoyed in the regiment, were appointed on different occasions to staff appointments both at home and abroad, and subsequently rose high in the service.

F. M. H.R.H. Duke of York, K.G., Colonel, 5 Sept. 1805.

	Appointed	Promoted to Maj.-Gen.	Promoted to Lieut.-Gen.
Harry Burrard, Lt.-Col.	16 Ap., 1804.	1 Jan. 1798.	1 Jan. 1805.
Hon. John Leslie, 1st Maj.,	16 Ap., 1804.	29 Ap. 1802.	23 Ap. 1808.
Hen. Wynyard, 2nd Maj.,	,, ,,	29 Ap. 1802.	25 Ap. 1808.
Wm. Thornton, 3rd Maj.,	,, ,,	29 Ap. 1802.	

CAPTAINS AND LIEUT.-COLONELS.

Wm. Caulfield Archer, Maj.-Gen.	E. W. V. Salisbury, died in Sicily.
Hon. Edmund Phipps, Maj.-Gen.	Hon. Philip Cocks.
Arthur Whetham, Maj.-Gen.	John Lambert, suby. Sir John.
Henry Warde, suby. Sir Henry.	M. C. Darby Griffith.
W. Hen. Clinton, suby. Sir Will.	John Francis Kelly.
Moore Disney.	Lord Charles Bentinck.
H. Fred. Campbell, sub. Sir Hen.	John Lord Proby.
Frederick Ch. White.	John D. Burnaby.
Henry Clinton, suby. Sir Henry.	Peregrine Maitland, sub. Sir Per.
William Anson, suby. Sir Willm.	Hon. Edward Capel.
Robert Cheney.	Andrew Gammell.
George Cooke, suby. Sir George.	Hon. F. G. Upton.
Hon. Fran. G. Lake.	Gordon George Donaldson.
G. Duncan Drummond.	Lord Frederick Bentinck.
Sir Thomas Richard Dyer, Bart.	Hon. J. F. Augustus Moreton.
Will. Wheatley, suby. Sir Willm.	Francis Todd.

Previously to the order for foreign service being issued, the pay of the non-commissioned officers and soldiers of the Guards was increased according to the following scale, by warrant of the 25th of June, 1806 :—

		s. d.		*s. d.*
Sergt.-Maj. and Quartermast.-Sgt.,	from	2 4¾	to	2 8
Sergeant	,,	1 10¼	,,	2 0
Corporal, after 14 years' service .	,,	1 4¼	,,	1 7
from 7 to 14 . .	,,	1 0	,,	1 6
below 7	.	.	.	1 5
Privates, after 14 years' service .	.	.	.	1 3
from 7 to 14 . .	,,	1 1	,,	1 2

The two battalions of the First Guards, first and third, under Colonel F. G. Lake and Colonel Moore Disney, forming the first brigade of Guards under General Wynyard,

1806.   were still at Chatham, in Lieutenant-General Ludlow's
        district, whose head-quarters were at Canterbury, with Henry
        Torrens, the future adjutant-general of the army, as his
        assistant adjutant-general. This brigade, of which Captain
July 8. Durnford was brigade-major, received orders on the 8th of
        July, about the time the British troops were crossing over
        to Italy, to complete to 120 men per company, and hold
        itself in immediate readiness for foreign service. A
        fortnight •passed before it received orders to move,
July 26. when, on the 26th and following days, it marched from
        Chatham, and embarked at Ramsgate, the first battalion
        1421 strong and the third battalion 1167. The fleet,
        having also on board a brigade of the line (52nd, 62nd,
        and 95th Regiments), anchored in the Downs on the 30th,
        but contrary winds detained it, and having been twice
        driven back, it did not finally set sail till the 17th
        of August, and anchored in Plymouth Sound on the
Aug. 21. 21st, when the troops were joined by another brigade
        of the line (45th and 87th Regiments) and by the 2nd
        Dragoons.

        More delays occurred in the progress of this expedition
to its destination. A portion of the homeward-bound fleet
from Quebec having been captured, an order was sent by
telegraph to detain the squadron, whereupon the brigade
of Guards, disembarking on the 2nd of September, at
Plymouth, marched to Bickleigh Down, on the road to
Tavistock, and encamped. While waiting here, the six
flank companies of the two battalions were formed into a
separate corps and placed under the command of Colonel
Henry Clinton, First Guards. The senior captain was
appointed to act as major, Captain Miller as adjutant, and
Sergeant-Major R. Colquhoun of the third battalion as the
quartermaster of these flank companies.

        The following were the officers of the first and third
battalions on proceeding to Sicily in 1806:—

1ST BATTALION, FIRST GUARDS.

Major-General Hon. J. LESLIE, Commanding.

CAPTAINS & LIEUT.-COLS.	LIEUTS. & CAPTAINS.	ENSIGNS.
King's, Col. R. Cheney.	Hon. W. Stuart,	E. Stables, and W. Cheney.
Gren., Col. W. Anson.	R. Bingham, H.	Townshend, & Earl of Tyrconnel.
3. Maj.-Gen. W. Archer.	H. Askew.	S. Lambert & R. Ellison.
4. Col. M. Disney.	S. Martin.	W. H. Milnes & T. Grant.
5. „ H. Clinton.	W. Sotheby.	A. Higginson & Cartwright.
6. Lt.-Col. Drummond.	J. West.	E. Wynyard & T. Streatfield.
7. „ Hon. P. Cocks.	H. Fetherstonhough.	G. Read & H. Hunter.
8. „ Lord Proby.	J. Colquitt.	G. Colquitt & J. Poulter.
9. „ Hon. F. Upton.	E. Davenport.	W. Whitmore & Thistlethwaite.
10. „ Ld. C. Bentinck	R. Clitherow.	G. Ramsden & G. Higginson.

Light Infantry,—

Lieut.-Col. J. Lambert. J. Speddings, J. Warrender, and F. J. Needham.
Lieut.-Col. Donaldson. J. R. Udny, H. Packe, and Jos. Latour.

Adjutant, Captain C. Murray.

3RD BATTALION, FIRST GUARDS.

Major-General WILLIAM THORNTON, Commanding.

Gren., Lt.-Col. E. W. Salisbury.	Thomas, Sambrooke Anson,°and J. H. Rigg.	
2. Brig.-Gen. W. H. Clinton.	Jones.	G. Clutterbuck & E. Grose.
3. Colonel H. F. Campbell.	F. D'Oyly.	W. Cooke & T. Robbins.
4. Lt.-Col. G. Cooke.	Maj. A. Barnard.	F. Trench & T. Best.
5. „ Hon. F. G. Lake,	A. W. Durnford.	C. Allix & J. Gunthorpe.
6. „ Hon. E. Capel, Hon. J. Macdonald, Hon. J. Stanhope & R. Marsack.		
7. „ Gammell.	H. D'Oyly.	L. Kortnight & F. Cunliffe.
8. „ Hon. J. Moreton.	Lord Saltoun.	C. Montgomery & T. Rous.
9. „ F. Todd.	T. Dorville.	R. Adair & H. Joddrell.

Light Infantry,—

Lieut.-Col. J. Burnaby. Capt. E. Sebright, G. Clifton, and J. Reeve.

Adjutant, T. Aubrey.

The Hon. J. Leslie and William Thornton, the regimental majors of the first and third battalions, and the three senior captains of companies in the regiment being major-generals, and the next two, Warde and W. H. Clinton, brigadier-generals, they were all returned on the staff, and the command of the three service battalions as now constituted devolved upon the following officers :—

First Guards	Flank Battalion	725 strong,	Lt.-Col.	H. Clinton.
	1st Battalion	919 „	„	F. G. Lake.
	3rd Battalion	915 „	„	M. Disney.

Total strength of Brigade . . 2559 under Maj.-Gen. H. Wynyard.

The brigade thus reconstituted, embarked for the second time on the 13th of September, and the fleet sailing on the 24th, under Sir John Duckworth, in the " Royal George," was off Cadiz on the 21st of October; on the 23rd it anchored in the Bay of Tangiers, and on the 1st November in Tetuan Bay, when both officers and men were strictly cautioned, if they landed for provisions, that the slightest marks of familiarity or disrespect to the Moorish women would be attended with the most fatal consequences.

Among the transports carrying part of the light infantry battalion of the First Guards, was a collier brig, the " Christopher," which carried away her foremast in a gale in the Bay of Biscay, thereby losing her convoy. The captain sailed for three weeks by his own reckoning, perfectly ignorant of his position, when one evening, just before dark, Sergeant-Major Colquhoun, the acting quartermaster, reported to the commanding officer that he thought the sea had this day very much changed colour. The commanding officer spoke on the subject to the captain, who laughed at the idea, declaring they were more than 100 miles from land. However, he hove the lead with the deep-water line, and found himself, to his great astonishment, in ten fathoms. No one knew where they were, but the transport was anchored, and the commanding officer ordered the men to be served out with ammunition, to be prepared for all eventualities, when on boats coming off, they found they were off the mouth of the Guadalquiver, close under the batteries of Rota. They were towed out during the night and put in charge of a brig-of-war, which took them safely to Gibraltar. The habits of observation of this non-commissioned officer had thus saved the lives of many of his officers and comrades.

Contrary winds had very materially detained the progress of the fleet, and it was not till the 2nd of December, that, after coasting along the Island of Maritima, the Guards entered the Bay of Messina, nearly three months after they had finally sailed from the shores of England ; but, instead of landing, an order came off for the transports carrying the

Lipari

Vulcano

Milazzo

MESSINA

Cape Faro

Scylla

Calabria

Reggio

Pellaro

Alcita

C.Calava

C.Orlando

Naso

Patti

Light Battalion in 1806

Light Company 1807

Melia

STRAITS OF MESSINA

MEDITERRANEAN SEA

2d. Camp

Taormina

along the Coast

Aci

Posts along the Coast

CATANIA
Head Quarters
of GEN: WYNYARD

Plain
of
Catania

Augusta

1807
Flank Batt.
& Camp
CLINTON

SYRACUSE

C. Passaro

EXPEDITION
TO
SICILY
AND OCCUPATION OF
EAST COAST
BY
FIRST GUARDS
1806 & 1807.

Scale of Eng. miles
5   0   5   10   15   20

brigade to proceed immediately to Catania, and there dis-   1806.
embark their men. They left Messina the same day, and Dec. 2.
on the afternoon of the 4th anchored off Catania, where the
whole of the First Guards, including the flank companies,
disembarked on Friday the 5th of December; when six
companies of the third battalion, under Colonel Disney,
were temporarily sent to Syracuse.

The flank battalion First Guards was at first sent to Mel-
lazzo, on the north coast, where it was still quartered towards
the end of 1806; but upon the arrival in Sicily of Colonel
Clinton, who was to command that battalion, and who, as
above recorded, had been detained on his voyage out, it
proceeded to Syracuse, to replace the six companies of the
third battalion under Colonel Disney, when the right wing
of this latter battalion was detached to Augusta, and the left
wing to Contessa, near Messina.

Some slight changes subsequently took place, and at
the beginning of 1807 the brigade of Guards was stationed
as follows :—The flank battalion, six companies, under
Colonel H. Clinton, at Syracuse; first battalion, eight companies, under Colonel F. G. Lake, and left wing, third battalion, at Catania; right wing, third battalion, under Colonel
Henry F. Campbell, at Augusta, between Syracuse and   1807.
Catania; and on the 8th of May a detachment was made
from the third battalion at Catania of two officers and sixty
men to march northwards to Taormina, the site of an
ancient Roman theatre, half-way between Catania and
Messina. At a later period the light companies of the
brigade were detached still further north to Contessa, within
three or four miles of Messina. The several battalions of
the First Guards were thus distributed in the principal
posts along the east coast of Sicily, extending from Messina
to Syracuse, for about eighty or ninety miles.

Major-General Wynyard fixed his head-quarters for some
time at Catania as a central spot, being about sixty miles
from Messina and twenty-five from Syracuse, and was here
left in command of the district, while General Fox, the
Commander-in-Chief, resided at Messina; Captain Colborne,

1807. the future Lord Seaton, serving on his staff as military secretary. General Fox had had on frequent occasions to circulate orders to the troops with respect to dress, but he specially informed General Wynyard that these orders were by no means intended to apply to the troops under his command.

The whole island of Sicily is mountainous with the exception of a plain at the base of Etna to the south, called the Plain of Catania, extending from that town to Augusta and Syracuse ; the twelve miles nearest Syracuse are however only undulating, not mountainous.

At the beginning of the year 1807, the British forces in the island, including Wynyard's brigade of Guards, amounted to 18,000 men, and there were also about 14,000 Neapolitan troops available in the event of an attack, but on the occa-

Jan. 12. sion of a *feu de joie* being fired on the 12th of January, in honour of the Sicilian king, no joy was manifested by the population, and it appeared probable that the protection afforded by England to the Sicilian court would only render the British troops obnoxious to the inhabitants.

The military plans of the British Government were naturally much influenced by the varying phases of the war in northern Europe. In October, 1806, the Prussian monarchy had been overturned by the battles of Jena and Austerlitz, and the Russians had retired to the Niemen ; but the Russian emperor having refused to ratify a peace, and there being rumours of Russian successes in Poland, the Sicilian court, incited by the queen, was clamorous for an attack upon Naples, with the assistance of the British army. General Fox, however, had no confidence in this project of the ex-queen of Naples, and though resolved to keep a firm hold on Sicily, both he and the Government at home declined to risk the army in such a doubtful enterprise, and the project was rendered still more impracticable in the spring by the British Government withdrawing 5000 men of regiments of the line from Sicily to send to Alexandria, while at the same time it sent a fleet to the Dardanelles to counteract the influence that the French Emperor was

exerting over the minds of the Turks, to induce them to   1807.
act in the field against the Russians. Such a reduction
of the forces in Sicily effectually prevented the remaining
part of the army being disposable for active operations
on the continent; notwithstanding which, the queen, in the
spring of 1807, took the desperate resolution of invading
Calabria single handed, but her troops were ignominiously
defeated on the 28th of May.

The expedition to Alexandria, though reinforced in May
by 2000 more men, was also unsuccessful, and it returned
to Sicily in the following October much reduced in
numbers.

Sir John Moore, who was second in command, under May 2.
General Fox, had been conspicuous during the last few years
in perfecting the drill and discipline of the troops placed
under him in the several camps in England, particularly
of the 52nd Regiment, which he had personally trained.
On the 6th of April of this year he inspected Colonel
Clinton's flank battalion of the First Guards at Syracuse,
and expressed himself on the occasion as much pleased with
the attention of the officers and men, adding that the
battalion moved better than any other he had seen in
Sicily, excepting only the 52nd; a high compliment,
when it is recollected that that regiment was of his own
creation.

The light companies of the Guards had not been many
months at Contessa, when the French, who, since the battle
of Maida, had remained in Calabria, suddenly marched a
large force down to the straits of Messina, commenced the
siege of the castle of Scylla, where there was a British
garrison, and taking possession of Reggio, a town on the
coast, nearly opposite the cantonments of the light companies of the Guards at Contessa, began collecting boats
and making preparations, apparently, to invade Sicily. A
party of an officer and thirty men of the Guards was established at a place called Milia, about six miles from the
Guards' cantonments, in order to give the alarm should any
landing take place in that quarter, and posts of a corporal

B B 2

1807.   and three men were placed at intervals to communicate along
the coast to a particular point three miles from Milia, which
was visited every night by the captain of the day, though the
sudden freshes in the rivers running down from the hills
rendered the carrying out of this duty at times very
hazardous.

During their somewhat monotonous stay in Sicily, such
of the officers as could procure leave, made shooting
parties or exploring expeditions over the island, visiting
the ancient temples, Girgente, and others, describing them
and making their remarks thereon in a true antiquarian
spirit. A first-rate pack of hounds also enabled many to
indulge in their favourite national pastime.

In the course of the summer, instructions arrived from
Lord Castlereagh, directing General Fox's attention to the
possibility of an invasion of Naples in conjunction with the
Neapolitans, but leaving it to his discretion to carry out the
proposal ; the measure was, however, abandoned, as the idea
was so ill received in the island, that disturbances were expected, when the general would have been called upon to
quell the tumult, thereby increasing the feeling already
existing amongst the population against the British, for the
support which their presence was giving to the Sicilian
Government.

General Fox, whose brother had died in the previous
July 10.   year, resigned his post in Sicily on the 10th of July, 1807,
and returned to England at the beginning of August, whereupon the command devolved upon Sir John Moore. On
the 17th of that month the news arrived of the defeat of the
Russians at Friedland, after which there was not a soldier
on continental Europe in arms against France. Sir John,
therefore, with his isolated force in Sicily made preparations
for meeting what he looked upon as inevitable—an immediate attack from the French.

Sickness became very prevalent ·amongst the troops towards the end of August, owing to the sultry weather; for
three months the thermometer averaged eighty degrees,
many men were in hospital, and more in an unfit state for

duty, and amongst the officers who fell victims to the climate was Colonel Salisbury of the First Guards, who, dying on the 16th of September, was buried on the 17th in the centre of the church of San Filippo.

1807.

Sept. 17.

We now come to the events that caused the sudden recall of the First Guards and other troops from Sicily towards the end of the year 1807. For the last three years, Spain had been at war with Great Britain, and the Spanish fleet had not only assisted the French emperor in his preparations for the invasion of England, but had fought against her at the battle of Trafalgar.

It had lately become known that Napoleon had signed an armistice with the Emperor of Russia, which resulted in the treaty of Tilsit, since which the French emperor had been engaged in completing that "continental system," which was intended to ruin the commerce of Great Britain by excluding her ships from all the harbours of Europe. The Prince Regent of Portugal at first acceded to the emperor's demands, but when the British ambassador demanded his passports, and a British fleet blockaded the Tagus, the Portuguese prince changed his policy, and declined to adopt any longer exclusive measures against the oldest ally of his country. The emperor, with his insatiate desire of conquest, now determined to subject the whole Spanish peninsula to his sway. He concluded a treaty with Spain, by which it was agreed that the combined armies of the two nations should over-run and divide Portugal; large forces were assembled at Bayonne, and, in 1807, Napoleon having decreed that the house of Braganza, as the reigning house of Portugal, had ceased to exist, directed Junot to march on Lisbon. Upon these circumstances coming to the knowledge of the British Government, anxious to support their old Portuguese ally, they sent orders to Sicily early in October, 1807, directing Sir John Moore to proceed with 7500 men of his army to Gibraltar, where he would receive further directions as to their ultimate destination. The brigade of First Guards, and some regiments of the line, which were to form part of the expedition, were ordered

November.

1807.   to embark without delay. The flank battalion, under Colonel
Henry Clinton, embarked at Syracuse on the 18th of October,
and the transports with the first and third battalions, under
their brigadier, Major-General Wynyard, from Catania and
Augusta, embarked on the 19th, joining the other battalions at Syracuse on the 20th.   Sir John Moore arrived
there on the.26th, and having gone on board the "Queen,"
the fleet got under weigh on the 27th, and after waiting the
arrival of the transports with the remainder of the troops
from Messina, the fleet sailed on the 30th, for Gibraltar,
leaving Sir John Sherbrook with 6000 men to protect
Sicily.

Throughout the month of November, the fleet, with the
brigade on board, beat about the Mediterranean, sometimes
becalmed, at others detained by strong gales and contrary
Dec. 1.   winds; at last, on the 1st of December, after a six weeks'
passage, they anchored at Gibraltar, where Sir Hew
Dalrymple was governor; here it was ascertained that since
Sir John Moore's departure from Sicily the "Volage"
frigate had carried out a dispatch to him, directing him not
to leave that country; also bringing Colonel Disney's
appointment as brigadier-general, with orders that he should
return to Sicily.   Sir John Moore was now made acquainted
with the object of the expedition, by the original orders
received at Gibraltar, directing him to proceed to Lisbon,
where he was to have been joined by 8000 men under
General Spencer, to support the fortunes of the king and the
Prince Regent of Portugal; but the French were by this
time within a few marches of Lisbon, and the Prince Regent,
seeing the futility of resistance, had quitted the capital,
with the rest of the royal family; and with 18,000 adherents,
embarked on the 29th of November for the Brazils.   On
the same day, Junot, with 1500 worn-out troops, entered
Lisbon without opposition.

Sir John Moore, after deliberating on the expediency of
proceeding to Lisbon to confer with Sir Sydney Smith,
who was off the port, as to whether a landing would be of
advantage to the country, sailed northward, and on his

arrival, hearing then for the first time of the state of affairs 1807.
in Portugal, that the Prince Regent had fled, and that the
French were in possession of the town, went back to Gibraltar, and leaving two regiments of the line on the rock,
he sailed again on the 15th of December with the Guards
and remainder of his troops for England, to receive further
orders. On the arrival of the fleet at St. Helen's on the
28th, the first and third battalions First Guards landed at
Portsmouth, whence they marched to Deal barracks, arriving
there in the first days of 1808, and both battalions remained in quarters there till the month of September,
when they were again ordered on foreign service. The
other troops that returned with the First Guards to England at the end of 1807, viz., the second battalion 20th,
first battalion 35th, second battalion 52nd and 78th, were
all landed at Portsmouth in January, 1808, and three
months later, when Sir John Moore was dispatched to
Sweden with an army to assist the king of that country,
the battalion of the 52nd was the only one of the above
corps that accompanied him.

The discipline of the several battalions of the First
Guards during the time they remained in Sicily had
been well maintained; the exertions of the officers and
men were unremitting, and the former had been fully
taught their duties. The flank battalion was instructed
by Colonel H. Clinton in light infantry drill, and the men
gained much credit for the manner in which they performed
the movements. Captain Durnford, who had hitherto acted
as brigade-major to the first brigade, being now promoted
to lieutenant-colonel, Captain Cooke, adjutant of the third
battalion, received the appointment.

While these events were occurring abroad, great fears
of riots had been entertained in London during the summer
of 1807, consequent upon the excitement arising from the
Westminster election, and the democratic proceedings of
Sir Francis Burdett; the three second battalions of the third
brigade were all confined to barracks, with artillery, on the
occasion, but fortunately the precautions taken, rendered
their services unnecessary.

1807.　The second battalion First Guards, under Lieutenant-Colonel Wheatley, in which were all the recruits of the regiment, was inspected on the 9th of November by Lieutenant-General Sir Harry Burrard, the lieutenant-colonel, then commanding the troops in London, who issued the following regimental order on the occasion :—

Lieut.-General Sir Harry Burrard requests Lieut.-Colonel Wheatley will acquaint the officers and non-commissioned officers of the 2nd battalion 1st Regiment, that he has much reason to approve of the movements and soldierlike appearance of the battalion at the inspection on the parade this morning, and that it gives him great satisfaction to observe that they had greatly improved since he saw them last.

Lieut.-Colonel Wheatley takes this opportunity of making known his approbation of the conduct of the battalion since it has left Knightsbridge barrack; the steady, quiet, and soldierlike behaviour of the men in quarters and when on duty has gained them much credit.

1808.

1808.　In consequence of his promotion to lieutenant-general, in May, 1808, the first brigade was now deprived of the services of General Wynyard, the second major of the regiment, who had so ably commanded them, as their brigadier, for the last five years, and under whom they had obtained so much credit, both in England and abroad. He took leave of his regiment in the following feeling and complimentary terms :—

"DEAL, *May* 11, 1808.

"Major-General Wynyard, having this day received the official notification of his promotion to the rank of lieutenant-general, and of his removal, in consequence, from the command of the first brigade of Guards, takes the earliest opportunity of expressing his gratitude and thanks to the officers, non-commissioned officers, and privates for the kind and ready attention they have at all times paid to his wishes and commands.

"Major-General Wynyard is at a loss to express all he feels at the recollection of the continued and flattering approbation he has received from H. R. H. the Commander-in-Chief of the appearance and state of discipline of the brigade under his command, all of which he feels he owes so entirely to the excellent conduct of those under his orders, who have thus by their regularity and attention obtained for themselves and their commander those repeated expressions of satisfaction and praise.

" The lieutenant-general is now under the painful necessity of taking his leave, but amidst the regret he feels at being separated from the society and the command of so fine a corps, he experiences a consolation in the conviction that upon no occasion, during the five years he has had the honour to command the first brigade of Guards, has he acted otherwise than with the view of promoting the comfort and advantage of. every individual in it; with this reflection, therefore, of satisfaction, and with a hearty and ardent wish that happiness and success may everywhere attend them, he bids them farewell."

The following appointments were made in May, 1808, amongst the senior officers of the First Guards :—Major-General Warde, the senior captain and lieutenant-colonel, succeeded General Wynyard in the command of the first brigade, and Major-General Henry Campbell was at the same time appointed to command the second brigade of Guards until the return of Major-General Moore Disney from Sicily. The relative position of these officers in the regiment as captains of companies was,—Warde, Disney, and Campbell.

In consequence of the several battalions of the Foot Guards being divided into three brigades, each commanded by a major-general, the duties of the field officer in brigade-waiting were temporarily dispensed with this year, but an adjutant and quartermaster - in - waiting continued to be appointed monthly.

May 23.

CAMPAIGN OF 1808 IN THE SPANISH PENINSULA.

At the same time that Junot marched on Lisbon, the French emperor had directed 50,000 troops, without any notification to the Spanish king, to march towards Madrid; the frontier fortresses were soon in possession of the French, and Murat entered the capital of Spain on the 23rd of March,

1808.
•

1808, whereupon the king was forced to abdicate in favour of his son, and with him proceeded in the month of April to Bayonne to meet Napoleon, who deprived them both of their crown, conferring it at the same time on his own brother, Joseph Bonaparte. But the treacherous character of this invasion roused the public mind in Spain, and, in May, the populace of Madrid becoming exasperated, and a severe conflict taking place with the French troops, which terminated in a cold-blooded massacre of Spanish prisoners in the Prado, the indignation of the country burst out, and the flame of patriotism was kindled throughout the land.

Aug. 1.

The military resources of Spain were at this time in a very low state: the ill-organised Spanish troops were capable of offering but feeble resistance to the veterans of France, and finding their country at the mercy of the French emperor, the Supreme Junta, in June, appealed for British sympathy and aid. The British government listened to the appeal, and peace with Spain was proclaimed in London on the 5th July. On the 12th, an army of about 10,000 men, under the command of Sir Arthur Wellesley, sailed from the British shores, landing at Mondego Bay on the 1st of August.

The Guards formed no portion of this first expedition ; it was not till four days after it landed in Portugal that, as will be seen, two battalions received their orders to hold themselves in readiness for foreign service.

The plan of the British government was first to drive the French out of Portugal, and then advance into Spain. On the 17th of August, Sir Arthur, with 12,000 men, attacked and drove the French, under Laborde, from a strong position at Roliça, and being reinforced, on the 20th of August, by two additional brigades from England, under Brigadier-Generals Anstruther and Ackland, was preparing to advance upon Lisbon, when Junot met him on the 21st at Vimiera, and in this engagement the British General was again completely victorious. Sir Harry Burrard, who formerly commanded the first brigade of Guards, and was still the lieutenant-colonel of the First Regiment, having been sent out to Portugal, arrived the day previous to the action, but, with creditable forbearance, refrained from taking the command during its progress. Now, however, he stopped the pursuit, for the purpose of waiting for the large reinforcements expected with Sir John Moore.

The following day the French General proposed an armistice, which was assented to by Sir Hew Dalrymple, who in the meantime had arrived from Gibraltar, and as senior officer assumed the chief command. A treaty was subsequently signed at Lisbon, commonly called the Convention of Cintra, by the terms of which it was stipulated that the French should evacuate Portugal, and be transported to France. The articles excited so much indignation in Great Britain, where an unconditional surrender had been expected, that an inquiry into the conduct of the general was instituted. On the departure of Sir Hew Dalrymple, the command of the army, now amounting to 28,000 men, again devolved upon Sir Harry Burrard, but this officer was himself shortly superseded by Sir John Moore.

Early in August, while Sir John Moore advanced from Lisbon with the troops under his command, the British government had determined to send out a further reinforcement of 10,000 men from Great Britain, including a brigade of Guards, so as to operate in the north of Spain with a British army of 30,000 infantry and 5,000 cavalry, and on the 5th of that month the first and third battalions of the First Guards, commanded respectively by Lieutenant-Colonels Cocks and Wheatley, and forming the first brigade to which Major-General Warde had lately succeeded on Wynward's promotion, were accordingly ordered to be in readiness for foreign service, with a view to joining Sir Arther Wellesley. These battalions had been quartered at Deal ever since their return from Sicily, and they now embarked at Ramsgate on the 8th of September, of the following strength :—

		Capts.	Subs.	Staff.	Sergts.	Drms.	Privts.
First Guards.	1st batt.	7	32	5	80	26	1361
	3rd batt.	9	28	5	67	21	1113
		16	60	10	147	47	2474

1808. on which occasion their new brigadier had occasion to issue the following order :—

"Sep. 11.—Major-General Warde cannot avoid taking this opportunity of expressing his highest approbation of the conduct of the whole brigade during the embarcation ; he can only add that they have behaved as he expected, like themselves."

As soon as embarked, they sailed for the general rendezvous at Falmouth, reaching that harbour on the 22nd of September. The assembled troops, to the number of 10,000, under the command of Sir David Baird, were now organised into four brigades, as follows :—

Maj.-Gen. Warde's	1st and 3rd battalions of 1st Guards,
„ Manningham's	1st, 26th, 27th, and 31st regiments,
„ Mackenzie's	51st, 59th, 60th, 76th, and 81st regiments,
Brig.-Gen. Craufurd's	14th, 23rd, 43rd, 2nd battalion, 95th,

Oct. 8. and having re-embarked, the fleet sailed on the 8th of October, anchoring off Corunna on the 13th of the same month.*

* The following return shows the number of British troops already landed at the end of August, and the number, including the First Guards, that landed in the course of the following two months :—

Date.	Strength.	From where.	Landed at	.	Under the command of.
1808. Aug. 1,	9,394	Cork.	Mondego.		Sir Art. Wellesley.
Aug. 3,	4,713	Cadiz.	Mondego.		Gen. Spencer.
	14,107				
Aug. 20,	4,702	Harwich.	Maceira.		Ackland and Anstruther.
Aug. 29,	11,324	Baltic.	Maceira.		Sir John Moore. Sir Harry Burrard.
	30,133				
Sept. 1,	672	Gravesend.	Lisbon.		Gen. C. Stewart.
Sept.	1,129	Gibraltar.	Tagus.		
Sept.	1,023	Madeira.	Tagus.		Gen. Beresford.
Oct. 13,	11,069*	Falmouth.	Corunna.		Sir David Baird.
„	1,622	„	Lisbon.		part of Sir David Baird's.
Oct. 30,	2,021	Portsmouth.	Corunna.		
Dec. 1,	672	England.	Lisbon.		
	48,341				

* Including brigade of Guards.

In the note below are the names of the officers of the two battalions of Guards, as they stood in the month of December following, during the hardships of the winter campaign, as well as in the final battle of Corunna.* In the First Guards, besides Lieutenant-General Burrard, the lieutenant-colonel; Major-General Whetham, the third major; Major-General W. H. Clinton, and five brigadier-generals, who were all on the staff of the army; Colonels Anson, Cheney, and Lord Proby, Captains Wheatley, F. D'Oyly, R. H. Cooke, Stanhope, Sotheby, and J. Stanhope, and Ensigns Burrard, Wyndham, Churchill, and Dukenfield, all held staff appointments. The companies

1808.

---

* 1st Battalion, commanded by Hon. P. Cocks.

Captains & Lieut.-Cols.	Lieuts. & Captains.	Ensigns.
King's, C. R. Cheney.	E. Stables, W. Cheney, and J. Warrender.	
Gren., Lord Ch. Bentinck	R. Bingham, R. Townshend, and Earl Tyrconnel.	
3. Brig.-Gen. Disney.	S. Martin.	Milnes & Churchill.
4. „ White.	F. H. Stanhope.	Grant & Thorton.
5. „ H. Clinton.	Clitheroe.	G. Higginson & Wyndham.
6. Wm. Anson.	C. Bisshop.	Ellison & Dukenfield.
7. Phil. Cocks.	R. A. Dalzell.	Hunter & Brydges.
8. J. Lambert.	J. West.	Streatfield & Poulter.
9. Griffith.	W. Sotheby.	A. Higginson.
10. Lord Proby.	Colquitt.	Evans & Molley.
Light } G. Donaldson.	F. Needham, K. Evans, and R. Marsack.	
Infy. } Lord F. Bentinck.	J. Udny, H. Packe, and J. Lautour.	

Adjutant, Captain Murray.

3rd Battalion, commanded by Col. Wm. Wheatley.

Gren., P. Maitland.	J. Hanbury, C. Thomas, and W. P. Elphinstone.	
2. Brig.-Gen. H. Clinton.	Jones.	Gross & Clements.
3. „ Campbell.	F. D'Oyly.	Hurst & Stevenson.
4. George Cooke.	Miller.	Best & Hutchinson.
5. W. Wheatley.	R. H. Cooke.	Allix & Gunthorpe.
6. J. F. Kelly.	H. D'Oyly.	Duncomb & Peachy.
7. Ed. Capel.	J. Macdonald.	Burrard & Fitzroy.
8. — Moreton.	De Courcey.	Rous & Brooke.
9. Francis Todd.	T. Dorville.	Adair & Blunt.
Light Infy., J. Burnaby.	G. Clifton, Lord Saltoun, and J. Reeve.	

Adjutant, Wm. Miller.

1808. whose captains were general officers, as seen in this list, were commanded in the field by their lieutenants.

October. Early in October the main body of the army under Sir John Moore advanced from Lisbon, by Almeida, towards Salamanca, which wás the point of concentration of the British; and Moore, after passing Ciudad Rodrigo, which he made his head quarters for a few days, reached Sala-
Nov. 13. manca on the 13th of November.

. In the arrangements for taking the field in Portugal, Sir John Moore had been cordially assisted by Sir Harry Burrard, who still remained in the country. This assistance, Sir John was the first to acknowledge in his despatch to government, in which he says,—" I cannot conclude without mentioning the very great assistance I receive from Sir Harry Burrard, who acts with a degree of candour, of which few people would be capable under such circumstances. He seems on this occasion to put himself aside, and to give everything to me and to a service he thinks the most important, with as much liberality as if he himself were personally concerned in the conduct of it." An acknowledgment as honourable to the officer who tendered it, as to the receiver.

The emperor was now in Spain at the head of no less than 300,000 men. In the course of the autumn the Spanish army of the north, under Blake, had been defeated at Espinosa; another large force had been dispersed by Soult near Burgos; the Spanish Generals, Palafox and
Dec. 4. Castanos, were routed at Tudela, and on the 4th of December Napoleon was in Madrid.

Moore, perceiving that assistance from the Spaniards was now hopeless, and that the French in Spain were in overwhelming numbers, resolved to return again to the Tagus, but upon the earnest representations of the British minister, Freer, though against his own better judgment, he was induced to change his plans, and not only to remain, but to advance still further into the country in order to offer some hindrance to the French armies advancing into the south. He sent orders to Baird and Hope to join him

To illustrate
CAMPAIGN of CORUNNA
1808.9
RETREAT from BURGOS
and
MARCH OF 1st GUARDS
from
CADIZ to SALAMANCA 1812.
AND
ADVANCE of the ARMY 1813.

Scale of British miles.

with all speed at Astorga, and decided upon throwing him- 1808.
self on the communications of the French, and succour
Madrid.

In the meantime the Junta of Corunna had refused to
allow Baird's division with the Guards, which had arrived
there from Falmouth on the 13th of October, to land
without the sanction of the Central Junta, and that authority did not arrive for several days. The first battalion of
the First Guards disembarked at Corunna on the 28th, Oct. 28.
1300 strong, and the third battalion on the following day,
1127 strong. Sir David Baird on landing called upon his
division to act in harmony with the Spanish people, and
respect their customs; and General Warde addressed his
own brigade of First Guards upon the same subject in the
following terms:—

" Major-General Warde feels confident that every attention will be paid to the general orders of the day by the
brigade under his command; but at the same time he requests them to consider how high their character already
stands for good conduct and discipline, and to recollect the
very honourable position they hold, both as his Majesty's
Guards and the Right Brigade of the British Infantry; that
it will not only be necessary for them to behave well, but
by their uniform good conduct he hopes and trusts they will
set an example worthy of imitation."

The spirit and discipline of the two battalions was excellent, and is thus noticed by a writer of the period :—" The
conduct of the officers and soldiers of the Guards was highly
to their credit from the time they disembarked; fewer excesses were committed by those men than many regiments
of similar numbers, and their officers preferred sharing
with them their quarters, to profiting by the billets offered
them. Out of 2500 men, when they were put in motion,
they only left 20 sick at Corunna : other regiments not half
their number left twice as many."

Upon the division leaving Corunna the brigade marched
by Corral and Ordinez to Santiago, arriving there the 2nd

1808.

Nov. 2.

Nov. 19.

Nov. 30.

of November.* They were generally quartered in the convents of the Friars, and very hospitably treated. On the 7th and three following days they marched by wings to Lugo, whence after halting two days they advanced to Villa Franca, where they arrived on the 19th of November; and continuing their route by Bembibre and Maxanelle reached Cambanos in the vicinity of Astorga on the 23rd and 24th of November. Sir David Baird now divided his force into two divisions, one of which was placed under Major-General Warde, when the command of the brigade of First Guards temporarily devolved upon Colonel William Anson, one of the acting majors; the flank companies being formed into a battalion under Colonel John Lambert.

Baird, being informed at Astorga that the enemy was in force at Rio Seco, halted to concentrate his troops, and received orders from Sir John Moore,—who for the second time felt the precariousness of the British advanced position in the Peninsula,—to fall back on Corunna and sail for the Tagus; he obeyed without reluctance, for he had already found out that no reliance could be placed on the information or judgment of any Spanish general. The First Guards retired on the 30th of November, moving towards Villafranca and Nogales; the six flank companies, under Colonel Lambert, were detached from the main column on the 1st of December to proceed to Cacabolos, and rejoined it at Herrerias. Orders were subsequently received from head-quarters countermanding the retreat, but directing Sir David Baird to prepare magazines for the army on the road to Corunna; whereupon the division again advanced, the brigade of Guards arriving at Astorga for the second time on the 14th of December, at Benevente on the 16th, and Mayorga on the frontiers of

---

* The Guards and another brigade had now marched for St. Jago. It seems they were to make three stages of this route, resting one night at Carrol, a very filthy and small village, the second night at Ordenez, consisting of a church and three wretched farmhouses. The stages were about ten miles each. —Extract from the "Royal Military Chronicle," vol. iv. pp. 17, 18.

Leon and Castille on the 20th, where the flank companies, as before mentioned, were again incorporated with the battalions.

While Sir John Moore was waiting for intelligence, the following circumstance, creditable to the Spanish character, took place :—

Lord Proby, of the first battalion First Guards, serving on the staff, was at Tordesillas reconnoitring, when a patrol of French cavalry came into the town, and remained there some time. Every man in the place knew that Lord Proby was there, for he had been two days amongst them, yet not a man betrayed him ; and when the cavalry left the place, and he came into the street, they all testified their satisfaction, declaring that, though they had no arms, they would have died rather than have allowed him to be taken.

In the meantime, Moore, having advanced from Salamanca on the 12th of December, marched by Alargos and Toro, and on the 20th effected a junction with Baird at Mayorga, where the army, consisting of 23,500 infantry, 2000 cavalry, and sixty pieces of artillery, was now concentrated. Here the first and third battalions of the First Guards again came under the command of Sir John Moore. Napier, in his History, after referring to the severity of the weather and the length of the marches, thus describes the British force : — "A more robust set of men never took the field ; the discipline was admirable, and there were but few stragglers. The experience of one or two campaigns alone was wanting to make a perfect army."

Colonel Moore Disney, now brigadier-general had, as before mentioned, returned to Sicily, and arrived at Messina at the beginning of the year 1808, on the 16th of January. A few days afterwards he was put in command of the citadel and garrison of that town, and remained in command till the 13th of April, when Sir J. Stewart arrived and took command of all the forces in the Mediterranean. General Disney continued in Sicily to the end of July, when he was ordered home to take command of a brigade. He sailed August 25th, and on his arrival at Lisbon on the 6th

1808. of October, was put in temporary command of a brigade of the line, consisting of the 2nd, 3rd, 6th, and 50th Regiments, with orders to join Sir John Moore's army in Spain. Proceeding by Abrantes with his column, he had reached Nov. 27. Castel Branco by the 27th November, when he received a confidential communication from Brigadier-General Anstruther, stating that circumstances had occurred in the country rendering a retrograde movement of the British Dec. 3. troops necessary. On the 3rd of December, General Disney, having been appointed to the command of another brigade (28th, 91st), forming part of the reserve, under Major-General Paget, left Castel Branco, and, proceeding by Guarda and Almeida, eventually joined the main army at Toro on the Douro.

Major-General Warde had now resumed the command of the First Guards, and occupied with them, at Majorga, a magnificent convent. The right of the main army was on the 17th at Toro, and General Disney, with his brigade of the line and the rest of the reserve, in front. General Disney continued his march northwards, and having on the 21st reached Grajal, two or three miles distant from Sahagun, which the brigade of Guards now occupied, placed himself at once in communication with his old comrades. Upon the French advanced guard showing itself in the neighbourhood, the 10th and 15th Hussars, under Lord Paget, were sent forward, and drove the enemy's cavalry off the field. As the French, however, continued their advance, and had taken possession of the bridge over the Carrion, the Guards' brigade, with the rest of Baird's division, were ordered on the night of the 23rd of December to attack that position ; the whole division was ready formed to march off at eleven o'clock, when Sir John Moore received intelligence that the object of his advance into Spain had been so far accomplished, that the French had been thereby deterred from entering the southern provinces of the country. Moore's advance from Lisbon had, in fact, paralysed the plans of the emperor; the French corps *en route* for Valencia, Badajoz, and Saragossa were arrested on their march, and Napoleon had postponed all other considerations that he might assemble every available man to crush the British army. On the 22nd, he was with 50,000 men at the foot of the Guadarrama range, on the 26th at Tordesillas, but he was one day too late to fall upon the British army, for Sir John Moore having gained his object in diverting Napoleon from his course, and knowing that he was not strong enough alone, unaided by his allies, to compete with the combined French armies, had already determined upon retreating into Gallicia. On the 23rd of December the army, now united, had been ordered to advance, as above referred to, in two columns, against the French at Carrion, on the river of that name, but a few hours later it received counter-orders, and on the following day, the 24th, part of it commenced its march towards Corunna, soon putting the river Esla between it and the enemy.

The Guards, with Baird's division, retired on the 25th by Valencia and San Juan, and, preceded by the rest of the infantry, crossed the Esla the next day, occupying Villa Manian, where they halted two days to give the main body time to effect a passage at Benevente; on the 29th they reached Astorga, where Hope's and Fraser's divisions had already arrived. The brigade of Guards was lodged in the episcopal palace of this town, and the men occupied the entire surface of the numerous galleries and corridors, as well as the large court-yard of this fine building. At four the next morning, Baird's division, preceded by Hope's and Frasers, was again *en route;* the weather was severe; many stragglers dropped behind, and it was necessary to halt frequently. It was late in the evening before the column reached Manzanel, a small village surrounded by snow-clad mountains; but, at ten at night, before the men could obtain anything to eat, the retreat was continued, and early on the 31st of December the troops arrived at Bembibre, where the worn-out soldiers broke into the wine-cellars, and great excesses were committed; the halt however here was only for a few hours.

The weather was wild and stormy, rain and snow had

Margin notes: 1808. December. — Dec. 25. Retreat to Corunna. — Dec. 30.

1809. made the roads almost impassable, and a British army in retreat presents a lamentable contrast to an advancing force. Proud and confident then in their courage and discipline, the soldiers look upon retreat as a disgrace; discipline becomes relaxed, and the national vice of drunkenness prevails. This retreat formed no exception, for numbers perished or were taken prisoners from their own reckless conduct.

The emperor, having effected a junction with Ney's corps, advanced to and occupied Astorga with 70,000

Jan. 1. men on the 1st of January, being thus two days' march behind the British army; but receiving intelligence while here that the Austrians were again about to appeal to arms and threaten his hold on Germany; he immediately countermarched a portion of his army then in Spain, and returned himself to Paris, leaving Soult and Ney to follow up the pursuit of the British army.

The advance of a body of 1200 French cavalry on the

Jan. 3. 3rd of January, obliged the army to withdraw through Cacabolos and form on the other side of the river; when the French cavalry were checked in their career by the artillery, and a smart fire was opened between the riflemen on both sides; the army then reformed column of route and retired through Villafranca four leagues to Alilea, where it arrived about one in the morning of the 4th. At seven the troops were again *en route* for Santa Maria, four leagues distant, the road a continual ascent over the mountains separating the province of Leon from Castille; a thaw had supervened, the roads were bad, strewn with broken-down carriages, dead horses, mules, and even men and women, all this in the midst of a mixture of rain, sleet, and a biting cold wind, a truly melancholy scene. On the

Jan. 5. 5th the army marched through Santa Maria, four more leagues, to a rising ground beyond Constantine, and failing in their efforts to break up the. bridge, were followed the whole day by a strong body of French cavalry and riflemen; but the steady appearance of the 28th Regiment, under Brigadier-General Disney, and a few shots from a six-pounder, prevented the French advance. The bullocks drawing the carts with the money-chests, knocked up this 1809. day, and 90,000 dollars were thrown down a precipice.

In the evening of the 5th, the troops, having passed Nogales, arrived at Lugo, and after two days' repose took up a position in front of the town, in which Sir John Moore remained two more days, determined to await the enemy's attack.

On the 7th the British chief issued a stirring order to the Jan. 7. army, appealing to the honourable feelings of the soldiers, calling upon the commanding officers to restore discipline, and to the credit of the troops, no sooner was there a chance of fighting than they rejoined the ranks with vigour and cheerfulness, and 19,000 soldiers were under arms when the enemy appeared. The British general rode down the ranks and saw his soldiers awaiting in confidence and discipline the long-wished-for issue. When Marshal Soult arrived, about midday, in front of the British position, he opened fire on their centre, but soon found he had more than a rear-guard to contend with, and his guns were silenced. After making a feint on the right, a column and five guns attacked the British left, but these were repulsed by some companies of the Guards and General Leith's brigade, and Soult, knowing Ney was approaching, would make no further general movement in advance till his arrival. Lieutenant-Colonel Donaldson, Captains Packe and Latour, of the light companies of the first battalion, and Ensign Blunt of the third battalion, were the officers of the First Guards more prominently engaged on this occasion, when the conduct of the Guards called forth the thanks of their brigadier in the following words :—

" Lugo, *January 8th.*

" Major-General Warde takes the earliest opportunity of thanking those officers, and the part of the brigade who were engaged in the affair of yesterday for their very cool and gallant conduct."

On the morning of the 8th the British army was still Jan. 8. in position about a mile in front of Lugo, formed in order of battle, in vain awaiting the advance of the enemy ; but

Jan. 8.

the French marshal, though with 22,000 men under his command, would not attack.

Order had now, it is true, been restored in the British army, but the magazines were failing, and Moore, conscious that no useful result would be attained even by any temporary success, as the Spaniards were no longer in the field, resolved to continue the retreat that same evening, and on the next day, the 9th, before quitting Lugo, he issued the following order calling upon the men to make fresh exertions :—

"HEAD-QUARTERS, LUGO, *9th January*, 1809.

" It is evident that the enemy will not fight this army, notwithstanding the superiority of his numbers, but will endeavour to harass and tease it upon its march.

" The commander of the forces requests that it may be carefully explained to the soldiers that their safety depends solely upon their keeping their divisions and marching with their regiments ; that those who stop in villages or straggle on the march will inevitably be cut off by the French cavalry, who have hitherto shown little mercy even to the feeble and infirm who have fallen into their hands.

" The army has still eleven leagues to march, the soldiers must make an exertion to accomplish them; the rear-guard cannot stop, and those who fall behind must take their fate."

Shortly after dark on the evening of the 8th, the British had withdrawn from their position, and, marching through Lugo, recommenced their harassing retreat. Major-General Paget's division, followed by the brigade of Guards and Baird's division, moved off in a terrible storm. The men of the corps first in retreat, to avoid the inclemency of the night, filled the buildings on the road-side, and had to be forced on. It was daybreak on the 9th before the Guards arrived at Vaamondas, six leagues further to the rear, where the army took up another position. The sufferings of the men during the day and night were frightful ; they lay scattered over a bleak and desolate heath with nothing to protect them ; they lined the ditches to escape the cutting sharpness of the tempest; many perished; regiments got mixed together and stragglers came in slowly; after a few hours' halt, the main body continued their retreat, and arrived at Betanzos on the evening of the 9th.

In the midst of the difficulties of this day's march, the brigade of Guards preserved some order and discipline; the reserve covered the retreat, and these noble soldiers, who were in frequent conflict with the enemy, lost fewer men than other divisions. The following extracts respecting the conduct of some of the corps are from the works of contemporary writers :—

" The corps in which there was the least straggling were the artillery, the Guards, and the reserve. The Guards were the strongest body of men in the army, and consequently suffered least from fatigue; besides, they are strictly disciplined, and their non-commissioned officers are excellent." " On the 9th of January the march was unusually irregular; the Guards, artillery, and reserve are stated to have distinguished themselves by their patience and discipline." " Yet there were fewer irregularities committed by the artillery, and the Guards, than by many regiments of the line, and amidst the turmoil, the reserve preserved order."

After halting on the 10th, the army continued its march on the morning of the 11th, Major-General Disney's brigade of the 28th and 91st Regiments still forming the rear-guard, and it was actively engaged in protecting the rear of the army at the bridge over the river at Betanzos, which they had in vain attempted to blow up.

The army continued its march on the 12th, and the knowledge that this was to be their last day's march, and the expectation that a trial of strength would shortly take place before embarking, had the effect to some extent of restoring discipline in the ranks ; and at length, in the course of the day, the army reached Corunna. The following account by an eye-witness of the arrival of the first and third battalions of the First Guards in presence of their commander-in-chief, who was so soon to give up his life for his country, is worthy of record.

The late Sir Robert Arbuthnot relates that he was with several other officers at Corunna, standing near Sir John Moore, who was watching the troops coming in, when Sir John called his attention, saying:—" Arbuthnot, look at that body of men in the distance; they are the Guards, by the way they are marching." They watched them and saw them march into Corunna by sections, their drums beating, the drum-major in front flourishing his stick, the sergeant-major at the head, and the drill-sergeants on the flanks keeping the men in step, exactly as if they were on their own drill-ground at home. Sir Robert said: "It was a fine sight, and one he should never forget." These two battalions, with the rest of Baird's and Fraser's divisions, occupied the town itself, while Hope's division was quartered in the suburbs, and the reserve at El Burgo.

Jan. 14.

The transports for the conveyance of the army to England not having yet arrived in the harbour of Corunna, the several divisions, 14,500 strong, after two days' rest, moved on the 14th from their quarters in the town and took up a position in order of battle on a ridge about two miles distant. Baird's and Hope's divisions were formed in line; Baird's on the right, and from the direction of the ridge, obliquely approaching the enemy's position, so that a great battery on the French left enfiladed it. The Guards, under Sir Henry Warde, were in column in support of Baird's right, this being the weak point of the position; Fraser's division was posted a short distance in its rear, while Paget with the reserve was in rear of the centre: and here the British army awaited for

Jan. 15.

two more days the enemy's attack. At last, on the 15th the transports entered the harbour of Corunna; the stores of the army, and the greater part of the artillery were shipped in the course of the night, and the necessary preparations were made to embark the infantry as soon

Jan. 16.
Battle of
Corunna.

as it was dark on the 16th. About two o'clock on that day, the French army under Soult, advanced in three columns, covered by skirmishers, against the British position; attacked the left column, carried the village of Elvina, and dividing, one portion attacked Baird in front

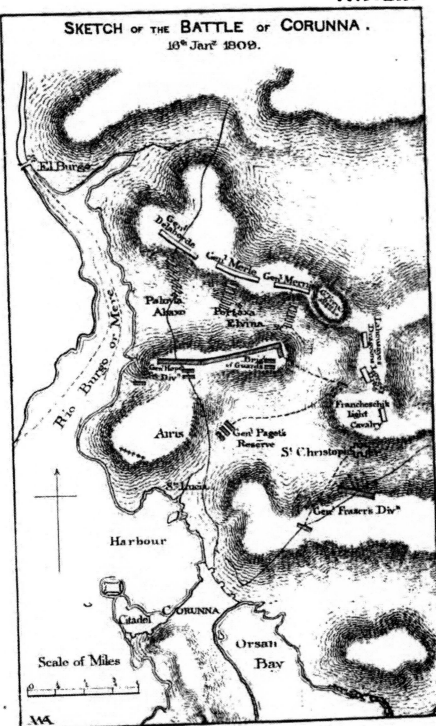

SKETCH of the BATTLE or CORUNNA.
16th Janr 1809.

El Burge

Genl Delborde

Genl Merle

Genl Mermet

Palavia Abaxo

Portida Elvina

Genl Hope's Divn

Bridge of Guardia

Genl La Houssaye's Cavalry

Franceschi's light Cavalry

Airis

Genl Paget's Reserve

St Christophilis Divn

Rio Burgo or Mere

St Lucia

Genl Fraser's Divn

Harbour

Citadel

CORUNNA

Orsan Bay

Scale of Miles

0   1   2   3

while the other attempted to turn his right. If this attack succeeded, the ruin of the British army was inevitable; the 4th Regiment on the right of Baird's line was therefore thrown back on its left, and opened a flank fire on the advancing column, while the reserve descended the valley and checked its advance. The 42nd Highlanders and 50th Regiment, forming the right centre of Baird's line, advanced and stormed the village of Elvina, when Sir David received a bullet in his arm, which forced him to leave the field, and Sir John Moore observing at the same time that an interval was left in the line, by the advance of those two regiments, sent orders to the brigade of Guards to move forward and occupy it; the first battalion of the First Guards immediately deployed and advanced down the hill to the assistance of the regiments in Elvina, the third battalion forming in support. As Captain Harding, who had carried the order to the Guards to advance, was, on his return, reporting to Sir John that he had executed his wishes, and pointing out to him the approaching line of the first battalion, Sir John received a mortal wound, a cannon shot carrying away his left shoulder. The troops, undismayed by the fall of their gallant commander, continued the action under Sir John Hope, upon whom the command of the army now devolved. The reserve on the extreme right having, at length, overthrown the French column, and approached the great battery on the French left, and the British left wing having also repulsed the attack made upon it, the army continued to advance beyond its original position, driving the French before them. By five o'clock, the enemy, giving up all hopes of any success against the British line, confined themselves to a distant cannonade, under the protection of which the French marshal withdrew his troops. By six o'clock the firing had entirely ceased and the enemy was retiring in confusion, after which the several brigades reoccupied the position they held in the morning.

Sir John Moore was carried off the field by six soldiers of the First Guards and 42nd Highlanders, the two regiments that were nearest to him when he fell, and being brought into Corunna, he died in the course of the evening, but not without expressing great satisfaction that he had beat the French. He was interred at his own request in the northeast bastion of the citadel, by the side of his old friend and comrade Brigadier-General Anstruther, formerly of the Third Guards, who had commanded a brigade during the retreat, but had succumbed from fatigue and illness on the day the army reached Corunna. The funeral service was read over the grave of Sir John Moore by the Rev. H. J. Symonds, one of the chaplains of the First Guards.

The British troops had retired 250 miles in the face of a superior force in the worst season of the year, and though from want of transport, they had destroyed many supplies, rather than that they should fall into the enemy's hands, they did not suffer one reverse or the loss of any trophies. Their Spanish allies, so far from assisting, treated them often inhospitably, frequently closing their doors against the wearied and hungry soldier; but in spite of all difficulties, they eventually defeated the French in a pitched battle, which enabled them to continue and complete the embarcation without further interruption. History affords few parallels to the like discipline under such disadvantageous circumstances.

The retreat to the ships commenced at ten o'clock at night, with great order and regularity, for Sir John Hope considered, notwithstanding the defeat of the enemy, that it was incumbent upon him to carry out an operation which had been commenced under the orders of Sir John Moore; and, with the exception of the brigades of Generals Hill and Beresford, which remained as a rear-guard to cover the embarcation, the whole army with the brigade of Guards proceeded on board during the night. The two brigades of Hill and Beresford, embarked the following day, the 17th, though not without being exposed to a partial fire of artillery from a battery brought by the enemy on to a height commanding the harbour. As Sir John Hope had succeeded to the command upon his two senior officers being carried

off the field, it was upon him that devolved the duty of
writing the official account of the late action, announcing
to the government the defeat of the enemy, and the evacuation of Spain.

He also issued a general order acknowledging the services
of the troops, of which the following is an extract :—

" His acknowledgments are in a peculiar manner due to
Major-General Lord William Bentinck and the brigade,
consisting of the 4th, 42nd, and 50th Regiments, which sustained the weight of the attack. Major-General Manning-
ham with his brigade, consisting of the Royals, 21st and
81st Regiments, and Major-General Warde with his brigade
of Guards, will also be pleased to accept his best thanks for
their steady and gallant conduct during the action."

Owing to the immediate sailing of the British army after
the action, and the departure of the several regiments to
their respective quarters on their return to England, no
general return of casualties in the battle of Corunna is to
be found. From the muster-rolls of the regiment, however,
it appears that the first battalion First Guards lost five men
and the third battalion eight killed on the day of the battle ;
many appear also to have subsequently died of their wounds,
as during the following weeks the first battalion lost by death
eighty-six men, the third battalion fifty-four; but in these
numbers are included those who died from natural causes,
as well as from the fatigues of the late campaign. The
numbers that fell into the hands of the enemy during the
retreat were, sixty-nine of the first and fifty-six of the
third battalion.

The total loss experienced by the army of Sir John
Moore during the campaign, including the advance, the
retreat to Corunna, and in the subsequent action, was about
4000 men, of whom 800 found their way to Portugal and
were formed into battalions of detachments.

The fleet encountered a terrible storm on its passage to
England, the ships were scattered and many wrecked, but
the transports carrying the brigade of First Guards anchored

1809. safely in Portsmouth harbour on the 25th of January, and the men, on landing, were marched to Chatham, where, on
Feb. 8. the 8th of February, they at length found a temporary repose only from their labours, for, having received numerous transfers in the course of the spring from the second battalion in London, these battalions were, as we shall see, again sent on foreign service in the summer.

Feb. 22. On the 22nd of February, Major-General H. Warde, an officer conspicuous for knowledge of his profession and military abilities, and not given to praise except where it was due, issued the following order to his brigade :—

" CHATHAM, 22nd *February.*

" Major-General Warde has anxiously waited the assembling of the brigade at Chatham to express in the very strongest manner possible, not only his approbation, but his most sincere thanks to the officers of all ranks for their hearty support and assistance upon all occasions, and to the non-commissioned officers and privates of the brigade for their general very good and exemplary conduct, their unremitting exertions, and their patience under many severe trials during the late most harassing and arduous service in Spain. Were he to add one word of his own respecting their conduct in the action of the 16th of January near Corunna, after the truly handsome remarks of Lieutenant-General Hope in the general order of the 18th ult., he should consider it as superfluous, and on his own part the height of presumption. Yet he may state with sincerity, should his future military employment remove him from the first brigade of Guards, he shall ever reflect upon his having commanded them in Spain with a heartfelt satisfaction and pleasure and pride to hear his name coupled upon such an occasion with so truly an honourable and respectable corps, for whose welfare, happiness, success, and honour, whether present or absent, he must ever feel the most lively interest."

After the embarcation of the British army, Soult's and Ney's corps remained at Corunna for about a month for the

purpose of restoring discipline; Soult then marched on 1809.
Oporto, which he stormed on the 29th of March. The
government at home, in the meantime, foreseeing the necessity of sending further reinforcements to the Peninsula, had,
at the end of the year 1808, prepared another expedition
under Major-General Sherbrook, composed of the second
brigade of Guards, viz., Coldstream and 3rd Regiments, under
Brigadier Henry Campbell, First Guards, and of the 87th
and 88th Regiments, and this expedition had sailed on the
15th of January, 1809, encountering the same gales that over- Jan. 15.
took the fleet bringing home the first brigade of Guards from
Corunna. It was delayed thereby for a month at Cork, after
which it proceeded to Cadiz, where the authorities objecting
to its presence, the fleet conveyed the troops to the Tagus,
and the second brigade of Guards was landed near Lisbon on
the 13th of March. The rest of the troops of the line which March 13.
had served under Sir John Moore were also sent back to
the Tagus as soon as they were recruited; and with other
additional reinforcements sent out from time to time from
England, formed that army in the field destined to oppose
the further progress of French arms in Portugal. Sir
Arthur Wellesley, who was sent out in command, arrived
in Lisbon on the 22nd of April, when, in addition to his April 22.
military command, he was invested with supreme authority
in the kingdom. The British army in Portugal now
amounted to about 18,000 men, to which may be added
about 20,000 native troops in British pay.

After being at the head of the British army at home for
fourteen years, H.R.H. the Duke of York, for reasons
unnecessary to recapitulate here, resigned his post of Commander-in-Chief, on the 18th of March, 1809, and for the March 18.
following two years that appointment was held by Sir
David Dundas.

Sir Arthur Wellesley lost no time in putting his troops
in motion; he crossed the Douro near Oporto in face of
Soult's army on the 12th of May, Hill's division establishing May 12.
itself in the town, while Sherbrook's, with the second
brigade of Guards, consisting of the first battalions of the

1809. Second and Third regiments, under Brigadier-General Henry Campbell of the First Guards, threatened the enemy's rear. It will not be out of place here to refer to Sir Arthur's report of the conduct of these two battalions during **May 13.** this campaign. In his despatch of the 13th of May to the Duke of York, he says: "The troops have behaved remarkably well in every instance, and I cannot conclude this letter without telling your Royal Highness, that the brigade of Guards are in every respect the example and the object of admiration of the whole army. They have not yet been engaged with the enemy; but I have no doubt but that they will acquit themselves as well in that respect as they do in all others." It is but fair, when recording on all occasions the credit the First Regiment of Guards was gaining for itself whenever it had an opportunity, to put on record also that their comrades in the other two regiments were equally upholding the character of the brigade in other fields; and it may be remarked that a system which invariably produced such soldiers was not one to be lightly cast aside, for however much in the present day men, even in high rank, may deny the existence of an *esprit de corps* rising superior to all self-considerations, they may rest assured that such is not the feeling that then animated, and still exists in, the brigade of Guards.

In consequence of the successful advance of the British troops, Soult was now compelled to make a precipitate retreat over the mountains to Braja and Orense, losing his artillery and baggage, and 6000 men, and Sir Arthur Wellesley followed up this blow by marching against Marshal Victor and on Madrid, where he effected a junction with the Spanish general Cuesta. The Anglo-Spanish army advanced **July 22.** on the 22nd of July to Talavera, and on the 28th fought the battle in which the French attack was completely defeated, and for which victory Sir Arthur Wellesley was created Viscount Wellington. The British general then turned north towards Soult, but finding that the French marshal had collected 50,000 men in the mountainous country at Navalmoral, and that it was impossible to depend upon Spanish promises, either as regarded supplies or co-operation, he retired to Almarez and Merida, in Estremadura, where he placed his army in cantonments.

Sir Arthur in this campaign satisfied himself that the defence of Portugal and the success of the British army must depend upon his own strategy, and upon the conduct of those over whom he had direct authority, as he could not rely upon his plans being carried out by any generals, except those who were under his own immediate orders. He accordingly directed the formation of the Lines of Torres Vedras to cover Lisbon; the construction of forts to defend the mouth of the Tagus; and he insisted, as marshal-general of Portugal, upon an army of 30,000 Portuguese being placed at his disposal, to the command of which General Beresford was appointed with the rank of marshal: and many regiments of which it was composed were placed under the command of British officers.

EXPEDITION TO WALCHEREN.

The services of a brigade of Guards were again put into requisition, in the summer of 1809, to join in an expedition to the Island of Walcheren, and the two battalions of the First Regiment lately returned from Spain were ordered to hold themselves in immediate readiness. The following circumstances gave rise to the determination on the part of the British Government to send this force abroad:—

Since the Belgian provinces had been converted into part of the French empire, Napoleon had created a considerable arsenal at Antwerp; and being master of the Scheldt, he continually threatened England on its left flank. At the latter end of May the British Government determined to attempt the destruction of this standing menace, as well as to make a diversion in favour of Austria. Antwerp was at the time badly garrisoned, troops having been withdrawn to reinforce the grand army at Vienna, towards which Napoleon was hastening in his victorious career. The intentions of the British Government were to capture or

EXPEDITION
to
WALCHEREN
July & August 1809.
and
CAMPAIGN of 1814.

Brig.-Gen. M. Disney, commanding 1st brigade of Guards.
Brig.-Gen. H. F. Campbell, commanding 2nd brigade of Guards.
Brig.-Gen. Charles White, on the Staff in Sicily.
Brig.-Gen. H. Clinton, Dep. Adjutant-General in Ireland.

1809.

The next three available senior officers,* not general officers, viz., Col. Wm. Anson, Col. George Cooke, and Col. William Wheatley were in command of the 1st, 3rd, and 2nd battalions respectively.

Lieut.-Col. Hon. Edward Capel was appointed Assistant-Adjutant-General, and Capt. Richard H. Cooke, Brigade Major, Capt. French, Assist.-Quartermaster-General, and Capt. Elphinstone, D. A. A.-Gen. of the 1st brigade, all of the First Regiment.

In addition to these, Lieut.-Col. Dalzell, First Guards, was appointed Judge-Advocate to the expedition, and the following Subalterns of the regiment were also on the Staff:—

Capt. F. D'Oyly, A.D.C. to Brig.-Gen. Disney.
  ,,   J. G. Woodford, A.D.C. to Lord-Lieutenant in Ireland.
  ,,   Edward Wynyard, A. A.-Gen. in Sicily.
  ,,   Hon. J. Stanhope, A.D.C. to Commander-in-Chief.
  ,,   Marquis of Tweeddale, on the Staff in Portugal.
  ,,   Hon. F. Stanhope, A.D.C. to Lt.-Gen. Sir Arthur Wellesley.
Ensign Duckenfield, A.D.C. to Major-Gen. Warde in India.
  ,,   Fitzgibbon, A.D.C. to Major-Gen. Payne.

The army, 21,000 strong, was organised in four divisions, under Lieutenant-General Sir John Hope, the Earl of Rosslyn, Lieutenant-General Grosvenor, and the Marquis of Huntly.

Lord Chatham thought it necessary, as a preparatory measure previous to more extensive operations, to obtain possession of some commanding point on the north side of South Beveland, from which to advance and take the enemy's batteries in rear, and thus force the French fleet, which was off Flushing, to move up the river, for fear of their retreat being cut off; by which means also the approach of the British fleet to Flushing would be facilitated; and for this purpose he selected Sir John Hope's division, which was the reserve of the army, and was thus composed :—

Brigade of Guards.—Major-Gen. Disney	3070
1st and 2nd battalions 4th, 28th Regiment.— Major-Gen.	
Earl of Dalhousie	2538
20th, 92nd, 7th Vet. battalion.—Major-Gen. Sir Wm. Erskine	1653
	7261

* Col. Robert Cheney was sick.

1809. To Admiral Sir Richard Keats was assigned the charge of transporting this division, and as it was to precede the July 28. rest of the army, it sailed from the Downs on the 28th of July; the Earl of Chatham, with the other divisions, sailing on the 29th and 30th.

Aug. 1. The grenadiers and first battalion of the First Guards, and the other regiments of Sir John Hope's division, who had been conveyed some distance up the river in boats, owing to the difficulty of navigation for larger vessels, landed without opposition on the morning of the 1st of August, on the north side of South Beveland, between Wilmenduye and Cattendyke, and as soon as a line was formed the grenadiers of the Guards, and a detachment of the 95th, moved forward to Cloeting, pushing on strong patrols to Goes, and leaving three companies of the 20th at Cattendyke. Goes capitulated, and was occupied by part of the 92nd Regiment, the enemy retiring towards Batz. The Guards remained that day at Capelle and Boulingen, and Erskine's brigade at Hexendenkinder and Goes. The third battalion of Guards did not land till the following day, the 2nd of August, when the division already on shore again advanced, the Guards to Vaarden, the 4th Regiment to Hanswardt; the grenadiers of the Guards then pushed on to Kruyningen, surprising seventy or eighty of the enemy and making them prisoners without loss to themselves. The Dutch evacuated Vaarden, and subsequently, on the 4th of August, as the British continued their advance, abandoned the town and important fort of Batz, on the low ground opposite to and commanding the entrance of the Scheldt, leading direct to Antwerp, which lay about twenty miles south, whereupon the Guards took up a position between Cattendyke and Batz. It was a surprise to Sir John Hope that this fort, considering its strength and position, should have been thus evacuated, for it was difficult to account for the officer in command, with 600 men, not making some resistance, though it is possible that the Dutch were already aware of the ally that must eventually come to their aid, in the unhealthy climate of the low country now occupied by the British army.

The communication by water was now entirely free for the fleet between Walcheren and South Beveland, and Sir John Hope at once urged the importance of the presence of the flotilla near the fort. Its absence was soon felt, for on the 5th and 8th of August the enemy commenced, though with little effect, to bombard the fort from twenty-five gunboats. It was on the occasion of this bombardment that a private soldier, a grenadier of the First Guards, John Skinner by name, distinguished himself by an act of gallantry which would in these days have earned for him the Victoria Cross. Twelve guns had been spiked and left by the French in Fort Batz when they retired. John Skinner, in the midst of the bombardment, offered to unspike them with tools made by himself, so that they might be turned upon the enemy's flotilla of gunboats, and having received the sanction of his commanding officer, Colonel Rainsford, to make the attempt, he carried it out successfully. In acknowledgment of this act, he was presented by the Duke of York and the officers of his regiment, on his return to England, with a medal purposely struck for the occasion. On one side of it he is represented on a cannon, with the following inscription :—" John Skinner.—Presented by the Duke of York and the officers of the First Regiment of Foot Guards for his soldierlike conduct." On the obverse is the flotilla bombarding the fort. During these operations eighty guns and a quantity of ordnance stores had fallen into the possession of General Hope's division. On the 9th of August the Earl of Rosslyn's division landed on South Beveland, when, as senior officer, the earl assumed the command.

While these operations were being successfully carried on against Fort Batz, the troops under the immediate command of Lord Chatham had landed, on the 30th of July, without opposition, at Veere, on the north-east shore of the island of Walcheren, after the fire from the mortar and gunboats had driven the enemy from their defences. The town of Camour was immediately cannonaded, and soon surrendered, and on the 4th of August Fort Rammekens succumbed to General

Fraser. This was an important acquisition, as it enabled the flotilla to advance, and prevent succour being thrown into Flushing, which was at once invested, and after a bombardment, by which the town was set in flames, it capitulated on the 15th, the garrison marching out with all the honours of war on the 18th of August.

On the reduction of Flushing, Lord Chatham, with head-quarters, moved to Goes, in South Beveland, and subsequently to Fort Batz, joining Sir John Hope's division with the brigade of Guards; but the most dangerous enemy to the British troops began now to make its appearance, for a low fever had already broken out, occasioned by the fatal miasma arising from the inundations.

The first part of the expedition having been successfully accomplished, the attack on Antwerp was the next object to carry out; but Louis Buonaparte had in the meantime arrived in the country with reinforcements, and Bernadotte had assumed the supreme command of the French troops thus augmented. The strength of the enemy in the citadel of Antwerp and its neighbourhood was now about 11,000 men; between Antwerp and Bergen-op-Zoom, 15,000; and in Bergen-op-Zoom, Breda, and Tholen, and on the left bank of the Scheldt, 11,000 more, making a total of 37,000 men. The effective force of the British army was about 30,000, but of this number, in the event of the siege of Antwerp being undertaken, 6000 would be required to remain in Walcheren, and 2000 in South Beveland. It would also be necessary to mask Bergen-op-Zoom and Breda; 10,000 or 12,000 men would be required to cover the siege, leaving only 10,000 men for the siege itself. The Admiral Sir Richard Strachan had expressed his opinion that the fleet could not move higher up the Scheldt as long as the two forts of Lillo and Liefkenshoek, situated on opposite sides of the river, half-way between Fort Batz and Antwerp, were in possession of the enemy; and though the navy would co-operate, yet their capture was a military measure, and in consequence of the advanced state of the season, and the shortness of the supply of water in the fleet, he asked for an immediate decision as to what the army   1809. could undertake.

A memorandum, on the above comparative strength of the hostile forces, was accordingly submitted for the opinion of the seven lieutenant-generals of the army. On the 27th of August they came to the decision that the siege of Antwerp was impracticable, and that no advantage would result from the reduction of the Fort of Lillo, or from any minor operations. In consequence of this decision the expedition was at an end; orders were given for the evacuation of South Beveland, and by the 4th of Sep- Sept. 4. tember no troops were left in the Scheldt, except a small garrison at Walcheren, under General Don. The first brigade of Guards landed in England at the beginning of September, and moved to their former quarters. They had suffered much from sickness, both officers and men bringing with them the seeds of disease from which many suffered to the latest hour of their lives; none had fallen in action, but many a grave was filled from the " Walcheren Fever" contracted in this fruitless campaign.

By a return made out five months later, at the beginning of February, 1810, it appears that, of the ninety-one officers of the First Guards, one died of fever on service, and two on their return, all of the first battalion; and that of the 2574 non-commissioned officers and men of that regiment, twenty-one died on service, and 208 on their return. In the whole army no less than sixty-seven officers and 4000 men died of the fever, and at the date of the report in February above 200 officers and 11,000 men were still in hospital.

Lieutenant-General Don, who was left in command at Walcheren for a time to prevent the enemy's fleet escaping from the river, having subsequently received orders to evacuate the island, destroyed the basin of the harbour with the naval defences on the 10th of December, and embarked for England.

After the return of the officers from the Corunna campaign, the brigade, in 1810, set up a private club of their own, of which the Dukes of York, Cambridge, and Gloucester, and nearly all the general and field officers of the Guards then in London became members. The loyalty at such a club was naturally very great, and when the *Times* in subsequent years, made use of disrespectful language towards Queen Caroline, it was resolved at a meeting convened by Sir Henry, the future Lord, Hardinge, to exclude that paper. The only place of meeting that the officers of the Guards, prior to 1810, had as a club, was in a small room in the St. James Coffee-house, at the bottom of St. James Street, described as a miserable little den, the floor sanded over like a tap-room of the present time ; but this, though a strong contrast to the luxurious habits now obtaining, did not prevent its being the resort of many of the wits of the day.

Contemporaneously with the campaign of 1809 in the Peninsula, and with the expedition to Walcheren, Napoleon, who had left his marshals to conduct the operations against the British in Spain, found on his arrival in Paris that Austria, subsidized by Great Britain, was bent on resuming hostilities, and in April heard that the Archduke Charles, Generalissimo of the Austrian armies, had passed the Inn and opened the campaign. Napoleon joined his army on the 17th, and, defeating his enemies at Landshut, Eckmuhl, and Ebensberg with his usual fortune, was, by the 10th of May, once more in Vienna. He crossed the Danube, but, being worsted in the desperate and bloody battles of Aspern and Essling, on the 21st and 22nd of that month, was compelled to withdraw for a time to the isle of Lobau on the Danube. After six weeks spent in reorganising his army, and collecting stores and *matériel*, he burst forth from Lobau on the 5th of July, crossed the Danube unopposed, and immediately attacked the Archduke. The combat was desperate, and both armies bivouacked on the ground where they fought. The next morning commenced the stern conflict of Wagram, in which, after eight hours' severe fighting, the Austrians were eventually forced to give way, although they were not routed. On the 10th, Prince John of Austria brought proposals for an armistice, which were agreed to and signed at Znaim on the 11th of July; a treaty of Peace was subsequently ratified at Vienna on the 14th of October, and the emperor returned to Paris.

1809.

October 14.

CHAPTER XXIII.

1810.

EXPEDITION TO CADIZ.

1810. EXPEDITION TO CADIZ—SECOND BATTALION OF FIRST GUARDS JOINS IT
—GENERAL GRAHAM ON WORKING PAY—DEFENCE OF CADIZ—CAMPAIGN
IN SPAIN—1811. SIEGE OF CADIZ—MAJOR-GENERAL DILKES—BATTLE
OF BARROSA—DESPATCHES—GOOD CONDUCT OF GUARDS AND OTHER
TROOPS—DUKE OF YORK REINSTATED AS COMMANDER-IN-CHIEF—SIEGE
CONTINUED BY THE FRENCH—ROYAL BADGES ON COLOURS OF GUARDS—
RECEPTION OF CAPTURED COLOURS—THIRD BATTALION SENT TO CADIZ
TO JOIN THEIR COMRADES—BADAJOS—SALAMANCA—FRENCH RETIRE
FROM BEFORE CADIZ—THIRD·BATTALION FIRST GUARDS MARCH TO SE-
VILLE, THENCE THROUGH SOUTH OF SPAIN TO SALAMANCA—BURGOS—
FIRST BATTALION FIRST GUARDS SENT OUT FROM ENGLAND—LANDED
AT CORUNNA—MARCHES THROUH NORTH OF SPAIN AND JOINS THIRD
BATTALION—CAMPAIGN—RETREAT FROM BURGOS AND SALAMANCA INTO
PORTUGAL TO VISEU, THENCE TO OPORTO.

1810.

Siege of
Cadiz.

THE southern provinces of Spain had been saved for a
time by the bold advance of Sir John Moore in 1808, and
again by the march of Lord Wellington towards Madrid
after the battle of Talavera; but the subsequent retreat of
the British general into Portugal, and the defeat of the
Spanish army at Ocana, thirty miles S.S.E. of Madrid, on
the 16th of November, 1809, opened the road for the French
to Cadiz, and no force remained in Spain capable of resisting the enemy in the field.

The British government aware of the importance of
preventing the French obtaining possession of the strong
fortress and noble harbour of Cadiz, had sent General
Sherbrooke there in the autumn of 1808 with 4000 men,
and Major-General Mackenzie followed him with a brigade
in February, 1809, but neither of these expeditions landed,
being recalled for the defence of Portugal. At this time

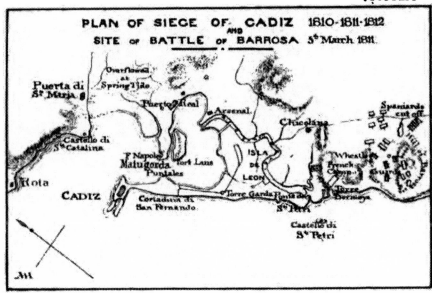

PLAN OF SIEGE OF CADIZ 1810-1811-1812
SITE of BATTLE of BARROSA 5ᵗʰ March 1811

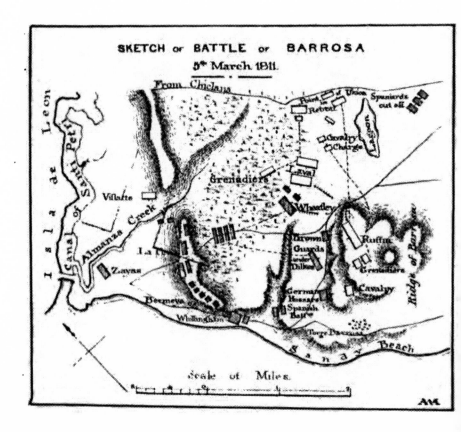

SKETCH of BATTLE of BARROSA
5ᵗʰ March 1811

there were only a few guns mounted on the ramparts of 1810.
Cadiz, while no less than 400 ought to have been in position; and there were only 5000 militia in garrison, with a
few enrolled peasants under the guise of artillerymen.

The French army of the south was now commanded by
Marshal Soult; Cordova and Seville in Andalusia had been
captured, and Cadiz appeared to be within his grasp, when the
Duke of Albuquerque, who was in the valleys of the Sierra
Morena, retreated by forced marches, and with 8000 men
threw himself into Isla de Leon, near Cadiz, on the 3rd Feb. 3.
of February, 1810, and by his energy saved the place, for by
this time the garrison amounted to 14,000 men. Marshal
Victor, however, followed the Spaniards with such diligence that he reached Chiclana, within a few miles of Cadiz,
only two days later, and on the 10th of February summoned Feb. 10.
the town, but in vain, to surrender. The French marshal then
saw that it would be necessary to besiege it in due form, and
proceeded to surround the bay with lines of contravallation.
Rota, Santa Maria, Puerto Real, and Chiclana were fortified,
and entrenched camps established in the most suitable positions, the principal one being at Chiclana, near Barrosa.

As the second and third battalions of the First Guards
subsequently took part in the long defence of Cadiz, a
description of the position is here given. A deep inlet of
the sea, the Santa Petri, was the first Spanish line of
defence; the second was the Isla de Leon, an irregular
triangle, the apex called Torregardo, pointing to the city,
the base resting on the Santa Petri, the right on the harbour, the left on the sea. The Isla, which is about seven
miles long, and half a mile broad, was marshy, except a
ridge four miles in length, on which the town of La Isla
stood. A narrow isthmus about five miles long connects
Cadiz with the apex, and across this isthmus is a cut called
the Cortadura, defended by the unfinished fort of Fernando.
A tongue of land projected from the eastern shore of the
harbour, and separated the inner from the outer harbour;
this tongue was cloven by a canal called the Trocadero; and
at the extreme point stood the fort of Matagorda, opposite to

1810. which, at 1200 yards' distance, on the isthmus leading to Cadiz, stood a powerful battery called Puntales. From Cadiz to Matagorda was 4000 yards; and from Matagorda the French could completely command the upper or inner harbour, as well as the forts of Fernando.

Lord Wellington having visited Seville in December, 1809, had drawn up a memorandum advising the completion of the work on the isthmus called Cortadura, in order to secure the communication between the Isla and the town, and recommended the construction of another strong work at the Torre d'Ercole (Torregorda). He subsequently expressed an opinion that "if the Isla was lost the town would not, and probably could not, hold out a week; and, on receiving information of the French advance upon Cadiz, he despatched Major-General Sir William Stewart with 2000 men (79th, 84th, and 89th regiments) to assist in its Feb. 11. defence. This brigade arrived on the 11th of February, and was soon joined by a Portuguese regiment 1300 strong, while the government at home also resolved to send Lieutenant-General Graham out from England with an additional reinforcement of 5000 men, of which a portion of the third brigade of Guards under Major-General Dilkes of the Third Regiment was to form a part. The remainder of the third brigade was to be left in England under the command of Brigadier-General Henry Campbell, who was to report to Major-General Disney, commanding the home district. The several companies for service were ordered early in March to be in readiness, and on the 7th of that month six companies of the second battalion First Guards, under Colonel Sebright, and three from each of the second battalions of Coldstream and Third Guards, under Lieutenant-Colonel Onslow of the latter regiment, left London for Portsmouth; and having embarked on board transports there awaiting them, were landed at the Isla de Leon March 24. on the 24th of March, with the rest of the reinforcements under Lieutenant-General Graham, who immediately assumed the chief command in the Isla, where all the allies were quartered. The British commander at once commenced adding to, and strengthening, the works, in which he was well supported by the Duke d'Albuquerque, till the latter was superseded, being appointed Spanish ambassador in London, where he died in January, 1811, on which occasion 800 men of the second brigade of Guards followed him to the grave in Westminster Abbey.

Fort Matagorda, which had been dismantled by the Spaniards, was hurriedly placed in a state of defence, but after an obstinate defence of fifty-four days, it was found, from its isolated position, to be quite untenable, and at the end of April was abandoned to the French, who, although they held it for upwards of two years, were unable to make it available in their attack upon the town, in consequence of the accurate and well-directed fire of the allies to which it was exposed.

The British and Portuguese, as well as the Spaniards of all classes, showed much zeal in working at the defences; and it was estimated that the construction of the requisite redoubts and defences would necessitate the labour of 4000 men for three months. Delays however arose, from the reluctance of the Spanish authorities to agree to the plans proposed, and the Junta would not, or could not, furnish the requisite tools. At a later period General Graham authorised working pay to be given to the troops under his own command, and in a general order that he issued to that effect, he laid down the principles upon which he acted in language so sound, that its perusal will be useful to every officer and soldier.

" It is needless to remind the troops under his command that this kind of service is one of the most essential duties of a soldier, and, like every other, ought to be cheerfully and diligently performed. Though the men will work under the immediate direction of the officers of engineers, it is nevertheless the bounden duty of every officer and non-commissioned officer present, to be vigilant during the whole time, and to prevent any negligent or improper conduct in the men. It is his intention, however, gradually to increase the working parties to as great a number as

1810.   possible, and for the convenience of the execution of those works at a considerable distance, a camp will be formed, where the same detachments will remain at least a week before being relieved.

"It is as much a soldier's duty on service before an enemy, to work as to fight without any additional pay. No man has any right to any additional allowance of any kind on account of this service, but the Lieutenant-General, following the practice established in Minorca, where General Sir Charles Stuart directed that all those men who were not marked down idle or disorderly should receive as an indemnification for the wear and tear of necessaries, sixpence per day (the day to be reckoned eight working hours), will order that the proper department should pay the men employed on the works at that rate, upon the certificate of the commanding officer of engineers."

May 22.   In the month of May a question appears to have arisen between Brigadier-General Dilkes and the principal medical officer of Cadiz, as to the right of the latter to inspect the hospital of the brigade of Guards, and the question was referred, through General Graham, to Lord Wellington, who, in his reply of the 11th of June from Colorico, entered fully into the whole subject, recognising that the management of the Guards' Hospitals was upon a different principle, but as he imagined only as far as regards finance.

The British force in Cadiz had been raised in July to 8,500 men, but in October, Lord Wellington, hard pressed, sent for some of the regiments, reducing thereby the garrison to 5000 ; before the close of the year, however, it was again reinforced from Gibraltar and Sicily.

October.

The French made great exertions to complete their attack ; 130 gun-boats having escaped out of the Guadalquivir, were, by Soult's orders, transported overland on rollers from Santa Maria to the Trocadero Canal, and huge mortars, which threw shells 5000 yards, were placed in position, but only an occasional shell fell into the city, creating much alarm but doing little mischief. One of these mortars now stands as a trophy upon the parade at the

Horse Guards. The great object of the French marshal 1810. was to overpower the fire of Fort Puntales, and establish himself between the Isla and the city, but as long as the allies held the great redoubt of Cortadura, General Graham considered the communication could not be interrupted.

Such was the state of affairs at Cadiz at the close of 1810, in the defence of which the six companies of the second battalion First Guards, besides three from each of the other regiments, all under General Dilkes, continued to take a share; but important events had been occurring in Portugal, and it is necessary, though the First Guards took no part in them, to keep in view the progress of the campaign in that part of the Peninsula.

SUMMARY OF CAMPAIGN. 1810.

The French had opened the campaign of 1810 in June by the sieges of Ciudad Rodrigo and Almeida, both of which, held by the Spaniards, soon surrendered, and in September, September. Massena, at the head of 60,000 French, advanced into Portugal, whereupon Wellington retired and took up a strong position on the heights of the Sierra de Busaco. The French marshal attempted to force it on the 27th of September, but was vigorously repulsed and driven down the mountain.* After this defeat, however, Massena succeeded in turning the British left, and Wellington continued his retrograde movement towards Lisbon. On the 10th Oct. 10. of October the British general entered the entrenchments of the far-famed lines of Torres Vedras, previously pre- Torres pared, and which evinced so much foresight on his part. Vedras. 55,000 British and Portuguese troops were here assembled; in vain did Massena examine every feature in the line of defence, seeking for a weak point; for five weeks the baffled marshal remained powerless to attack either in front or flank; the country had been so much desolated that his supplies began to fail; the wet season, and with it, sickness, had set

---

* Captain the Marquis of Tweeddale, then in the First Guards, was Depty.-Assist. Q.M.G., and was present in the battle of Busaco, Sept. 27, 1810.

1810.   in ; and, at last, Massena being forced to turn his back on

Nov. 14.   those impregnable lines, moved his army into winter quarters in the vicinity of Santarem.

1811.

1811.   The apathy of the Spanish authorities with regard to the siege of Cadiz was still conspicuous at the commencement of the following year; and while General Graham praised the exertions of the British engineers and soldiers, he complained that the Spaniards endeavoured to prevent the execution of some of the most essential measures of defence.

January.   In the month of January the allied commanders determined to attempt to force the enemy to raise the siege, for which purpose their united forces were to embark, and land at Tarifa, whence they were to fall upon the rear of the French camp at Chiclana ; while a Spanish force in the Isla should throw a bridge over the San Petri and threaten the French lines in front. The allied force destined for this operation amounted to 14,000 men, of whom 4300 were British.* The brigade of Guards, under Major-General Dilkes, 1221 strong, with a detachment of the 95th Regiment, having embarked at Cadiz, landed at Algesiras and marched to

Feb. 28.   Tarifa on the 28th of February, but unfortunately General Graham waived his right to command on this occasion, and allowed that duty to be assumed by Don Manuel de la Peña.

March 3.   The army advanced on the 2nd and 3rd of March by Casas Viegas and Vegas de la Frontera, and about noon on the

---

* The British force was thus constituted :

Brigade of Guards, 6 comps. First Regt., 3 comps. 2nd, 3 comps. 3rd, Brig.-Gen. Dilkes	1221
1st Bat. 28th, 2nd Bat. 67th, 2nd Bat. 87th, and 2 companies Portuguese, under Colonel Wheatley	1764
Detachments of 3rd Bat. 95th, and 47th (2 cos.), Lt.-Col. Ch. Barnard	594
2 comps. 2nd Bat. of 9th, 2 comps. 1st Bat. 28th, 2 comps. 2nd Bat. 82nd, Lieut.-Col. Brown's Battalion of Infantry. . .	475
Besides engineers, 47, 1 compy. of Roy. Staff corps, 33 . .	80
Hussars	150

Total   4314

Artillery, 10 guns.

5th of March reached the heights of Barrosa, four miles   1811.
from the sea mouth of the San Petri.

The ridge of Barrosa stretches about a mile and a half
from the coast, being bounded on the left by the cliffs, on
the right by the Forest of Chiclana, and in front by a pine
wood, beyond which rises a narrow height called Bermeya,
which could be reached by moving through the wood or by
the beach under the cliffs. Though the troops had marched
all night, a distance of twenty miles, La Peña sent the
Spanish vanguard to the mouth of the San Petri, where it
effected a junction with the troops on the Isla, and General
Graham was directed to follow that body. This was contrary to his advice, as he wished to hold the ridge, foreseeing that the enemy would come out to fight; he however
obeyed, and with Dilkes's brigade of Guards and Wheatley's
brigade, marched off left in front over the heights, leaving
the flank companies of the 9th and 82nd Regiments,
under Major Brown, with the baggage, on the hill; but no
sooner had Graham entered the wood than La Peña led
off his Spaniards by the sea-road to San Petri, leaving the
Barrosa ridge unprotected and covered with baggage.

The French in the meantime were intently watching Battle of
these movements from the Forest of Chiclana, and Marshal Barrosa.
Victor observing the detached manœuvres of the allies, Mar. 5.
suddenly advanced into the plain with 9000 well-trained
soldiers and fourteen pieces of artillery. A Spanish peasant
informed General Graham that the enemy were coming
round the wood, and were in the plain they had just quitted.
The brigade of Guards, under Dilkes, was at once faced-
about, when the second battalion First Guards being then
in front, formed line to the right, the men filing into line
under a galling fire as they came out of the wood; the three
companies of the Third Guards, under Barnard, were formed
in support in second line, while Wheatley's brigade, with whom
were the three companies of the Coldstreams, under Colonel
Jackson, who were told off to cover Duncan's guns, formed
on the left. When General Graham debouched into the
plain, he found the key of the position already in pos-

session of the French, and the Spanish rear-guard flying towards the sea, La Peña nowhere visible. The situation was desperate, and the small handful of British soldiers, not half the number of their opponents, completely isolated. Graham, making up his mind at once to assume the offensive, rode forward, and, waving his hat, said, " Now, my lads, there they are, spare your powder, but give them steel enough." Covered by the fire of Duncan's guns, the little army advanced against the foe. Dilkes, with the Guards and part of the 67th Regiment, forming the right wing of the British, marched rapidly against the French general Ruffin's column, bringing up his right shoulders on the march, while Wheatley's brigade advanced against the right of the French under Laval. The Guards had to cross a deep hollow, under a severe fire, before they could close with the enemy; they came up in loose skirmishing order, but "in fighting mood," and, without stopping to reform, rushed up the hill, on the crest of which their gallant opponents met them, and for some time a severe and doubtful conflict raged. Ruffin fell mortally wounded; Sebright, commanding the 2nd battalion First Guards, was carried off the field wounded, when Colonel Sambrooke Anson assumed the command of that battalion. Brigadier Dilkes had his horse killed under him, but the British Guards and their comrades bore resolutely on with an "incessant slaughtering fire," driving the enemy before them. Wheatley's brigade on the left was equally successful, a determined charge of three companies of the Coldstreams and 87th Regiment overthrew Laval's first line, driving the French 8th Regiment, whose eagle was captured, upon their second line, whereupon the broken columns of the French commenced retiring from the field. They made one more attempt to turn, but Duncan's guns forced them to continue their retreat, and the British troops, who had been twenty-four hours without food, were unable from exhaustion to pursue them further.

During the whole day no Spanish soldier fired a shot or drew a sabre to assist their outnumbered allies. Short and fierce had been the conflict which was fought not many miles from the memorable Cape Trafalgar; it lasted but one hour and a half, and in that time 1243 British and near 3000 French were either killed or wounded.

The casualties in the 2nd Battalion First Regiment of Guards were two Ensigns, two Sergeants, thirty-one Rank and File killed. One Lieutenant-Colonel, three Captains, four Ensigns, eight Sergeants, 169 Rank and File wounded; total, 216 casualties. The Officers killed were Ensign Commerell and Ensign Eyre, acting aide-de-camp to Colonel Wheatley; of the eight wounded, six were severely so, viz., Lieutenant-Colonel Sebright commanding, Captains Stables and Colquitt very severely, and Ensigns Sir H. Lambert, Cameron, and Vigors: the two slightly wounded were Captain Adair and Ensign Field. The detachment of 2nd Battalion Coldstreams had three Ensigns and fifty-three Rank and File killed or wounded; 2nd Battalion Third Guards, three Officers, ninety-nine Rank and File killed or wounded.

The following are extracts of reports of the action by Brigadier-General Dilkes, commanding the Guards brigade, and by Lieutenant-Colonel Hon. Sambrooke Anson, First Guards, who succeeded Sebright in command of the 2nd Battalion 1st Regiment.

Extract from the report of Brigadier-General Dilkes:—"About two hours after the reserve had been ordered to halt in close column on the east side of the heights of Barrosa, on the morning of the 5th of March, I received Lieut.-General Graham's orders to proceed, together with Colonel Wheatley's brigade, towards Santi Petri,—this was done, and the column began its march left in front over the height, and descending the other side entered a fir wood, so thick as to be nearly impracticable for the guns and mounted officers. Having advanced about a mile, N. Reade, a staff-officer, overtook me, seeking General Graham, informing me that the enemy had made his appearance on the heath or plain we had quitted; the deployment was soon after effected under all disadvantages (the detachment battalion forming a second line to the 2nd battalion of First Guards). At this time an application being made for a party to cover the guns, I sent three companies of the first-mentioned battalion for that service. The line was advanced obliquely to the right, towards a body of the

1811.
March 5.

enemy already occupying the heights we had lately passed over, a heavy fire of artillery and musketry being kept up on both sides; but our line continuing to advance, I may say with distinguished gallantry, that part of the enemy's force immediately opposed to us withdrew towards another corps on his right. Our army still advanced, bringing up their right shoulder, and threatening his left, so that at last he formed that flank *en masse*, continuing his retreat down the hill, and ascending another rising ground, halting occasionally and keeping up a severely destructive fire. When fronted at one time, I perceived him push forward two or three divisions from the *masse*, as I conceived, to charge our line, whose well-directed fire still advancing, obliged him to desist. Unfortunately, our men were so completely exhausted by their march, &c. &c., as to be quite unable to return the compliment." *

Extract from the report of the Hon. Sambrooke Anson, First Guards:— "Almost immediately after this, I assumed the command of the battalion, Lieut.-Colonel Sebright being wounded, and it continued to advance in the same manner to prevent its being outflanked by the French infantry, which was extended considerably, apparently with that view, as well as being threatened by a body of their cavalry, which might also have charged its flank, but which did not avail itself of the opportunity. I conclude they must have been kept in check by a part of the detachment battalion of Guards, and I believe the 67th Regiment, who had hitherto formed a second line, in endeavouring to get into the general one to the right, for at this time they came up and joined in the determined advance against the enemy's left; in this order the line proceeded to the brow of the hill, when the retreat of the French became general." †

Lieutenant-General Graham remained for some time on the heights he had so desperately won, hoping that La Pena, with his 12,000 men, would pursue the enemy, who were retiring in confusion; but it was in vain, and, disgusted with the conduct of his ally, the gallant General at last returned with his wearied troops to the Isla. The victory had reflected lustre on the British arms, but the blood had been shed in a profitless contest.

There was much correspondence on the subject of the absence of the Spaniards during the whole action, and their not even coming forward to complete the defeat of the enemy;

* Supp. Disp. Duke of Well., vol. vii. p. 126.
† Supp. Disp. Duke of Well., vol. vii. p. 130.

but the subject does not come within the scope of this work.   1811.
Had the Spaniards acted up to their promises, and to the March 5.
plan originally laid down by the commanders, the enemy
might have been forced to raise the siege, and all the •
advantages have been gained that had been anticipated; all
the more honour, however, to the British for defeating
the enemy single-handed.

The despatches written home on the occasion do full General
justice to the indomitable perseverance of the British Graham's
Guards. General Graham, after describing the attack of despatch.
General Wheatley's Brigade, adds :—" Meanwhile the right
wing was not less successful. The enemy, confident of success, met General Dilkes on the ascent of the hill, and the
contest was sanguinary, but the undaunted perseverance of
the Brigade of Guards, of Lieutenant-Colonel Brown's Battalion, and of Lieutenant-Colonel Norcott's and Major
Anderson's detachments, overcame every obstacle, and
General Ruffin's division was driven from the heights in
confusion, leaving two pieces of cannon. No expression of
mine could do justice to the conduct of the troops throughout. Nothing less than the almost unparalleled exertions
of every officer, the invincible bravery of every soldier, and
the most determined devotion to the honour of his Majesty's
arms in all, could have achieved the brilliant success
against such a formidable enemy so posted. . . Where
all have so distinguished themselves it is scarcely possible to discriminate any as most deserving of praise.
Your Lordship will, however, observe how gloriously the
Brigade of Guards under Brigadier-General Dilkes, with
the Commanders of the Battalions, Lieutenant-Colonel
the Hon. C. Onslow and Lieutenant-Colonel Sebright
(wounded), as well as the three separate companies under
Lieutenant-Colonel Jackson, maintained the high character
of his Majesty's household troops."

The Duke of York thus expressed himself in answer to a Mar. 29.
letter received from Brigadier-General Dilkes :—

" I take the earliest opportunity in my power of acknowledging the receipt of your letter of the 9th of March, and

of thanking you for your obliging attention in communicating to me thus early what relates to the distinguished
conduct of my gallant old friends the Guards under your
command in the glorious and severely-contested action of
the 5th. While congratulating you and them on the successful result of an action in which their efforts were so
conspicuous, and so deserving of the admiration with which
all have viewed them, I cannot conceal my deep feeling of
regret that it has been attended with so severe and painful
a loss of officers and men, which upon this occasion
perhaps makes a deeper impression upon me, as many of
the latter were old soldiers and faithful companions, whose
meritorious exertions I have myself witnessed, and had
occasion to approve upon former services.

"I have read with great satisfaction in Lieutenant-
General Graham's despatch the high and well-earned
encomiums bestowed upon your conduct, and that of the
officers and men engaged under your command; and as a
brother Guardsman, a title of which I must ever be proud,
and colonel of the corps, I trust I shall not be considered
as exceeding the limits of my station in requesting that
you will yourself receive and convey to the brigade under
your orders my sincere and cordial .hanks for having so
gloriously maintained, and indeed, if possible, raised, the
high character of a corps on whose welfare and success,
collectively and individually, I shall never cease to take the
warmest interest."

The Duke of York also desired Lieutenant-General
Sir Harry Burrard, the Lieutenant-Colonel of the First
Guards, then commanding the Guards in London, to convey
to the brigade, the sense H.R.H. entertained of the conduct
of the Guards on the above occasion, which was done in the
following words :—

" BRIGADE ORDERS.   *30th March,* 1811.

" Lieutenant-General Sir Harry Burrard has received the
commands of the Duke of York to convey to the brigade of

Guards his Royal Highness's entire approbation of the conduct of the Brigade at Cadiz, in the action under Lieutenant-General Graham, on the heights of Barrosa. The Duke has already written to Brigadier-General Dilkes and to Colonel Wheatley on the gratifying subject, that the officers and men who so gallantly fought, and nobly conquered, on that day may be made acquainted with the admiration, which the recent proof of their undaunted courage and steady discipline has excited in the mind of his Royal Highness, whereby all the efforts of the French, notwithstanding their great superiority in numbers, were repulsed and defeated.

1811.

March 5.

" The lieutenant-general is highly gratified in being thus honoured with the commands of H.R.H., and, in common with his brother soldiers and all good Englishmen, he feels an honest exultation on this glorious occasion; on which he has only further to observe that the same steady discipline and cheerful obedience which crowned the exertions of officers and men on the 5th of March must, on all future occasions, reward that valour of· which his · Majesty's Guards have ever given such distinguished proofs."

The illness of the King having become much aggravated towards the end of the year 1810, an Act of Parliament was passed on the 5th of February, 1811, declaring H.R.H. the Prince of Wales Regent of the kingdom ; and one of the earliest acts of the Prince Regent was to desire Lord Liverpool, the Secretary of State for Foreign Affairs, to convey to General Graham H.R.H.'s sense of the conduct of the Army on the late occasion, which he did in the following terms :—

May 26.

" Downing Street, 30th *March*, 1811.

" The Prince Regent has likewise felt the highest gratification in observing the unanimous spirit with which the Officers and soldiers under your command and in execution of your orders, and the steady discipline and unconquerable valour which at length accomplished a decided victory over an enemy nearly double their numbers, and of long experience and high reputation in war . . . and his Royal Highness has commanded me to desire you will accept upon your part, and would convey to the Officers and soldiers serving under your orders upon the 5th of March, H.R.H.'s thanks for the brilliant exploits performed on that day, exploits which have never been surpassed in the military annals of Great Britain."

Sir David Dundas, the Commander-in-Chief at home, expressed himself as follows to Lieutenant-General Graham:

" His Royal Highness has observed with very peculiar gratification, the combined display of discipline and bravery which appears to have eminently marked the conduct of his Majesty's troops in this distinguished action, and in which, under your able guidance, they have most deservedly earned the gratitude and admiration of the country."

Lieutenant-General Graham, in communicating the above letters and orders to the troops under his command, stated, " that he need not assure them that the performance of this duty is most gratifying to him. If, as he felt at the time, he could not do justice to the incomparable behaviour of the troops, he has now at least the satisfaction of knowing that the faithful recital of the facts has excited in the hearts of their countrymen the sentiments of admiration and gratitude they so well deserve, a noble reward for a soldier."

This record of the appreciation of the conduct of the troops engaged cannot be more fitly terminated than by adding, that Lord Wellington declared in strong terms " his admiration of the principle of the attack, and of the distinguished bravery which won the battle." The Houses of Lords and Commons passed a vote of thanks to the army, and the city of London voted swords to Generals Graham and Dilkes.

The Second Battalion First Guards shared in conjunction

with their comrades the above encomiums of the Prince
Regent and of Sir David Dundas, but it was more peculiarly
honoured by the opinions expressed above of its merits by
the Duke of York as their Colonel, who was himself a good
judge of those qualities in the field which are deserving of
favourable mention.

Shortly after the Army returned to the Isla, Colonel
Wheatley rejoined the Second Battalion First Guards, and
assumed the command, but owing to the severe losses sustained by that corps in the late action, it was ordered home;
and the Third Battalion of the Regiment, commanded by
Colonel G. Cooke, now completely recruited from the severe
losses it sustained in the Corunna campaign, and in the mias-
matic marshes of South Beveland, received orders in March
to embark for Cadiz, and relieve their comrades. Six companies of the Third Battalion accordingly marched from
London for Portsmouth on the 2nd of April, and disembarking at Cadiz on the 27th, occupied the St. Helena barracks. April
Two days afterwards General Graham inspected them on
the Glacis, when certain men of the Second Battalion, who
were selected to remain at Cadiz, were incorporated with the
Third. On the embarcation for England of the remainder
of the Second Battalion, which was delayed till the 4th of May 4.
May, Brigadier-General Dilkes issued the following Brigade
Order, dated April 29th :—

" Brigadier-General Dilkes cannot suffer the Brigade to
be thus broken up, without requesting the Officers and men
will accept his assurance of the high sense he entertains of
their general conduct, and of the cheerfulness and alacrity
with which they have discharged their duties upon all occasions, and of the consequent gratification he has derived
from a command at all times honourable, but since the 5th
of March he has felt still more elated with it. He now with
pleasure repeats his admiration of the gallantry exhibited
by them on that day. Fortunate are those who participated
in the glory of it, himself doubly so.

" To those who continue under his command, the Brigadier-General expresses his satisfaction at still retaining

1811. them; to those who are now separated from him he offers his assurance of heartfelt good wishes for their happiness and success, wherever the fortune of war may conduct them."

Lieutenant-General Graham also issued the following order on the 3rd of May, the day before the departure of the Second Battalion for England :—

G. O.   " CADIZ, *May 3rd*, 1811.

May 3.   " The Brigade of Guards under the command of Briga. dier-General Dilkes having been ordered home, and to embark according to General Orders of yesterday, it will readily be imagined, that however desirous the Lieutenant-General is that this Brigade should enjoy repose, and should have an opportunity of recruiting the severe losses it has sustained, he cannot part with it without sincere regret at the loss of so valuable a corps.

" It is doing no more than strict justice to declare in this public manner, that he considers the conduct of this Brigade as most exemplary during all the time he has had the honour of their command; while their behaviour in the field was such as to secure to them the admiration and applause of their country.

" Their exertions on the 5th of March, in the opinion of the Lieutenant-General, can never be overrated. It is not less creditable to them as good soldiers, that he has it in his power to make an agreeable report of their conduct in quarters. He requests that the Brigadier-General, the Officers, Non-Commissioned Officers, and soldiers of the brigade will accept his best thanks, and be assured of his best wishes on every occasion."

The attention of his Royal Highness the Prince Regent was, at an early period of the Regency, called to the Colours and badges borne by the three Regiments of Foot Guards; March 11. and on the 11th of March of this year, his Royal Highness, in the name of the Sovereign, was pleased to confirm, by Royal Warrant, the original grants made, in 1661, by Charles II. to his original two Royal Regiments of Foot Guards, under Lord Wentworth and Colonel Russell, and

same time, Major-General Dilkes returned home, and was
appointed to the command of the Third Brigade of Guards
in the home district (London),* but, as will be seen, he was
not long left to repose. During the summer of 1811,
Lieut.-General Graham, who had infused energy into the
defence of Cadiz, and saved it from the enemy's grasp, was
removed to the command of a Division in the field under
Wellington, and was at first succeeded by Major-General
Disney, First Guards; but this officer returned home in
November, and the command at Cadiz eventually devolved
upon Major-General George Cooke, First Guards.

The Spaniards themselves made no efforts, and laid all
their losses to the fault of the British Government and its
Generals, but the mutual dissatisfaction that had existed for
some time, did not break out till after the battle of Barrosa.
The duties of the Third Battalion at Cadiz underwent very
little variation in the course of the year. The construction
of a redoubt was entrusted to them, for which purpose
they found eighty men daily, while a detachment of seventy-
five men, relieved weekly, was stationed at Cantera. The
monotony of the Siege was occasionally relieved by a bombardment from the French lines, but no attempt was made
to storm the entrenchments. The only event of importance
was the gallant defence of Tarifa in December, under Colonel
J. B. Skerrett; Colonel Lord Proby, First Guards, being
second in command. The successful result of this defence
was mainly owing to the persevering skill of General
Sir Charles Smith, of the Royal Engineers, which eventually caused the French under Marshal Victor to raise the
siege of that town, on the 4th of January, 1812. In the

23rd June, 1811.

* His Royal Highness the Prince Regent has been pleased to appoint
Major-Gen. Dilkes to serve upon the Staff of the Home District, and will
command the brigade of Guards.

The Duke of Cambridge is pleased to approve of commandants of Battalions
continuing to take part of the duty of Field Officers in brigade waiting as
directed in orders of the 5th of Feb. 1811.

When the Prince Regent shall give commands which shall require immediate execution, the acting F. O. in waiting will issue the necessary orders,
reporting the same to the Commanding Officer of the brigade.

1811.   same month, an expedition under the command of Colonel J. Lambert, of the First Guards, was sent to Carthagena, and upon that officer being relieved in the following April, he returned to Cadiz.

OPERATIONS IN THE PENINSULA, 1811–12.

March.   Nothing decisive occurred beyond the Portuguese frontier in the year 1811. Soult had captured Badajos from the Spaniards on the 10th of March, and Massena was driven out of Portugal in the same month, but, upon hearing that Lord Wellington had gone to the south, he advanced again to relieve Almeida,· then besieged by the British. Wellington, however, suddenly returned and met him with inferior forces at Fuentes d'Onoro, when a stern conflict ensued, but the British succeeded in maintaining the village, and two days later the French retired.

In the meantime, Marshal Beresford having invested Badajos on the 8th of May, Soult advanced to its relief, and Beresford encountered him on the 15th of that month on the ridge of Albuera, when the bloodiest contest of the war took place. As usual, the Spaniards failed in offering the requisite assistance, and the whole force of the enemy fell upon the British. The French were, however, defeated with great slaughter, but of 7500 British soldiers 4300 were also struck down. Soult now united his army to that of Marmont, who had superseded Massena, and their superior forces compelled the British to raise the siege of Badajos. The French marshals, however, soon separated again, and during the remainder of the year, Wellington, by a series of brilliant manœuvres, maintained himself on the frontiers of Portugal; Soult returned to Seville, and General Hill, after surprising Gerard at Arroyo del Molinos, was left undisturbed in Estremadura.

1812.   The Siege of Cadiz continued during all the first months of the year 1812, but nothing of importance occurred there till the month of August; it will therefore be useful to continue the *précis* of Lord Wellington's operations up

to that period, which had such a paralysing effect upon the   1812.
French armies of the south.

Lord Wellington suddenly invested Ciudad Rodrigo in
the month of January, and after twelve days' open trenches
it was taken by storm.*   He subsequently moved south to   Jan. 14.
Badajos, which fell after a siege of twenty-one days, the
British suffering terrible losses in the breach.   Having
now two large fortresses to secure his communications,
Wellington crossed the Agueda and advanced against
Marmònt, who retired to Salamanca.   After several days
spent in manœuvring, the hostile armies encountered each
other on the 22nd of July.   The eagle-eye of the British   Battle of
chief detected Marmont in a false manœuvre in extending   Salamanca.
his left and weakening his centre, of which he took advan-   July 22.
tage and suddenly fell upon him, gaining, though not without a severe contest, one of the most decisive victories on
record.   The French fled in confusion, and two eagles, six
colours, sixteen guns, and 7000 prisoners·were the trophies   .
of the day.   The enemy retreated in the direction of Burgos,
and Wellington moved on Madrid, entering the capital on
the 12th of August, where the war-worn veterans obtained a
brief season of repose before moving to the attack of
Burgos, and orders were at once sent to General Hill, in
Estremadura, and General Cooke, in Cadiz, to act on the   September.
offensive.   ·

War had at length broken out between the Emperor of
Russia and Napoleon, and, on the 24th of June, the French
crossed the Niemen: the battle of Smolensko, fiercely   Smolensko.
contested, was fought on the 16th of August, and though   Aug. 16.
the Russians for a time maintained their ground, they
subsequently continued their retreat towards Moscow.
The sanguinary battle of Borodino took place on the   Borodino.
7th of September, in which 80,000 men were killed or   Sept. 7.
wounded, and both sides held their ground, but the Russians

---

* Captain Hon. James Stanhope, of the First Guards, who, as aide-de-camp
to Lieutenant-General Graham, was present at the siege of Ciudad Rodrigo,
was wounded on the 14th of January.

eventually retreated through Moscow, and, on the 16th of September, Napoleon slept in the palace of the Kremlin, occupying a city which his enemies had made into a funeral pile.

SIEGE OF CADIZ.

Siege of Cadiz.

While Wellington was advancing with giant strides into the heart of Spain, driving the enemy before him in the north, the resolute defence of Cadiz gave strength to the Spanish cause in the south, keeping the French armies in Andalusia on the alert, and preventing reinforcements being sent to the usurping king at Madrid.   On the 16th of May 16.   May, 1812, the town was subjected to a serious bombardment from thirty gun-boats that Soult had collected in the Trocadero canal.   This bombardment against the town and shipping was repeated on the 4th of July, but the French July 4.   marshal's attention was soon taken off the siege by the landing of troops from English vessels on the coast of Grenada.   No alteration however took place in the respective positions of the besieged and besiegers until the month of August, when, the bombardment becoming serious, opposition to British influence within the walls increased, but the time for deliverance was approaching; the victory of Salamanca in July, and the subsequent occupation of Madrid by the British army, depressed the spirits of the French, and rendered it necessary for King Joseph, if he wished to save his kingdom, to concentrate his armies of the North and South.   For this purpose, Joseph, after retreating into Valencia, sent Soult positive directions to come with all his forces to the assistance of the army of the centre, for the recovery of Madrid; and about the same time Wellington sent orders, as above referred to, to General Cooke to make a direct attack upon the French lines round Cadiz.

Aug. 9.   Previous to these last orders being received, Colonel Skerrett, the brave and gallant defender of Tarifa, had, under former instructions, been ordered to embark at Cadiz with 4000 troops, and land on the coast to the north,

and marching thence on Seville, to force the French to 1812.
withdraw from before the town. Six companies of the Aug. 9.
Third Battalion First Guards, under Colonel Peregrine
Maitland, who was appointed second in command, formed
part of this expedition. The detachment of Guards accordingly marched on the morning of the 9th of
August from their old quarters on .the Isla de Leon to
Cadiz and embarked the same day. On the following
morning the expedition sailed for Huebro, on the coast,
seventy miles to the north-west, arriving there in the
middle of the night of the 11th. .During the day the
troops were put into boats, and after thirty-six hours spent
in them, the Guards were landed at Huebro on the night of
the 13th, the rest of the army and stores being landed on
the 14th and 15th. On the 16th the troops began their
march up the country towards Seville, threatening the communications of the French round Cadiz, and, after halting
that night at Trigeras, moved, on the following day, to
Niebla, expecting to find the enemy, but the place was
deserted ; whereupon Skerrett continued his march on the
18th and 19th through Palma and Villa Abber to Man-
zanilla, where the troops rested on the 24th. From this
place a detachment of the Guards and of other corps was
despatched at 11 at night, which attacked the enemy at
St. Lucar la Major, near Seville, driving in their outposts
without any loss to themselves.

Soult now found himself obliged to abandon the siege of
Cadiz, and on the 25th of August, after destroying the
immense works at Chiclana and the Trocadero, as well as
1000 guns, and stores in proportion, he retired in all haste
from before the town, taking the route to Seville, when, after
a blockade by land of upwards of two years and a half,
the defenders, amongst whom were still four companies of
the Third Battalion First Guards, gained the glorious reward
of their constancy and perseverance. Napier describes the
defence of Cadiz as a curious episode in the war, and after
speculating upon the question whether the Spaniards would
have defended it without British assistance, remarks that,

1812.   notwithstanding the glorious battle of Barrosa, Cadiz was
always a heavy burden on Lord Wellington, and that the
forces there employed would have done more service under
his immediate command.

Aug. 26.   Skerrett's corps, including the six companies of the Third
Battalion First Guards, under Maitland, preceded by the
light company of the Guards, under Colonel Colquitt, with
some Hussars, having marched all the night of the 25th
from San Lucar, reached the heights to the north of Seville
on the following morning.   They fell in with the advanced
posts of the enemy about three miles from Seville, drove
them in, and about seven in the morning moved to the attack
of the place.   Seville is situated on the south bank of the
Guadalquivir, and the allies approached it from the north,
through the suburbs of Triana.   The Spaniards were
directed to turn these suburbs on the right flank, while the
Attack on   British and Portuguese attacked in front.   The British
Seville.   column advanced for more than two miles at the double-
quick, and were just in time to drive the French from the
bridge with the bayonet, as they were trying to cut it.   As
soon as the Spanish column had reached its destined point,
the British cavalry and artillery advanced at a gallop, followed by the Grenadiers of the Guards, the rest of the
infantry bringing up the rear.   The enemy abandoned the
gate, and the allies followed rapidly to prevent the destruction
of the bridge; for a moment they were checked by a heavy fire;
but the Grenadiers of the Guards advanced, and drove everything before them, while the flanking columns made the
enemy's position on the other side of the river untenable.
The bridge was injured, but not to such an extent as
to prevent the Grenadiers of the British Guards, and some
Spanish troops, who led the column, from passing it.   The
enemy's forces, which consisted of eight battalions and two
regiments of cavalry, retired with precipitation on the road
to Cordova, leaving behind them 200 prisoners, their baggage, and their treasure.   Colonel Skerrett thus expressed
himself in his despatch on the conduct of the troops
engaged on this occasion:—

" The conduct of every officer and soldier has been above 1812. praise. Where all have behaved well it is difficult to dis- Aug. 26. tinguish. I must, however, mention the detachment of the King's German Legion, commanded by Cornet Wiebolt; the artillery, by Captain Roberts ; the detachment of the 95th, by Captain Cadoux, and the grenadiers of the First Regiment of Guards, by Captain Thomas. To Colonel Maitland, First Guards (second in command), I am much indebted, from the commencement of this service ; and in the attack of Seville his military talents, intrepidity, and zeal were particularly conspicuous. I am also much indebted to Lieutenant-Colonel Colquitt, commanding a detachment of the First Regiment of Guards."

The remaining four companies of the Third Battalion Sept. 1. First Guards, under Colonel Lambert, left the Isla on the March of 3rd Batta- 1st of September by the more direct route for Seville, and lion. on their arrival at Xeres, a few miles from Cadiz, the inhabitants received them with acclamations. They halted here till the 6th, waiting for the Infantry Brigade under Lord Proby. On the 7th, after a march of twenty-seven miles over a flat country, under a burning sun, they arrived at Utrera, within a day's march of Seville, where, on the 11th, they were joined by the six companies of the Battalion that had entered Seville on the 26th of the previous month.

These six companies, after halting four days in Seville, had marched two leagues to Alcala, where they remained till the 7th of September, when they moved for two days to Mayrena, returning on the 9th to Alcala, and on the 11th, after a march of three leagues, they joined their other four companies at Utrera. While the Third Battalion First Guards remained in this town, the 95th Regiment and part of the artillery were stationed at Alcala, and the cavalry, the 47th and 87th British, and 20th Portuguese Regiments, and a brigade of guns remained at Head Quarters in Seville. Colonel Colquitt, who had been severely wounded at Barrosa, died of fever while the battalion was at Utrera, greatly lamented by his brother officers. After a week's halt in this

1812.

Oct. 17.

Arrival of 3rd Battalion at Talavera.

town, the Battalion received orders to join Wellington's army in the north of Spain; it moved accordingly to Seville on the 19th, and after again halting some days, Skerrett's brigade commenced its march on the 30th for Truxillo, passing Los Santos, Villafranca, Guarema, and Medellin, where is a fine old castle and a magnificent bridge over the Guadiana, which had escaped the ravages of war. On the 11th of October they halted at Mayados, and next day at Truxillo, arriving at Talavera by Almarez on the 18th. The march had been long and the weather hot; but the troops were cheered by the splendid scenery through which they passed, and were elated by the successes attending the British arms. A detail of this march is appended in a note.*

In the meantime Wellington, with very inadequate means, had invested Burgos, on the 19th of September. Several breaches were made by explosions, and five assaults took place at different times; but no permanent lodgment could be made.

It will not be out of place here to record the high

---

* Sept. 19, To Seville, five leagues, joined the division. German recruits to remain in Cadiz, where Gen. Cooke is to remain in command.

20—29, Remain at Seville till the .

30, March to Guillena, three leagues, bivouac.

Oct. 1, To Ronquilla, four leagues, bivouac.

2, To Santa Olalla, four leagues, bivouac.

3, To Monasterio, four leagues; on this march entered Estremadura.

4, Sunday, to Fuente de Cantos, three leagues.

5, To Los Santos, four leagues; had marched to this day 223 miles.

6, Halt.

7, To Villa Franca, two leagues.

8, To Zarsa, five leagues, pass the Muschat river.

9, To Guarema, two leagues.

10, To Medellin.

11, Cross the Guadiana, march to Mayados, four leagues.

12, To Truxillo, six leagues.

13, Halt (total, 316 miles).

14, To Taraicijo, four leagues.

15, To Naval Moral, six leagues, crossing Tagus by pontoons at Almarez.

16, To Cabyada, four leagues.

17, To Orapeza, two leagues.

18, To Talavera de la Reyna.

19, Halt (404 miles).

character that the First Battalions of the Coldstream and   1812. Third Guards were gaining for themselves at this siege. Frequent complaints appear to have been made to the Commander-in-Chief of the manner in which the working parties performed, or rather did not perform, their duties in the trenches, so much so that Lord Wellington on the 1st and Oct. 1. 3rd of October issued stringent orders on the subject; but the seventh paragraph of the latter order was to this effect: "At the same time that the Commander of the Forces notices this misconduct of the working parties, he is happy to make an exception in favour of the Guards, who, he is informed, have invariably performed this duty, as they have every other in this army, in the most exemplary manner. 8. The officers and soldiers of the army should know that to work during a siege is as much part of their duty as it is to engage the enemy in the field;" and at a later period he added:

"It is impossible for me to represent in adequate terms my sense of the conduct of the Guards and German Legion on this occasion. If it had been possible to maintain the posts which they had gained with so much gallantry, those troops would have maintained them."

The Commander-in-Chief, in a subsequent despatch, expressed himself as follows: "I had every reason to be satisfied with the conduct of the officers and men during the siege of Burgos, particularly with the Brigade of Guards."

At last, after thirty-eight days' siege, and a brilliant defence on the part of the enemy, the combined movements of the reorganised French armies compelled the British General to raise the siege. King Joseph and Soult, who had united their forces, were now marching with 56,000 men on Madrid, from the side of Murcia, in the south-east, while Souham was within a few miles of Burgos, at the head of a considerable force.

The retreat from Burgos had commenced on the 22nd of October; on the 24th the army halted behind the confluence Oct. 24. of the Carrion and Pisuerga rivers, and while in this posi-

1812.
Arrival of 1st Battalion to join Wellington's army.
Sept. 13.
Sept. 26.

tion, the First Battalion First Guards, under the command of Colonel M. C. Darby Griffith, joined it from England. This Battalion had returned home after the Walcheren campaign, in 1809, and in the early part of September of this year was ordered to hold itself in readiness again for foreign service. It was inspected by the Duke of York in Hyde Park on the 7th of September, when it marched to Portsmouth, and on the 13th embarked on board the " Alfred " man-of-war, for Corunna, where it disembarked on the 26th of the same month.

The following were the officers present with the First Battalion, September, 1812 :—

Colonel M. C. DARBY GRIFFITH, Commanding.

CAPTS. & LIEUT.-COLS.	LIEUTS. & CAPTS.	ENSIGNS.
Lieut.-Col. Hon. A. Upton.	Capt. R. Clitherow.	J. L. Duckenfield.
H. Askew.	J. Hanbury.	Ed. Poole.
Hon. W. Stuart.	H. Packe.	Ed. Penruddocke.
Hon. G. Macdonald.	J. Lautour.	Newton Chambers.
E. Sebright.	S. Lambert, Adjt.	H. B. Trelawny.
H. Wheatley.	G. Ramsden.	L. Boldero.
T. P. Tinling.	R. Marsac.	P. Clarke.
R. T. Bingham.	H. Joddrell.	Hon. A. De Roos.
	H. Stables.	W. Burrard.
Qr.-Mast. Hodder.	A. Higginson.	A. Viscount Bury.
Surgeon Nixon.	J. Davies, 3rd B.	Hon. W. Dawson.
Assist.-Surg. Bacot.	T. Brooke.	Edward Clive.
„ „ Armstrong.	T. Grant.	Adjutant,—
	B. Charlewood.	Samuel Lambert.

Colonel Dalzell, of the First Battalion, was Assistant-Adjutant-General of the Home District ; Captains the Earl of Tyreonell, Stanhope, and Allix ; and Ensigns Milnes, Vernon, and Sir Henry Wheatley, of the same Battalion, were A.D.C.'s to several General Officers. (Extracted from Monthly Returns.)[1]

It had been the original intention of the Duke of York that the Third Battalion, then at Cadiz, should proceed by sea to Lisbon, with the rest of the troops from that town, and be there brigaded with the First Battalion, to be sent thither from England, and Lord Wellington had issued directions for carrying out this proposal, but the subsequent orders to the Third Battalion to proceed from Cadiz by route, and join the army in the field, and other exigen-

cies of the service, would not permit this arrangement   1812.
to be carried out, and on Lord Wellington subsequently
writing to Lord Bathurst, desiring that the First Battalion
should be sent to Corunna, its destination was eventually Sept. 10.
altered to that town. The 91st Regiment, 950 strong, was
to be temporarily brigaded with it, and placed under
Lord Dalhousie, while a draft of 250 men for the several
Battalions of Guards already in the Peninsula was to accompany the expedition. Lord Bathurst wrote to Lord Wellington on the 10th of September, as follows : " The Duke Letter of
of York is much disappointed at the First and Third Earl
Battalions of First Guards not meeting at Lisbon to be Bathurst
brigaded there. It was a favourite object of his, and made of Welling-
him consent so readily to the sending the First Battalion. ton.
If you can bring them together conveniently, pray do." Sept. 10.

With the view to carrying out this plan, Lord Wellington
wrote to Lieutenant-Colonel Bourke, on the 21st of Sep- Sept. 21.
tember, as follows :—

" Sir,—I wish the First Battalion First Foot Guards to Villa Toro,
move through Gallicia, as already arranged ; but, instead of near
turning off from the high road at Villa Franca, as directed Burgos.
when the enemy was in possession of Astorga, and it was supposed they would maintain that position, I wish them now to
proceed to Astorga on to Benavente. Mr. White must make
provision for them till they will arrive at Benavente. At
Benavente, or before they will arrive there, a Staff Officer
of this army shall meet them, and they will receive further
orders for their march.

" The messenger who takes this has a letter from the
Quartermaster-General, for the commanding officer of the
First Battalion First Foot Guards, of which I enclose a
duplicate, in case there is any mistake about that with
which he is charged.

" We took by storm on the 19th the outwork of the
Castle of Burgos, with some loss.

" I have, &c.,

" WELLINGTON."

And on the 29th of September Lord Wellington, in reply to Lord Bathurst, wrote : " I beg you will mention to the Duke of York that I will take care to bring the two Battalions of the First Regiment of Guards together."

Further correspondence took place at this time between Lord Wellington and the Duke of York, with reference to the future command of the Division of Guards, when the two Brigades should be brought together.

The First Battalion First Guards having landed at Corunna, commenced its march by wings on the 30th of September, traversing historic ground well known to many still in the ranks, recalling melancholy yet proud recollections. They halted at Lugo on the 5th and 6th of October, and were at Astorga on the 16th. The marks of destruction were everywhere visible as they advanced. At Astorga they found the castle destroyed and a great portion of the town levelled with the ground; the noble cathedral much damaged; the chapter-house in ruins. On the 19th they reached Benavente, in a flat country, half' deserted, where they found the convent they had occupied in 1808 destroyed, and the castle burned. As the Battalion marched along it was received with special marks of joy. At Ampadia, on the 23rd of October, seven men, dressed fantastically in jackets and silk brocade, and their hair adorned with ribbons, met them with rustic music, dancing before them, while the governor, alcades, and priests came out to do them honour. On the morning of the 24th the Battalion was on the march for Palencia, when the Commanding Officer received intelligence that Lord Wellington was retreating from before Burgos, and that the enemy were close upon them. He accordingly turned off to the right, and following the line of the canal, arrived at Duenas, where he joined the main body of the British army, and marching thence through the British and Spanish lines, the Battalion bivouacked, with the rest of the Division of Guards, on the right of the allies.

No sooner had the First Battalion joined the main army, than it came in contact with the French, for on the next

morning the First Division, of which it formed a part,   1812.
marched to the left to support the Fifth, then engaged
with the enemy, who were attempting to cross the Pisuerga
river. On the following day, the 26th, the retreat was
continued, in a southerly direction, towards Valladolid, the
First Division halting at Cabeson. On reaching Valladolid,
on the 29th, it was reported that the French had crossed at Oct. 29.
Tordesillas, upon which the First Division was ordered to
that place.

Wellington had intended awaiting the arrival of Hill's
corps, in a strong position, between Tordesillas and Rueda;
but on the 6th of November the army fell back again to Nov. 6.
San Christoval, seven miles north of Salamanca, the First
Division moving to Villares de la Reyna, three miles nearer
that town.

While these events were in progress, Skerrett's little
army, with the Third Battalion First Guards, moved from
Talavera de la Reyna on the 19th of October, and marching Oct. 19.
due east by Toledo, reached Puente Largo on the 26th,
where it fell in with Hill's corps, which, since the battle
of Salamanca, had been occupied in opposing the return
of King Joseph and Soult to Madrid, and while here the
Third Battalion First Guards was removed from Skerrett's
command, and attached to the Fourth Division, under Cole,
forming part of Hill's corps.

In consequence of the raising of the siege of Burgos,
Hill was now, by order of Wellington, making preparations
for a retreat from the advanced position he had occupied, and
the outposts of the Fourth Division (which was selected as
his rear guard) were, on the 27th of October, engaged with
Soult's advance on the Jarama. Hill resolved, in order
to protect his retrograde movement towards Wellington's
army, to blow up the bridge across the Tagus at Puente
Largo, and the Third Battalion First Guards was employed
in covering this operation, and in keeping the enemy in
check; the engineering work proceeded slowly, for want
of mining tools, and on the 29th the Battalion, on being Oct. 29.
relieved in this duty by Skerrett's brigade, consisting of

1812.   the 47th and 87th Regiments, marched to Clempo Suelos, south of Madrid. On the 30th the enemy attacked in force, and the attempt to blow up the bridge having failed, the French tried to carry it at the point of the bayonet, but were vigorously repulsed by the 47th Regiment. The Third Battalion First Guards, though present in support on this occasion, was not engaged. During the next twelve hours, owing to a sudden fall of four feet in the river, the fords became practicable, and the British position consequently untenable ; the Division therefore continued its retreat, marching all night towards Madrid, and halted

Nov. 1.   outside the town. On the 1st of November General Hill destroyed his stores and blew up the Retiro, and on the same day, the Third Battalion First Guards, still forming part of Cole's rear guard, marched through Madrid, and

Nov. 2.   halted on the 2nd at Alvara, the enemy entering Màdrid as soon as it was evacuated. On the 4th the Battalion, marching by the Escurial, crossed the Guadarama mountains, and proceeding thence through the province of Old

Nov. 8.   Castille, and across the Tormes river on the 8th, reached the heights of San Christoval, in the vicinity of Salamanca, on the 9th, which position Wellington himself had reached

Nov. 11.   the day before. On the 11th, the Third Battalion proceeded to a cantonment at Aldea Seco, about a league from Salamanca, having marched 640 miles from Seville, and here the First and Third Battalions First Guards again met, and were brigaded together under the command of Major-General Howard, Lord Wellington having thus, in the midst of his more serious duties, carried out the expressed wishes of the Duke of York. In a note is appended a detail of this march of the Third Battalion from Talavera to Salamanca.*

The Third Battalion received well-earned compliments, both on leaving Skerrett's brigade in October, and Cole's

* Oct. 20, To Cebella, four leagues, crossing the Albucherche river.
21, To Torrigos.

22, To Toledo, four leagues, crossed the Guadarama, running into the Tagus, two leagues from Toledo.

Division on the present occasion, in the orders issued by those Officers, and which were expressed in the following terms, of which the Regiment may well feel proud :—

DIVISIONAL ORDERS, COLONEL SKERRETT IN COMMAND.

" PUENTE DEL LARGO, 26th *October*, 1812.

" Colonel Skerrett cannot take leave of the Guards without requesting the officers and soldiers will accept his acknowledgments for their perfect discipline and highly soldierlike conduct while he has had them under his command."

Oct. 23, Halt.

24, Villa Seca, three leagues.

25, Sunday, to Añoru, one league.

26, To the park at Aranjuez, four leagues. Owing to alarm, Lord Hill ordered bridge to be destroyed.

27, Halt.

28, The enemy occupy the town and gardens of the palace on the opposite side of Tagus.

29, Retired at one in the morning over Jarama river, and take post in the Madrid road in rear of the Puente Largo, which the English were preparing to destroy; in evening march to Pozalos.

30, The French attack Puente Largo, the mines of which failed, and French were repulsed with loss by the 47th Regiment. Saltoun joined head-quarters as orderly officer, and retired to Aravaca, six leagues.

31, Head-quarters retire to Escurial, six leagues.

Nov. 1, Sunday, halt. Palace at Escurial much destroyed.

2, Head-quarters retire to Espinau, five leagues.

3, To Larajos, four leagues.

4, To Villa Nueva de Gomes, three leagues. Skirmishing between our rear and the French advance.

5, S. joined the battalion, and retired to Fonte Viros, four leagues.

6, Retire one and a half league to Panaranda.

7, Alba de Tormes, five leagues, take post.

8, Crossed the Tormes, and take post near site of battle of Salamanca, two leagues from Alba de Tormes.

9, March to Salamanca, three leagues. Guards quartered in a convent. First time under cover, except at Cien Pozuelos, since we left Añoru. (636 miles.) Here joined Lord Wellington's army, which had retired here from Burgos.

10, Halt.

1812.

" Fourth Division Orders, 9*th* Nov. 1812.

" Lieutenant-General Cole requests Colonel Lambert will express his sincere thanks to the Battalion of Guards under his command for their exemplary conduct during the short time they have been attached to the Fourth Division. When straggling and every species of irregularity was committed by the troops, they alone remained uncontaminated, and he trusts that their example may recall the Fourth Division to its former good conduct."

The Brigade of First Guards, and the Second Brigade, consisting of the First Battalions of the Coldstream and Third Regiments, were at once formed into a Division.

Major-General H. F. Campbell, of the First Guards, who had formerly commanded the second Brigade, had been promoted to a Division, and Colonel Hon. T. Fermor,* of the Third Regiment, was now placed in temporary command of it till Major-General Hon. Ed. Stopford,† also of the Third Guards, should come out. Major-General G. Cooke, of the First Guards, had been ordered to remain for a time at Cadiz ; Major-General William Wheatley, who had commanded a portion of the Guards so gallantly at the battle of Barrosa, died at the Escurial on the 1st of September; and Major-General Richard Hulse, of the Coldstream Guards, also died a week later, on the 7th, at Arevalo; and the command of the First Brigade of Guards, viz., of the First and Third Battalions First Guards, was in consequence now bestowed, as above recorded, on Major-General K. A. Howard, of the Coldstreams.

The united British army now mustered 64,000 men and seventy pieces of artillery; the three French corps 95,000 men with 120 guns. Notwithstanding this disparity, Wellington offered battle, and on the night of the

Nov. 13.   13th to 14th of November, the Brigade of the First Guards, and the rest of the First Division, under Sir Edward Paget, took up a position on the far-famed Arapiles, near Aldea Tejada, to secure the passage over the Zurgain. Soult, how-

---

* The late Lord Pomfret.   † Second son of the Earl of Courtown.

ever, refused, and made a demonstration against the allied 1812.
right, passing three Divisions over the Tormes, and
threatening their communications, upon which Wellington,
after destroying his stores, retired to Valmuya. On the 17th
the First Division halted at San Munos, on the Huebra, Nov. 17.
where the active pursuit of the French ceased from want of
the necessary supplies. On the 18th it marched by very
bad roads to San Spiritus; on the 19th to Ciudad Rodrigo;
and on the 20th, the First Guards, passing through that
town, crossed the Agueda; when the First Battalion was
cantoned at Carpes, and the Third Battalion, after a very
fatiguing march, arrived at Gallegos, near the Portuguese
frontier.

This retreat from Salamanca had been very severe,
and the army generally was much in want of rest. The
weather had entirely broken, the rain fell in torrents, a
thick mist prevailed; the ground was so saturated with
rain that the troops could hardly move; the roads were a
mass of mud; sometimes the troops were under arms without rations, at others they had to cook the meat in embers,
and eat boiled acorns as a substitute for bread. The result of
these hardships was considerable relaxation of discipline: and
much irregularity, straggling, plunder, marauding, and the
usual concomitants of a retreat ensued. The British General
issued a severe order censuring the troops, and attributing
their conduct to the inattention of the officers. No exceptions were made in this order, but it is satisfactory to know
and to record, that however just this order may have been
generally, yet Lord Wellington himself owned subsequently
that neither the Division of Guards nor the Light Division
merited the condemnation. Napier, the historian, writes:
" Nevertheless, Wellington's circular was not strictly just,
because he excepted none from blame, though, in conversation, he admitted it did not apply to the Light Division nor
to the Guards." And in comparing Moore's retreat with
that from Burgos, Napier says, " the justice of the re-
proaches was proved by the exceptions. The reserve and
Foot Guards in Moore's campaign, the Light Division and

1812.　Foot Guards in Wellington's, gave signal proof that it was negligence of discipline, not hardships, that caused the losses in the other regiments."

The Third Battalion First Guards had had the advantage of being long in the field, and was in a magnificent state of discipline. Since leaving Cadiz, on the 20th of August, the men had been constantly on the march, a distance of 650 miles. They had shown proofs of discipline in the Isla, they had exhibited their prowess in the field, and their steadiness under fire at Barrosa and in the attack on Seville, and they had received the thanks of their generals for their discipline on the march. After remaining for eight days at Gallegos, in the vicinity of Ciudad Rodrigo, the army continued its retreat towards Portugal, and the Nov. 28.　First Brigade of Guards, marching on the 28th to San Pedro and Val de la Mula, and passing the site of the battle of Fuentes d'Onor, crossed the frontier. On Sunday, the 29th, the Third Battalion was quartered at Medo, and the First Battalion, after crossing the river Coa, reached Castello del Mendo ; the two advanced thence, by short and easy marches, by Lamegal, Alverea, Francesco, Aguiar de Beira, through Asamel, Villa Formosa, and Tugal ; and on the Dec. 8.　8th of December marched into cantonments, the First Battalion in Viseu, the Third Battalion in Mordao, Spraida de Rondio, and adjacent villages. Viseu is built on uneven ground, with narrow and crooked streets, the vicinity being very beautiful, bounded on the north-west by the Sierra de Mula, and on the south-east by that of Estrella. Here the brigades, after their sufferings and hardships, were enabled to enjoy for a time relaxation and repose from their labours. An itinerary of the march of the Third Battalion First Guards from the neighbourhood of Salamanca to Viseu, is here inserted.*

---

* Nov. 11, March at 3 P.M. to cantonments at Aldea Seca, one league, and join the Guards' Division. First Battalion

First Guards and Second Brigade of Guards cantoned at Villares, about one mile to our right.

The campaign in Russia was at this time drawing to its 1812.
terrible close. Napoleon, was still at Moscow, in the early
part of October, trying to induce the Emperor Alexander to
open negotiations, but no answer was given to his proposals, and the only notice taken, was an order to the
Russians to fall upon the French with all their forces,
as soon as they should begin to retire. Napoleon left the
Kremlin on the 20th of October with 100,000 men and Oct. 20.
600 guns; a fierce and bloody battle was fought at Milo
Jaroslovitz, in which the French remained masters of a
ruined town, but, being still threatened on both flanks,
were forced to continue their retreat. On the 9th of

Nov. 12, Halt.

13, Halt. Sick sent to Ciudad Rodrigo.

14, March in afternoon to Salamanca, one league. March
at ten at night, one league,
and took the right of the
position.

15, Sunday, retired two leagues,
and bivouac.

16, Retire two leagues, and
bivouac.

17, Retire three leagues. A
cannonade and sharp skir-
mishing at a ford. The Light
Division lost several men
and four or five officers. Bivouac.

18, Retire six leagues. Very bad
roads; in many places sheets
of water. Bivouac near St.
Spiritus.

19, Retire three leagues on the
Agueda, at Ciudad Rodrigo.
Bivouac half way between
Ciudad and Gallegos.

20, Gallegos.

21, 22, Sunday.

23, Halted till 27th.

28, Marched to San Pedro, Val de
la Mula, two leagues. Passed

site of battle of Fuentes
d'Onor, and entered Portugal. Immediate striking difference in language and
manners of the people.

29, Sunday. To Medo. First
Battalion to Castello del
Mundo, two leagues. Crossed
the Coa river at Castello,
bivouac.

30, Lamegal, three leagues.

Dec. 1, To Cirijos, three leagues.
First Battalion to Alveira.

2, Halted.

3, To Francesco, three leagues.

4, To Aguiar de Beira, three
leagues.

5, To Asamel and Tugal, two
leagues.

6, Sunday, to Mondaô and ad-
jacents, two leagues.

7, Halt.

8, Went into cantonments, the
First Battalion in Viseu, the
Third Battalion in Mondaô,
Spraida de Rondio, and ad-
jacents; had at this place
marched from Huelva, 800
miles, computing the Spanish
league at four English miles.

1812.   November winter set in with its usual severity, the snow
fell, the winds howled through the forests, the men had
no shelter, and but little food.   The Emperor was at
Smolensko on the 9th of November, and with the Old
Guard quitted it on the 14th, arriving the next day at
Krasnoi.   Ney brought up the rear, over ground strewn
with the dead and dying and every species of munition of
Nov. 27.   war, and joined Napoleon on the 20th.   On the 27th he
crossed the Beresina, the passage of which, by many of
the corps, was attended with such terrible results.   The
Emperor left the remains of his army at Smorgoni on the
5th, and, travelling night and day, arrived in Paris on the
Dec. 19.   19th of December.   Ney had entered Kovno on the 13th
alone, himself the last of the rear-guard, and the Grand
Army ceased to exist.

CHAPTER XXIV.

PENINSULAR WAR—CAMPAIGN OF 1813.

1812—A LOW FEVER BREAKS OUT IN THE ARMY WHILE IN CANTONMENT.
1813—FIRST BRIGADE SENT TO OPORTO—CAMPAIGN OF 1813—BATTLE OF
VITTORIA—SIEGE AND CAPTURE OF ST. SEBASTIAN—PASSAGE OF THE
BIDASSOA—BATTLE OF THE NIVELLE—ADVANCE TOWARDS BAYONNE—
BATTLE OF THE NIVE—BRITISH ARMY ESTABLISHED IN FRANCE—PASSAGE
OF THE ADOUR. 1814—INVESTMENT OF BAYONNE—ABDICATION OF
NAPOLEON—SORTIE FROM BAYONNE REPULSED—PEACE OF PARIS—RETURN
OF THE BOURBONS—FIRST AND THIRD BATTALIONS OF FIRST GUARDS
RETURN TO ENGLAND—MARCH OF THE ALLIES TOWARDS THE RHINE—AN
EXPEDITION OF 8,000 MEN SENT TO HOLLAND UNDER SIR THOMAS GRAHAM
—A BRIGADE OF GUARDS WITH IT, INCLUDING PART OF SECOND BATTALION
FIRST GUARDS—CAMPAIGN IN HOLLAND—STORMING OF BERGEN-OP-
ZOOM—ADVANCE OF ALLIES INTO FRANCE—ENTRY OF GUARDS INTO
ANTWERP—SUSPENSION OF ARMS—CONVENTION OF PARIS.

THE First Infantry Division of the British Army now 1812. consisted of the First Brigade of Guards, under Major-General Howard, Captain Millar, brigade major; of the Second Brigade of Guards, under Major-General Hon. E. Stopford; and of two other Brigades, consisting of the first, second, and fifth Battalions of King's German Legion, under Major-General Lowe, and first and second King's Light German Legion, under Colonel Halket, the whole under Lieutenant-General Hon. Sir William Stewart, who was not a Guards officer. Captain Carey le Marchant, of the First Guards, was appointed Aide-de-Camp to the Lieutenant-General.

The First Brigade of Guards had not been long in their winter quarters, enjoying a well-earned relaxation after their long marches from Corunna and Cadiz, before the reaction from hard work to ease produced sickness, and a low fever broke out amongst the men. From the following return of the state of the two battalions on the 25th November,

1812. within a few days of their arrival at Carpes and Gallegos, it appears they had nearly 700 sick out of 2541 men present with their corps ; they had but 176 effective men to supply the deficiency attached to the 2nd Battalion in England.

Corps.		Effect.	Sick.	Total.	Want-ing to com-plete.	Esta-blish-ment.	Means of reinforce-ing the regiment.	R. & F. for im-mediate service.
1st Ft. Gds.	{ 1st Bat.	996	377	1373	247	1620 }	2nd Batt.	176
	{ 3rd Bat.	849	319	1168	182	1350 }		
		1845	696	2541				

1813. The proportion of 696 sick to 1845 effectives appears a very serious one, being about 1 in 3½, but it was small compared to the sickness of the army generally, in which there were 18,000 sick to 31,000 effective, or about two to three, while one regiment had above 700 sick and 500 effective.

The Light Companies of the First Guards presented a very great contrast in health to the rest of the army. The light company of the Third Battalion, quartered since the

Jan. 12. 12th of January, in advance at Spraida, covering the rest of the army, had retained its health throughout, and at the beginning of February had only eight men on the sick list. As sickness, however, was still very prevalent through-out the winter, and was only partially alleviated by the return of fine weather, the several Battalions of Guards were, on the 18th of February, removed to the neighbour-ing villages, but neither change of air nor the approach of spring checked the progress of disease, and at last Wel-lington ordered them to Oporto, about sixty miles distant, in the hopes that change of scene and sea air might restore them to health.

March. Previous to their moving, however, a question of Guards' privileges arose, with reference to the right of General Officers not of the Guards, commanding Divisions to which Brigades of Guards were attached, to inspect the accounts of the Battalions composing those Brigades. Major-General Howard, who was commanding the First Brigade, viz., the two

Battalions of the First Guards, and the commanding officers of those Battalions appear to have made no objection to showing their accounts when requested to do so at a recent inspection by Lieutenant-General William Stewart. Lieutenant-Colonel Alex. Woodford and Lieutenant-Colonel Guise, commanding the Coldstreams and third regiments, both of the Second Brigade, appear to have demurred to such a proceeding as contrary to custom. After some correspondence between General Stewart and Lord Wellington, the latter gave his opinion on the subject in a letter of the 17th of February, to the effect that if Major-General Howard and the officers of the First Regiment of Guards had submitted the books of the first regiment to his inspection, he thought there could be no doubt upon the subject, and that, upon communication with the commanding officers of the second brigade of Guards, they would consider the matter in the same light. The matter was, April 7. however, by his desire referred to the Duke of York at home, who, on the 7th April, after laying down as a principle that such lieutenant-general had an undoubted right, *if he shall see occasion*, was of opinion that unless he had reason to suppose the existence of some improper proceedings, it would be unadvisable to exercise that right, as the accounts of the Guards being on a different principle, an examination of them by an officer who had not experience in the details of the system, could lead to no beneficial results.

The brigade broke up from its cantonments on the 26th Mar. 26. and 27th of March, and on arrival at Oporto, on the 1st of April, occupied the St. Ovadio Barracks, a grand pile of buildings with a large open space around it. The sick moved on the 7th of that month by Lamego and Rego on the Douro, and thence down its left bank to Oporto. The salutary effects of the change were soon apparent, and the numbers in hospital rapidly decreased, but the effective state of the first brigade of Guards, now under Major-General Howard, of the Coldstreams, was still very low, the First Battalion having only 355 men, and the Third 430 men, fit for duty.

At the end of May, Major-General Howard, the Brigadier, May. was promoted to the command of the first Division, thereby

1813.   avoiding the difficulty above referred to, and Major-General John Lambert succeeded him in the command of the First Brigade of Guards; Major-General Disney, third major, continued in command of the Home District.

The main body of the army took the field towards the end of May. At that time the First Brigade of Guards were beginning to recover from the fatal sickness, and the men began again to look like soldiers; but since the month of December the deaths had been averaging four or five per day. With these severe losses it was decided to leave the brigade at Oporto some time longer; and it was not till a month later that, on the 24th of June, they received orders to take the field and join the main army. By the month of July, as shown by the following return, the First Guards had actually buried, since the beginning of the year, 800 out of 2500 men.

June 24.

RETURN OF RANK AND FILE OF FIRST REGIMENT OF GUARDS THAT DIED OF FEVER IN PORTUGAL FROM JANUARY TO JULY, 1813.

	1st Batt.	3rd Batt.	Tot.
To 25th January	43	22	65
,, 25th February	142	45	187
,, 25th March	No return; included in April.		
,, 25th April	169	99	268
,, 25th May	121	69	190
,, 25th June	58	16	74
,, 25th July	15	2	17
			801

During the time the two Battalions of the First Guards had been stationed in Oporto, they had obtained the good-will of the inhabitants, and supported the credit of the regiment by their discipline and conduct; and when the governor of the city, Sir A. Trant, learnt that the route had arrived directing them to join the left wing of the allied army under Sir Thomas Graham, he issued the following memorandum bearing testimony to the merits of the regiment :—

Memorandum issued in Garrison Orders by Brigadier-General Trant, Governor-General of the Province and City of Oporto.

"*June,* 1813.

" Major-General Lambert, commanding First Brigade of " Guards of His British Majesty, having communicated to

1813.

" the Governor the order which he hâs received for the
" march of the said brigade to join the army in the field,
" the Governor cannot let pass this opportunity without con-
" veying to the Major-General, through the medium of this
" garrison memorandum, the sense which the inhabitants of
" Oporto unanimously entertain of the conduct of the
" Brigade during the three months it has been stationed in
" this city. Not one instance has occurred in that interval
" which may be alleged as complaint in the slightest
" degree against any individual of the Brigade, nor can any
" more convincing proof be offered of the strict discipline
" observed in the Battalions which compose it than the
" fact that not one non-commissioned officer or soldier
" has been apprehended at any time by the day or
" night guards of the garrison in a disorderly state of
" intoxication.

. " The governor hǒlds forth this exemplary conduct to the
" troops under his immediate command at Oporto and its
" district, and being desirous also of having (it) recorded
" as a testimony of the harmony which does, and he trusts
" ever will, continue between the troops and inhabitants
" of this kingdom and their faithful British allies, he ·
" directs that this memorandum shall be inserted in the
" order books of the several corps stationed in the Partido,
" requesting at the same time that Major-General Lambert,
" as his senior officer, will excuse the liberty he has taken
" in his quality of governor of this city in communicating
" through so public a channel the sentiments and opinions
" which both his duty and his inclination have prompted
" him to express in the terms above-mentioned.

" Signed,   " W. MILLER, Brigade Major,
" First Brigade of Guards."

Major-General Disney issued the following Regimental
Order to the First Guards in England :—

" Major-General Disney has great pleasure in commu-
" nicating the (above) memorandum issued by Sir A. Trant

1813.   " on the First Brigade of Guards receiving their orders to
" march from Oporto, as an additional testimony of the
" good conduct for which the Guards have always been, and
" he trusts ever will be, distinguished.   Courage is the
" attribute of every British soldier, and in this they may
" be equalled but not excelled by any regiment in His
" Majesty's service.   It is for their regular and orderly
" conduct that the Second Brigade of Guards have been so
" frequently and deservedly held up by Lord Wellington as
" a pattern to the rest of the army, and for which, indeed,
" the First Brigade has already rendered themselves con-
" spicuous in their march from Corunna and Cadiz, and
": General Disney feels convinced that they have only to be
" as well known to his lordship as their brother soldiers of
" the Second Brigade to be as highly praised."

Before describing the march of the First Guards through
the north of Spain in the summer of 1813, it is necessary
to advert briefly to the progress of the allied army under
Lord Wellington, before whom the French were at this time
retiring in confusion to the frontiers of France.

May.   The British general had determined in May to operate
upon the French right, by marching through Tras os
Montes in the north of Portugal.   For this purpose a corps
of five divisions, 40,000 men, under Lieutenant-General
Sir Thomas Graham, forming the left wing of the army,
May 22   crossed the Douro and reached Braganza on the 22nd of
that month.   Lord Wellington then advanced with his own
corps of 30,000 on Alba and Salamanca; thence he turned
northward towards Zanura, and the two armies united at
Carcagales on the 30th and 31st.   The Spanish troops
under General Freyre, having also effected a junction, the
allied army in the field on the right bank of the Douro
amounted to 90,000 men and 100 guns, and on the 4th
of June Wellington commenced his ever-successful march
towards the frontiers of France.

June 4.   King Joseph was at Valladolid with 52,000 men and 100
guns, but the strategical position of the British general
enabled him, by continually pushing forward his left, to

compel the French to abandon without serious resistance   1813.
every position in succession. Wellington was at the Carrion on the 7th, and on the 12th of June in sight of Burgos. June 12.
The enemy blew up the castle and retired, anxious to place
the defile of Parnorbo between himself and the allies, but
Sir Thomas Graham acting on the left, and marching by a
route hitherto regarded as impracticable, crossed the Ebro
at Frias on the 15th, and getting into the rear of the French June 15.
right, cut them off from the coast. Wellington was thus
enabled to establish for himself a new base of operations
on the sea, and the British fleet entered Santander.
It was at this time that orders were sent to Oporto for the
first brigade of Guards to move up to the front. Sir
Thomas Graham still pushed on, driving back Reille's
corps of 8,000 men at Osma to Anana, and òn the evening
of the 20th he halted at Marguia. By a series of clever June 20.
strategical movements Wellington gained the decisive Battle of
battle of Vittoria on the 21st of June, when a total rout of $\frac{\text{Vittoria.}}{\text{June 21.}}$
the French army ensued, 151 guns were captured on the
field, and stores of every description fell into the hands of
the conquerors. The French general, Foy, conducted the
retreat, vigorously pursued by Graham; and after throwing
a garrison into San Sebastian, crossed the Bidassoa into
France. Graham invested San Sebastian on the 9th of July,
and on the 24th made an attempt to storm it : the assault, First
however, was repulsed with heavy loss to the assailants.   assault
    Soult had recently arrived from Germany to take com- Sebastian,
mand of the French army, and having reorganised his $\frac{\text{on San}}{\text{July 24.}}$
forces, again advanced with the view of turning the British
right, and relieving Pampeluna, upon which Wellington
converted the siege of San Sebastian into a blockade, met
the French, and, after a series of combats which lasted from
the 25th to the 30th of July, carried the position in front of
Sorauren, forcing the enemy to a disastrous retreat, and on
the 2nd of August the French were driven across the Aug. 2.
frontier, thus abandoning the Spanish Peninsula.
    The siege of San Sebastian was at once renewed, but
the fire was not opened   l the 26th August, before which

1813.   time the First Brigade of Guards, whose march from Oporto will now be recorded, arrived on the scene of action, and on the 18th of August marched into camp, joining the First Division.*

Leaving Lieutenant-Colonel Tinling at Oporto in charge of the sick, the regiment, under the brigade-command of Major-General Lambert, commenced its march from Oporto on the 29th of June, proceeding by Amarante, Villa Real, Mirandella, Braganza, and Palencia, where it arrived on

July 23.   the 23rd of July, the men all in very good health, and marching as well as they ever did, not a single man left behind. From Palencia, instead of following the direct road to Burgos, it took a northerly course, through Saldana to Reynosa and by Medina to Osona. At this place were found many traces of the retreat of the French, and after marching over the battle-field of the 21st of June, the regiment passed through Vittoria. On the 10th of August it

Aug. 11.   halted at Zobrano, and on the 11th passed by the Puerto de Francia, where was packed all the artillery captured in the battle and during the subsequent retreat, amounting to 210

Aug. 18.   guns. On the 18th of the same month, as above stated, the First Guards marched into camp at Oyarzun, two miles from Irun, and joined their comrades of the Second Brigade, in the left wing of the allied army under Sir Thomas

---

* March of first brigade to join the army from Oporto towards Irun :—

1813.				1813.			
June 30.	Villa Longa.	.	2 leagues.	July 11.	Izada	. .	3 leagues.
July 1.	Penafiel	. . 4	,,	,, 12.	Halt.		
,, 2.	Amarante	. 4	,,	,, 13.	Vimiosos	. . 3	,,
	Cross River Tamega.			,, 14.	Alcanizes .	. 4	,,
,, 3.	Campeao	. . 3	,,	,, 15.	Corvejales	. 4	,,
,, 4.	Villa Real	. 2	,,	,, 16.	Andavias	. 2	,,
,, 5.	Halt.				Cross the Esla.		
,, 6.	Parado de Pinho	3	,,	,, 17.	Cozeses	. . 3	,,
,, 7.	Murca	. . 2	,,	,, 18.	Toro	. 3	,,
,, 8.	Lamas	. . 3	,,	,, 19.	Halt.		
,, 9.	Mirandella	. 2	,,	,, 20.	Tudra .	. . 3	,,
	Cross the Tua.				—		
,, 10.	Masada de Ca-					67 leagues,	
	valleros	. . 4	,,			or about 268 miles.	

Graham.   On the 28th of August they advanced still nearer
to Irun, whence they acted as a covering force to the troops
of the fifth division, who were carrying on the siege of
San Sebastian.

The camp was well situated, about one mile from Irun, in
an old wood upon the face of the mountain, whence the
Bidassoa, the French lines, St. Jean de Luz, and Bayonne
in the distance, were visible.   The Second Brigade was
encamped on the left of the First, and further still the
Germans.   The Bidassoa, from low water to half-tide, was
fordable, but the ground in front of the Guards camp was
very strong, and there was not much likelihood of the enemy
attacking that side of the position.   Major-General Lambert having thus brought the First Guards from Oporto to
the French frontiers, resigned his command on being appointed to a brigade in the sixth division.   Colonel Peregrine
Maitland succeeded to the First Guards Brigade, and
Lieutenant-Colonel Hon. W. Stuart to the Third Battalion.

The left wing of the allied army, under Sir Thomas
Graham, was now composed of the First Division under Major-
General Howard ; the Fifth Division under Major-General
Sir James Leith; Lord Aylmer's brigade ; and a Spanish
army under Don Manuel Freyre.   The fifth division, consisting of Major-Generals Hay's and Robinson's brigades,
was employed in carrying on the operations of the siege of
San Sebastian ; the first division formed the covering force
and guarded the line of the Bidassoa from the Crown
mountain to the left, while Freyre's Spanish corps was
posted to the right, on the heights of San Marcial.

The order of battle of the first division was thus constituted.   The First Guards on the right, Hinuber's Germans
on their left, then Stopford's second brigade of Guards, and
the German light infantry on the extreme left.

By the 30th of August the enemy's guns on the ramparts
of San Sebastian were silenced, and the walls apparently
breached in two places ; the assault was, therefore, fixed to
take place on the following morning.   Lord Wellington had
been displeased with some indiscreet opinions expressed by

officers of the fifth division since the failure on the 24th of
July, respecting the practicability of storming the breach, and
thought that the men of that division would be discouraged.
He accordingly ordered 400 men of the first division—viz.,
200 of the division of Guards and 200 of the King's German
Legion—and 350 of the fourth and light divisions " to
show the way to the breach if it should be practicable."
The storming party of the Guards, consisting of 100 men of
the first and as many of the second brigade, under the
command of Lieutenant-Colonel R. H. Cooke of the First
Guards, marched at 6 P.M. from camp, with the other detachments from the division, and encamped about two miles
from the fortress. They moved off again about two in the

morning of the 31st, and occupied the ruined convent of
St. Bartolomeo, where they remained till half-past nine.

Sir James Leith commanded the assaulting columns, and
would not suffer the volunteers to lead the way, but placed
them in support to Robinson's brigade. The troops were
exposed to a heavy fire in advancing to the breach, the
appearance of which proved to be fallacious, as it could
not be entered except in single file. They attacked in
succession, and with determined gallantry, tried to effect
a lodgement, but were struck down by hundreds. The
Volunteers had demanded " why they had been brought
there if they were not to lead the assault ? " and at last, let
loose, they went like a whirlwind to the breach and swarmed
up the ruins. But at first all in vain; many were struck down
on the crest, and, though repeated attempts were made,
none but the dead or wounded remained on the summit.

At last Graham ordered the artillery to open over the
heads of the assailants, and clear the ramparts. Fortune
now rescued these heroic soldiers from their desperate
position. A shell ignited a quantity of powder and com-
bustibles, which the enemy had prepared to spring in the
event of the ramparts being gained; under cover of the

explosions, the dauntless stormers forced their way on, and
with irresistible power at last entered the town. The
governor retired to the citadel, and, on the 9th of Sep-

tember, after a gallant resistance of more than a week, surrendered the charge he had so faithfully defended.

Major-General Hay, under whose immediate orders the men of the first division fought, expressed in his despatch to Sir Thomas Graham his great satisfaction at the gallant and judicious conduct of Lieutenant-Colonel Cooke, commanding the detachment of Guards.

The losses of the division of Guards on this occasion were :—

		Officers.		Men.			
		Kd.	Wd.	Kd.	Wd.	Missg.	Total.
First Guards { 1st Battn..	.	1		9	11	3	24
{ 3rd Battn.	.		1	10	22	3	36
		1	1	19	33	6	60
Second Guards, 1st Battn.	.		1	3	20	5	29
Third Guards, 1st Battn..	.			1	20	12	33
					Total	. .	122

The casualties among the Officers of the First Guards were one officer, Ensign Burrard, of the first battalion (a son of Sir Harry Burrard), severely wounded (since dead), and one officer, Ensign Orlando Bridgeman, wounded. According to Lord Saltoun there were, in round numbers, 150 casualties amongst the 200 Guardsmen.*

The total losses were 1500 men.

Soult made one more attempt to relieve the fortress on the morning of the assault, by threatening the allied left : but it was easily repulsed. During this attempt the First Division was drawn up in support, in rear of Irun, but was not engaged. The enemy withdrew within their own frontier on the same day.

Before the British army enter France it is necessary to recount the chief events which had taken place in Germany, for the necessities of the French emperor in that country

* Lord Saltoun, who was in the third battalion of Guards, says—"We (the Guards) sent a detachment of 1 lieutenant-colonel, 2 captains, 4 subalterns, and 200 men, fifty of whom returned." 150 volunteers of the light division, and 200 volunteers of the fourth division.

had considerable influence upon the war on the Spanish
frontiers.   After the disastrous retreat of the French from
Russia, Prussia had joined the Russian alliance, and Austria
was secretly preparing to do so likewise.   Napoleon, however, rapidly collected another army of 200,000 men and

**May
2 and 21.**   350 guns, with which, in the month of May, he fought and
gained the battles of Lutzen and Bautzen; but after the
news of the battle of Vittoria reached Vienna, Austria

Aug. 27.   openly espoused the cause of the allies, who, on the 27th of
August, were again defeated with heavy loss at Dresden.
From that time however Napoleon's good fortune seemed to
forsake him.   The allies, 250,000 strong, again opposed

**Battle of
Leipsic.**   him at Leipsic, and after three days' combat, gained a de-

Oct. 18.   cisive victory, which eventually obliged the French Emperor

Nov. 4.   to retire across the Rhine, and the allies subsequently

Dec. 20-31.   entered France at different points.

October.   Wellington remained inactive for a month after the fall of
San Sebastian, waiting for the policy of the Allies in Germany to develop itself, for as they had not then decided
upon the invasion of France, he hesitated to embark in
such an undertaking before he could depend upon a diversion
in his favour on its eastern frontier.   Urged, however, by
the British government to make such a diversion himself
in favour of the continental sovereigns, who were then preparing for the final blow against the French emperor at
Leipsic, he commenced operations early in October, by
forcing the passage of the Bidassoa, and thus treading, for
the first time, the soil of Southern France.

A considerable range of mountains rose opposite the
allied position, separating the valleys of the Bidassoa and
the Nivelle rivers.   Wellington's plan was to seize, with his
right and centre, the highest point of these mountains, La
Rhune, and its dependent ridges, while on his extreme left
he would obtain possession of Fuenterabia.   The French
position to the north of the Bidassoa was already very strong
by nature, and Soult had strengthened it with additional
works.   He anticipated that the allied Anglo-Spanish army
would attack his centre and left, and he was therefore busy

little prepared for the bold movement which Wellington executed of passing the Bidassoa at its mouth at low water, where the tide rises sixteen feet, and the sands are half a mile broad. The services of the First Division of Guards and of the Fifth Division, together with some foreign troops, forming the left wing of the allied army, were brought into requisition to carry out this part of the attack.

The previous instructions for the left wing were, that the two brigades of Guards and Bridagier-General Wilson's Portuguese brigade should pass the Bidassoa, by the ford, at the ruined bridge, and by two fords a little lower down the river, the lower one of which is called the Vado de las Nasas de Abaxo, and is near the point where the chaussée from Irun first comes upon the banks of the river. Some of these battalions were to pass at a ford a short distance above the ruined bridge, and all were to commence their advance upon the fords at the same time that the fifth division from Fuenterabia began to move forward. They were to assemble before break of day, near Irun, be kept concealed as much as possible until the moment of attack, and then move forward simultaneously to the various fords. A rocket from the steeple of Fuenterabia was to be the signal for the advance of the Brigades of Guards, as soon as the Fifth Division was ready to move, for, as the river bends to the right below the bridge of Irun, it was necessary that the division on the extreme left should slightly precede the rest of the attack. Part of the 12th Light Dragoons, with the Brigade of artillery attached to the First Division, and a Brigade of reserve artillery, were to pass over with these columns, while other guns were to cover the passage from the most available heights of San Marcial, Lord Alymer's brigade forming the reserve to the first division, behind the slopes of that mountain. The first object of the Guards after crossing was to establish themselves upon the opposite hill called Montagne de Louis XIV., and on other advantageous points, keeping up a communication on their left, if possible, with the Fifth Division. The troops were all to be in position at seven o'clock in the morning, low water being expected at a quarter past.

It is considered that among the many daring operations of the war, the passage of the Bidassoa may be ranked amongst the boldest, as the confidence of the General in his various combinations for the attack, and in the manner in which he knew they would be carried out by the troops under his command, must have been great indeed, when it is kept in mind that a failure in the execution of them might have carried with it a disastrous defeat, for no sooner were the troops across than the rising tide would prevent their return for several hours.

At three o'clock in the morning of the 7th of October the First Division was under arms, and, leaving its tents standing, passed through Irun, and arrived at the rendezvous at the appointed time, without having been observed by the enemy, in which they were much assisted by a violent thunderstorm, which burst over the French position. Upon the signal being given, the advance of the First Division was made; not a shot had yet been fired; the several fords were approached, and the French were completely taken by surprise. Under cover of a heavy fire of artillery from the heights of San Marcial, the right column of the First Division, viz., Wilson's Portuguese, supported by the two Battalions of First Guards, crossed the river in front of the lower heights of San Marcial, taking the higher right hand fords according to previous orders, and advanced upon the enemy. The left column, or Second Brigade of Guards, preceded by the German light infantry, crossed the river at the ford, near the broken bridge, and formed on the right of the Fifth Division, covering the formation of a pontoon bridge for the passage of artillery. The right column of the Fifth Division, after crossing the river, drove the French from the village of Andaya on the right bank, and continued to advance rapidly on Croix de Bouquet. The French, opposed to the First Brigade, under Maitland, did not await the close approach of the British Guards, but retired, leaving three guns in their

PLAN OF THE PASSAGE OF THE BIDASSOA.

October 7th 1813.

A. Ford of Naxas de Abaxo
B. Café Republicain

FUENTERABIA

Columns of 5th Division

Irun

Andaya

hands; and the left column of the First Division drove the
enemy from the Café Republicain, and from the Louis XIV.
mountain, also upon Croix de Bouquet, which was the key
of the position. After a severe struggle, in which the 9th
regiment met with considerable opposition, the heights were
won, and the enemy, being outflanked by the left column of
the Fifth Division, gave way; the First Brigade of Guards,
continuing its advance, encamped for the night on the
heights they had gained, to the right of the high road
leading to Urrugne.

The Commander-in-Chief, in his despatch relative to this
part of the action, states that he had particular satisfaction
in observing the steadiness and gallantry of all the troops.

It is recorded that during the advance of the Light Infantry of the First Guards, under Lord Saltoun, some
French wounded were passed, lying by the road side. Lord
Saltoun observed one of his men go up to one, and after a
moment, put his bayonet through him. He immediately
rushed at him, enquiring what he was doing to the wounded
Frenchman. " It's no Frenchman, sir," was the reply; " it's
that Evans who deserted the night before the battle of
Corunna." The man was sent to the field hospital, but
died the next day. The accusation was correct, he had
deserted in January, 1809, had taken service with the French
at the commencement of the war, and now, towards its close,
in 1813, met his death from the hands of his former comrades, by whom he would not have been recognised, had he
not, on seeing the uniform of his old regiment, called
out to them for a drink of water. A curious instance of
retributive justice for the crime of desertion.

The fighting had been more severe on the right of the
British line, though the French there were also taken by
surprise. The Light Division and Giron's Spaniards
assaulted the ridge called Bayonette, held by Taupin's
division, and, after a severe contest, carried all before them,
in spite of the height of the mountain and strength of the
works. Freyre's Spaniards had, in the meantime, won the
Mundane Hill, and, by advancing on St. Jean de Luz, by

Joliment, cut off Taupin's line of retreat. The French had succeeded in repelling the attacks made upon the great Rhune Mountain; but Wellington, having made fresh combinations, the French, under Clausel, abandoned its defence on the following day.

The First Guards suffered no loss during these operations the Coldstreams had 2 rank and file killed, and 8 wounded the Third Guards, 9 rank and file wounded, and 2 missing The total losses of the British were—79 killed, 490 wounded

The British army was now in complete possession of the formidable position occupied the day before by the enemy who retired, and took up a new position for the defence of the line of the Nivelle.

The health of Sir Thomas Graham had been failing for some time: and having thus assisted in establishing the allied British and Portuguese forces within French territory, he resigned the command of the left wing the day after the passage of the Bidassoa, and was succeeded by Lieutenant-General Sir John Hope, who had arrived from Ireland the previous day. In consequence of the proximity of the armies, there was much outpost duty for the light infantry companies of the Guards, and the advanced sentries of the opposing armies often stood at night within thirty yards of each other.

So long as the town of Pampeluna remained in the hands of the French, Wellington had hesitated to advance further but after a blockade of four months, that town surrendered

on the 31st of October, and the British General was now in a position to carry the war into the enemy's country.

The French position extended from the seaport of St Jean de Luz, on their right, nearly due east for about twelve miles, to the hills in front of Souraide and Espelette and every available point was strengthened by earthworks The left of the French first line rested on the Nivelle extending to the right of the Choupara and Mandarin mountains, while Claudet's corps occupied the heights of Ascain and Arnots, between which were the camp of Sar and several strong redoubts.

Since the passage of the Bidassoa, Wellington had observed that Soult had been careful to secure his right flank in front of St. Jean de Luz on the Nivelle, by a triple line of works, that rendered it impregnable; he therefore determined to make only a feigned attack, with his left wing, now under Sir John Hope, on that part of the enemy's line, while he forced the enemy's left, and threatened the rear of his right, thus compelling him to withdraw from the strongly-entrenched position in front of St. Jean de Luz.

The previous instructions to Sir John Hope to regulate the attack of the left wing of the army were to the following effect:—He was to operate in three columns. The left column, composed of Halkett's German light infantry, was to act between the heights of Urrugne and the sea coast, fronting northwards towards Socoa Fort; the centre column, or Fifth Division, and some other troops were to occupy the most advantageous points upon the left bank of the rivulet, which runs between the heights of Urrugne and those of Siboure, and when halted were to face towards Siboure and St. Jean de Luz, while the right column, composed of the two Brigades of Guards, were to threaten the front of the encampment, which the enemy occupied, on the right bank of the rivulet of Urrugne, and on the British right of the high road leading from that village to St. Jean de Luz, keeping up at the same time the communication on their right with Freyre's Spaniards, who were to attack Ascain. Sir John was particularly instructed that it was not intended that the operations in that quarter should be pushed forward as a real attack.

The First Division was still under the command of Major-General Howard, while the First Brigade of Guards was commanded by Major-General Maitland.

The weather had now for some time been wet, which delayed the projected attack against the enemy; but, at length, the morning of the 10th of November broke gloriously on a day which was destined to be one of victory to the allies. During the previous night 100,000 men, with nearly 100 guns, were moved into positions, previously arranged, with so much secrecy, that again the enemy was unaware of the vicinity of so many troops awaiting, in silence, the signal for battle.

Nov. 10.
Battle of the Nivelle.
About three o'clock on the morning of the 10th of November, the First and Fifth Divisions descended from the heights on which they had been so long encamped, and advanced to the verge of the line of outposts, where they arrived about an hour before dawn. The French picquets, forming the advanced posts of Reille's and Villatte's divisions, were strongly entrenched, and a large redoubt defended the rising ground in front of Urrugne. At the given signal of three guns being fired from the Alchabia mountain, 100 guns opened upon the French position, and the army advanced to the attack. On the left, Halkett's German light infantry moved round the hill, whilst the picquets of the First Division, under Lieutenant-Colonel West of the First Guards, made a brisk attack in front, driving the enemy from his advanced position down the hill to the verge of his entrenchments. The Brigades to the left of the First Division moved direct upon Urrugne, while Maitland's Brigade of Guards and Hinuber's Germans advanced against the heights behind Urrugne, which extend towards Ascain. A continued fire was kept up by the light infantry of the First Guards and Germans, but they received no orders to storm the works in their front, as Wellington adhered to his original plan. Sir John Hope, however, had now gained the heights commanding Siboure, so that he was in a position to take advantage of any forward movement the right centre of the enemy might make. He kept up this false attack till nightfall, engaging the attention of Reille's and Villatte's Divisions, and thus preventing them from sending succour to the centre of the French army under Clausel.

While the First and Fifth Divisions held their ground on the left, the rest of the army advanced, and drove the enemy from their several positions along the whole front, gallantly overcoming all opposition, and seizing the bridges of Ascain and Arnots over the Nivelle. After some seven

ATTACK
ON THE RIGHT OF THE
FRENCH POSITION
on the
NIVELLE
BY THE LEFT WING OF THE
ALLIED ARMY
Nov! 10ᵗʰ 1813.

The Nivelle

Sᵗ JEAN DE LUZ

Suburbs of Sibourre

Socoa Fort

INTRENCHED CAMP OF THE FRENCH

Urrugne Rivulet

ALKETS GERMAN LIGHT INFANTRY

5ᵀᴴ DIVISION

Urrugne

5ᵀᴴ DIVISION

GUARDS

1ˢᵀ DIVISION

4ᵀᴴ DIVISION

CAMP OF LEFT WING AFTER PASSAGE OF THE BIDASSOA

Scale of British miles

struggles, and a stubborn resistance on the part of the enemy, the latter retired on all sides, abandoning their entrenched camp of St. Jean de Luz. During the action, Soult arrived with a large body of troops at Serres, and threatened the allied centre, but the position of Hope's wing prevented his giving any assistance to Clausel, and Sir John followed the retreating French as soon as he could cross the river. Lord Wellington, in his despatch, after describing the brilliant attack of his centre and right, adds, " Although the most brilliant part of this service did not fall to the lot of Lieutenant-Generals Sir John Hope and Don Manuel Freyre, I had every reason to be satisfied with the mode in which these general officers conducted the service of which they had the direction."

Owing to the duties assigned to the two brigades of Guards, their losses were trifling; but Captain Charles Allix, First Guards, acting brigade-major of the first brigade, was severely wounded, and Captain William Miller resumed his post. The total losses during the day's operations were above 200 killed, and nearly 2300 wounded.

The French now retired to the heights of Bidart on the road to Bayonne, and prepared to defend the passage of the Adour, and on the 11th the British army moved forward. The First Division, after passing over the strongly-fortified position in front of St. Jean de Luz, came in sight of that town about twelve o'clock, and, descending into the valley, and, fording the river above the town, advanced the same afternoon to within eight miles of Bayonne. The First Guards' Brigade at once took post about one and a half mile distant from, and to the right of, the high road. The enemy's right rested at Anglet; their centre on the ridge of Beyres, and their left on the entrenched camp of Bayonne, near the confluence of the Nive and the Adour.

Bayonne is covered to the south by Vauban's old entrenched camp, and here Soult's right, in three divisions, under Reille, was posted, touching the Lower Adour, and supported by a flotilla. A swamp was in his front, and several fortified posts were pushed forward near Anglet, two miles from Bayonne. Clausel's three Divisions extended from the entrenched camp to the Nive, covered partly by the swamp, a fortified house, and an inundation near Urdanis; D'Erlon's four divisions extended up the right bank of the Nive; D'Armanac was in front of Ustaritz; and Foy, at Cambo.

Lord Wellington, who found his position between the Nivelles and the Nive too contracted, soon made dispositions to force the line of this latter river, so as to establish himself on the left bank of the Adour, but the state of the weather delayed their execution, and while awaiting a favourable change, the First Brigade of Guards returned to St. Jean de Luz, where Lord Wellington had now established his head-quarters, and were quartered in the suburb of Siboure. An Officer of the Guards, writing from St. Jean de Luz on the 28th of November, after giving an account of the state of affairs, and of the two Brigades of Guards in particular, refers to a report that was current in the town, that Napoleon was coming to Bayonne to take command of the French armies against Lord Wellington, and he then adds,—

"I am sure that there is not a man in the army, from Lord Wellington himself to the lowest soldier, that would not think it the happiest day of his life to be fairly placed in front of the French with Bonaparte at their head. If ever there was a day when British soldiers would be more than themselves, that day would certainly be the one."

How truly was this assertion verified eighteen months later on the field of Waterloo.

Wellington now proposed to pass the Nive with his right wing, and place it on the Adour, while, to conceal his intentions, Sir John Hope was to make a demonstration with his left wing of 24,000 men, against the entrenched camp at Bayonne, occupied by Reille and Villatte.

Battle of
the Nive.

The duty assigned to the left wing of the British army, after reconnoitering the position and strength of the enemy in front of Bayonne, was to examine the mouth of the Lower Adour, with a view to hereafter throwing a bridge

Boucaut

St Etienne

R. Adour

BAYONNE

R. Nive

BAY OF BISCAY

SKETCH
illustrative of operations
OF LEFT WING OF ALLIED ARMY
on the Nive in vicinity of Bayonne
December 1813
and passage of the Adour Feb 1814

AA Entrenchments thrown up by British to protect the Left of the Army

Scale of English Miles

across that river. The two Brigades of Guards paraded, at
two A.M. on the 9th, and were soon *en route* along the coast
road to take up their position. The morning was wet and
dreary, and after a fatiguing march, the Brigades halted at
Barouillet, in front of Bidart, until they were joined by the
rest of the Division. The fifth Division crossed the valley
between Biarritz and Bidart, their left resting upon the sea.
At eight o'clock the First Battalion First Guards advanced,
covered by the Light Infantry and by the fire of Artillery,
and became at once engaged ; the enemy soon began to
retire, contesting every inch of ground, every hedge, and
every bank ; by one o'clock, the Light Infantry having driven
the enemy through the village of Anglet, and down the
slopes of the entrenched camp, the First Division gained
the heights on the right of the road near that village.

While the attention of the French had been thus engaged
with Hope's army, Hill and Beresford were enabled to
pass the Nive near Ustaritz and Cambo, when the enemy
fell back without resistance, and Wellington having thus
succeeded in the object of his attack, viz., the gaining a
field for operating against the French left, directed Hope's
troops, which had so materially assisted in attaining that
object, to commence, about six o'clock in the evening, their
return to St. Jean de Luz. The Fifth Division, which formed
the rear-guard, halted at Bidart, leaving a Portuguese
brigade in advance at Anglet; and the same night the First
Brigade of Guards, under Maitland, reached its former
quarters at Siboure, the southern suburb of St. Jean de Luz.

Sir John Hope reported to Lord Wellington that he had
reason to be most perfectly satisfied with the manner in
which the officers commanding the several columns had
conducted their advance, and particularly with the manner
in which the connection was kept up between the columns.

Wellington's left was now separated from the rest of his
army by the Nive, and Soult was not slow in seizing his
opportunity. He sallied forth from Bayonne on the morning of the 10th of December, at the head of 60,000 men,
against Hope's wing. Reille, driving the Portuguese from

Anglet, advanced towards Barouillet, while Clausel on his left attacked Arcange, occupied by Kempts' Brigade of the Light Division, who maintained their post all day. The sound of heavy firing in front, and the arrival of an Aide-de-Camp, warning the Guards and the troops in rear, that the attack was serious, the Guards pushed on rapidly to the scene of action, and took their place in line; but the state of the ground having prevented the enemy deploying his forces, the attack was already repulsed, and a renewal of it was prevented by the arrival of three Divisions near Ustaritz, on the left of the enemy's attack. The First Brigade, however, remained that night in Bidart.

The French again attacked the outposts of the left wing on the 11th, and after passing the tanks, penetrated the first line; but when Aylmer's brigade arrived on the ground, Soult withdrew his troops behind the Etang de Chartreuse, opposite Barouillet. The Guards relieved the 5th Division in front line that night, the latter forming on the same ground from which the Guards had moved.

The two Brigades of Guards at once took up a position in front of Barouillet, the first Brigade, under Maitland, being near a farmhouse on the brow of a hill, separated by a narrow ravine from the heights which had so often been the scene of contest, and which were still held by the French. The picquets of the third battalion First Guards were posted in a thick coppice wood on the slopes of the hill, while those of the first, on the extreme right, commanded by Captain West, were in a large orchard to the right of the farm-house. The First Battalion First Guards, under Colonel Askew, was formed on the high ground to the rear, while the Third Battalion, under Colonel Stuart, was to the left, in rear of the farm, with some artillery. A picquet of the First Guards, under Lord Saltoun, occupied a hut to the left, to watch the road which led from the enemy's position, and to keep up the communication with the Second Brigade, in front of the mayor's house.

The night of the 11th was dark and wet, and when morning broke the French appeared in great force, and

more troops were coming up. About ten o'clock, a strong
line of tirailleurs was seen advancing from the west along
the brow of the ravine in front of Maitland's First Brigade of Guards; the artillery opened fire; and, the outposts becoming engaged, the skirmishing was kept up
during the greater part of the day in front of both Brigades,
occasioning a loss of about 200 officers and men. Lieutenant-Colonel Coote Martin, commanding the picquets of
the First Battalion, First Guards, was shot while giving some
directions in the orchard, and almost immediately afterwards Captain Charles William Thompson, of the same
Battalion, an officer of much promise, fell mortally wounded,
while leading on his men. Captain Streatfield was slightly
wounded about the same time, and Ensign Lautour
severely. The following is the last stanza of a dirge
written to the memory of Captain Charles Thompson:—

> " Weep not, he died as heroes die,
>   The death permitted to the brave;
> Mourn not, he lies where soldiers lie,
>   And valour envies such a grave."

Wellington, referring in his despatch to this attack against
his left, states that the Division of Guards, " under Major-
General Howard, conducted themselves with their usual
spirit."

Marshal Soult, finding he could make no impression on
the allied left, under Sir John Hope, and that the British
position on the left bank of the Nive was secure, and believing that they would be occupied in strengthening it still
further, retired behind his entrenchments; but he was not
without hope of eventual success, and though he had so far
failed, he resolved, after leaving only a cordon of outposts in
front of Hope's troops, to pass 35,000 men quickly through
Bayonne during the night, with the intention of attacking
Hill's corps the following morning on the right of the Nive.
The British general, however, in expectation of such an
attack, sent Marshal Beresford, with three Divisions, early
in the morning of the 13th, to Hill's assistance. That
General had only 14,000 men under him, but he held his
ground at St. Pierre, and repelled every attack until the three

1813.
Dec. 13.

Divisions arrived, with Wellington at their head. The French attacks then became gradually feebler, and at two o'clock Wellington ordered a general advance; the French retreated fighting, and during the night Foy's division retired across the Adour, and were sent to reinforce Reille, opposed to the British left.

Action off
Bidart.

While the fight was raging at St. Pierre, on the 13th, the enemy reinforced their advanced posts in front of the First and Fifth Divisions, and firing was kept up with little intermission till the afternoon. The First Brigade of Guards, the Coldstreams, and Lord Aylmer's Brigade were those chiefly engaged. Sir John Hope reported that they had conducted themselves extremely well, and expressed his thanks to Major-General Howard, commanding the Guards Division. To Major-General Stopford and Colonel Maitland, commanding the two Brigades of Guards, to Lord Aylmer, and Major-General Bradford, Lord Wellington also expressed himself in terms of approbation. Captain Carey le Marchant, of the 1st Guards, Aide-de-Camp to Lieutenant-General Sir William Stewart, was severely wounded on the occasion.

The following is the return of casualties in the army under the command of Lord Wellington during the operations connected with the passage of the Nive, from the 9th to the 13th of December :—

	Officers.	Sergts.	Rank and File.	Total.
Killed . . .	32	15	603	650
Wounded . . .	233	215	3459	3907
Missing . . .	17	14	473	504
		Total		5161

The First Brigade of Guards returned to St. Jean de Luz after these several actions, and as the enemy made no further attempts during the remainder of the year 1813 to molest the British, the beginning of the following year found the allied armies firmly established on French soil.

The following are the names of the senior officers of the First Guards, and of those of the two Battalions taking part in the operations in the south of France ; showing also those employed on the Staff.   Part of the 2nd battalion was at this time in Holland.

OFFICERS OF THE FIRST GUARDS, JANUARY, 1814.

H.R.H. Frederick, Duke of York, Colonel.

Hon. J. Leslie, Lieut.-General, Lieut.-Colonel of the Regiment.

Battn.

1. WilliamClinton,1stMajor.	Lieut.-General, staff in Spain; removed from Sicily.
2. M. Disney, 2nd Major.	Major-General, commanding Third Brigade of Guards.
3. H. F. Campbell,3rdMajor.	Major-General, on the staff.

CAPTAINS AND LIEUT.-COLONELS.

1. F. G. White	Major-General, staff in Ireland.
2. William Anson	Major-General, staff in Spain.
1. Robert Cheney	Major-General, staff at Hull.
3. G. Cooke	Major-General, staff in Holland.
3. John Lambert .	Major-General, staff in Spain.
1. M. D. Griffiths	Major-General, on leave from commander-in-chief.
2. J. Kelly	Major-General, on leave from commander-in-chief.
2. John, Lord Proby	Staff in Spain.
3. Per. G. Maitland	Commanding first brigade of Guards in Spain.
3. Hon. Edward Capel	Staff at Cadiz.
2. Andrew Gammell	Lieutenant-General, on leave from commander-in-chief.
1. Lord Fredk. Bentinck	On leave from commander-in-chief.
1. Hon. Arthur Upton	Staff in Spain.
1. Henry Askew	Commanding 1st Battalion, Spain.
3. Hon. William Stuart	Commanding 3rd Battalion, Spain.

1. Godfrey Macdonald.	Spain.	2. Hon. James Macdonald	Holland.
3. Hon.H.T.P.Townshend	Spain.	2. Henry Parke	Holland.
1. I. P. Tinling	Spain.	2. Henry D'Oyly	London.
3. RichardHarveyCooke	Spain.	3. John G. Woodford	S. Spain.
3. Edward Stables	Spain.	2. Thos. Dorville	Prisoner of war.
3. Francis D'Oyly, *s.*	Spain.		
1. Robert Clitherow.	Spain.	2. George Fead.	Spain.
3. John Hanbury.	Spain.	2. Charles Thomas	Spain.
2. George Clifton	Holland.	2. Alex. Lord Saltoun	Spain.
2. Leslie G. Jones.	Holland.	2 John Reeve	Spain.

FIRST BATTALION, FIRST GUARDS.
Lieutenant-Colonel Askew, commanding.

CAPTAINS AND LIEUT.-COLONELS.	LIEUTENANTS AND CAPTAINS.	ENSIGNS.
Hon. W. Stuart.	J. Lambert.	Edward Clive.
Hon. G. Macdonald.	G. Ramsden.	William F. Johnstone.
I. P. Tinling.	R. H. Marsac.	F. F. Luttrell.
S. C. Martin.	H. E. Joddrell.	E. P. Buckley.
J. D. West.	G. Colquitt.	T. Brown.
R. Clitherow.	A. Higginson.	Ch. F. Lascelles.
—	T. Brooke.	Edward Poore.
ADJUTANT.	T. Grant.	S. W. Burges.
Samuel Lambert.	B. Charlewood.	R. Batty.
—	J. B. Evans.	J. Home.
SURGEON.	G. Higginson.	—
Thomas Nixon.	Lord J. Hay.	QUARTER-MASTER.
—	H. E. Hunter.	G. Hodder.
ASSISTANT SURGEONS.	R. Thoroton.	
John Bacot.	T. B. Barrett.	
A. Armstrong.		

THIRD BATTALION, FIRST GUARDS.
Hon. Wm. Stuart, commanding.

CAPTAINS AND LIEUT.-COLONELS.	LIEUTENANTS AND CAPTAINS.	ENSIGNS.
Maitland.	C. Thomas.	L. A. Fox.
Hon. H. T. Towns-hend.	A. Lord Saltoun.*	Hon. O. Bridgeman.
R. W. Cooke.	J. Reeve.	T. Starke.
Edward Stables.	R. Adair.	Ch. P. Ellis.
J. Hanbury.	T. Streatfield.	James Simpson.
—	J. H. Davies.	A. F. Viscount Bury.
	Edward Grose.	P. J. Percival.
ADJUTANT.	Hon. R. Clements.	W. Vane.
James Gunthorpe.	Ch. W. Thompson.	J. O. Lautour.

QUARTER-MASTER.	ASSIST.-SURGEON.	ASSIST.-SURGEON.
R. Colquhoun.	R. Gibson.	William Lambert.

SUBALTERNS ON THE STAFF.—FIRST BATTALION.

Major E. Wynward, wounded, Brigade-Major Third Brigade.
Major Hon. J. Stanhope, staff in Holland.
G. R. Molloy, staff in Spain.

* Lord Saltoun was promoted into the Second Battalion, but remained in France attached to the First Battalion.

C. H. Churchill, staff in Spain.
J. H. Hutchinson, wounded, attached to second battalion.

THIRD BATTALION.

Captain W. Miller, Brigade-Major Third Brigade of Guards.
W. H. Milnes, Aide-de-Camp to Lieut.-General Lord William Bentinck.
Ch. Allix, Staff in Spain.
Lord Charles Fitzroy, Staff in Spain.
Henry Vernon, Aide-de-Camp to Major-General Anson.
Ensign Phillimore, wounded, Second Battalion.
Surgeon Curtis, wounded, Second Battalion, Holland.

1814.

Soult employed himself during the subsequent short period of inaction in strengthening his position, protecting the passages of the rivers Bidouse and Gave d'Oleron, and making demonstrations. On the 3rd of January, 1814, he Jan. 3. attacked the British position on the Joyeuse, and shortly after appeared in force in front of the left wing. The brigades of Guards were immediately despatched from St. Jean de Luz to the outposts of Barouillet, where they relieved the Fifth Division, which then took ground to the right. As no attack, however, was made by the French, the Guards returned to St. Jean de Luz, leaving Lord Aylmer's brigade in charge of the outposts. On the 14th of January this brigade was relieved by the First Guards, Jan. 14. who in succession were relieved by the Second Brigade. The soldiers on outpost-duty were employed in constructing a line of entrenchments along the front of the left wing, for the defence of the ground behind Barouillet, and this duty was performed by the several battalions in rotation for three days each, but was much impeded by the wet and stormy weather that prevailed during the whole month.

The left wing of the army was now destined for the investment of Bayonne, and although this duty prevented their taking part in the operations under Wellington's immediate command, which led to the several actions of Orthez, Garris, Aire, and Tarbes, during the forward movement of the right and centre of the army towards Toulouse, duties assigned to it were of no less importance.

The light companies of the Brigade of Guards were r placed under the command of Lieutenant-Colonel L Saltoun, who had been promoted to a company at the end the year 1813. This promotion would have sent him to home battalion, but, anxious to continue on active servi he applied for, and at the beginning of February, 18 received, the above command, which he retained with gr credit to himself to the end of the war.

Lord Wellington had for some time been maturing expedition well worthy of his former reputation. believed that Soult felt convinced that the British ar could not pass the Adour, and least of all, that the attem would be made at its mouth below Bayonne : neverthele it was here that the British general had determined to m the attempt. For this purpose he collected at Socoa, near Jean de Luz, forty of the ordinary French trading vesse or *Chasses-Marées*, ostensibly for commissariat purposes, a loaded them with materials for constructing a bridge boats. With a view to concealing his design, and while Ho with his left wing, showed a bold front towards Bayon Hill was directed, in the second week of February, to ts advantage of a sharp frost to attack the enemy. He did on the 16th, driving the French advanced posts back to : Palais, on the Upper Bidouse, when Soult retreated behi the Gave d'Oleron, with his left resting on Navarreins, leavi a garrison under Thouvenot in Bayonne.

While the necessary arrangements for the passage of t Adour were being completed at a distance from the futu scene of operations, the two Brigades of Guards, und Maitland and Stopford, advanced, on the 15th of Fe ruary, to the plateau near Biaritz, and took up a positi facing the town with the rest of Hope's troops; the fi Brigade, on the right of the road to Bayonne, occupying, wi a detachment, the chateau of Pucho ; the 5th Division, their right, extending from Bussussary to the Nive, wh Hinuber's Germans and Stopford's Second Guards' Briga were on the left. The light Companies of the Guards, and the light Battalions of the German legion, were on the advanced posts; the sentries of the First Brigade being posted a short distance from Anglet, which was occupied by the enemy; while Aylmer's brigade with Campbell's Portuguese were in support at Bidart.

In a week's time, all arrangements for forcing the passage of the river being completed, Sir John Hope, at midnight, on the 22nd of February, advanced, with 28,000 men, including the two Brigades of Guards, twenty guns, a Feb. 23. rocket troop, and eighteen pontoons. On approaching Anglet, the first division turned to the left towards the coast, preserving strict silence, for though the night was dark, they were within musket shot of the enemy's sentries. The lane by which they were moving was narrow and muddy, with deep ditches on either side, and their progress was delayed for a time by the upsetting of an 18-pounder. Stopford's and Hinuber's Brigades proceeded to the mouth of the river with the pontoons, and at daybreak the light infantry of the First Guards advanced along the plateau, driving the enemy from Anglet into their camp. Maitland's Brigade followed, advancing through the Bois de Bayonne, dragging the 18-pounders with them, and debouched near to the eastern beacon. Here they formed under cover of the sand hills, close to the inundation or marsh, on the west front of the enemy's camp, opposite Boucant. The guns were put Passage of in position on the extreme left, near the Adour, fronting the the Adour. right flank of the enemy's camp. The First Guards, with their guns, were now in a position both to resist any attempt of the enemy to disturb the formation of the bridge, and to cover the subsequent passage of it, by their comrades. On the appearance of this column the enemy's gunboats and a frigate opened fire, but they were soon driven higher up the river by the fire of the battery and rocket troop.

It was intended that the arrival of the *Chasses-Marées* from Socoa, and the Column with the pontoons, should have been simultaneous, but the former were delayed by bad weather. Sir John Hope, however, determined to

attempt the passage at once with the means he had
hand.   While, therefore, the attention of the enemy w
fixed upon the movements of the First Brigade in the
front, a pontoon raft was formed, by means of which, a
aided by some boats, six companies of the Third Guard
two of the Coldstreams, and two of the 60th, were ferri
over to the right bank and landed without opposition, und
Major-General Stopford.   The French, under Gener
Thouvenot, came up a little before dark, their drums bea
ing the *pas de charge*, but they were firmly met by Sto
ford's men, who, waiting till they were tolerably clos
received them with a rolling fire in their front, while t
rocket troop and guns on the sand hills on the southe
bank opened fire upon their left flank.   The enemy we

routed, and on the following morning, the 24th, the r
mainder of the Second Brigade of Guards, the German
and Portuguese crossed over under cover, both of th
comrades who had preceded them, and of the First Guar
who still remained on the south bank, to prevent any inte
rutpion in that quarter by a sortie from the town.

The flotilla of *Chasses-Marées* appearing in the Ado
about noon of the 24th, the construction of the bridge w
immediately proceeded with, the boats were anchored for
feet apart, about three miles below Bayonne, and the brid
was completed without further opposition.   This gre
undertaking was entrusted to Colonel Sturgeon and Maj
Todd, and while it was in progress the First Brigade
Guards, after showing a front towards Bayonne, were t
last of the First Division to cross over, not by the new bridg
but by the same temporary means employed by their co
rades on the previous day—a tedious operation, for on
twelve men could cross at a time in one of the pontoo
boats, the rapidity of the tide rendering the pontoon r
useless.   It was dark before the last men of the Briga
were ferried over, and it was not without much difficul
that the last boats were prevented from drifting out
sea.

Sir John Hope lost no time in investing the Citad

SORTIE FROM BAYONNE
14th April 1814

KING'S GERMAN LEGION

HINUBER

CASTENAU

STOPFORD
BRIGADE of GUARDS

MAITLAND

S. ESPRIT

Principal places of attack

RIVER ADOUR

BAYONNE

Inundated by the Enemy

Inundated by the Enemy

lying on the right bank of the river, a bend in which 1814.
favoured the operation by shortening the extent of ground Investment
to be occupied, and a marsh ' partly protected the line of Bayonne.
he took up.   At seven o'clock on the morning of the Feb. 25.
25th of February, the First Division and Bradford's Portuguese advanced towards the Citadel in Battalion columns of
companies, each Brigade at deploying distance.   The First
Guards on the right, with their right resting on the Adour,
halted for a short time at Boucant, while the centre and
left brigades moved gradually round, forming in succession
to their right, till the extreme left rested on the Adour
above the town.   While this was going on to the north of the
river, the Fifth Division, which still remained on the south
bank, crossed the Nive, and took up a position between the
Nive and the Adour, thus completing the investment, and
severing all communication between the town and country.
An attack was also made on the enemy's entrenched camp, to
prevent the garrison from interfering with the construction of
the bridge, which was completed by the morning of the 26th, Feb. 26.
and it continued to be used by the allies till the end of the
war as the principal means of communication between the
Spanish frontier and Bordeaux.

No sooner was the bridge secure, than Sir John Hope
determined to contract his lines round the Citadel.   The
enemy had strongly entrenched himself in the village of
St. Etienne, situated on a ridge, along which ran the roads
from Bordeaux and Peyhorrada ; and this village was
further protected by the fire from the Fort.

The troops moved forward in three columns, converging
on the Citadel.   The right column, consisting of the two Battalions First Guards, advanced in *echelon* of battalions from
the left ; the Third Battalion leading, halted for a time on the
slope of some high ground, when, upon a pre-concerted signal
of the display of the Third Battalion Colours, the first Battalion advanced also ; the enemy immediately opened fire, and as
soon as the First Battalion had crossed a marshy ground in
its front, Maitland moved his whole Brigade forward together,
covered by Light Infantry, and drove the enemy within their

entrenchments. The brigade was now within 900 yards of the
citadel, the right resting on the Adour, at the Convent of St.
Bernard, which, on being occupied by the light companies of
the First Regiment, was converted into a strong post by
their commanding officer, Lord Saltoun, it being supposed
that the enemy would make a vigorous sortie to attempt to
retake it, and destroy the bridge of boats. The left column,
consisting of the Second Brigade of Guards, was equally
successful in taking up its advanced position; the centre,
which moved forward upon the village of St. Etienne, met
with considerable opposition, but the French were eventually
beat back into the Citadel, with the loss of one of their guns.

During the month of March Sir John Hope made every
preparation for an attack upon the works, but no heavy
artillery arrived. Every house had been turned into an
entrenched post, which was the more necessary as, from the
accuracy of the French gunners, no sentry could expose
himself with impunity.

As Bordeaux and the adjacent country now exhibited a
strong disposition to declare for the Bourbons, Wellington
was induced, on the 8th of March, to despatch Beresford
March 12. with a force to that city, which he entered on the 12th, and
was well received by the municipality. After remaining
there a few days, Beresford left Lord Dalhousie with the
seventh Division, and rejoined his chief on the 18th,
viâ Bigorre. Wellington, after driving the enemy in a
hardly-contested action from Tarbes, continued his advance
by easy marches, arriving on the left bank of the Ga-
ronne above Toulouse on the 27th, where Soult had
entrenched himself upon ground already strong by nature.

March 27. While these events were occurring in the south of France,
the plains of Champagne had become, since the beginning
of the year, the theatre of a desperate struggle, and France
was now suffering the mortification she had so long inflicted
upon other countries, of seeing an enemy on her own soil.
The brilliant genius and indefatigable energy of Napoleon
never shone forth with greater *éclat* than now, when he was
contending with inferior forces against the overwhelming

numbers of the allies. Engaging his opponents in detail,
and constantly victorious without any permanent results, it
seemed as if success still ·clung to his standards, only to
lure him on, by reliance on his star, to a more certain ruin.
He left Paris on the 27th of January, and though beaten at
La Rothiére on the 1st of February, he was victorious on
several other occasions during the month. On the 21st, at
Arcis sur Aube, with 55,000 men, he received the shock of
100,000 of the allies, and retired without confusion behind
the Aube. As a last resource he moved north, in order to
reinforce his army by the garrisons of the frontier, thus
leaving Paris open, and entrusting its defence to Joseph.
The allies then advanced with such an irresistible force of
250,000 men, arriving before the city on the 29th of March, March 29.
that two days later Paris capitulated. Napoleon, on receiving
this intelligence, retired to Fontainebleau, and, after several
fruitless attempts at negotiation, abdicated the throne of April 6.
France on the 6th of April. Two military events, however,
occurred in the south of France in the interval between
the Emperor's abdication and the receipt of official information of the cessation of hostilities, that must now be referred
to, viz., the battle of Toulouse, and the sortie from Bayonne,
in both of which many lives were fruitlessly sacrificed on
both sides.

The defence of Toulouse had been honourable to the
French marshal, both for the display of his ability and for the
constancy with which he endeavoured to stem the tide of
invasion ; but it was also glorious to the allies, who, on the
10th April, four days after the ¦Emperor's abdication, April 10.
stormed the fortified heights, and drove the French before
them into the town. On the 11th, Soult abandoned the
town, and on the following morning Wellington entered it in
triumph. On the same afternoon messengers arrived announcing the deposition of the Emperor, from whom also
came a formal injunction to his Generals to stop all further
hostilities.

Sir John Hope, while still investing Bayonne, had received
information, on the 7th of April, of the fall of Paris ; and
though it was not sufficiently authoritative to warrant his

1814. making a formal communication thereof to the Governor, yet he made it known at the outposts. The French commander, however, paid no attention to the notice, which he was justified in thinking might be intended to deceive him. Another whole week elapsed when, at one o'clock on the

April 14. morning of the 14th of April, a deserter from the Citadel informed General Hay, whose brigade of the Fifth Division had been recently removed to the right bank, and who was, on this night, Major-General in charge of the outposts, that a sortie was projected. Hay at once sent the man to General Hinuber, who put his Brigade under arms, and forwarded the intelligence to Sir John Hope, and ordered his own brigade to form at Boucant, in case of alarm.

Sortie from Bayonne. In accordance with this information, a strong force of about 3000 Frenchmen, under cover of the guns from the ramparts, sallied out of the Citadel, about three o'clock on the morning of the 14th, and vigorously attacked the picquets of the left and centre of the allied investing force, these being furnished respectively by General Hay's brigade and by the Second Brigade of Guards. The picquets of the First Guards covered the right of the line. It was so dark that it was impossible to tell friend from foe. On the left the rush was so impetuous that the enemy quickly carried the church and village, except one house, held by a detachment of the 38th Regiment, which was maintained, until the Germans, in company with Hay's brigade, which had rallied, recovered the post, and drove the enemy back to their entrenchments. General Hay was, unfortunately, killed in this affair, while giving directions for the church to be defended to the last. In the centre the enemy also succeeded in driving in one of the picquets, after a sharp resistance, compelling the other picquets of the Second Brigade to fall back, by which the left rear of the First Brigade became exposed to the enemy's attacks. Major-General Stopford was wounded on this occasion, when the command of the Second Guards Brigade devolved upon Colonel Guise.

Maitland's Brigade of the First Guards, as before described, was on the British right, and there the attack had not been so vigorous. The picquets fell back upon their supports, and Lieutenant-Colonel Hon. H. Townshend, First Guards being severely wounded, while bringing up his company to their assistance, was taken prisoner. The enemy at once began to destroy the entrenchments, when Major-General Howard gave directions to Colonel Maitland to advance with his Brigade of First Guards to the support, and co-operate in recovering the ground between the right and St. Etienne. Maitland had formed his Brigade on the hill above the convent, in readiness to fall upon the enemy in flank, if he attempted to push on in the direction of Boucant, and to penetrate to the bridge; but when it was found that the attack was entirely directed against the lines opposite the citadel, and that the enemy had penetrated to the left rear of his picquets, he advanced with the Third Battalion First Guards, against the French in the hollow road and field, of which they had taken possession. The night was so dark that they could only make them out by the flashes of their muskets. The Battalion had been ordered to lie down, and, orders being sent to Lieutenant-Colonel Woodford to make a simultaneous attack with the Coldstreams, the signal was given to charge: the two Battalions sprang to their feet, and, with loud shouts, dashed against the enemy, dislodged them from the hill, and re-occupied all the posts which the British had before possessed. The French did not stand to receive them, and, fearing they might be cut off, commenced a retreat. When morning dawned a most destructive fire was opened upon their retiring columns as they crossed the Glacis, and they were eventually forced to seek refuge in the citadel, having lost nearly 900 men in this, the last military operation of the war. Lieut.-General Sir John Hope was, unfortunately, taken prisoner, when moving up with the reserve, in consequence of which the report of the sortie was made by Major-General Howard, Commanding the Division of Guards, who, in his despatch of the 15th of April, said that to Major-Generals Hinuber and Stopford, and Colonel Maitland, commanding

1814.

Sortie from Bayonne. April 14.

1814. Brigades, as well as to Colonel Guise, he begged to express hi
best thanks for their exertion and promptitude in the affair
and Colonel Maitland expressed his satisfaction at the con
duct of both officers and men, and the greatest regret at th
Lieutenant-General's misfortune. The casualties amongs
the allies were nearly as great as amongst the enemy
amounting to 150 killed, 457 wounded, and 236 missing
but the losses of the First Guards Brigade were small i
proportion to those of the other Brigade, being three office
wounded, three men killed, thirty-seven wounded, and fiftee
missing. There were no casualties amongst the officers
the First Battalion First Guards. The three in the Thir
Battalion were, Lieutenant-Colonel Hon. H. Townshen
severely wounded, and taken prisoner; Lieutenant an
Captain J. P. Percival, and Walter Vane, both also severel
wounded. There were, altogether, sixteen casualties among
the Guards officers, and 490 amongst their men, as show
in the following return, and no less than nine officers of th
Guards subsequently died of the wounds they received o
the occasion : an unnecessary loss which was much deplore
for the news of the abdication of Buonaparte had bee
received the day before, and a suspension of hostilities ha
been expected that Sunday.

CASUALTIES IN THE TWO BRIGADES OF GUARDS AT THE SORT
FROM BAYONNE, APRIL 14TH, 1814.

		OFFICERS.			SERGEANTS.			MEN.		
		K.	W.	M.	K.	W.	M.	K.	W.	M.
First Guards {	1st Battn.	0	0	0	0	2	0	1	4	0
	3rd Battn.	0	3	0	0	1	2	2	30	13
Coldstream .	1st Battn.	2	5	0	1	11	2	31	111	82
Third Guards.	3rd Battn.	2	3	1	0	8	0	35	98	56
		4	11	1	1	22	4	69	243	151
			16			27			463	

Total　.　. 5

Lieutenant-Colonel Hon. A. Upton, of the First Guar

had been acting throughout these operations as Assistant 1814. Quarter-master-General to Sir John Hope.

The official news of the abdication of the Emperor did not reach the camp of the allies till the 18th of April, April 18. when it was at once communicated to the Governor of the Fortress; a convention was agreed upon between Lord Wellington and Marshal Soult, for the suspension of hostilities, and at mid-day on the 20th, the allies in front of Bayonne, hoisted the Bourbon standard, saluting it with twenty-one guns. The French garrison of Bayonne hoisted the tri-colour, and fired two shells, which was the only indication of hostility that they showed. On the 27th an Aide-de-Camp from Soult arrived with the official intelligence of the suspension of hostilities, upon which an armistice was signed, and on the following day the white flag April 28. was displayed from the Fortress, and saluted by the French, the allied army, then under arms, echoing back the salute.

The Brigades of Guards still remained encamped for above six weeks in the vicinity of the Citadel. Peace was signed at Paris on the 30th of May; the official account of its May 30. signature reached Bayonne on the 9th of June; three days after which, on the 12th, salutes were fired by the governor June 12. at daybreak, at mid-day, and at sunset, in celebration of the event. Orders were at the same time received for the First Brigade of Guards to march to Bordeaux, whence they were to embark for England. In accordance with these orders, they broke up their camp on the 16th of June, and, marching through the country of the Landes, arrived, on the 21st, at Bellevue. On the following day they entered Bordeaux by the " Hospital Militaire," passing by the Palais Royal and cathedral. Here the brigade remained for a month, and, at length, on the 23rd of July, the First and July 23. Third Battalions, embarking in large boats, descended the river to the mouth of the Gironde, where H.M.S. " Tigre," " Belle Poule," and " Freya," frigates, were ready to receive them. These ships sailed on the 26th and 27th of July, reaching Portsmouth at the beginning of August, when the troops being landed, the two Battalions of First

1814.
Aug. 10.

Guards marched to London, arriving there on the 9th and 10th of August respectively.

EXPEDITION TO LOW COUNTRIES, BERGEN-OP-ZOOM.

In order not to interfere with the account of the last events of the Peninsular War, we have hitherto omitted all reference to an expedition to the Low Countries, set on foot by the British government towards the end of the year 1813, in which the Second Battalion of the First Guards, as well as the Second Battalions of the other two Regiments of Guards took a part.

1813.

Upon the retreat of the French army into France, after the battle of Leipsig, and the consequent advance of the allied sovereigns towards the Rhine, Napoleon had found himself under the necessity of withdrawing a considerable number of troops from Holland and the Low Countries. The Dutch, seizing the opportunity, resolved to throw off the French yoke; the people of Amsterdam on the 15th of November rose *en masse* with the cry of " Orange Boven," hoisting the Orange colours, and proclaiming the Stadtholder, while other towns followed their example. The intelligence of this rising reached the British Government on the 21st of November, at the same time as the news of the successful passage of the Bidassoa, and the subsequent entry of the allies, under Wellington, into France, whereupon they determined without delay to organise an expedition of 8000 men, to be placed under Sir Thomas Graham, who had now recovered from his illness, and to give the Dutch material support, both in asserting their independence and in driving the remainder of the French forces out of their country. On that same day orders were issued for several Regiments to hold themselves in readiness for immediate embarcation; and on the 22nd the whole of the Third Brigade of Guards in London, consisting of the three Second Battalions, was assembled, with the view to drawing out every available man for service. The Second Battalion First Guards was then above 1300 strong, and by the

Nov. 15.

Nov. 21

following month was increased, principally by volunteers 1813.
from the militia, to 1600 men, but many of these were
recruits. A Battalion, however, was formed above 800
strong, with 16 officers, divided into six companies, and
placed under the command of Colonel Lord Proby. The
drafts selected from the Coldstreams and Third Guards
were equally divided into six companies each, commanded
respectively by Lieutenant-Colonel Adams of the Coldstreams, and Lieutenant-Colonel William . Rooke of the
Third Guards ; Colonel Lord Proby, First Guards, was
put in command of this brigade ; that of the second battalion First Regiment devolving for a time upon the next
senior officer, Lieutenant-Colonel George Clifton.

The following officers were with the service companies
of the Second Battalion in the month of January, 1814 :—

OFFICERS OF 2ND BATTALION FIRST GUARDS, JANUARY, 1814.

Colonel Lord Proby, Commanding.

CAPTS. & LIEUT.-COLS.	LIEUTS. & CAPTS.	ENSIGNS.
George Clifton.	James Lindsay.	Robert Batty.
L. G. Jones.	J. L. Duckenfield.	J. Home.
Hon. Jn. McDonald.	H. W. Powell.	R. Masters.
H. Packe.	Sir H. Lambert, Bart.	Aug. Dashwood.
	H. B. Trelawny.	Wm. Barton.
Surgeon W. Curtis.	J. Bulteel.	J. O. Honyman.
Assist.-Surg. Harrison.		Edward Pardoe.
		C. Chambers.

Major Wynyard, of the First Battalion, remained Brigade-Major to
the Third Brigade in England ; Captain Desbrowe was appointed
A.D.C. to Major-General G. Cooke, in Holland, and Captain Lord
Bury was removed to the staff in Holland, from the South of France.

Two hundred men, exclusive of recruits, fit only for home
service, were all that remained of the First Guards to perform
the London duties, so that on the 22nd of November the Nov. 22.
Nottingham militia were ordered from the Tower to take
the duties at the West-end. They were relieved by the
West London on the 23rd, and these, in their turn, on the
24th, by the Staffordshire militia, brought up on purpose Nov. 24.
for that duty. After this many militiamen volunteered into

1813. the First Guards, so that towards the end of the year additional company was added to each of the battalions.

The above Brigade was at once despatched to H land; the ships sailed from Greenwich on the 24th

Dec. 6. November, arriving at Scheveling on the 6th of Decemb where the troops landed and marched to the Hague. T Prince of Orange also left England on the 26th November, and, landing at Scheveling on the 30th, h preceded the Guards to the Hague. The allies, exhaust with the severity of the late campaign in Germany, and no condition to continue in the field from want of shoes a clothing, had gone into winter quarters. It was consider however, that notwithstanding the inclemency of the weath the British Guards should move to the front, and take u position in line with them. After ten days, therefore, spe in the Dutch capital, and having seen the Prince of Oran

Dec. 16. firmly re-established, the Guards were re-embarked the 16th of December, and sailed to Willemstadt, fro

1814.
Jan. 9. whence, on the 9th of January, 1814, they proceeded Steenbergen, lying a few miles to the north of Bergen-o Zoom, where Sir Thomas Graham was enabled to effect junction with the allies cantoned on his left at Oudenbos and Breda. Early in January the French had assembl all their available forces at Antwerp, and occupied We Wesel and Hoogstraten in advance, when Blucher, then Breda, with his Prussians, proposed to drive them thenc so as to make a reconnaissance of Antwerp; and, at h

Jan. 10. request, Sir Thomas Graham moved forward on the 10 from Rosendaal to cover the Prussian right flank. Th Guards had landed in time to accompany this expeditio Two of the British Divisions reached Calmhout on t morning of the 11th, followed by the First Division, wi

Jan. 12. the Guards. On the 12th, Sir Thomas reached Capelle, the road from Bergen-op-Zoom to Antwerp; here the Fir Division, under Major-General Cooke, remained in reserv while part of the British troops advanced towards Merxen After being stationed a week at Capelle, the Guar returned to Steenbergen on the 19th of January, where tw

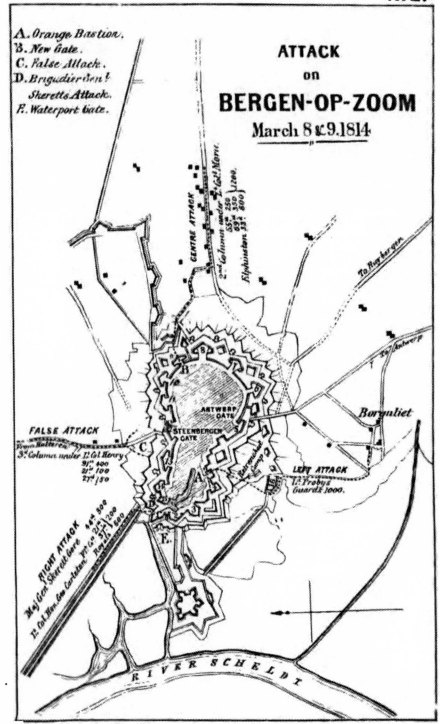

A. *Orange Bastion.*
B. *New Gate.*
C. *False Attack.*
D. *Brigadier Genl.*
   Skerett's Attack.
E. *Waterport Gate.*

ATTACK

on

BERGEN-OP-ZOOM

March 8 & 9.1814

CENTRE ATTACK

2d. Columns under Lieut. Morice.
55th. 250
55th. 330 } 1200.
69th. 300
Elphinston 331. 600

FALSE ATTACK
from Halteren.
3d. Column under Lt. Col. Henry.
91st. 400
21st. 100
21st. 150

ANTWERP GATE

STEENBERGEN GATE

RIGHT ATTACK
Major Gen. Skerett late
Lt. Col. Hon. Im. Carleton
44th. 300
2d. Gs. 200
37th. 500
Royal. 600

LEFT ATTACK
Lt. Proby's
Guards 1000.

Bergenliet

To Rozendaal

RIVER SCHELDT

days later they were inspected by His Royal Highness the
Duke of Clarence.

Further reinforcements for the Guards arrived from
England on the 3rd of February, which increased the
Second Battalion First Regiment from 800 to above 1000
men, viz.: to 18 Officers, 39 Sergeants, 12 Drummers, 952
Rank and File. The following additional officers came out
with the draft of the First Guards :—

> Lieutenant-Colonels H. D'Oyly and T. Dorville.
> Captain L. Boldero.
> Ensigns Hon. E. A. Edgecumbe, G. Fludyer, G. Thornton, and
> F. H. Needham.

After being thus reinforced, the Guards made another
forward movement towards Antwerp, now invested by Sir
Thomas Graham, who, on the 2nd of February, in concert with General Bulow, had made an attack on Merxem,
close to Antwerp, with the object of moving on that
town. The village of Braachstadt was speedily taken, and
batteries were erected on the 3rd, when fire was opened,
which continued on the 4th and 5th, but the defective
state of the mortars and ammunition from Willemstadt was
such that after three days' fire the attempt was given up,
and the troops returned on the 6th to their cantonments,
the investment of the town, however, being continued.

Sir Thomas had now a force of about 8000 men under his
command, and at the beginning of March arrangements
were made for carrying into execution a plan for seizing
Bergen-op-Zoom by a coup de main, garrisoned as it was by
5000 or 6000 Frenchmen. It was calculated that the
severe frost would have prevented the sluices being used to
raise or lower the water, and that the ice in the ditches of
the fortress would only be partially broken ; 4000 British
troops, of which 1000 were selected from the brigade of
Guards, were accordingly detached, on the 8th of March,
from the investing force of Antwerp, and marched secretly
to the neighbourhood of Bergen-op-Zoom, being told off
into four columns of attack, as follows, under the supreme
command of Major-General George Cooke.

1814.   MEN.

March 8.

1st Column, Detachments of the brigade of Guards, under
         Lord Proby 1000

2nd   ,,   55th, 250; 69th, 350; 33rd, 600; under Lt.-Col.
             Morice 1200

3rd   ,,   91st, 400; 21st, 100; 27th, 150; under Lt.-Col.
             Henry (21st) 650

4th   ,,   44th, 300; Flank columns of 21st and 37th, 200;
             and Royals, 600; under Brig.-Gen. Gore and
             Lt.-Col. Hon. George Carleton, accompanied by
             Major-General Skerrett 1100

                                        Total . . 3950

Storming   The first column, viz., the brigade of Guards, which was
of Bergen-
op-Zoom. accompanied on this occasion by Major-General Cooke,
formed the left of the line, and was destined to attack the
works between the Waterport and the Antwerp Gates. The
second column on its right was to attack the right of
the New Gate; the third to make a feint on the Steenbergen Gate, call off the attention of the enemy from the
more serious attacks, and be disposable according to circumstances; while the 4th or right column, accompanied by
Major-General Skerrett, the former temporary brigadier of
the Guards in the Peninsula, was to force the entrance of
the harbour, which was fordable at low water. As soon as
the fourth and Guards columns gained an entrance to the
fortress, they were to move along the ramparts, and, having
effected a junction, proceed to clear them of the enemy, and
assist the other attacks. The hour for the assault was
fixed for half-past ten at night, at which hour the
columns advanced. The 4th, under Carleton, after successfully gaining the interior of the enemy's works, near
No. 1 bastion, and opening the Waterport gate, moved with
part of its force along several of the bastions to No. 9, but
was here met by a most destructive fire; the ladders by
which it had entered were caught and thrown down by the
enemy, and it lost its three commanders, Skerrett wounded,
Gore and Carleton both killed, which caused it to fall into
disorder, and retire from its advanced position, after having
suffered considerable loss in killed, wounded, and prisoners.

The centre column also failing in its attack at B, against bastion 1814.
No. 9, was driven back, losing 200 men killed and wounded, March 8.
as well as its two commanders, Lieutenant-Colonel Morice,
and Lieutenant-Colonel Elphinstone, commanding the 33rd
Regiment. This latter corps was soon reformed under its
major, and moved to the support of the left or Guards
column, followed by the 55th and 69th Regiments. In the
meantime the Guards column, under Lord Proby, had
been so far successful that, having advanced from the
Antwerp road round the salient of the lunette (16) of the
entrenched camp, they had reached the broad wet ditch of the
unreveted fronts (2), (3), (4), without being discovered, but,
finding the ice, from the rise and fall of the tide, unfit to
support them at the point they were to have crossed, Lord
Proby was obliged to move them more to the right, towards
the ditch of the Orange bastion, at A, where a batardeau
preventing the action of the tide, allowed the ice to
form strong enough to bear them. The advanced, and
ladder parties of the Guards, under Captain Rodney and
Ensigns Gooch and Pardoe, at once proceeded across the
frozen ditch followed by the rest of the brigade. No time
was lost in placing the ladders against the demi revetment,
seventeen feet high, and the men soon swarmed up, gaining
possession of the ramparts without much opposition, beyond
a slight musketry fire from the flanks. Major-General
Cooke, with the commanding officers of artillery and
engineers, also entered at this point with the Guards.

In consequence of the delay in the hour of attack of this
column, owing to the necessary change that Lord Proby
had been forced to make in the point of attack, it was half-
past eleven before the Brigade had established itself on the
ramparts. The garrison, though surprised by the first
assault, was not thrown into confusion, and was soon again
in a position to resist. General Cooke, suspecting from the
quiet that reigned at the French posts opposite the other
intended points of attack, that the several columns had not
yet entered, formed the brigade of Guards on the ramparts
in column of sections, occupying at the same time some houses

in his front and in the adjoining bastions from which his men might otherwise have been much annoyed. The ladders by which the men had entered, were left standing against the scarpe, so that a ready communication with the exterior was ensured, and they were, in fact, used by the troops of the second column after their own attack had failed. A strong patrol of the brigade was at once sent off to the left towards the point at which the fourth column, under Skerrett, had vainly endeavoured to maintain itself, while part of the First Guards, under Lieutenant-Colonels Clifton and Jones, both of that regiment, was sent along the rampart to the right to secure the Antwerp Gate, between bastions (5) and (6), and to support, or endeavour to gain some intelligence as to the success or otherwise of the second column, under Lieutenant-Colonel Morice. Colonel Clifton reached the gate, but it could not be opened by his men, who were soon exposed to a murderous fire from the street leading to it, and it was also found that the enemy occupied an outwork commanding the bridge, which would have effectually prevented the use of the gate as an outlet. As the detachment under Clifton did not return, owing, apparently, to the enemy having got possession of the intermediate bastion (5), Lieutenant-Colonel Rooke, with a party of Coldstreams, was sent in that direction; this officer drove the enemy from the position they had taken up and reached the gate; but he also, found it useless to attempt to force it, as the work outside was still occupied by the enemy, and his party returned with some loss. Lieutenant-Colonel Clifton's detachment of First Guards, after having charged the enemy and captured a field gun, had been cut off after a very gallant resistance, exposed to a destructive fire on all sides, which cost the lives of many most valuable men and officers, amongst whom was Colonel Clifton himself, while the remainder, with Lieutenant-Colonel Jones, fell into the hands of the enemy. During the whole night the brigade of Guards, while still maintaining their position on the ramparts, suffered severely from the galling fire kept up upon them, from the houses still in possession

of the garrison, but they gallantly and unflinchingly held
their ground.

In the course of the night the Guards had been joined by
the 33rd, the right wing of the 55th, (the left wing was
left outside to remove their wounded), and by the second
battalion 69th, who all formed up to the left of the Guards.
General Cooke soon despatched the 33rd Regiment, under
Lieutenant-Colonel Muller, to the left, to the support of
the troops at the Waterport Gate, but, being all the
time uncertain what had occurred elsewhere, he deemed
it prudent to retain the remainder by him, and not attempt
to penetrate into the streets with the certainty of great loss
to the men.

The enemy, about six in the morning of the 9th of March,
directed their first attack against General Skerrett's column,
which, after a gallant resistance, was forced, by four times
their number, to abandon their hold of the Waterport Gate;
about the same time the garrison turned the guns of the
place upon the Guards, and on the other regiments, now
.reduced to about 1550 men, that still maintained their
position on the open ramparts. They witnessed the Royal
Scots, 600 strong, who felt success hopeless, followed by the
33rd, which had been sent by General Cooke to their assistance, retiring before the attack of the garrison, from the Waterport Gate, and the former regiment, in its retreat, finding
itself exposed to a cross fire, was forced to lay down its arms.
Major-General Cooke, then despairing of eventual success,
directed the Guards also to retire from their hardly-won
position. The retreat was conducted in the most orderly
manner, protected by the remains of the 69th and right
wing of the 55th Regiments, the latter corps, under General
Cooke's directions, repeatedly driving the enemy back; but
these weak battalions as they crossed the ditch were so
much exposed to the continued concentrated fire of musketry
and artillery, that the General found it impossible to withdraw them, and at ten o'clock in the morning, upon hearing
of the complete failure of the other attacks, he surrendered
in order to save the lives of the remainder.

Major-General Cooke, in his despatch to Sir Thomas Graham, reports " his highest approbation of all officers and men employed near him, particularly mentioning Colonel Lord Proby, First Guards; Lieutenant-Colonel Rooke,. commanding Second Guards; Lieutenant-Colonel Mercer, of the Third Guards, commanding the light companies of the brigade ; and Majors G. Muttlebury and A. Hog, of the 69th and 55th Regiments, as deserving his warm praise."

Lord Proby also, on the same day, issued a Brigade order from his head-quarters at Hogerheide, nine miles south of Bergen-op-Zoom, to which the Brigade had moved, returning his best thanks to the officers, non-commissioned officers, and privates of the detachment of Guards which had been engaged.   He· said he was equally satisfied with the gallantry which they had displayed in the assault, with their steady conduct during the many hours they maintained their position upon the ramparts, and with the soldierly and orderly manner in which they effected the retreat ; and he particularly remarked the excellent conduct. of the officers who commanded the advanced and the ladder parties, viz., Captain Rodney, Ensign Gooch, and Ensign Pardoe.

Captain H. W. Powell, who succeeded to the temporary command of the Battalion of First Guards upon the death of Lieutenant-Colonel Clifton, writes :—" Our people behaved most gallantly, and the conduct of the officers was most conspicuous."

The total loss of the British troops on this occasion was 300 killed and 1800 prisoners, or about half the troops engaged. Among the prisoners were many wounded.

The loss of officers of the First Guards was :—Colonel Hon. James Macdonald, killed.   Lieutenant-Colonel G. Clifton, severely wounded ; since dead.   Captain John Bulteel, severely wounded ; since dead.   Captains James Lindsay, J. L. Duckenfield, and H. B. Trelawny, and Ensign Edward Pardoe, all four severely but not dangerously wounded.   Major-General G. Cooke, Lieutenant-

Colonel L. G. Jones, Ensigns R. Masters, and J. O. Hony-   1814.
man, and Surgeon Curtis, prisoners.

It was credibly stated as one cause of the non-success
of this attack, that the governor of the place had received
notice of the intentions of the British commander, and had
made use of every available means to defeat them; but
though the final result of the assault was a failure, owing
to circumstances over which the general had no control, the
conduct of the Guards was as conspicuous for bravery and
discipline as on any former occasion. They succeeded in
the assault, and gained the ramparts they were ordered
to attack, maintaining themselves in this exposed position, with the other regiments that had followed them,
till their own General, finding that all hopes of taking the
place had vanished, owing to failure in other quarters, gave
the order to retire. Captain Powell wrote that, had more
supports been ready to come up, the place must have been
theirs.

Any further attempt against Bergen-op-Zoom was now
necessarily given up, and the troops were withdrawn from the
neighbourhood, moving the first day to Hogerheide, the
second to Calmhout, halfway between Bergen-op-Zoom and
Antwerp, and continued the investment of that latter
fortress, Calmhout remaining the head-quarters of the
British troops. The Brigade of Guards remained under
the command of Lord Proby, while Captain Henry Powell
retained the command of the second battalion First Guards
till Lieutenant-Colonel D'Oyly arrived to take it over.

Lieutenant-Colonel Jones, First Guards, proceeded on the
same day, with the sanction of the governor of Bergen-op-
Zoom, to the British head-quarters with letters from Major-
General Cooke, whereupon Major Stanhope was immediately sent back into the fortress, and an agreement for
an exchange of prisoners was made, agreeably to which
Major-General Cooke and the rest of the officers and men—
except the wounded, who remained in charge of British
surgeons in the fortress—returned to the British camp on
the 10th, the day after the failure, on the condition of their March 10.

1814.
March 11.

returning to England as soon as the navigation of the Scheldt should be opened; but events now rapidly succeeded one another, which made the above conditions to become a dead letter, and caused the Guards, as we shall see, in the course of a few weeks to form. part of the garrison of Antwerp.

The combined armies of Russia, Austria, and Prussia, under the command of their respective sovereigns, had been advancing on Paris. On the 9th of March the headquarters of Prince Blucher were at Laon, and, notwithstanding the strenuous exertions that Napoleon was making to stem the onward tide, he was gradually forced to retire on the capital, and on the 30th of the month the allies entered Paris, after a successful attack upon St. Denis, Montmartre, Romainville, and Belleville. The Emperors of Russia and Austria and the King of Prussia entered on the

March 31.

following day, proclaiming they would no longer treat with Napoleon; a provisional government was established

April 3.

pending the return of Louis XVIII.; and on the 3rd of April the senate decreed the deposition of Buonaparte, who at the same time formally abdicated the throne of France.

The Duke of Wellington, who had, as before recorded, been triumphantly advancing in the south of France, hearing of the entry of the combined armies into Paris, agreed to

April 14.

a suspension of arms with Soult, and, on the 14th of April, came for a few days to Paris, when the terms of a military

April 23.

convention were discussed. It was signed on the 23rd of April, and one of its articles stipulated that Antwerp should be forthwith evacuated by the French. Upon the commissioner of the allied powers at Antwerp expressing a wish that it should be occupied by British troops till the government was definitively settled, Sir Thomas Graham, now Lord Lynedoch, commanding the forces in the Low Countries, directed the Brigade of Guards, under Lord Proby, as well as the second Division, under Major-General Cooke, to

May 5.

march in. They accordingly entered on the 5th of May, 1814, and, after the several guards were relieved, the new

Printed in the United States
134934LV00003B/167/A